EUGENE ELY

EUGENE ELY

Pioneer of Naval Aviation

John H. Zobel

EDITED BY LaVerne Woods

NAVAL INSTITUTE PRESS
Annapolis, Maryland

Naval Institute Press
291 Wood Road
Annapolis, MD 21402

Library of Congress Cataloging-in-Publication Data

Names: Zobel, John H. (John Hiller), 1960–2017, author.
Title: Eugene Ely : pioneer of naval aviation / by John H. Zobel.
Other titles: Pioneer of naval aviation
Description: Annapolis, MD : Naval Institute Press, [2023] |
Includes bibliographical references and index.
Identifiers: LCCN 2023012902 (print) | LCCN 2023012903 (ebook) |
ISBN 9781682478370 (hardcover) | ISBN 9781682478394 (ebook)
Subjects: LCSH: Ely, Eugene Burton, 1886–1911. | United States. Navy—Aviation—Biography. | United States. Navy—Aviation—History—20th century. | Air pilots, Military—United States—Biography. | Test pilots—United States—Biography. | Curtiss, Glenn Hammond, 1878–1930. | BISAC: BIOGRAPHY & AUTOBIOGRAPHY / Aviation & Nautical | TRANSPORTATION / Aviation / History
Classification: LCC V63.E46 Z63 2023 (print) | LCC V63.E46 (ebook) |
DDC 359.9/84092—dc23/eng/20230627
LC record available at https://lccn.loc.gov/2023012902
LC ebook record available at https://lccn.loc.gov/2023012903

♾ This paper meets the requirements of ANSI/NISO z39.48-1992 (Permanence of Paper). Printed in the United States of America.

31 30 29 28 27 26 25 24 23 9 8 7 6 5 4 3 2 1
First printing

DEDICATION

HILLER B. ZOBEL
United States Navy, 1953–55

WEIGHTSTILL WILLIAM WOODS
United States Marine Corps, 1944–46

Anybody may be able to go up in an aeroplane,
but it requires skill and practice to come down
without damage to man or machine.

—GLENN H. CURTISS and AUGUSTUS POST,
The Curtiss Aviation Book

CONTENTS

FOREWORD

WHEN JOHN H. ZOBEL first contacted me, he was already deeply involved in researching the life of Eugene B. Ely, the aviation pioneer who, a hundred years earlier, had executed the world's first shipboard launch and shipboard landing.

Together we went over photographs of the full-scale replica of Ely's historic biplane that I had built and flown for the 2011 Centennial of Naval Aviation celebration. I told John I had read every piece on Ely I could find, most of which I had found either superficial or profoundly flawed.

John's disarming friendliness belied an intense energy and intellect. I was impressed by the depth and scope of his knowledge about the lives of Ely, Glenn Curtiss, Capt. W. I. Chambers, and others. Clearly, his account of Ely's life and historic flights would be far more accurate than anything that had previously been published.

Our collaboration was all too brief. An avid alpinist and distance runner, John closed his final chapter above 22,000 feet, at the summit of the highest peak in the Americas.

This exceptional work is his legacy. It is the definitive biography of Ely and an in-depth exploration of the far-ranging connections and undercurrents attending the birth of naval aviation. But it is also an object lesson in authorial integrity and commitment, crafted by a gentleman of consequence.

Fair skies and tailwinds on your westward flight, my friend.

— BOB COOLBAUGH
Commander, U.S.Navy (Ret.)
Carrier Pilot

AUTHOR'S NOTE

FOR MORE THAN A CENTURY, what little there was to be gleaned of the life of Eugene Burton Ely lay buried in piles of dusty newsprint. Audio recording was in its formative stage during his short lifetime, and the rare motion pictures of him are silent. Ely maintained no regular correspondence, particularly during the hectic eighteen months of his flying career. To the extent he wrote at all to friends and family, it was in brief telegrams or messages scribbled on postcards. In his twenty-four years, he committed almost nothing about his historic experiences to writing. He had no children and few confidants. For many years, what the world knew—or thought it knew—about Ely came from biographical sketches written after his death and was based, for the most part, on rumors and legends.

The popular origin story goes something like this: Henry Wemme, an automobile dealer in Portland, Oregon, acquired a biplane from manufacturer Glenn Curtiss but did not know how to fly it. Ely, sometimes said to have been a salesman for Wemme, imagined that flying could not be much different from driving, so he offered to try. He crashed the airplane on the first attempt and felt so badly that he bought the machine, quickly taught himself to fly, and immediately went on the road as a star exhibition aviator.[1]

Thanks to today's digital archives and powerful search engines, the modern researcher can disprove at least some myths. The colorful story above, for instance, is wrong in almost every respect. True, Ely flew without prior instruction; but Wemme never sold autos or airplanes, and Ely never worked for him. Nor did he crash on his first attempt. Ely's entry into the exhibition business was a calculated investment, backed by local businessmen. And he failed miserably on the exhibition circuit before finding success.

The legends of Ely's life arose in large part from the imaginative and often intentionally inaccurate journalism of his day. During Ely's boyhood in the 1890s, Joseph Pulitzer's *New York World* and William Randolph Hearst's *New York Journal* were competing mightily for readership and advertising revenue. Both newspaper devolved into "yellow journalism," a style that emphasized shock and scandal, sloppy research, fabricated stories and quotes, faked photos, press releases masquerading as articles—anything to attract the public eye. With improvements in journalistic standards, the practice gradually waned, but as late as 1926, Orville Wright could still complain that the newspapers were publishing "trivial, unimportant stuff and sensationalist matter," just to have "something to put next to the 'ads.'"[2]

Essentially free to print whatever they wished, early twentieth-century journalists were not above both promising and reporting impossible feats of flying. Aviators were usually en route to their next appearances by the time accounts of their activities and their remarks were published; if the record needed correcting, no one was around to do it. As Curtiss wryly observed, "I have noticed that newspaper reporters have a way of taking advantage of the time after a man has sailed to mis-quote him."[3]

Compounding the confusion was the tendency of exhibition aviators and their associates—including press agents, mechanics, and "advance men"—to supply the press with streams of colorful fabrications about the fliers and their supposed exploits. Exhibition flying was entertainment, and it was important to the aviators to maintain the public's interest. Ely's widow, by her own admission many years later, flat-out lied to newsmen, who wrote her tales as though they were fact. For instance, she was often quoted as saying she had flown many times with her husband, whereas a day-by-day examination of news reports reveals only one such occasion.[4]

The challenge for any biographer is to separate fact from fabrication; and given how indiscriminately news outlets of this period repeated and even corroborated one another's falsehoods, a researcher can easily be led astray. David McCullough recounts in *The Wright Brothers* how rapidly the press turned the brothers' telegram reporting their first successful flights—the longest just under three hundred yards—into a "ludicrously inaccurate account" of their having soared three miles over hills and waves, "an account that was almost entirely contrived."[5]

Louis S. Casey, former curator of aircraft at the Smithsonian Institution's National Air and Space Museum, commented on the "power of the press" to take a reporter's erroneous statement and cause it to be "forevermore . . . repeated by subsequent writers and historians." While tracking down details of the various Curtiss aircraft, he corresponded with Charles F. Willard, one of Ely's fellow aviators. "Do not believe all that those people [reported] write," Willard warned Casey, "because they did not know, and like all writers were looking for being the first with the latest."[6]

The contemporary news coverage of Ely's career has been exhaustively researched and collected in a work—*Eugene Ely, Daredevil Aviator*, by William Miller—to which the interested reader should turn for the many romantic and heroic stories about the man, flush with poignant, often flowery, and largely apocryphal quotes attributed to the famously laconic Iowan.

Given that so many of those stories are demonstrably inaccurate, we cannot take them at face value. In the present work, when a news source has purported to quote Ely or to summarize his thoughts or intentions, the passage is presented as fact only if independent confirmation exists. The author has not sought to debunk every fabricated story and unsupported "fact"—such a project would make for a long and tedious book—but rather to triangulate, to the extent possible, by examining multiple sources and photographic records and disregarding obviously impossible and improbable claims, to arrive at a record that is as accurate as one can reasonably hope for. Inaccuracies doubtless remain, for which the author assumes full responsibility.

Terminology in the early days of aviation was not yet standardized, and sources can readily be found that conflict with one another in the spelling of various words and phrases and even in the names bestowed on individual aircraft by their designers. In order to accommodate modern orthographical and typographical conventions, certain silent revisions have here been made: the spelling *Aide for Materiel*, for example, is used in preference to the earlier *Aid for Material*; the words *flier* and *flyer* always denote the aviator and the aircraft, respectively; and except when it appears in a direct quote, the word that was consistently spelled *aeroplane* in Ely's time is here spelled *airplane*.

INTRODUCTION

THROUGHOUT HISTORY, humans have always dreamed of the possibility of flight. In Greek mythology, Daedalus and his son, Icarus, escaped imprisonment by taking to the air on feathered wings. The mortal hero Bellerophon tamed the divine winged stallion Pegasus, offspring of the sea god Poseidon, and rode him to victory over the Chimera and numerous other monsters.

Such stories begin exhilaratingly enough but tend to end in hubris and the inevitable tragic downfall. When Icarus soared too close to the realm of the gods, the sun melted the wax that held his wings together, and he tumbled into the sea. When Bellerophon made so bold as to ride through the skies to Olympus unbidden, Pegasus threw him, and he fell to earth.

Some of these early dreams of flight may have had a practical origin. Egyptian and Phoenician cultures used the image of a winged horse to symbolize the sailing ships that carried men out past land's end on broad, billowing "wings." Indeed, the name "Pegasus" is thought to derive from the Phoenician word *sus*, meaning both "ship" and "horse."[1]

Millennia passed. Inventors and dreamers proposed any number of schemes for breaking the shackles of gravity. But the physical laws remained inviolable.

And then, quite suddenly, over the course of a single generation, ships truly did gain wings—not sails, but actual wings—and a handful of bold pioneers, at the controls of the new "air-ships," at last realized the dream of flight.

A young American from a farm in York Center, Iowa, found himself at the heart of that epochal transformation. Eugene Burton Ely was born in 1886 and lived just short of twenty-five years. His brief and remarkable life covered not only the most fascinating quarter-century in the evolution of powered transportation but also a watershed period in the evolution of sea power.[2]

Ely's ancestors had been active in the country's settlement and growth, and his family had a long association with the military and with higher education. At the time of his birth, a craze was sweeping the nation, fueled by the recent appearance of the first practical "safety bicycle." In contrast with the almost comically mismatched wheels of the old penny-farthing bicycle, it featured two equal-sized wheels, making it simpler and safer to use. Mechanical advantage was provided by a chain drive, with a gear ratio that allowed a rider on a sufficiently smooth road to pedal faster than a horse could trot.

By the turn of the century, a new craze was in full swing: the automobile. Its advantages over beasts of burden were obvious. But given the mechanical unreliability of the horseless carriage and the poor state of most country roads, debate raged over whether it had any practical application beyond city limits.

Then the Wright brothers proved the feasibility of heavier-than-air flying machines. The first glimpse of a man in flight stunned even seasoned journalists:

> Two strong [mechanics] are holding the machine down. It quivers like a thing of animation, held against its will, anxious to leap forward and upward.
>
> The word is given. The men drop back swiftly to evade the thin planes.
>
> "He's off!" someone shouts. . . . Suddenly a slight depression is reached in the ground ahead, the aviator ducks his machine downward for one last spring and shoots upward as if climbing an incline of blue ether. Higher and higher he goes and the gaping throng stretches its neck and gasps.[3]

America went from horse to safety bicycle to automobile to airplane in under two decades—and the next transformation in the transportation revolution, the one where Ely made his indelible mark, was in naval aviation.

Initially, few of the nation's highest-ranking political and military leaders grasped that airplanes could have much strategic value to the Navy. By proving that it was possible to fly off of and onto the deck of a ship at sea, Ely toppled that short-sighted view, and his pioneering flights made him famous across the world.

The world was changing rapidly, though, and his fame was as fleeting as it was meteoric.

Within eighteen months of the day he first laid eyes on an airplane, Ely had become one of the most accomplished, respected, and celebrated aviators in the sky. Within three years, the nation's attention would be focused on the Great War, in which aircraft were first widely deployed in combat roles. Within half a century, aircraft carriers had become the principal striking arm of the fleet.

But by then hardly anyone remembered the "son of York" who had spent two brief but glorious summers as the world's darling.[4]

CHAPTER 1

SON OF YORK

ON A BLUSTERY AFTERNOON in November 1910, American "bird man" Eugene Ely climbed onto the seat of the Glenn Curtiss *Hudson Flyer.* The biplane was perched on a makeshift wooden platform atop the foredeck of the scout cruiser USS *Birmingham*, which was lying at anchor in Chesapeake Bay waiting out a passing rainstorm. Eight men held down the flying machine's wings as the heavy engine behind the aviator roared to life.

Ely, age twenty-four, had been flying for barely seven months and was about to attempt the world's first airplane flight from the deck of a ship. He gave the signal for the men to let go, and the rickety machine sped off the thirty-seven-foot cliff of the ship's bow.

It shot toward the water.

The first Ely known to have set foot in the New World was a seaman on the *Mayflower.* Arriving with the Pilgrims in 1620, he was "hired to stay a year" and then returned to England when his "time was out." Any further details of his life, including his first name, remain unknown.

The next Ely stayed for good. Nathaniel Ely of Kent, England, son of a Cambridge-educated curate, crossed the Atlantic to Massachusetts around 1634. He was likely a Puritan attempting to escape religious persecution under King Charles I.

Another English immigrant to Massachusetts, possibly arriving on the same ship, was a teenager named Robert Harrington. Ely settled in Newe Towne (or Newtowne, later Cambridge) with his wife and their two children; Harrington settled in neighboring Watertown.[1]

For nearly two centuries the Ely and Harrington families remained in the Northeast. But at last, the expansion of the country began to pull them westward. In 1799 Lewis Ely and his family left their farm in New England and built the first cabin in Deerfield Township, Portage County, Ohio. There they stayed until 1852, when Asher Ely (Lewis's son) and his youngest son, Hanson Asher Ely, relocated their families to near Fond du Lac, Wisconsin.

Two years after that, Orson Harrington, a private-school–educated teacher and merchant, moved his family from New York to Indiana. There he taught school for a year before continuing on to Iowa and eventually settling near Williamsburg (at that time frequently spelled with a terminal *-h*), a region that would be home to seven or more generations of his family. Within ten years, Orson was farming, teaching school, serving in local government, and raising seven children together with his wife, Mary Wakely Harrington. Their fifth child was named Emma.[2]

Eugene Hanson Ely was born in 1839 to Hanson and his wife, Mary Titus Ely. In 1859, the same year Orson came to Williamsburg, Eugene enrolled in the classics department at Lawrence University in Appleton, Wisconsin, quite possibly the first member of his family in three centuries or more to attend college.

Still a student when the Civil War broke out, he enlisted as a private in a Wisconsin militia regiment and rose quickly to the rank of first lieutenant in the Indiana cavalry. He married Julia Lamb in 1863, and after the war ended, the couple moved to Iowa: first to a farm in Buchanan County, and then to Iowa City. Eugene found work as a superintendent of schools and as a publisher's representative.

At least two of his six children were students at the State University of Iowa (now the University of Iowa), where he was employed as a lecturer on Shakespeare and established "an enviable reputation as a scholarly student of the works of the immortal Bard." The second of his children to attend the university, Nathan Dana Ely, matriculated in 1883 but did not complete his sophomore year. Instead, "with pockets full of recommendations and cash," he went into teaching, as his father and his older sister had.[3]

On Christmas Eve 1885, the Ely and Harrington families were joined when Nathan Dana Ely married Emma Lois Harrington at her parents' farm, her childhood home. Emma was twenty-eight years old; Nathan had celebrated his twentieth birthday less than a week earlier. Ten months later, on October 21, 1886, Emma gave birth to a son, Eugene ("Gene") Burton Ely, named for his paternal grandfather and a maternal uncle.[4]

Orson Harrington, who by this time owned 551 acres of farmland in the fledgling community that he and his fellow New York transplants had named York Township, gave his daughter eighty acres of farmland, apparently her one-seventh share of his estate. The couple moved into "as snug and cozy a house as one could meet with," and Nathan Ely became a farmer on land that had belonged to his father-in-law.[5]

But he did not remain long on the farm. In 1887, Williamsburg businessman Michael J. Kelly won election to the Iowa Senate as a Democrat, and Nathan accepted a job as his secretary. For him, this marked the start of a permanent career move into the law and Democratic politics. Two years later, while the family was out, the Ely home burned to the ground. Arson was suspected.[6]

In 1892, without an undergraduate degree but with five years of political experience, Nathan returned to the State University of Iowa and enrolled in the law department. While attending law school, he once again lived with his parents in Iowa City. This was a practical matter: Iowa City was thirty miles east of Williamsburg over unpaved roads, and the fastest available means of travel between the two places was by horse and carriage. A one-way trip took the better part of a day. The strain on the young family, which now, in addition to Eugene, included Mary W. ("Maidie," born 1888) and Julia M. (born 1893), must have been substantial.

Following his graduation in 1895, Nathan formed a partnership with classmate Arthur G. Bush and opened a private law practice in Davenport, Iowa, on the banks of the Mississippi River, opposite the Illinois cities of Rock Island and Moline. In addition to the farm in Williamsburg, the family now maintained a home in Davenport.[7]

Davenport, fifty miles beyond Iowa City, was still farther removed from Emma's relatives. While Nathan was engaged with his legal and political career, she and the children often returned to Williamsburg. In July 1896, he was in Chicago attending the Democratic convention and Emma was at her parents' farm when a terrible accident occurred. According to a newspaper account, three-year-old Julia stumbled and fell into a bucket of boiling suds left unattended on the floor. She was horribly scalded and died from her injuries.[8]

On the world stage, Cuba was fighting for its independence from Spain, and the United States sent the battleship *Maine* to maintain a presence in Havana harbor. Late in the evening of February 15, 1898, an explosion sank the ship. More than 250 of her crew perished in what was described as "the worst disaster in the naval history of the United States." American newspaper stories spread rumors that Spain was responsible, and relations, already tense, deteriorated. President William McKinley proclaimed a blockade of the island on April 22, and three days later Congress passed a formal declaration of war.[9]

Nathan Ely, with no experience at sea, enlisted for a year with the rating "ordinary seaman." For a well-established community leader with an active two-person law practice to accept a posting at the second-lowest rating in the naval hierarchy, particularly a thirty-two-year-old married man with children, is surprising. Yet he departed in late May to join the U.S. fleet in Key West, leaving Bush to manage the practice and Emma to manage the family.[10]

A telegram he sent from Florida on May 30, 1898, indicates that he expected to be billeted aboard one of the blockade ships heading for the coast of Cuba. Instead, the screw sloop-of-war to which he was assigned, *Lancaster*, served as "station ship" at Key West, ostensibly participating in coastal defense against an attack that never came.[11]

Nathan evidently benefited from concessions to his age and status. A news story somewhat jocularly quoted him as saying that his role was "assistant surgeon, in about the fourteenth degree," and that "the only distinction between him and the common seaman" was "that he did not have to do scrubbing of decks or brightening brass." Another and perhaps more reliable story reported that he had been appointed "shipwrighter" and explained that the position meant "that Mr. Ely will mess [dine] with the officers of the boat and that he will have charge of the log book and will take the reckonings of longitude and latitude." Given that *Lancaster* remained at anchor in the Key West harbor throughout the war, that task would have presented no great challenge.[12]

Two weeks after reporting for duty, Nathan succumbed to heat prostration while on shore. Over the previous six years he had suffered severe headaches in hot weather, but this time his condition was reported to have been more severe and to have included vertigo.

Hostilities ceased on August 12, 1898, and *Lancaster* sailed the following week for Portsmouth, New Hampshire; but ordinary seaman Ely missed even that limited seagoing experience. A medical examination had found him unfit for naval service, and he was granted an honorable discharge, effective August 7.[13]

The would-be sailor headed back to Davenport. Passing through Birmingham, Alabama, on August 10, where his presence "excited a great deal of attention," he was hailed as a "jolly jack tar." The next day's newspaper, apparently confusing him with another sailor transiting Birmingham, identified him as a seaman from the battleship *Oregon* and cited his "graphic description" of the July 3 battle of Santiago de Cuba. The article concluded: "Ely was slightly wounded and afterward was taken sick with fever, and for this reason was given a furlough." The only remotely accurate part of the story was the fever.[14]

By August 13, 1898, the veteran was home in Iowa and back on familiar ground: playing a key role in the Second District Democratic congressional convention, telling colorful stories about Navy life, and openly criticizing the Navy's policy of requiring sailors to pay their own way home upon discharge. Davenporters welcomed him as a war hero. At a homecoming parade and banquet for soldiers and sailors in Moline, he was a featured speaker. A social services agency prevailed on him to "give the children a talk on the late war with Spain." Three years later, he would be elected "admiral" of the Davenport Fishing Club, chiefly because his "seafaring experience made him particularly fit for the office."[15]

In the ensuing years, he took up golfing and duck hunting and became a prominent booster of the University of Iowa football team. He and Emma went on to have one more child. Hubert D. was born in April 1900, when Emma was forty-three, Gene thirteen, and Maidie twelve.[16]

In January 1901, Gene graduated from the ninth grade at Davenport Public School No. 4 and was eligible to start classes at the high school. But the age of the automobile was dawning, and he had a knack for the mechanical. In 1904, when his former classmates were finishing their senior year of high school, he was already employed as a chauffeur.[17]

CHAPTER 2

RISE OF THE WHEELMEN

FROM THE INTRODUCTION OF THE WHEEL for transportation around 3500 BC until the early nineteenth century, there was little evolution in the technology of land transportation. The axle was developed in the Bronze Age, making animal-drawn wagons possible; eventually a suspension system to separate passengers from the joltings of the road was added. But until the innovation of the steam locomotive and railroad, all land transport relied in one way or another on the stride of a human or an animal. Toward the end of the nineteenth century, everything changed. In stunningly rapid succession first the bicycle, then the motorcycle and automobile, and then, incredibly, "heavier-than-air" flying machines burst into being. Over the span of a few decades, humans went from wobbling on high-wheeled bicycles to realizing the ancient dream of flight, and concepts of space and time were forever altered.

This astonishing transportation revolution blossomed over the course of a single generation. Many of the pioneers who designed and raced the newly developed bicycle also spearheaded the burgeoning motorcycle and automobile industries and designed and piloted the earliest flying machines, pressing the outer limits of the possible. Eugene Ely was born on the cusp of this breathtaking acceleration in technological development. His story—his brief, meteoric rise to fame—is deeply intertwined with the transformation of transportation and those who propelled it.[1]

Around 1870, English inventor James Starley began production of the first device generally known as a "bicycle" (from the Greek for "two wheels"). With its spoked metal wheels, solid rubber tires, and relatively light construction, it provided significantly more comfort than its wooden-wheeled, iron-tired predecessor, the velocipede or "boneshaker." And because the bicycle's top speed was directly proportional to the radius of the front wheel, to which the pedals were attached, that wheel soon evolved, growing until it reached its practical limit: the approximate length of the rider's inseam. The larger wheel made the vehicle more resistant to tipping sideways when in motion. Mounting and dismounting were awkward, however, and a sudden stop or high-speed turn could easily cause the rider to "take a header."

At the 1876 Centennial International Exposition in Philadelphia, Col. Albert Augustus Pope, a Bostonian and Civil War veteran, viewed several bicycles on display and was instantly enthusiastic. He began importing them from England and introduced his own model in 1878, the Columbia High Wheeler. Its innovations included the use of ball bearings in the wheel hubs and hollow steel tubes for the frame.

But as a practical matter there was almost nowhere for budding cyclists to use their new machines. After fifty years of growth, the railroads had become the principal means of long-distance overland transportation, leaving American intercity roads in woeful disrepair. Farmers still brought their crops to market by horse and wagon which could handle the less-than-ideal road conditions. Within cities, street railways functioned well. Legislation banning bicycles from city parks and streets began cropping up all over America.

When Newport, Rhode Island, "hosted a grand parade of a hundred cyclists" in May 1880, Pope used the opportunity to announce the formation of the National League of American Wheelmen, which "lobbied for a lifestyle in which roads, not rails, became the primary arteries of American recreation and commerce." The League quickly became a powerful national lobby associated with the novel Good Roads movement.[2]

Starley had experimented in England with chain drives on tricycles and quadricycles. His nephew John Kemp Starley applied the chain drive to a bicycle in 1885 and added a rear-wheel gearing system, eliminating the need for the enormous front wheel. The result, the Rover "safety" bicycle, featured front and rear wheels of equal size. And thus, the modern bicycle was born.[3]

A huge upsurge in bicycling followed. New techniques in mass production were already lowering retail costs to the point where workingmen could afford to buy two-wheelers, and the emergence of bloomers as an acceptable fashion meant that women, too, could ride. In 1887 the New York state legislature voted to permit bicycles to share the streets with carriages. The craze spread across the country in no time.[4]

In Ohio, Pope's National League of American Wheelmen counted among the members of its Dayton branch two brothers in the printing business: Wilbur and Orville Wright. Orville competed in bicycle races, and the brothers often used their mechanical skills to help friends with bicycle repairs.

The League's 1892 convention in Dayton apparently influenced the brothers' decision to transform their printing business into a bicycle sales, parts, and repair shop. In 1896 the Wrights began offering their own make of bicycle, with a frame built by means of an electrical welding device they had designed. One of the most useful innovations they introduced was a left-hand thread for the left-side pedal, to prevent it from working itself loose.

Around 1899, the Wrights developed a keen interest in the mechanics of powered flight—still strictly theoretical at the time—in particular, the difficulties of controlling an aircraft in motion. Their knowledge of bicycling informed their experiments with flight. They understood a bicyclist's critical need for balance, both on a straight road and when leaning into a turn; the chain-and-sprocket system for transmitting motive power; the importance of lightweight materials; and the interaction of wind resistance and aerodynamic shape. By 1900 the Wrights were wheelmen no more; they remained in the bicycle business through 1907 solely to finance their flight experiments.[5]

An aircraft changes direction in three dimensions through *roll* (rotation around the front-to-back axis), *pitch* (rotation around the left-to-right axis), and *yaw* (rotation around the top-to-bottom axis). The benefits of pitch and yaw control are easy to grasp. The value of roll control is sometimes harder to understand.

Extended flight is impossible without a system of lateral stability; that is, some way to control the extent to which the aircraft leans to one side or the other. Not only is this necessary for correcting inadvertent left-right tilts, such as those caused by puffs of wind, but it also provides a way to make tight banking turns. To change the direction of flight, it is not sufficient simply to turn the rudder as one does with boats, which take advantage of the fact that water resistance is much greater than air resistance. An airplane is turned by leaning it to one side while pulling the nose up, where "up" is a direction that is no longer precisely vertical (since the airplane is now tilted) but instead slants up and sideways.

Forerunners to the Wrights had devised solutions to pitch and yaw that took advantage of the resistance of the air to the machine's forward motion. Yaw could be controlled by manipulating a rudder (a flat piece hinged vertically, like the rudder of a ship), which would point the nose to the left or right. Pitch adjustments could be made by means of one or more rudders turned on their sides: tilting these "elevator planes" upward made the machine rise; tilting them downward made it descend. But the problem of controlling roll had defied solution, and it became the Wrights' main focus.

The accepted practice for addressing roll in a glider, employed by German aviation pioneer Otto Lilienthal and others, was for the aviator to shift the aircraft's center of gravity by sliding his body sideways. The Wrights knew this approach was impractical, the result often fatal. By contrast, a bird maintains equilibrium during flight by manipulating its wings to produce "dynamic reactions of the air." From this observation Wilbur Wright developed the concept of "wing-warping," a solution that no one, so far as the Wrights were aware, had thought of before.

The heart of the Wrights' wing-warping system was a pair of stiff yet flexible wings, both upper and lower, whose ends could be physically twisted in opposite directions under the aviator's control. Doing so would increase the aerodynamic lifting force on one side of the aircraft while decreasing it on the other, tilting the machine toward the latter side. Wilbur is said to have demonstrated the concept by twisting the ends of a long, narrow cardboard box, of the sort that might hold a bicycle inner tube; a similar demonstration can be made with an object such as a plastic ice cube tray.[6]

In 1900 the brothers traveled to the sand dunes and strong winds of Kitty Hawk, on the Outer Banks of North Carolina, to work with unmanned and manned gliders. There they achieved their first breakthrough: in-flight control of a glider.

But their wing-warping solution had the dramatic and undesirable side effect of also rotating the machine around its vertical axis: banking to the left pointed the nose slightly toward the right, and vice versa. In 1902 they solved the problem by linking the rear rudder to the wing-warping controls so that the necessary correction was applied automatically.

Their trials were so successful that in March 1903 the brothers applied for a patent on their glider, which the U.S. Patent Office quickly rejected. They had prepared the application themselves; the examiner found their drawings inadequate and their written description "vague and indefinite" and recommended that they hire an experienced patent attorney.

Undaunted, the Wrights continued their experiments, eventually developing a design in which an onboard engine drove a pair of propellers via a bicycle-inspired chain-and-sprocket linkage. On December 17, 1903, they achieved the world's first controlled, powered flight in a heavier-than-air machine. Within weeks they had engaged a patent attorney to help them protect their invention.

Convinced that wing-warping with automatic rudder control was the secret to lateral stability, the Wrights now expected to receive royalties from anyone who achieved flight using their method—or anything like it. They ultimately received a patent for their glider in 1906, which they used to wage a seemingly endless patent war against the rest of the aviation world, a war that some contemporaries and historians have blamed for retarding American aviation by many years.[7]

One of the men the Wrights set their sights on was Glenn Hammond Curtiss. As a youngster in the village of Hammondsport in upstate New York, Curtiss had won his first bicycle in a race sponsored by the *Hammondsport Herald* for covering a specified newspaper delivery route in the fastest time. He left school after eighth grade and in 1895 got a job with the Eastman Dry Plate and Film Company in Rochester, where his inventive genius increased efficiencies in the stenciling of roll film. Soon he was recruited by a local bicycle racing team and became an accomplished competitive rider.[8]

In 1900, just when the Wright brothers were beginning to move away from the bicycle business, Curtiss entered it. He began as they had: with a repair and spare-parts business that later expanded into manufacturing. Soon he was selling an engine he had designed that could transform a bicycle into a motorcycle. Although motorized cycles had been around since the 1860s, the light and powerful Curtiss engine was a leap forward.[9]

His business took a significant turn in the early summer of 1904 when he received a telegram order to deliver a motorcycle engine to Oakland, California. The purchaser, Thomas S. Baldwin—widely known as Captain Tom, though he had no formal claim to the title—was a former circus balloonist trying to perfect a one-man dirigible.

Like most contemporary designs, Baldwin's dirigible (from the French for "steerable [balloon]") featured a large, torpedo-shaped fabric envelope stretched over a rigid frame. Inside the envelope a buoyant gas provided lift, while an engine suspended beneath it drove a propeller. A rudder allowed the operator to steer left and right. To tilt the nose up or down, the operator clambered fore and aft along a narrow catwalk, shifting the airship's center of gravity.[10]

Although dirigibles had made successful controlled flights in Europe, the feat had yet to be accomplished in America. Heavy engines were a major hindrance. Baldwin constructed his *California Arrow* with help from James C. Mars (born McBride), a former circus acrobat and balloon parachutist. Diminutive and fearless, "Bud" Mars had the ideal build and temperament for an *aeronaut* ("air sailor"—a flier of lighter-than-air craft) and later an *aviator* ("one who flies as the birds do"—a flier of heavier-than-air craft).[11]

On August 3, 1904, the Baldwin-Mars dirigible, powered by a lightweight Curtiss engine and with Baldwin at the controls, flew a circuit over Oakland. With that sensational flight, Baldwin made the first powered flight in America that ended where it began, beating the Wrights in that regard by nearly two months.[12]

To pilot *California Arrow* at the St. Louis Louisiana Purchase Exposition in the fall of 1904, Baldwin hired A. Roy Knabenshue, a slim youth from Toledo, Ohio. The airship's effect on the city was huge, as "clerks deserted their desks, street cars were stopped, and all business was suspended until the machine passed." Knabenshue's ascensions, which included a maneuverability demonstration in which he flew in a figure eight, attracted thousands of spectators and were hailed as "the most successful ever made in the United States."[13]

In the wake of that success, Baldwin struck a deal to buy more Curtiss engines for his dirigibles. While Curtiss had no special interest in aviation at that time, he was interested in new markets for his engines. From bicycles to motorcycles to powered airships, Curtiss was now in the business of flight.[14]

The 1905 Lewis and Clark Exposition in Portland, Oregon, featured a Baldwin dirigible flown by seventeen-year-old Lincoln Beachey, a bicycle racer and motorcyclist from San Francisco. "There's really nothing to it," Beachey reportedly said of aerial acrobatics. "It's just the same as being on the ground, so far as nervousness is concerned."[15]

He left Baldwin's employ to tour the country with Knabenshue and became known for performing increasingly daring dirigible stunts. In June 1906 he circled the U.S. Capitol building and landed on the White House lawn. "It is safe to say," reported the *Washington Evening Star*, "that there was not a full hour's work put in by any of the employees of the government or any of the other offices within view of the flight from 10 a.m. till after 12." Less than a year after taking up flying, Beachey had become a national sensation.[16]

Although most Americans were aware, by 1906, of the Wrights' claimed ability to fly, there was general skepticism. While the exploits of Mars, Knabenshue, Beachey, and others with lighter-than-air craft such as dirigibles drew large crowds and were widely reported, the public had never seen a heavier-than-air machine actually fly. For some years after their Kitty Hawk breakthrough, the brothers did almost no flying in public. A public demonstration near Dayton in May 1904 failed because of weather and ground conditions; Wilbur Wright flew for more than twenty-four miles outside Dayton in October 1905, but the audience had been only some thirty people. It was no wonder that the public widely regarded powered flight as physically impossible.[17]

Curtiss, aware of the Wrights' claims and always interested in expanding his market, wrote a friendly letter to the brothers in May 1906, offering to supply them with lightweight motors "with which to carry on your work." The Wrights declined, although that September they met with him in connection with a Baldwin dirigible exhibition in Dayton. They showed him a few photographs of their machine but did not permit him to inspect the real thing.[18]

The bicycle craze that Albert Augustus Pope helped to spark in America was sweeping through Iowa around the time of Ely's birth. By 1891, bicycles were such a common sight in his hometown of Williamsburg that there was talk of forming a club. Four years later, the local paper reported the exciting news that Orson Harrington Jr., Ely's teenaged cousin, had bought "a handsome new bike."

In August 1888, Davenport had become one of the first cities in the United States to boast an electric street railway. Less than twelve years later, in May 1900, the city witnessed the appearance of another marvelous, highly anticipated new vehicle when a steam-driven two-seater automobile made by the Locomobile Company of America appeared on the streets. Local newspapers reported that its twenty-gallon water tank allowed the machine to cover up to thirty miles between fill-ups, traveling at the remarkable average speed of twelve miles an hour.

Its pioneering owner, Otto von Schaezler, was a leading citizen and a German immigrant. Though he later renounced his hereditary title, with newspapers making much of his American wife Mabel's decision not to move to Germany and take the title of baroness, he would nevertheless be known for the rest of his time in Iowa as "the Baron."[19]

Across the nation, vehicles like the Baron's had already become the subject of open ridicule. Newspaper editorials dismissed the newly termed *automobile* ("self-moving") as a poor substitute for the horse—and a fire hazard to boot—and were quick to point out that "horseless carriages, like bicycles, are dry weather vehicles, and not capable of making speed over bad roads." For most Americans, the horseless carriage had limited utility. A small minority took a broader view. Thomas Edison, in remarks reported across the country, said in early 1899, "I believe in ten years a horse will be a rare sight. The automobile is here to stay."[20]

The military soon envisioned various practical uses for the automobile. At a time when the standard method of communication between distant army units was the carrier pigeon, the Signal Service announced plans to conduct experiments in which electric horseless carriages paid out lengths of wire and served as power sources to facilitate telephone communication. Europeans were more farsighted, experimenting with motorcars as replacements for horses in transporting matériel such as heavy guns. By the turn of the century, the U.S. Army had adopted an "automobile gun" for field service.[21]

In December 1902, Ely's father, Nathan, fell while alighting from a Davenport streetcar. The incident made the news not only in Davenport but in Iowa City and Williamsburg as well. The initial diagnosis of a "sprain" changed to a wrenched back with headaches, then to "congestion [swelling] of the brain" requiring weeks of bed rest followed by a mandatory two-month vacation. So Nathan once again left home, this time to travel on his own throughout the Southeast. In February 1903 he wrote that he was recovering his health and enjoying a "trip on the Tennessee River"; in March he returned to Davenport.[22]

A few weeks after Nathan returned, Emma left town with Maidie and Hubert to spend the summer at her childhood home in Williamsburg. Soon sixteen-year-old Gene left Davenport, too. He was back in Williamsburg in August and by October was living full time on his own in nearby Cosgrove.

He soon found employment: Father Thomas Smyth, a Roman Catholic priest in Cosgrove, owned a car that he was unable to drive. In August 1903 the *Williamsburg Journal-Tribune* reported that Smyth "came up today with his new auto. The trip was made in short order. 'Gene Ely came along as chauffeur."[23]

Turn-of-the-century automobiles were specialized pieces of equipment, and owners frequently hired experts to operate and maintain them. Father Smyth's car, with its internal combustion engine and the ability to reach speeds exceeding 30 mph, was a far cry from the Baron's clunky, steam-powered Locomobile. Not yet seventeen when he first took the wheel, for the next year and a half, Ely sped around Iowa in his employer's car.

It is unclear where and how he learned to drive. The man generally supposed to have taught him is "Pete" Petersen. Born in Denmark in 1869, four years younger than Nathan Ely, Peder Christian Pedersen had changed the spelling of his name upon immigrating to the United States sometime after 1890. On a visit to Paris in 1899, he obtained a French driver's license. By the time he arrived in Davenport three or four years later, Petersen knew his way around motors and was soon driving in local races. By 1909 he owned a garage in Davenport.[24]

Once he had access to an automobile, Ely set about learning everything there was to know about them. According to a late 1904 newspaper story, "Gene Ely of Cosgrove, the well-known chauffeur, was in town for a couple of days last week repairing the automobile [of] Lyman Hanaford. Gene knows all about the gasoline wagons and can diagnose the ailments to which they are subject as correctly as any mechanic in Iowa." He was also cool under pressure. Once, when the gas tank of Father Smyth's car leaked and a spark set the machine on fire, Ely "succeeded in smothering the flames before much damage was done."[25]

Although automobiles were becoming an accepted sight around town, wagon drivers on rural roads considered them a nuisance. Horses could easily be spooked by the unfamiliar sight and sound, and a team would sometimes have to be unhitched and held even though the approaching "devil wagon" was still as much as a mile away. Father Smyth's car once overtook some farmers hauling coal who, cursing, threw chunks at its occupants as they passed.[26]

Father Smyth had a love of speed and encouraged it in his driver. In June 1904 the two of them were reported to have driven eight miles in fourteen minutes, an average speed of 34 mph. In August, it took them less than two and a half hours to cover about fifty-five miles of rough country roads not designed with automobiles in mind, an impressive average speed of about 22 mph. Two weeks later they did it again, 3 mph faster.[27]

At about this time Father Smyth upgraded to a larger, more powerful car—a splendid red 30-hp Franklin touring car with a back seat for two or three additional passengers. It was reputedly able to reach 60 mph—if only the dirt-and-mud roads of Iowa (and the absence of a windscreen) had allowed for such speed.

Stories abounded about the priest's "wild driver," such as the tale that he preferred to drive with chains on the tires even when the road was hard and dry, because of the extra startup traction they gave. He supposedly once roared across a bridge so fast that he failed to notice that some of the planks were missing.[28]

Schoolchildren idolized him. A local ten-year-old named Louis Rohret reminisced long afterward:

> All of us kids were always hoping that Father Smyth would invite us to go along on one of the trips he made. That happened to me and my friend, Willie McCabe. . . . [In December 1904] the two of us and two elderly ladies were in the back seat. Ely picked up a buddy of his . . . , who also sat in the back seat since Father Smyth always rode beside Ely. On the way home, Ely and his friend had it made up to scare the old ladies a bit. Ely turned and winked at his friend as he let the car out for a bit of speed.

What happened next was detailed on the front page of the *Iowa City Daily Press*:

> When six miles south of town and going at considerable speed, the steering apparatus failed to work properly, the guide sticking. The machine ran with much force into a bank at the side of the road, the shock of the impact throwing Father Smyth out, and shaking up the other occupants of the car. No one was injured, happily.
>
> The front wheels of the machine were wrecked, one being badly broken and twisted, while the other received a bent axle. A livery team was sent for here, and the party taken home by horse power of the ordinary kind.[29]

Somehow the car remained upright, but seat belts had yet to be invented, and Rohret marveled that the sixty-six-year-old Smyth was able to pick himself up after being tossed from the vehicle "like a mailbag." A head injury Ely later admitted sustaining at about this time in his life may also have occurred during the crash.[30]

Ely had come face to face with the consequences of losing control of a fast-moving machine.

But it was a different sort of risky behavior that shortly afterward ended his employment. According to Rohret, "Ely got a little too smart for the old priest" and began borrowing the car for extended periods, under the pretense of "making some difficult repairs to it." The fact that he was actually using it to "run races at the county fairs . . . finally got back to Father Smyth," who fired him.

The comings and goings of the speed-loving priest in the big red car continued to make the local news, but by the fall of 1905 there was no further mention of Ely as his driver.[31]

CHAPTER 3

FIRE AND EARTH

FOLLOWING HIS DISCHARGE as Father Smyth's chauffeur, it made sense for Ely to look for a similar type of employment, perhaps in one of the big cities to the east. With his experience in driving, racing, and servicing the big car, he could have sought a job at Franklin Automobile Company headquarters in Syracuse, New York. Another logical destination for an eighteen-year-old midwesterner with skills as a driver and mechanic might have been Chicago. In the end, however, he traveled in the opposite direction.

San Francisco was a long way away, but Ely was probably aware that since late 1904 Franklin had been planning to establish agencies (that is, dealership arrangements) there and in Los Angeles. And the pages of the *Williamsburg Journal-Tribune* were splashed with seductive advertisements: "Tens of thousands will spend their winter vacations in California; will you? There you can pick flowers and enjoy outdoor life all the year 'round."[1]

With no serviceable road through the Rocky Mountains, the only practical route west was by rail. Nine generations of Ely ancestors had taken nearly two and a half centuries to cover the 1,200 miles from Massachusetts to Iowa. Ely rode half again as far in a matter of days. The date of his departure is unknown, but he may have traveled with his cousin Orson Harrington, who—nearly thirty but without a family—left for San Francisco in mid-October 1905, intending to stay the winter. By April 1906 the two were evidently sharing lodgings in the city.[2]

Ely found a thriving automobile industry in California. People were more likely to own cars there than in the Midwest, and the roads were better built and maintained. But cars did not enjoy exclusive use of the streets: 1906 motion-picture footage of San Francisco's primary thoroughfare, Market Street, reveals a chaotic jumble of automobiles, pedestrians, streetcars, bicycles, and horse-drawn carts.[3]

Perhaps for that reason, Northern California had implemented speed limits that made driving scarcely faster than walking. Five years before Ely's arrival, in response to ordinances that restricted motor vehicle operation in favor of the "automobilists' worst enemy, the horse," a group of motoring enthusiasts formed the San Francisco–based Automobile Club of California. The club's efforts to secure a uniform set of laws governing automobiles' operation paid off in 1905 with statewide regulation, including precursors of modern driver's licenses and vehicle-registration systems.[4]

At the time, most San Francisco car dealerships were clustered along eight blocks of Golden Gate Avenue, between Octavia and Jones Streets. The location was deliberate: Golden Gate Avenue was the route most often taken by wealthy horse-carriage owners—prospective automobile purchasers—traveling from downtown to Golden Gate Park.

Within a few weeks of Ely's arrival, Franklin announced its first San Francisco agency. It may be that Ely had traveled to California specifically for that reason, aware that mechanics familiar with Franklin engines would be needed. Soon, however, he was working as a professional chauffeur.[5]

Few California automobile owners wished to operate and maintain the tricky, greasy engines themselves. This created a demand for drivers who could also perform repairs. Early in 1904, San Francisco drivers had organized the Chauffeurs' Association of California No. 1, later the California Chauffeurs' Association, which established a new three-tier wage scale. Each aspirant to membership had to pass a knowledge test, demonstrate skill at running a particular make of automobile, and agree never to exceed the speed limit in Golden Gate Park at night. The association soon had more than fifty members.

Ely received license number 2474, the thirtieth license issued by the State of California in 1906, and joined the association, giving as his address the Windsor Hotel, a few blocks east of the Franklin dealership. Within a year he was an elected officer.[6]

Dr. Morris Herzstein emigrated from Germany to the United States at the age of twenty-four. By 1905 he had become a well-known surgeon, a benefactor of the University of California, and the wealthy founder of the Waldeck sanatorium and nurses' training school, six blocks from the Franklin dealership and just up the hill from the Windsor Hotel. He ordered the sale of "all of his horses, carriages and harness" late that year, and within six months he had joined the Automobile Club and obtained his first two horseless carriages. In need of a full-time chauffeur, he hired Ely.[7]

In the early morning of April 18, 1906, San Francisco was rocked by an earthquake. Many buildings were destroyed outright, including Ely's hotel; Harrington recorded that "most of the roof was in our room when we got up." The devastating fires that followed burned for three days and covered nearly five square miles. An estimated seven to eight hundred people lost their lives.

The first report to Iowa County came from Harrington and Ely, "who wired to Mrs. Ely of Davenport to the effect that they had escaped and were well." On April 29, Orson composed a long letter to his sister-in-law Winnifred, which the *Williamsburg Journal-Tribune* printed in full. "I never was so near scared to death as I was that morning and own up to it," he confessed. "There are some four-story buildings that have settled down so the roof is about level with the pavements. . . . The fire commenced in several places all at once and we had no water, for the earthquake had broken every water and gas main in the city."

As both the hotel and the sanatorium burned to the ground, Ely and Harrington, driving Herzstein's two automobiles, reportedly helped convey all the patients north to safety on the other side of Nob Hill. The group spent the first night on Union Street, but according to Orson, "the fire came too close so we moved to a small park near the Presidio and camped two days" before moving again after the fires subsided. The city was under martial law, with a 10 p.m. curfew to curb rampant vandalism. "Several chauffeurs have been killed, been ordered to stop and did not. [The soldiers] stuck their old musket up in my face several times and you don't need to ask me whether I stopped for it's a certainty that I did and was glad to for that big gun didn't look good to me."

Years later, after Ely had achieved fame as an aviator, newspapers breathlessly recounted inflated tales of his San Francisco heroics, according to which he had set "a record of working forty hours without sleep" and had singlehandedly rescued all the sanatorium's patients—a number variously reported as sixty and "more than three hundred." He also, it was said, saved the life of a wealthy banker and later married the banker's daughter.[8]

Shaken and missing his family, Harrington returned to Williamsburg in May of that year, but Ely remained. California was where the automobiles were, and life in Iowa could never be the same again for him. By 1905 his parents had divorced—a rare occurrence at that time—and five weeks before the earthquake his father, Nathan, had married Mabel von Schaezler, who had divorced the Baron in 1901.[9]

In early November 1906, Harrington escorted Ely's siblings—eighteen-year-old Maidie and six-year-old Hubert—to San Francisco for the winter. (The record is unclear as to whether their mother, Emma, joined them.) The city was quickly rebuilding, and Ely was thriving there.[10]

With the Waldeck in ruins, Herzstein required little or no driving, so Ely became a chauffeur for Charles Conlisk, a wealthy Oakland socialite who held several high-profile business positions. Within a fortnight of the earthquake Conlisk relocated his office from Napa to San Francisco, publicly demonstrating his faith in the city's future.[11]

San Francisco's inaugural automobile show in February 1907 served as both a powerful symbol of the city's rapid rebound from the disaster and a marketing opportunity extraordinaire for the newly formed Automobile Dealers' Association of California. The seven-day extravaganza took place in the brand-new Coliseum near the panhandle of Golden Gate Park, opening with a "gala procession" of some 250 cars. "Great crowds" lined Van Ness Avenue to watch the "largest parade of the sort" that San Francisco had ever seen, while a band in a large vehicle played near the head of the procession. At the Coliseum, forty different makes of gleaming automobiles were arranged in a semicircle, ready to take passengers for test rides. The crowd "was refreshingly happy and good-natured," and the dealers were "delighted with the results," making many sales on the floor.[12]

The local automobile business was poised for growth. Even the earthquake proved no obstacle to the industry; the opportunity to rebuild seems to have led San Franciscans to embrace motor transportation with even greater enthusiasm. After the fire, many of the automobile dealerships consolidated into a main "Auto Row" along upper Van Ness Avenue, which had served as a firebreak. The center of Auto Row was at the intersection of Golden Gate and Van Ness, near where the Matheson Company of California did business.[13]

In early 1907, Ely bought two Matheson seven-passenger touring cars, intending to build a private chauffeur business. The combined purchase price of the two Mathesons exceeded $10,000, far beyond his means, so perhaps he borrowed the money or found financial backers. He had connections with several potential investors by that time, including Conlisk and Herzstein. Ely was swept up in the movement to demonstrate to the public just what an automobile could do.

Ely was legally entitled to charge five dollars an hour for the use of his Mathesons. Presumably he did the driving, but he may have employed a second chauffeur. His timing was fortuitous: on May 5, 1907, the streetcar operators of San Francisco began a nearly six-month strike, paralyzing the city's transportation system and putting automobiles at a premium. Ely had all the private chauffeuring opportunities he wanted, for a time, and continued to operate his car-hire business in San Francisco for the next year and a half.[14]

The best money to be made in the automotive business was in sales, and the best way to advertise was by racing. "We want endurance and reliability runs," said the president of the Automobile Dealers' Association, "to prove the reliability of the cars, and also hill-climbing contests. A reliability run, say of two hundred miles, to start and finish in San Francisco, would prove of great interest."[15]

The "endurance run" was the safest method of competition and provided the most useful information for prospective car buyers. It typically required the driver to travel a set distance over a specified time, strictly adhering to all speed limits and without stopping for engine repairs—as confirmed by an independent observer riding as a passenger or by sealing the engine compartment shut. In May 1907, fifty-four vehicles participated in the association's first contest, an all-day ninety-mile affair from San Francisco to Half Moon Bay and La Honda. One was an Auburn, driven by Norman DeVaux.[16]

A decade earlier, nineteen-year-old cycling enthusiast DeVaux had set out to ride a safety bicycle across the United States. Although the Good Roads movement was growing in popularity, it had not yet resulted in many truly good intercity roads, and the record for a transcontinental bicycle crossing was just over forty-one days. DeVaux and his friend John LaFrance pedaled out of Manhattan on June 1, 1896, and on July 8, "two tired and dusty wheelmen" arrived in San Francisco. Their elapsed time was thirty-seven days, fourteen hours, and thirty minutes—roughly one hundred miles per day over a route that was little more than a series of rutted wagon tracks and cow paths. Three decades later, their astonishing record still stood.[17]

DeVaux stayed in San Francisco, working as a salesman and chauffeur. He was an early convert to automobiles and was reportedly involved in building the first Cadillac; by 1903 he was a Cadillac salesman. In an echo of his cycling days a decade earlier, DeVaux was on a five-man team in the summer of 1906 that drove a Buick from New York to San Francisco in twenty-four days, eight hours, and forty-five minutes, shattering the previous record of thirty-three days. By 1907 he was manager of the City Hall Automobile Company and reporting robust sales of five to seven Auburn cars per week. Concentrating on headline-grabbing distance drives, he virtually single-handedly established the Auburn as a vehicle of the highest reliability.[18]

While DeVaux did not finish the inaugural La Honda endurance run on May 19, 1907, he made up for it the following week with a trip between Oakland and Fresno—two hundred miles that he covered in 11.5 hours, including meal stops. The *San Francisco Call*'s automotive editor called it "one of the most successful runs that has been made in some time."[19]

Del Monte (part of present-day Monterey), 120 miles down the coast from San Francisco, was one of the most popular destinations for social automobilists. In July it drew crowds for its auto races, including one in which each contestant drove a half-mile circuit while attempting to maintain a speed of precisely ten miles per hour—no easy task without a speedometer. The winner of that race in 1907, turning in a perfect time of three minutes, was Ely.[20]

Ely apparently met Mabel Ellen Hall on a ferry between San Francisco and Marin County when a mutual friend introduced them, likely in early 1907. Mabel was the eldest daughter of Henry Clay Hall, a local schoolteacher and principal, and Mary Locklan Hall. Born in Menlo Park in May 1890, Mabel was ten when the family moved to Corte Madera, a bayside lumber town in Marin County with little more than a general store.[21]

Ely was twenty when they met. He ran his own business and catered to the rich and famous but was nonetheless quiet and introverted. Mabel was petite, brunette, and dark-eyed—an outgoing high school student who turned seventeen that spring. They were married by the end of the summer.

The announcement of their engagement misidentified Ely as the son of "Congressman Ely of Iowa" and elevated his social status to "popular clubman." Mabel was underage and needed parental consent, which her mother—herself only fifteen when she married—willingly gave. The couple married on August 7, 1907, at St. Raphael Catholic Church in San Rafael, ten days after the engagement was announced. Ely's brother, Hubert, was back in Iowa with their mother, but Maidie apparently remained in San Francisco for the event. The couple honeymooned in Colorado—a luxury at the time, perhaps made possible by Conlisk or Herzstein.[22]

By the summer of 1907, automotive events were, according to the press, "coming along on the high gear." In addition to endurance/reliability runs and hill climbs, a third way to test an automobile's worth had been added: track races. These were by far the simplest type of contest to coordinate. Unlike the others, they required little advance planning and did not entail sharing streets with pedestrians, horses, and other automobiles. One event followed hard upon the heels of another, and dealers had to compete. Unwillingness to do so would be considered a sign of inability: "Success on the road, on the track or on the beach are capital to the makers of automobiles, likewise to the dealer," according to one dealer. "Those who fail to enter into the field of competition in some way or other fail to build up a reputation for their cars and incidentally to prove that what they say of them is true." But entry was no trivial undertaking. By one estimate, each race cost a dealer between $500 and $1,000—close to the retail price of the least-expensive automobiles. Just to break even, a dealer would need to sell one car for every race he entered.[23]

Dealers soon were agitating for restrictions on the number of races. "Every little place that has a track is bringing off automobile contests," went the refrain, and people started to worry about the safety of spectators. During races on the Tanforan track just south of San Francisco, where a reported five thousand spectators cheered the motorists, "once or twice the involuntary cry of horror went up as a machine was seen to skid when taking a turn at top speed."[24]

The days of track racing as a form of dealer advertising ended suddenly in northern California when two fatal crashes occurred within a week. At the state fair in Sacramento on September 14,

1907, Ernest Kelly smashed his Thomas Flyer into the fence and tore it up for seventy-five feet before his car flipped, ejecting him. He died the next day. A week later, at Del Monte, a Matheson car made its first appearance on the track, with Roy Rehms at the wheel. When one of his inner tubes blew, he attempted to avoid the fence and the spectators and cranked the steering mechanism too hard. His front inner wheel collapsed, and he was thrown clear. The body of the car rolled over him, crushing his skull.

The California Chauffeurs' Association took charge of Rehms' funeral. As an officer, Ely likely drove in the cortege. But any thoughts he may have entertained about racing his Mathesons on a track were squelched by a swift and widespread call to halt track racing in California. Dealers, owners, and the public agreed: speed contests would henceforth be confined to the roads, viewed as safer because they featured fewer turns.[25]

While initially successful, Ely's San Francisco automobile-hire business apparently fell on hard times in the wake of the so-called Panic of 1907, when a plunge in the New York Stock Exchange resulted in a wave of bankruptcies throughout the country. Ely soldiered on through the summer of 1908, after which he and Mabel decamped from San Francisco in one of his Mathesons. In October they reached Lakeview, Oregon.[26]

Lakeview was a small town on a high, dry plateau, just a few miles from the northeast corner of California. The local paper ran front-page stories promoting the real-estate market: "No section of Oregon, or of the Northwest, offers greater inducements to the homeseeker than does Lake County. Here are still lands for the taking to the hardy and venturesome." Despite headlines that asserted: "People Coming by Thousands," Lakeview was miles from nowhere—specifically, eighty miles north of Likely, California, and the connection with the railway to Reno.

Seeing an opportunity, Ely and a partner, W. Lucas Clapp Jr., began an automobile stage service between Lakeview and Likely. (Clapp had evidently spent time in San Francisco, but he was not a licensed California chauffeur; how he and Ely connected is unknown.) “This service will be a big improvement over the long tedious [twelve-hour] stage ride necessary heretofore,” proclaimed the newspaper. And the service was indeed immediately and hugely popular, often with all seats sold. Demand was so great that Clapp had to arrange locally for use of an additional automobile, at least until Ely’s second Matheson could be brought up from San Francisco.[27]

The business produced a steady income throughout the fall. But the work was grueling for both driver and automobile. Even though the one-way trip took four hours less by auto-stage than by stagecoach, it was still more than eight hours of “deep mud and heavy roads.” Once snow had closed the route for the winter, Ely and Clapp left the high plateau. Clapp returned to Lakeview in the spring of 1909 to resume the service, but Ely had other plans.[28]

In late 1908 Chanslor & Lyon, a prominent California motor-supply company, began offering a “perpetual trophy” to any stock car that established a new record for the round trip between San Francisco and Del Monte. The name of the driver of each successive record-breaking run over the approximately 240-mile course would be inscribed on a large silver challenge cup.

Since a stock car is one manufactured for sale to the public (although typically modified for racing), the challenge was surely of interest to every local auto dealer. And the choice of destination was not lost on the press: “Realizing how greatly the route is traveled by the wealthiest people, there is not an agent in the city who does not covet the record time over the distance.” But racers would need to apply the right combination of speed and guile; the rules stipulated that if “a contestant is arrested for exceeding the speed limit he will forfeit his chance for that particular trial.”[29]

The Hotel Del Monte, designated as the turnaround point, promised to award a miniature silver cup to each of the first ten record-setters. Since the first cup would by default go to whoever completed the run first, a drawing was held to establish the order of attempts. Each entrant was assigned a specific twenty-four-hour window in which to start his run or forfeit.

The first run was scheduled for New Year's Day, 1909, but when rain made the roads treacherous, that day's challenger and the next both declined to make a start. On January 3, the third driver made a "splendid" outbound run, reaching the hotel in just five hours and twenty-three minutes. But on the return leg, an axle broke fifteen miles from the finish line, giving the driver an undistinguished overall time of fifteen hours and forty minutes.

The next challenger to make the attempt, on January 7, 1909, was Norman DeVaux in a two-cylinder Auburn. Despite ongoing poor weather and "seas of mud" in places, he claimed the second cup with an impressive finish of twelve hours and twelve minutes. Six weeks later, his record was still standing.[30]

In mid-February, a notice appeared in the *San Francisco Call*: "The automobile enthusiasts of the Auto Vehicle Company will try to lower Norman DeVaux's record to Del Monte and return today. The start in the Tourist car will be made at 6 a.m. Bruce Aurandt will be at the wheel. He will be assisted in the run by E. Ely."

The Tourist, debuted by the Auto Vehicle Company of Los Angeles in 1907, was billed as "The California Car," built specifically for California conditions. Its advertising touted its "strength and power" and its domination in races against "many cars costing two or three times as much." Hazlitt L. Pelton, one of the best-known automobile men in northern California, was Tourist's manager for the entire northwest region of the country. But just how Ely came to meet him and to be involved in the competition—as a ride-along mechanic rather than a driver—is a mystery.[31]

At first light on February 19, 1909, Ely and Aurandt set off from Oakland over roads still in "frightful condition" from rain the previous night. They reached the Del Monte turnaround in slightly under six hours. Twenty miles into the return trip, Aurandt drove through Salinas

> in fine shape, and was 27 minutes ahead of the record, when, three miles beyond that place, he ran into the clutches of the law in the form of a country constable. The latter had drawn his wagon across the road and there was nothing for Aurandt

> to do but stop. Then began a funeral procession of his hopes back to Salinas, the county seat, where a judge relieved the record breaker of five good hard American dollars. By the time that the law had been satisfied it was too late to attempt to finish the run, and Aurandt and his assistant, E. Ely, toured leisurely homeward.[32]

There would be no silver cup for the Tourist; the ability of the "country constable" to spot any southbound speeder, wait for him to pass, and then block his path northward on the return leg made any further attempts futile.

By late March, Pelton apparently felt confident enough in Ely's driving skills to hire him to compete in the 1909 San Francisco Hill Climb, a much-anticipated public event sponsored by the San Francisco Motor Club. The route began near the intersection of 19th Avenue and Sloat Boulevard in the southwestern portion of San Francisco and made an arrow-straight shot north, ending around Q Street (present-day Quintara), a rise of 250 feet over one mile.

The competing cars, stripped of mudguards and other extraneous weight, were divided into four price classes, and there was a free-for-all as well. Competitors raced against the clock, one at a time. A custom telephone cable strung along the road formed the heart of a novel electromechanical timing mechanism, in which strings stretched across the start and finish lines triggered an electromagnet that physically tapped the start/stop button on a stopwatch. At the crest of the hill, a natural grandstand of earth afforded a view of the entire course. It made for an ideal venue and an ideal promotional event: exciting, competitive, yet with minimal risk to drivers or to the reported four to five thousand spectators.

Pelton had entered two Tourists, but only one ended up competing: a standard two-cylinder, in the $1,200 to $1,800 class. A photograph in a scrapbook kept by Mabel shows a relaxed and confident Ely cresting the hill, in marked contrast with the next day's headline: "Auto Racing Face Indicates Anxiety of Men Guiding

Automobiles." Although her annotation reads "Winning hill climb on 19th Ave San Francisco," he in fact finished in third place out of four, with an elapsed time of 1:41.6. Still, his average speed of over 35 mph was 5 mph faster than the Auburn, which had been entered in another class.[33]

Ely was developing a reputation as a skilled automobile racer. In early May 1909, a notice in the *Call* read: "Expert Ely of the Auto Vehicle Company is enthusiastic over Speare's oil. He says to [retailer Ollier] & Worthington that it cut down fully half the quantity necessary for lubrication on his Tourist cars." It was the first celebrity endorsement for the unassuming young Iowan who had made his way to Auto Row.[34]

CHAPTER 4

INTO THE AIR

THE AMERICAN MILITARY made its first foray into aeronautics during the Civil War, more than two decades before Ely was born. Thaddeus Lowe, a builder of spherical gas balloons, demonstrated that a man in a tethered balloon five hundred feet in the air could observe the movements of distant enemy troops and could, through telegraphic messages transmitted to the ground, provide accurate intelligence of anything "going on within a long day's march of [its] position in any direction." Charged by President Abraham Lincoln with overseeing aerial reconnaissance, Lowe, in his role as chief aeronaut of the Union Army Balloon Corps, was quickly dubbed the Civil War's "most shot-at man."[1]

The next chapter in military aviation was launched in 1896 by the Smithsonian Institution's third secretary, astrophysicist Samuel Pierpont Langley, who had designed a propeller-driven fixed-wing flying machine shaped something like a dragonfly. With his friend Alexander Graham Bell in attendance as witness, Langley successfully catapulted a scaled-down, unmanned model of his invention off a boat on the Potomac River. It flew for nearly a mile.

Assistant Secretary of the Navy Theodore Roosevelt, impressed by the potential military applications of Langley's Aerodrome (from two Greek roots: one meaning "air," the other signifying "run" or "course"), was instrumental in persuading the War Department to finance construction of a full-scale manned prototype. The cost was a then-staggering $50,000.

But Langley's attempts to scale up his model were stupendously unsuccessful. Twice in late 1903 the full-sized Aerodrome, with

Langley's assistant Charles M. Manly at the controls, swooped directly into the Potomac. "At no time," remarked the Associated Press after the first failure, "was there any semblance of flight." Manly survived; Langley abandoned powered flight and died not long afterward.[2]

Two years after the Aerodrome debacle, the Wright brothers tried twice to sell their new machine, by then known as the Flyer, to the U.S. Army. But the waste of $50,000 still stung, and the War Department was not interested in undertaking further expensive and risky aeronautical experiments. The brothers, affronted, began to make overtures to the British and French governments instead.[3]

Maj. George O. Squier of the Signal Corps, a student of aeronautics, had a different perspective. Squier believed that airplanes would "lessen the number of wars," because "the men who provoked" them would no longer be safe from the actual fighting and would therefore "think twice before launching a war." Having been named executive officer to Chief Signal Officer Brig. Gen. James Allen in July 1907, Squier lobbied for the formation of a body that would be dedicated to the military applications of aircraft. Within a month, the Aeronautical Division of the Signal Corps had been created and given "charge of all matters pertaining to military ballooning, air machines, and all kindred subjects," thus becoming an indirect ancestor of the U.S. Air Force.

By December 1907, Squier had persuaded his superiors to issue a specification and solicit bids for one dirigible and one heavier-than-air machine, of the type that was by now being called an "aeroplane." (The word *aeroplane* originated as the two-word phrase "aero plane," used to designate an approximately flat object subjected to a high-speed airflow at a shallow angle. Though the term was initially used specifically to denote the wing of an aircraft, it evolved to refer to the entire machine. Similarly, the word *aerodrome* gradually came to denote not a vehicle but an "aerial track"—what would come to be called an *airstrip*—by analogy with *hippodrome*, a place where horses are run.)[4]

Meanwhile, Glenn Curtiss was continuing to design and manufacture engines for motorcycles and dirigibles at a facility he had constructed in his hometown of Hammondsport, New York, at the southern tip of Keuka Lake. In January 1906, at the newly formed Aero Club of America's special aeronautical exhibit for the New York Automobile Show, he displayed a selection of lightweight engines suitable for dirigible airships.

Alexander Graham Bell, like his late friend Langley, had long been interested in the possibility of human flight. Since 1902 he had been testing kite designs powerful enough to lift a man, and now he was working on how to attach an engine-driven propeller without adding insurmountable weight. In the literal shadow of "Captain Tom" Baldwin's dirigible *California Arrow*, which was suspended from the ceiling at the auto show, he inspected Curtiss' engines. Soon afterward, he ordered one.[5]

Although Curtiss recognized the value of his engines to aeronauts, he initially seems to have been more interested in their ground-based applications. In January 1907 he took an eight-cylinder 40-hp motor designed for an airship customer and attached it to a custom-built seven-foot motorcycle frame. On the firm sand of Florida's Ormond Beach, he covered a mile in 26 2/5 seconds—a speed of just over 136 mph, making him "the fastest man in the world." It was not until six months later that he made his first flight, going up in one of Baldwin's dirigibles at Hammondsport in order to gain a better understanding of the dynamics of the machine.[6]

By the spring of 1907, Bell had hired two Canadian mechanical engineers to assist him, both recent graduates of the University of Toronto: J. A. D. "Douglas" McCurdy (whose father and brother had both been assistants of Bell's) and McCurdy's friend Frederick W. "Casey" Baldwin (no relation to Tom). Then field artillery officer and West Point graduate Lt. Thomas E. Selfridge, anticipating the creation of a military air service, requested permission to work with Bell in designing flying machines. Bell asked his personal friend,

Theodore Roosevelt, who was now president, to have Selfridge assigned to temporary duty with him.[7]

The team's initial hurdle would be adding a propeller to one of Bell's kites. For that task they reached out to Curtiss, who agreed to deliver Bell's engine in person and to provide instruction on its use. In mid-July 1907, one month after his inaugural flight in the dirigible, Curtiss arrived at Bell's estate on Cape Breton Island, Nova Scotia. He left about a week later but remained actively involved in the group's work, both remotely and in person. On September 30, the five men drew up the charter that would create the Aerial Experiment Association (AEA). Its stated purpose was simple: "To get into the air."[8]

Beginning with Bell's kite, the group worked sequentially on a number of projects, dividing their time between Nova Scotia and Hammondsport. They built a glider, added a motor, and christened it *Red Wing* for the color of the silk fabric that covered its wings. Other than a few photographs of the Wright Flyer, none of the AEA members had seen a working airplane. As a result, *Red Wing* resembled nothing that had come before, except in having a biplane configuration—two wings stacked vertically.

Casey Baldwin drew the winning lot to fly it at frozen Keuka Lake on March 12, 1908. Once the motor was warmed up, the ground crew let go of the wings, and *Red Wing* skittered over the ice for two hundred feet, jumped twenty feet into the air, remained aloft for a little over three hundred feet, and crashed. Hammondsport residents had just witnessed one of the first public flights of a heavier-than-air machine in the United States. Baldwin, happily, was uninjured.

To *Red Wing*'s successor, christened *White Wing*, were added wheels, a forward elevator, and the AEA's first attempt at a system to provide lateral control. The outermost few feet of each wing were replaced by a triangular surface, hinged along the forward edge and controlled by cables. These were a form of what French aviators had already taken to calling *ailerons* (from the French for "winglets"), and they were there to control rotation around the machine's front-to-back axis. Rotating an aileron downward increased the aerodynamic lifting force on its side of the aircraft; rotating it upward decreased it. Changing the lifting force on one side with respect to the other caused the plane to roll.

Curtiss' knowledge of bicycling and motorcycling was evident in the design of *White Wing*. The cables that operated the ailerons were attached to an innovative metal framework, hinged to the seat, that cradled the aviator about the shoulders, allowing him to tilt the airplane to one side or the other simply by leaning his body in the desired direction, like a cyclist leaning into a turn.

In May 1908, Lieutenant Selfridge took *White Wing* aloft and became the first U.S. Army officer to command an airplane, however briefly. Curtiss, too, took a turn and established a record for the longest public flight in America: 339 yards, which he accomplished in two hops.[9]

Curtiss was in charge of constructing the next machine, *June Bug*, with which he hoped to win a trophy offered by *Scientific American* for the first public flight in America of one kilometer or longer. In a practice flight on June 25, 1908, he exceeded the stipulated kilometer, and the AEA requested a formal trial at Hammondsport. Charles Manly, who had twice ridden Langley's ill-fated Aerodrome into the Potomac, would act as official starter.

On Independence Day 1908, with Curtiss at the wheel, *June Bug* flew into history. The flight covered more than a full mile, handily winning the trophy. Human flight had become a practical reality.[10]

Wanting to push the technology further, the AEA now began considering the possibility of building an airplane capable of takeoffs and landings on water. Curtiss and McCurdy fashioned a pair of pontoons for *June Bug*, rechristening it *Loon* to honor its aquatic habitat, but the waterbird failed to take wing.[11]

When the Army had solicited bids for a dirigible and an airplane in December 1907, "Captain Tom" Baldwin was the obvious and only bidder for the dirigible. For the heavier-than-air machine, the

Wrights, in their third attempt at selling their invention to the War Department, quoted a heavily discounted price of $25,000. This bid was accepted, contingent upon the successful completion of acceptance tests to verify that the machine would meet the Signal Corps' specification, which called for a minimum speed of 40 mph, the ability to stay aloft for at least an hour, and a carrying capacity of two men—the exact claimed capabilities of the Wrights' machine.

The acceptance tests for the Baldwin dirigible and the Wright airplane were held in August and September 1908 at Fort Myer, in Virginia, just west of Washington, D.C. They were conducted under the auspices of the Army's Aeronautical Board, chaired by Major Squier, with the expectation that during the tests each board member would be given a ride in the airplane.

One of those board members was Selfridge, who had by now been assigned to the Aeronautical Division of the Signal Corps and was one of the most experienced aviators not just in the Army but in the world. Even setting aside the obvious conflict of interest, the Wrights resented his presence at the acceptance tests for what they saw as his history of underhanded attempts to coax trade secrets from them. Months earlier, he had written to them on behalf of the AEA seeking construction advice, to which Wilbur had responded with useful information that he now regretted sharing. Orville's assessment was more blunt: "I don't trust him an inch."

Curtiss, who had been selling motors to Baldwin since 1904, helped prepare the dirigible for the test and flew it on test day. The Army accepted delivery. The German government promptly ordered a Baldwin dirigible as well, presumably not as an ordinary customer but to study its flight characteristics and construction. Given the success the Germans had already been having with Count Ferdinand von Zeppelin's airship designs, the purchase was likely made in anticipation of war with the United States or one of its allies.

Orville Wright was also at Fort Myer, making his demonstration flights in the Flyer. On September 9, 1908, he established a world endurance record, which he then broke on each of two subsequent attempts, staying aloft both times for more than an hour. Twice he took board members up: first Lt. Frank P. Lahm, and then Major Squier. His third passenger would be Selfridge.[12]

On September 17, Wright took off with Selfridge beside him and began circling the parade ground. Suddenly, one of the propellers cracked lengthwise. The fierce vibrations that resulted caused the second propeller to foul a wire, snapping the blade off, and the machine pitched up briefly and then made a dive to the ground.

Both men were pinned underneath the wreckage. Orville sustained serious injuries. Selfridge, his skull crushed, became the first person ever to die in an airplane crash.[13]

The first true road race in Northern California was the California Grand Prize Auto Race, held on May 9, 1909. A dozen cars took part, including Ely in a Tourist, entered by Pelton only three days before the race. DeVaux showed up with an Auburn after the entry deadline and was turned away.[14]

The course consisted of a roughly fifty-mile loop stretching northwestward from Santa Rosa, only one lane wide at times. Local law enforcement, far from lying in wait for speedsters and reckless drivers, kept the roads clear. Unlike in the Del Monte challenge and most track races, the machines were competing not against the clock but against one another, all at once. The race featured a staggered start, with one car speeding away down the dusty road every sixty seconds.

Ely, the last to leave, had an inauspicious start: he jumped the gun and had to back up to the line, costing him seven seconds. But he "made a great run and was well up with the time made by the leaders"—until a failure in the Tourist's ignition system brought him to a complete and ignominious halt. Repairs cost him an estimated sixteen minutes, but he "was determined to fight it out to the end" and ultimately crossed the finish line in last place.[15]

This performance, however, was in no way considered a failure, especially given that six of the twelve starters had been unable to finish. "The Tourist's time was somewhat slower than that of the other cars," said *Motor Age* magazine, "but, nevertheless, it arrived, and considering the number of high-grade cars that were hung up along the road and failed to cross the finishing line at all, this was something."[16]

Just days before the Santa Rosa race, Pelton, the Tourist dealer, had declared his own "Tourist Cup" open for competition—a perpetual cup to be held by whoever established a new Oakland-to-San Francisco record. On May 11, 1909, one of DeVaux's Auburns made the first claim to the prize. His driver sped around the bay in 2 hours, 19 minutes, and 32 1/5 seconds, nipping four minutes off the existing record. Five days later, veteran Stoddard-Dayton driver Fred Wiseman, another bicycle racer-turned-driver, lowered the mark a further ten minutes.[17]

Pelton sent his new best driver out to claim the trophy. As the sun rose on the morning of May 22 Ely and his mechanic set out over the comparatively empty roads. They made good time to San Jose, but as they began the northward run to San Francisco, they rounded a left-hand curve and encountered a farmer driving a horse team in the opposite direction, hauling what was later reported to have been a wagonload of cherries.

> Ely had slackened his speed to less than 20 miles an hour as the view at the turn was obstructed. As he went around [it,] the driver of the [horse] team instead of holding to his side of the road pulled to the left directly in front of the car. Ely was swinging wide on the turn to prevent just such an accident. It was impossible to stop the momentum of the car, and it shot into the wagon, wrecking two of the [wagon's] wheels and throwing the driver from his seat to the steering wheel of the automobile. The only damage to the automobile was a puncture in the radiator.

No one was hurt, but Ely's chance at breaking the record was gone. He continued on to San Francisco at a more leisurely pace. It was his first reported crash since the ditching of Father Smyth's Franklin nearly five years before, and the greater maturity in Ely's driving is apparent: slowing down, anticipating the danger, and taking the turn wide.[18]

The outcome could have been much worse, as events the next morning underscored. Fred Wiseman, determined to beat his own record, was within a mile of the site of Ely's run-in with the cherry wagon and traveling at an estimated 60 mph when he hit a sudden rise in the road, sending his Stoddard-Dayton airborne. The automobile slammed into a tree and he and his mechanic were thrown free. Wiseman reportedly retained such a grip on the wheel that it snapped from the steering column. Miraculously, the pair survived.[19]

Ely made a second attempt at the record that same morning, six minutes behind Wiseman. Near the site of Wiseman's crash, however, and no doubt because of it, the streets were no longer empty. The Tourist

> reached San Jose in good time and was about to leave when two blocks from the hotel Ely ran into two officers of the law who were waiting for him with drawn revolvers. Ely thought under the circumstances that it was best to stop. He lost eight minutes appeasing the officers of the law, and then proceeded on his way. He got as far as Burlingame [fifteen miles from the finish] with the record well in hand when the engine dropped. It was found that it had been loosened when it struck the cherry wagon the day before.

Ely would not get another shot at the record. Three weeks later Pelton abruptly resigned from the Auto Vehicle Company and permanently closed its northern branch. With the demise of the Tourist in San Francisco, Ely decided to look elsewhere for employment.[20]

Nevada City, a California gold rush town located some sixty miles northeast of Sacramento and eighty miles southwest of Reno, apparently offered opportunities for a professional driver, and by August 4, 1909, Mabel had joined Ely there. In early September the following note appeared in the *San Francisco Chronicle*, under the headline "GOOD FEAT OF AN E-M-F":

> Just what can be done with a high-class automobile was proven a few days ago at Nevada City. A transportation company operating there, using a large six-cylinder car, found itself suddenly unable to transport its passengers on account of the disabling of its car on one of the steep grades. E. B. Ely, who drives a Studebaker E-M-F "30," was prevailed upon to loan his car to the transportation company. The car made the round trip from Nevada City to [Forest City] on schedule time, carrying four passengers up and five down without a hitch.

No Studebaker E-M-F was ever registered to Ely; most likely the reporter confused it with the Matheson, which it slightly resembled.[21]

But by late fall the steep roads into the mining hills would not have been fit for driving, and near the end of October 1909, the local paper reported that the Elys had gone to San Francisco "to witness the Portola celebration." This Mardi Gras–like festival, ostensibly to commemorate the 140th anniversary of the arrival in San Francisco Bay of Gaspar de Portola, California's first governor, was also a celebration of the city's phoenix-like rebirth from its ashes. Warships from five nations, including Germany and Japan, filled the harbor, and a holiday was declared for five days of masked balls, athletic competitions, fireworks, confetti, and parades. It was a "festival of fun," a "glorious, glittering, fantastic dream," and events included a procession of some 150 automobiles, beginning at Auto Row, with costumed drivers and prizes for the best-decorated cars. But it was the automobile races that would have interested Ely. A reported 200,000 spectators witnessed "the greatest event in automobiling ever held in the West" in a series of races run in laps around Oakland. The winning driver of the signature 258-mile race averaged 64.51 miles an hour, setting a new world's record.[22]

The Bay Area racing season produced one final automobile meet. San Jose had built a brand-new track in furtherance of its aspiration to become "the center of coast auto racing." For the first time on any California track, the turns would be banked, in theory making it possible to take them safely at higher speeds.

The standing record for a lap of a one-mile track was a little under fifty-five seconds. Observers believed that Ely, who had been recruited to drive a new gasoline (rather than steam) model of the White automobile, had a legitimate shot at bettering it. A story in the *San Francisco Call* added luster to his credentials by asserting baselessly that he had driven Fiats in races overseas.[23]

A crowd reported at ten thousand showed up to watch the San Jose races on November 28, 1909. Ely finished third in a ten-mile event for cars with a stock chassis "stripped of all extra parts and running as light as possible." The showpiece of the day, however, was the fifty-mile free-for-all. Ely had high hopes, which went unrealized: "Five cars started . . . and several smart brushes occurred, but the Thomas had the power that enabled it to draw away on each occasion. [Thomas driver W. H.] Turner drove recklessly with little regard for track rules and there were several narrow escapes from collisions. Ely in the White, which ran very consistently and finished second, filed a protest . . . on the ground of foul driving."[24]

Ely "ran a smooth, pretty race and went as steadily as a clock," even if he did not break the mile-a-minute pace he had hoped for—Mabel's scrapbook notes that he covered the fifty miles in "54 min 26 2/5 sec.," two minutes and twenty seconds behind the winning time. As for Turner's reckless driving, within a day or two "the White gas car entrants withdrew their protest." The second-place prize was $150—welcome money for a man who had been without a steady job for at least a month. But whether he knew it or not, Ely's automobile racing career had just come to an end.[25]

By 1909 enormous cash prizes were being offered in Europe for significant flights. One of the largest was the $5,000 Gordon Bennett prize, offered by the publisher of the *New York Herald* (and its European edition) for the fastest airplane speed at an international air meet to be held that summer. By offering such prizes, publishers hoped to associate their newspapers with the cutting-edge aviation industry, thereby increasing both readership and advertisers.

Having reached and surpassed its stated goal—"to get into the air"—the AEA now faced the question of whether and how to exploit its work. "Government contracts and exhibition work seem to be the two most promising sources of revenue," Curtiss wrote in a letter to the other members on February 15, 1909. Of the two, the latter seemed to him far more potentially lucrative in the near term: "There are now several cash prizes offered. . . . I think prize chasing and exhibition work should go hand in hand." That was not to say that new markets would not arise. "Probably by another year the machines will become more standardized," he added, "and a certain amount of business may be expected from private parties for machines for sport." The members discussed forming an "Aerial Development Company" with an eye toward securing government contracts and prizes, while at the same time preparing for what Curtiss saw as "the large volume of business which is bound to come later."[26]

Bell, however, was of two minds. On the one hand, the idea of an exhibition company interested him. On the other hand, recalling the mass of patent litigation that had followed his invention of the telephone, he was concerned that any enterprise that generated revenue from the construction or public exhibition of airplanes would draw a lawsuit from the Wrights.

The brothers insisted that they had not merely built a new machine, but that through their invention of a "balancing device," they had solved the problem of lateral stability. Their innovation, they believed, was so groundbreaking that it should be granted broad "pioneer patent" status. If, as they claimed, controlled flight was possible only by wing edge deflection in conjunction with manipulation of a vertical rudder, then their patent should cover all aircraft designs, even those that did not involve wing-warping.[27]

The AEA's deliberations were cut short by a public announcement on March 3, 1909, that Curtiss intended to form a manufacturing corporation with inventor Augustus Herring. The articles of incorporation were filed on March 19, and on the last day of the month Bell, McCurdy, and Casey Baldwin met in Nova Scotia and, as their minutes reflect, "reluctantly" and "regretfully" voted to disband the AEA.[28]

Curtiss brought to his new Herring-Curtiss Company the world's first purchase order for an American airplane. Two months earlier he had secretly agreed to build a machine for the Aeronautic Society of New York (later The Aeronautical Society), a splinter group of heavier-than-air enthusiasts who had felt "smothered" by the Aero Club's focus on lighter-than-air craft. At the time he signed the $5,000 contract, he had only ever built experimental aircraft and had no commercial airplane manufacturing capability. Nevertheless, the Society viewed him as the designer "most likely to turn out something good" and chose him over all his competitors—including the Wrights.[29]

In designing this new machine, known as Curtiss No. 1 (alternatively Herring-Curtiss No. 1), Curtiss retained the three-wheeled undercarriage as well as the characteristic canard, a forward elevator for controlling pitch (so named by French aviators because it resembled the outstretched neck of a duck in flight). But he abandoned the notion of pivoting wing tips, replacing them with trapezoidal ailerons located midway between the upper and lower planes. This configuration, which could be distinguished on sight from that of the Wright models, would provide a useful defense should the Wrights threaten litigation.[30]

The Aeronautic Society of New York took delivery of the new machine, christened *Golden Flyer* for the color of its wings, and designated two members to receive instruction from Curtiss himself. One was Charles Forster Willard, a young automotive engineer who had recently collaborated on the construction of a monoplane that never flew. Curtiss sat him in the *Golden Flyer* and explained the controls, after which Willard took off on a short, conservative flight. (Decades later, Willard insisted that he did not in fact fly the machine on that first day, but it appears he was mistaken.)

The other student aviator was Alexander Williams. He took off too steeply, turned too sharply, and stalled, landing upside down and doing considerable damage to the machine. Williams escaped with only a broken arm and thumb, but he never flew again.[31]

While the *Golden Flyer* was still under construction, it was announced that the Gordon Bennett Cup race would take place August 22–29, 1909, in Rheims, France. Aero Club president Cortlandt Field Bishop, a wealthy financial backer of the Herring-Curtiss Company, badly wanted Curtiss to enter the race and to represent the club. Curtiss doubted the ability of the *Golden Flyer* or any of his other airplanes to win the speed prize, but he offered to build and enter a faster machine if he could keep any money he won, and if the Aero Club would cover any expenses over and above his winnings. Bishop agreed.

Curtiss set sail for Europe on August 5, 1909, bringing with him an unproven and unnamed airplane that had been designed and built in less than four weeks. Constructed largely on the model of the *Golden Flyer*, it featured a powerful but barely tested 50-hp V-8 motor. Aside from an extra propeller, Curtiss brought no spare parts.

But just as he arrived and was beginning his practice flights, news spread that the Wrights had filed lawsuits claiming patent infringement against the Herring-Curtiss Company, the Aeronautic Society, and Curtiss individually, seeking injunctions and damages. Curtiss did not appear to be overly troubled; in a letter home he wrote that the sentiment at Rheims was that the suit was "only bluff."

The tournament, a "Grande Semaine d'Aviation," held before grandstands accommodating 50,000 spectators, lived up to its promise. Forty-four airplanes were entered. Five were Wright Flyers produced in Europe under franchise agreements; Curtiss was confident he could beat them. At one point, he counted twelve wrecked machines on the ground below him. At the time, there were not a dozen flyable airplanes in all the United States.[32]

The official speed record would be established late in the week by flights of two complete circuits of a ten-kilometer rectangular course. Curtiss was the sole American; his primary rivals were an Englishman and three Frenchmen, including prohibitive favorite

Louis Blériot, who had crossed the English Channel at more than 40 miles per hour. The motor in Blériot's machine reportedly generated eighty horsepower.[33]

Curtiss immediately established the average speed that others would have to beat: 46.5 mph. The next three competitors all failed to match it. Then it was Blériot's turn. He shot around the course, but his final time was nearly six seconds slower. Curtiss, hailed as "King of All Aviators," returned home with the Gordon Bennett Cup and $15,000 in prize money, representing his winnings from Rheims and from a second event in Italy.[34]

In September 1909, New York would be hosting a celebration commemorating the three hundred–year anniversary of Henry Hudson's upriver sailing voyage to Albany and the approximate centennial of Robert Fulton's retracing of that route by steamship. In connection with the celebration, Joseph Pulitzer, publisher of the *New York World* and an aviation enthusiast, offered a $10,000 prize for the first flight made by airplane or dirigible from New York to Albany. The prize was more than had been offered for any flight in the United States, but the distance, roughly 150 miles, was nearly six times as far as anyone had ever flown. There were no immediate takers.

The commemoration commission had asked the Wrights and Curtiss each to stage an exhibition. Before Curtiss left for France, he agreed to accept $5,000 for a twenty-mile roundtrip flight from Governors Island, just south of the island of Manhattan, up the Hudson River to Grant's Tomb. The flight was to be made no later than October 2. Wilbur Wright demanded $15,000 to make one flight of ten miles, or alternatively an hour's duration, between September 25 and October 9.

Curtiss expected to use the powerful eight-cylinder machine, now known as the "Rheims racer," to fulfill the New York obligation, but his partner, Herring, had committed it for display in department stores in New York, Philadelphia, and Boston for $9,000, and it would be unavailable for eight weeks.[35]

To make his contractual flights in New York, Curtiss oversaw the construction of a new flying machine. Because the machine was not going to race, it would not need so powerful an engine as the Rheims racer. The Hammondsport factory, which had in the meantime received orders from private parties for two airplanes, turned out Herring-Curtiss No. 5 for Curtiss, with a 25-hp four-cylinder engine. It was informally known as the "Hudson-Fulton" machine, and its design would be the template for the next four Herring-Curtiss machines.[36]

Unlike the Wright Flyer, which needed plenty of wind to stay aloft, the lightweight Herring-Curtiss models depended on calm air. But the weather was unsettled during the period when Curtiss was to make his flights. He arrived in New York on September 27, and two days later he took the Hudson-Fulton machine up for the first time. It was a short, early-morning flight witnessed by almost no one, and he had difficulty getting airborne, which he blamed on an inability to work up enough speed on the soft ground. Wilbur Wright, no doubt to Curtiss' annoyance, made two flights that day with ease, closing by circling the Statue of Liberty.

High winds kept both men grounded over the next several days. Determined to redeem himself, Curtiss postponed his return to Hammondsport and made one more attempt on October 3, the day after his contracted end date. It amounted only to a disappointing hop around the airfield. The following day Wright made a triumphant flight to Grant's Tomb and back, earning his full $15,000; Curtiss, by contrast, had to threaten suit to recover even half of the $5,000 he had been promised.

As for a flight upriver to Albany during the celebration, only Tom Baldwin and another dirigible balloonist even made the attempt to claim Pulitzer's prize. Baldwin's dirigible went into the Hudson off Manhattan; the other aeronaut was forced to land near White Plains.

The *New York World* extended its prize offer for a year.[37]

CHAPTER 5

ROAD TO THE SKY

IN THE FIRST DECADE of the twentieth century, the development of the automobile led quickly to the establishment of an automobile manufacturing industry. In the wake of the successful Rheims meet, it was expected that an airplane manufacturing industry would soon follow. "Manufacturers believe sportsmen of every country will now begin to buy aeroplanes," the *Morning Oregonian* proclaimed, "particularly as the number of actual flights [in Rheims] during the week, estimated at over 1300, were without a single fatal accident. This demonstrates that flying is no more dangerous than was automobiling in its early stages."[1]

Curtiss had predicted in his letter to the Aerial Experiment Association (AEA) in February 1909 that "a certain amount of business" could be expected in the sale of machines "for sport." But by the time he returned from France at the end of the summer, he was convinced that public exhibitions presented greater immediate opportunities than manufacturing. He wrote in October that the exhibition business was "assuming such stupendous proportions . . . that it seems to me worth organizing and going after." What he meant by "organizing," it turned out, was creating a new exhibition entity that was entirely separate from Herring-Curtiss.

This would have several advantages. The Herring-Curtiss partnership had been troubled almost from the beginning. Duped into believing that Herring held valuable patents and could secure significant financing from investors, Curtiss had signed over to the new company all his Hammondsport manufacturing assets, along with all his real estate (business and personal) and his patents and inventions. Now he needed a way to disengage from Herring and regain control of those assets.[2]

On October 7–10, 1909, he demonstrated the Hudson-Fulton machine at a celebration of St. Louis' centennial. Hampered daily by nearly incessant wind and rain, he made only brief, low-altitude hops, typified by a sunset flight on October 9 in which he "rose gradually to 25 feet in the air," skimmed along the field for half a mile, and landed after some forty seconds. The crowds were evidently satisfied by the novelty of a man airborne, but in the end the organizers reportedly declared that Curtiss' flights were not "successful" and withheld a portion of his contracted $6,000. Even so, he received more for a few minutes of flying than the retail price of a Herring-Curtiss machine.[3]

After Rheims, aspiring young aviators flocked to Curtiss. At Curtiss' next stop in Chicago, Charles Keeney Hamilton tracked him down. Hamilton, like Bud Mars, was a balloonist and parachute jumper. By 1909 he was flying dirigibles and was returning from an exhibition tour in Japan when he read the results of the Rheims meet. He rushed to find Curtiss and begged him to teach him to fly.

Hamilton, age twenty-four, stood barely five feet tall, had a shock of red hair, and weighed one hundred pounds—a significant advantage in operating underpowered airplanes. Curtiss was intrigued by the intense young man. If Hamilton could become a competent flier and serve as a second aviator, Curtiss could double the money from the exhibition business. He gave Hamilton basic on-the-ground instruction in Chicago and told him he should come to Hammondsport if he was serious about flying. Hamilton headed straight to Keuka Lake and was waiting there for Curtiss upon his return.[4]

Hamilton was a quick pupil. On what was reported to be only his third attempt, he flew the four-cylinder Hudson-Fulton machine for more than twenty-five consecutive minutes—five minutes shy of Curtiss' longest flight to date. Curtiss had found what he was looking for: someone to pilot the machine at exhibitions while he operated the trickier and more powerful Rheims racer himself.

Rather than hiring Hamilton or selling him a machine, Curtiss proposed to lease one to him, with Hamilton paying Curtiss 60 percent of his net earnings from exhibition flying. The reason for this arrangement, Curtiss later explained, was that he did not wish to be held responsible for Hamilton's "venturesome" flying.

It is certainly true that if Curtiss had taken Hamilton on as an employee, then each time he flew, the Wrights could have claimed that the company was liable for patent infringement. And if Hamilton were to own the machine outright, he might decide to fly it against the company's other aviators at competitions. Whatever his motivation, Curtiss would use this lease arrangement with all his exhibition fliers.[5]

To manage and publicize his planned exhibitions, Curtiss hired twenty-one-year-old Jerome Fanciulli, one of the founders of the Washington (D.C.) Aero Club. Despite his youth, Fanciulli, a former *Washington Post* reporter, was an influential newsman. He was the Associated Press' first aviation specialist, and he already knew both Curtiss and the Wrights. He had witnessed the accident at Fort Meyer in which Lieutenant Selfridge died, and during the Hudson-Fulton celebration he had been the only reporter present for the first of Curtiss' two aborted flight attempts.[6]

With the hiring of Fanciulli, the business that would eventually be incorporated as the Curtiss Exhibition Company was effectively launched. Appearances followed at once. In mid-November, Curtiss took the Hudson-Fulton machine—the Rheims racer was still on display and unavailable—to an exhibition in Covington, Kentucky, across the Ohio River from Cincinnati. Charles Willard, his star pupil from the Aeronautic Society of New York, joined him with the *Golden Flyer.* A month later, the Hudson-Fulton machine was sent to St. Joseph, Missouri, for Hamilton's first engagement.

Six years after the Wrights' success at Kitty Hawk, Americans in cities and towns across the eastern half of the country were witnessing heavier-than-air flight for the first time. But the West had yet to see a flying machine.[7]

Ernst Heinrich Wemme was a farmer's son with minimal education. Born in Saxony in the German Confederation in 1861, he emigrated to America around 1879, intending to stay only temporarily. After a succession of short-lived unskilled jobs in Chicago he traveled to Portland, Oregon, in 1882 and, as E. Henry Wemme, entered into the business of stitching and mending awnings and canvas bunk bottoms. Before the century was out, his Willamette Tent and Awning Company was doing a huge volume of business, including supplying prospectors during the Klondike gold rush and the U.S. Army during the Spanish-American War.

Shrewd real estate investments in the growing city made Wemme one of its wealthiest citizens, and in 1899 he took delivery of a Locomobile, as Baron von Schaezler would do in Davenport a year later. It was the first automobile seen in Portland, and the "pioneer automobilist" reportedly claimed that more horses bolted during the year he owned it than had in the preceding twenty.[8]

He soon tired of lurching over the bumpy streets of Portland in the little Locomobile and replaced it with a larger, more powerful model. But the experience made him "a 'first in Oregon' good roads enthusiast." He became an inveterate car collector, ultimately owning nearly three dozen vehicles over a sixteen-year period. In 1905 he joined local automobile buffs in forming the Portland Automobile Club.[9]

The first automobile show in North America was held in New York in 1900. San Francisco made a splash with its own show in 1907. In March 1909, the Portland Automobile Club brought the city up to date with Portland's inaugural automobile show. Deemed a "gigantic success," it was precisely the automotive awakening Wemme and others had hoped for. Dealers reportedly doubled their orders to manufacturers, and rumors circulated that an automobile manufacturing plant would be coming to the

Pacific Northwest. Amid this boom, Wemme was elected president of the club.[10]

By late November 1909, after nearly five years in the Bay Area, Ely—having driven his last automobile race and without a steady job—was ready to look elsewhere for employment. He found it in Portland, courtesy of Norman DeVaux.

DeVaux had recently severed his connection with Auburn and moved from San Francisco to Portland. There he took up the Oregon and Washington agency for Buick, the maker of the automobile he had driven in his record-breaking 1906 cross-country trip from New York to San Francisco. He soon made a name for himself in Portland automobile circles with such feats of driving skill as piloting a Buick up a hill "hitherto considered impossible." In mid-October 1909 he traveled to Auburn headquarters in Indiana with Robert Simpson, a popular salesman on Portland's modest Auto Row, and helped Simpson get a position as Auburn's dealer for Oregon.[11]

In January 1910, Ely, a veteran of many races against Auburn automobiles, accepted a position as "shop foreman" at Simpson's Auburn dealership and moved into a boarding house two blocks away. He arrived just in time for the second Portland Automobile Show, which opened at the Portland Armory on January 24—coincidentally only two weeks after Glenn Curtiss had brought the West Coast its first airplanes.[12]

While Ely was traveling north to Portland, Curtiss was heading southwest to Los Angeles. The newly formed Aero Club of California had arranged a grand aviation meet, and Curtiss had agreed to headline it. The exhibition would also feature Willard and Hamilton. It would be the first time the three aviators would appear together.[13]

The Los Angeles meet was to be held south of the city, in an open area known as Dominguez Field, and could legitimately be called "international" because a handful of French aviators, including Rheims contender Louis Paulhan, had agreed to participate. But on January 3, 1910, just a week before opening day, federal judge John R. Hazel granted the Wrights a preliminary injunction in their patent infringement case.

Lateral stability in a Wright aircraft was achieved by physically distorting the wings, whereas Curtiss aircraft used pivoting control surfaces—a fundamental difference. Nevertheless, Judge Hazel ruled that the Wrights' patent claims were "entitled to a broad and liberal" interpretation that did not require "narrowing to the details of construction." Until the suit was resolved, Herring-Curtiss was prohibited from manufacturing or selling any more airplanes, and Curtiss himself was explicitly prohibited from flying anywhere in the United States "for commercial purposes," including at competitions and exhibitions.[14]

Since the previous October, Wemme had been busy raising funds to acquire and improve a private toll road that had once been a part of the Oregon Trail. Known as the Barlow Road, it connected Portlanders with the lower slopes of 11,249-foot Mount Hood, a stunning, glacier-covered pyramid about sixty miles to the east. The original road had been constructed in 1846 for pioneers seeking an overland alternative to the dangerous business of rafting the swift Columbia River, and it was long overdue for improvement.

According to one estimate, the number of cars in Portland had tripled in the year since the Portland Auto Club's inaugural automobile show. Given the strong attendance projections for the second show, Wemme and his associates in the Good Roads movement saw tremendous fundraising potential for the road project.[15]

At the same time, with America going aviation-mad, it seemed to Wemme that the mere presence of a flying machine, even one that was not actually flying, would help to promote the show. No matter that no one in town owned one. He had owned the first horseless carriage in Portland; he could own the first flying machine, too.

On January 3, 1910, he ordered a new airplane from the only American manufacturer selling them at the time: Herring-Curtiss.

Coincidentally, his order was placed on the same day that Judge Hazel ordered the company to cease manufacturing and selling new machines.[16]

During the appeal of the court's order, the parties agreed to a suspension of the injunction against Curtiss, provided that the defendants posted a $10,000 bond. Herring-Curtiss put up the money, and Curtiss was free to fly at Dominguez Field. On opening day, the organizers gave him the honor of making the first public flight on the Pacific coast.[17]

Crowds as large as 40,000 to 50,000 thronged to the meet each day. Although they saw no Wright machines, it was hardly a Curtiss-only event. The French team brought two Blériot monoplanes and two biplanes designed by Anglo-French aviator Henri Farman. Local enthusiasts trotted out a number of homegrown designs of varying airworthiness. Balloons and dirigibles also filled the sky.[18]

The meet demonstrated the potential of the airplane far beyond its use for competitions and entertainment. The surveillance capabilities of airplanes became apparent when Curtiss used a string-operated camera to take some of the world's first photos from a heavier-than-air craft. A second seat was added to the Rheims racer, and Fanciulli, at his own insistence, became the first passenger in a Curtiss machine.

Lt. Paul Beck of the United States Army also rode with Curtiss one day, and later with Paulhan, with whom he dropped sandbag "bombs" on targets from a height of 250 feet. "Every war office in the world was watching," the *Los Angeles Times* story opened. To the spectators, the bomb-dropping exercise was perhaps "only an amusing little game," but two artillery captains sent as observers recognized it as "the raising of the curtain on the war drama of tomorrow."[19]

The Dominguez meet also saw the dawning of what soon became known as "sensational" or "spectacular" flying and would later develop into the style known as aerobatics. Hamilton took it up quite by accident one day when, hundreds of feet in the sky, his engine unexpectedly quit. He calmly put the nose down and glided safely to earth, a maneuver that gained instant fame as the "Hamilton Glide." It became a central element of his repertoire, which also included moves that journalists dubbed the "pelican soar," "swallow dive," and "eagle dash." The appeal of such maneuvers to audiences was at least partly because the limited technology of the day made them inherently risky.[20]

In the final tally of prizes at Dominguez, either Curtiss or Paulhan won almost every event, followed by either Willard or Hamilton. The only exceptions were starting and landing in a twenty-foot square, in which Willard received a perfect score, and an event that Hamilton won for making the slowest lap of the course. This was no gag: a reduction in airspeed meant a decrease in lift and maneuverability and therefore a smaller margin of error.

An overwhelming success, the Dominguez meet also marked a permanent transfer of public enthusiasm from the lumbering dirigible airship to the nimble airplane. "Gas bag doings have become commonplace," wrote a journalist. "The aeroplane is the real thriller." Watching Paulhan swooping through the air, daredevil dirigible pilot Lincoln Beachey reportedly remarked to his partner, Knabenshue, "Roy, our racket is dead."[21]

From the Wrights' point of view, every Curtiss airplane that took to the air at the meet, as well as every Farman and Blériot, was infringing on their patent. The Aero Club of America's headquarters became the "storm center of discussion" about the dispute and was flooded with "telegrams of inquiry and protest."

To most observers, the brothers' argument seemed specious, given that the claims in their patent specifically encompassed only biplanes with rectangular wings that were controlled by being warped. Biplanes equipped with ailerons, those with tapered wings, and monoplanes—in other words, every airplane flying at Dominguez—had no wing-warping mechanism, and no need for one.

An undesirable side effect of banking an airplane is that it tends to repoint the machine's nose to the left or right, a problem known today as adverse yaw. To counteract this effect, the solution described in the Wrights' patent involved a vertical rudder that moved automatically, in tandem with the wing-warping controls. Adverse yaw is much less pronounced on aircraft equipped with ailerons than on those that use wing-warping, and Curtiss airplanes had no need at all for a compensating rudder, let alone for the Wrights' automatic one. To prove the point, Hamilton briefly disabled his rudder at the Dominguez meet and demonstrated that he could still roll left and right at will without deviating from straight-line flight, a feat not possible in a Wright airplane.

In glossing over these and other glaring differences between the competing technologies, Judge Hazel might as well have been granting the brothers exclusive rights to the very notion of flight. That was Curtiss' position ("They don't own the air, you know," he reportedly remarked), and the aviation community generally supported him.[22]

During the ten months following its incorporation on March 19, 1909, the Herring-Curtiss Company had built and shipped nine machines, assigning a serial number to each. But the numbering system was at times inconsistent, confusing, and even self-contradictory. Numbers were not necessarily assigned in the order in which the machines were completed, and new machines were not always shipped directly to their buyers.

With regard to the numbering of the first six machines, there is today little disagreement, though certain facts can only be inferred. No. 1 was the *Golden Flyer*, owned by the Aeronautic Society of New York and usually operated by Willard. No. 2 was the eight-cylinder Rheims racer, usually piloted by Curtiss. Nos. 3, 4, and 6 were sold and shipped to private buyers Arthur P. Warner, James E. Plew, and F. Louis de Riemsdyk, respectively.

No. 5 was the Hudson-Fulton machine, which Curtiss had debuted in New York in September 1909, and which Hamilton had been flying since October of that year. Some sources refer to it as the "Arnold Machine" because of Herring's attempt to sell it to a "Mrs. H. Arnold," the pseudonym he gave to Harriet T. Rathbone (née Arnot), the wealthy sister of one of his associates. In addition to the machine, Herring arranged an option for her on several hundred shares of Herring-Curtiss stock. But he neglected to disclose his plans to Curtiss.

Perhaps recognizing Mrs. Rathbone's too-sudden interest in aviation for what it was—a ruse to give Herring greater control of the company or, at the very least, a way to make a privately owned machine available to Hamilton, who could then use it to compete with Curtiss on the exhibition circuit—Curtiss attempted to cancel the sale. When Herring vetoed that move, Curtiss added a clause to the contract stipulating that the machine could not be flown in public "for amusement or advertising purposes" and sent it to Mrs. Rathbone on Wednesday, December 1, 1909, with the warning, "We cannot hold aeroplane No. 5 for you after Saturday." Not surprisingly the sale fell through, and Hamilton continued to fly the machine for Curtiss.

For a number of reasons, Curtiss continued to insert this new provision into Herring-Curtiss sales contracts. Although it presumably dissuaded any buyers who wanted to make public flights for money, it also limited the company's liability in the event that the Wrights ultimately prevailed in their lawsuit. At the same time, it minimized competition with Curtiss' own fliers at airshows, and it might even force the company into bankruptcy—which would give Curtiss a convenient, legal way to disentangle himself from Herring.

After No. 6, the record becomes quite muddy. There is, in particular, a good deal of confusion surrounding the provenance of Nos. 7 through 9, the so-called Harmon, Johnson, and Wemme machines.

The paper trail is clear enough at first. On November 23, 1909, Long Island millionaire and amateur aviator Clifford B. Harmon ordered a machine, referenced in the contract as No. 7. On December 21, Herring-Curtiss' new California agent, Col. Frank H.

Johnson of San Francisco, placed an order for eight machines: seven for resale and one (No. 8) for his personal use at Dominguez Field. On January 3, 1910, Wemme ordered a machine, later identified as No. 9. None of the three would be flown for money (Wemme's machine would not be flying at all), so Curtiss' prohibition against paid exhibition flights was presumably not an issue for any of the buyers.[23]

It appears that five Curtiss machines found their way to the Dominguez meet in January 1910. Willard brought the *Golden Flyer*, Curtiss the Rheims racer, and Hamilton the Hudson-Fulton machine. Harmon's No. 7 was shipped to Los Angeles from Hammondsport on New Year's Eve; Curtiss flew it on opening day. Three days later, "Curtiss received a new machine at the grounds."[24]

That same day, Johnson began to "assemble his Curtiss machine . . . preparatory to flight." Most likely this was the machine that Curtiss had just received, but in any event it was not Johnson's No. 8. Herring-Curtiss had already informed him that a new machine could not reach him in time for the meet and had agreed to lease him an existing machine in the interim.

A week earlier, four short days after Wemme's purchase order was received, Herring-Curtiss had reported shipping him "One Complete Aeroplane," presumably drawn from existing inventory at Hammondsport. The fact that it never arrived in Portland suggests that it was temporarily rerouted to Los Angeles for Johnson's use.

In the end, it hardly mattered; Wemme never took delivery of that machine. Instead, in mid-January he announced that he had sent an agent to Dominguez in search of the "best airship he could find for the money"—not a new machine but "one of the prize-winning aeroplanes." He may have decided that since it would only be going on static display, a prize-winner would prove a better draw.[25]

But later a story circulated that after placing his order, Wemme had discovered that express shipping an airplane from Hammondsport to Portland, even if not via Los Angeles, could add over 20 percent to the $5,000 price and still might not guarantee its arrival in time for the show. According to this story, he canceled the order and began looking for something more immediately available and cheaper to ship.

Whichever story is true, his options were limited. Most of the Curtiss machines at Dominguez Field were spoken for. The Aeronautic Society of New York sold the *Golden Flyer* to Toledo dirigible impresario Charles J. Strobel. Hamilton was scheduled to go on tour with two machines: an unspecified four-cylinder machine, probably the one Johnson had been using, and the far more powerful Rheims racer. Willard, who had signed a lease "for exhibition work," would be touring with another four-cylinder machine. Harmon, perhaps to avoid becoming entangled in the Wright-Curtiss dispute, ultimately canceled his order, returned his machine to Curtiss, and bought a Farman biplane instead. On January 22, 1910, Curtiss at last delivered the first of the machines for which Johnson had been waiting more than a month, along with a new contract of sale that somewhat disingenuously continued to list it as "number eight." It was actually No. 7—Harmon's hand-me-down.[26]

Wemme's representative reached Dominguez Field on January 15, 1910, and within a few hours Herring-Curtiss recorded receipt of a check for $500 as a 10 percent deposit on "Aeroplane Number Nine." Despite its new serial number, the machine that Wemme purchased was not a new machine at all but "No. 5," the Hudson-Fulton machine. "Insist that it be a prize winner," he had instructed his agent, and the Hudson-Fulton had indeed won first prize—in the slowest-lap contest.

On January 23, 1910, one day before the opening of the auto show, Wemme's machine reached Portland and was taken to the Armory gymnasium. There it was assembled by Walter E. Donnelly, a Portland mechanic without practical aviation experience but with an interest in the subject. Also on display was a machine that had been invented by a local enthusiast. Admission to the airplane room would cost an additional twenty-five cents over the fifty-cent price of admission to the auto show, with all proceeds to be donated to the Mount Hood road fund.

The auto show would almost certainly have given Ely his first chance to inspect a working airplane, particularly since his new employer, the Auburn dealership, had three cars on display there. However, there is no record of whether he took advantage of the opportunity.[27]

Public interest in "the airship that won the big contest in Los Angeles" was high, and over the six-day run of the auto show, the presence of a third or more of the visitors was credited to the airplane display. Reportedly, however, the fund's take fell short of the $2,000 Wemme had been expecting.

Determined to squeeze every last penny out of his purchase, he had the machine put on display in Portland's Meier & Frank department store: admission, ten cents. Later he had it reassembled down the street in a room designated "Aviation Hall," where it remained for two additional weeks. In the latter half of February, it was exhibited in Seattle, but by then Wemme, suffering from a chronic health issue, had departed for an extended stay in Hot Springs, Arkansas.[28]

After the Dominguez meet closed on January 20, Curtiss returned to Hammondsport to address his deteriorating relationship with Herring and to strategize on the appeal from Judge Hazel's order in the patent lawsuit. Invitations to participate in exhibitions had been pouring in from other American cities, fueled by the publicity from Dominguez. Curtiss could not let the opportunities pass. Hamilton and Willard had proven themselves to be competent aviators, so he left them in the West to fill exhibition dates.[29]

Hamilton's first stop was San Diego. He arrived with the Rheims racer on January 22 and reportedly made a forty-minute flight, during which he crossed the border into Mexico. He also carried a number of passengers across the aviation field, using the new seat in which Fanciulli had ridden at Dominguez.

One of those passengers was Whipple Spear Hall, a twenty-eight-year-old Oakland socialite eager to experience flight. More than twice Hamilton's weight at a reported 235 pounds, Hall claimed after the flight that he was now the heaviest man ever to have ridden in an airplane. The two men had met by chance twelve months earlier, aboard a ship bound from San Francisco to Honolulu. Hamilton and his wife were en route to Japan for his dirigible tour, Hall and his wife were en route to China for sightseeing.[30]

From San Diego, Hamilton went north to Bakersfield for a one-day appearance on January 29. Next, he and Willard joined up in Fresno, where a new Curtiss four-cylinder machine—perhaps No. 8, the machine leased to Willard—had arrived a week earlier. Hamilton demonstrated it first; then he switched to the Rheims racer and the two aviators thrilled the crowds with the spectacle of two machines in the air at the same time. The reported fee for their joint appearance was a healthy $9,100.

After Fresno they flew at a five-day meet in Phoenix; then Hamilton continued on to solo appearances in Tucson, El Paso, and Douglas, Arizona. In the wake of Dominguez, it was reported, the "whole Southwest got the aviation fever." Hamilton took with him both the Rheims racer and a machine with a four-cylinder engine and left Willard with the new four-cylinder machine.

While Ely was establishing himself in Portland, Mabel Ely had been living with her parents in Corte Madera, California. One day she saw a full-sized replica of a Farman biplane on display at the Emporium, a San Francisco department store. According to her later recollection, when she discovered that the exhibit would be moving to Portland, she wrote to her husband and urged him to see it for himself. There is no record of Ely's having done so, but he certainly had the opportunity. On February 14, 1910, the exhibit opened, free to the public, in the same department store where Wemme's machine had previously been on display at ten cents a peek.[31]

But Portland, like many parts of the country, had gone "aeronutty." Mere static displays, free or otherwise, were no longer adequate to hold the public's interest. What people wanted to see was something that had never before been seen in Oregon: a flying machine in flight.[32]

In light of his fundraising goal for the Mount Hood road, Wemme requested an exception to the Herring-Curtiss contract provision against paid exhibition flights. Fanciulli responded that if such flights were to be made, it could only be "by one of our demonstrators"—meaning Curtiss, Willard, or Hamilton. So Wemme arranged an "aviation meet" in Portland for the weekend of March 5–7 and secured Hamilton's participation for $3,000.[33]

The meet would be held at a country club. The railroads offered special rates in order to give "every person in the state . . . an opportunity to witness this great event." Army officers from nearby Vancouver Barracks arranged to attend; a brigadier general was quoted as saying that the experiments at Dominguez had proven that "it will be only a few years now before flying machines will show their ability to drop a dynamite cartridge within a prescribed circle of five feet." With the local newspaper glibly (if baselessly) promising that rain, "no matter how hard the downpour, does not interfere with flying an aeroplane," attendance was predicted to reach 50,000. Again, there is no record of whether Ely was among them.[34]

For additional entertainment, promoters promised "one of the most spectacular races in the history of speed contests. . . . It will be between Hamilton in his Curtiss biplane and a Buick automobile with a 30-horsepower engine, driven by Norman DeVaux, of the Northwest Buick Company." Although the track was likely to be muddy, DeVaux had reportedly expressed confidence that the Buick would emerge victorious.[35]

Mechanic Walter Donnelly brought the "Wemme machine" back by train from Seattle for the meet. It had not been flown since Dominguez, two months earlier, and an unspecified "break" had to be repaired.[36]

Hamilton arrived from Arizona on March 3 to much fanfare. Reporters swooned over the "daring little aviator." Immediately recognizing Wemme's machine as the Hudson-Fulton machine he had until recently been flying, Hamilton wired Curtiss: "OLD AEROPLANE HERE."[37]

The meet opened two days later. Although Hamilton had brought with him the Rheims racer and his four-cylinder machine, Wemme had insisted that *his* airplane have the honor of making the first flight in Oregon, so Hamilton climbed aboard and made a straight flight a few hundred feet long. He then switched to the Rheims racer and gave an exhibition that delivered "a series of thrills on a graduating scale upward." None of the flights was longer than five minutes or higher than five hundred feet, reportedly because Hamilton intended "merely to exhibit the capabilities of an aeroplane in his hands." Nonetheless, to those who were seeing a flying machine for the first time, the sight was nothing short of remarkable: "Higher and higher he goes and the gaping throng stretches its neck and gasps." Later that day he handily won the race against the Buick. DeVaux, who may have recognized it as a contest he could not win, opted out of driving.[38]

Hamilton had made flying look easy; emboldened, mechanic Donnelly decided to take a turn with the Wemme machine. "His work consisted of [rolling] along the ground, occasionally rising two or three feet in the air." At some point Donnelly probably thought he was on the verge of ascending. But as the machine hopped along, the crowd pressed too close, and the would-be aviator was forced to swerve. He struck a pedestrian and a mounted police officer and knocked down several other people. The machine "turned over on its side, sustaining a few unimportant breaks," and Donnelly was reportedly "thrown from his seat headlong to the ground." He was fortunate not to have been injured. The front-page sub-headline the next day read: "Walter Donnelly, Amateur, Runs Amuck with Plane," and the entire fiasco underscored just how difficult it was to operate a flying machine.[39]

On the final day of the meet Hamilton deigned to make a second short flight with the Wemme machine, but he "came down after flying 100 yards, saying that the horizontal rudder"—that is, the elevator—"was not adjusted properly." Though skeptics winked that perhaps he "did not care to advertise Wemme's machine," the complaint could have been legitimate. Hamilton knew better than anyone how the machine in which he had made "his sensational flights at Los Angeles" was supposed to fly.

After the meet, the machine was shipped to Spokane, for static display at yet another automobile show.[40]

On his way to Portland, Hamilton had wired Curtiss that he had a buyer for a four-cylinder machine. His friend Hall, who had flown as a passenger with him in San Diego and had clearly caught the aviation fever, had just handed him a $500 deposit.

After Portland, Hamilton's tour took him north to the state of Washington, where Hall caught up with him. On March 12, Hamilton survived a spectacular crash into a pond at Seattle's Meadows racetrack, near the site of present-day Boeing Field. Hall accompanied his friend to the hospital and was seen physically supporting him when he reappeared in public the next day, limping and temporarily grounded. A few days later, Hamilton's own manager sued him for breach of contract, alleging that the aviator had made himself unfit to fly "by reason of too frequent libations . . . in lively company" the night before the crash.[41]

Hamilton recovered faster than the Rheims racer did; ongoing repairs cost him a day of flying in Tacoma. The next day, with the machine back in working order, he made "three absolutely perfect and remarkable flights" before departing for Vancouver, British Columbia, and then Spokane.[42]

Hall, still determined to become an aviator himself and undeterred by Hamilton's mishap, paid the balance of the purchase price for the four-cylinder machine. On March 18, he attempted his first solo flight in an empty area south of Seattle. "Though he did not get more than ten feet from the ground he was in the air for about 300 feet and the flight was considered successful for the first attempt at manipulating a machine."[43]

"Wemme Tires of Biplane," the headline ran. He had owned Oregon's first flying machine for only nine weeks, but he had never once seen it in the air. He had been in Arkansas during the entirety of the

Portland exhibition, and other than for Hamilton's two brief hops and Donnelly's crash, it had not left the ground since its arrival. The exhibition itself had resulted in a financial loss, reportedly because no more than six thousand people paid admission while more than ten times that number slipped onto the grounds or watched for free from nearby hillsides. Wemme had had enough. He was ready to sell.[44]

At the time, only four people were flying publicly in America, all in Herring-Curtiss airplanes: Curtiss, Hamilton, Willard, and Hall, the last of whom had yet to master his machine. Whoever bought Wemme's airplane and got it off the ground could claim to be among the first half-dozen professional aviators in the country.

CHAPTER 6

FLYING LESSONS

SPRING 1910 BROUGHT FINE WEATHER, and as word spread about the Dominguez meet, the demand for flying exhibitions grew across America. Curtiss welcomed this development, and in April he made his first foray into staging an exhibition. Held in Memphis, the event featured Curtiss, Charles Willard, and a new pupil making his first public flights: Bud Mars, the circus acrobat who had helped Tom Baldwin build the airship *California Arrow* in 1904.[1]

A decade older than Charles Hamilton and Willard and three years Curtiss' senior, Mars, at thirty-five, was said to be "training himself to operate a Curtiss biplane on the ice at Hammondsport" around the time Whipple Hall was learning to use his own machine. Mars concluded the Memphis meet by losing control of his machine (one patterned on the Hudson-Fulton) in gusty winds, crashing into a parked car, and demolishing the airplane. Luckily, no one was injured.[2]

The trouble caused by wind would become a familiar theme of aviation exhibitions. Early airplanes were constructed of metal, hardwood, bamboo, and coated fabric. With their limited stability, and lacking a closed fuselage to resist twisting forces, they flew at the mercy of any wind.[3]

The lead story out of the Memphis exhibition was that Curtiss had lowered his world record for quick-starting (the time or distance from the moment the airplane started rolling forward to the moment it left the ground) to just under six seconds.

Spring also brought another lawsuit against Herring-Curtiss. On April 1, 1910, three Hammondsport creditors initiated an involuntary bankruptcy proceeding against the company. While Curtiss denied any secret agreement with the creditors to bring the action as a means to enable him to regain control of the company and eliminate Herring, the suit in fact furthered his interests.[4]

Following Curtiss' victory in Rheims and his exhibition flights in the United States, his was the name the public increasingly linked with airplanes. The Wrights lagged behind in entering the exhibition business, and by late 1909 they recognized that they needed to act.

In early 1910, they invited dirigible pilot Roy Knabenshue to assemble and manage a team of fliers, and opened a "flight school" in Montgomery, Alabama, where they were rumored to be teaching half a dozen U.S. Army officers. In truth, the Wrights brought just one man to Montgomery: their Dayton neighbor, twenty-one-year-old Walter Brookins, whom they began to train that March.[5]

Perhaps as a sales device, Henry Wemme authorized Walter Donnelly, who had crashed the Hudson-Fulton machine ignominiously at the auto show in March, to take another crack at getting the airplane aloft. On the morning of April 12, Wemme headed out to Twelve Mile House, a horse track and makeshift airfield. A "party of motorists," potential buyers, accompanied him. One of them was "automobile man" Ely.

Whether Ely had viewed the Hudson-Fulton machine while it was on display in Portland, and whether he traveled to Twelve Mile House that morning specifically intending to fly it, are matters of conjecture. Colleagues from the Auburn dealership were also present. But whether by plan or simply opportunity, it was not the hapless Donnelly who took the Hudson-Fulton aloft that morning. Instead, Ely, the chauffeur, seated himself at the controls of the biplane. What happened next made the front page of the *Morning Oregonian*:

> One moment seated in an aeroplane on the ground without thought of trying to fly, and the next to be shooting through the air at the rate of 35 miles an hour when the men holding

> it down suddenly let go, was the sensation experienced by [E.] B. Ely, a local automobile man. . . .
>
> The machine was the Curtiss biplane owned by E. Henry Wemme. It was recently taken to the Twelve-Mile House where Walter E. Donnelly, the amateur aviator, was to practice with it. Ely, with a party of motorists, including Mr. Wemme, went out yesterday to inspect the air craft. The engine was started and Ely, who is interested in heavier-than-air flying, seated himself at the steering-wheel of the machine. The thin-bladed propeller was soon making 1200 revolutions a minute and the machine quivered from the vibrations and strained to be free.
>
> Suddenly, whether as a joke or by accident, those holding it stepped back. Ely had just elevated the altitude rudder and in less than 10 seconds the aeroplane was 30 feet in the air.
>
> Ely was able to bring it to the ground easily and gracefully after flying about 200 yards. It was the first time Ely had ever even sat in the seat of an aeroplane.[6]

While that final statement was true, the flight was clearly no accident. Ely flew because he intended to. The mere act of taking off could never have occurred without his active participation: springing the hand lever that lifted a restraining bar out of the ground and signaling the handlers to release their hold on the wings, keeping the engine at full throttle as the machine rolled across the ground, pulling back on the wheel to become airborne, and holding the wings level by leaning his upper body left and right against the aileron controls. His climb to thirty feet within ten seconds could have happened only by design.[7]

It is difficult to overstate the significance of Ely's accomplishment. He had no instruction in flying and had not studied aerodynamics, yet his first flight covered five times the distance that Wilbur Wright's had. Glenn Curtiss' first flight, though half again as long as Ely's, had included a touchdown along the way. Operating the machine that Curtiss had not been able to get airborne in New York, that Hamilton had crashed repeatedly in late 1909, and that Donnelly had driven into a crowd on the ground—the same model that Mars had crashed into a parked car—Ely made flying look effortless.

The following day the *Morning Oregonian* reported: "Ely, with his associates in the local selling branch of Auburn automobiles, has an option on the Wemme machine. The option calls for test trials with a view of determining its flying capabilities. In the event that Ely masters it, and he has already shown unusual aptitude, it will be purchased by the Auburn people and exhibition flights will be made with it."[8]

The flaw in that plan, though there is no indication Ely was aware of it, was that Wemme's purchase of the machine three months earlier had included the express restriction that public flights for amusement or advertising purposes were prohibited, other than for certain sanctioned events. Making exhibition flights could invite lawsuits against Ely and the "Auburn people" (Wemme's legal successors in interest), not only from the Wrights but also from Curtiss.[9]

That issue would remain a purely academic one if Ely could not master the machine. The day after his first flight he was in the air again, making several short, straight runs no more than ten feet off the ground. Two years later, Curtiss would write,

> One of the most important things that should be developed in the beginner, and, at the same time, the most difficult, is the sense of balance. Every one who has ever ridden a bicycle knows that the sense of balance comes only after considerable practice. Once a bicycle is under way the balance is comparatively easy, but in an aeroplane the balance changes with every gust of wind, and the aviator must learn to adjust himself to these changes automatically. Especially is a fine sense of balance necessary in making sharp turns.[10]

On Ely's fourth attempt, traveling at an estimated 30 mph, he rose to thirty feet, but the wind pushed him off course. When he tried to turn, the wind tipped the machine too far, and it fell to the ground. Far from panicking, Ely "maintained remarkable coolness and shut off the motor just as the machine struck." He emerged unscathed.

Damage to the machine was estimated at fifty dollars, and repairs were expected to be completed within a couple of days.[11]

Ely had just learned an important lesson: not to make a cross- or downwind turn low to the ground. The simple act of rolling into a turn was a complex exercise in balance and control, requiring the aviator to turn the control wheel, pull back on it, and lean sideways, all while keeping the foot throttle pressed down. To stop rolling or to reverse the roll angle, the aviator had to lean "uphill" while continuing to maintain altitude through judicious use of the elevators. The challenge of getting the fragile biplane aloft, keeping it under control in flight, and landing it safely required athleticism; it has been described as a "flying pectoral and upper-arm exercise machine." It also required muscle memory. As Curtiss explained, "With all of these movements it is no wonder that the aviator's mind must be active—there is no time to think, every movement and act must be absolutely accurate and the body must be under full control."[12]

On April 17, with the machine repaired, Ely made more than half a dozen straight practice flights. "No accidents occurred and Ely expressed himself as being well pleased with the result." He compared it to "learning to ride a bicycle" and expressed his intention to continue trying, in hopes of making an extended flight within a few days.[13]

But Ely's first crash had taught him caution regarding wind conditions, and over the next ten days he prudently made no such attempt. It was not until fifteen days after his first experience with the machine, once the wind had abated, that Ely made "a graceful rise from the earth." Quickly discovering that his tail rudder was not responding, he "immediately lowered the altitude rudder and came to the ground, alighting easily."[14]

The news story of that aborted flight claims that Ely had "recently purchased the Curtiss aeroplane owned by E. Henry Wemme." It is certainly the case that within a week, three Portland investors had formed the Portland Aeroplane Company with capital stock of $5,000—the price Wemme was asking. The corporate directors and officers were Robert Simpson, Ely, and Colburn Barrell—all associated with the Portland Auburn dealership. Hartman Price would act as the advance agent, securing bookings for Ely wherever he could find opportunities, and Walter Kaufman would serve as mechanic. The day after the test flight, one of the Elys responded to the 1910 census by listing Gene's occupation as "aeronaut." (The fact that the birthplaces of Ely's parents are listed as "unknown" suggests that the respondent was Mabel, who had by then moved to Portland.)[15]

No sooner was the company formed than Ely, as vice president, signed a contract with the Sutherlin Commercial Club, which planned to hold an aviation meet some 170 miles south of Portland on May 17–19. The meet's highlight would be the exhibition of a biplane invented by a local man, J. W. DePries. But DePries had yet to fly, and the promoters hedged their bets by hiring Ely, "an experienced aviator." Scarcely two weeks after his initial attempt at flight, Ely had committed to exhibition flying.

Under the terms of the Sutherlin contract, Ely agreed to make two flights each day. In return, he would be entitled to half the daily gate receipts (at fifty cents a head) and half the grandstand sales (an additional ten cents a head). Apparently, neither party was aware of the restriction in the machine's contract of sale. A tent city and "an immense dining hall" would be erected to house the anticipated throngs. The Southern Pacific Railroad announced special rates for round trips to Sutherlin. With such a buildup, Ely and the other "Auburn people" may well have expected to recoup their investment in a matter of weeks.[16]

The initial report from the Sutherlin meet was favorable. DePries and his biplane failed to appear, but "Ely, the man-bird," reportedly made a "thrilling" flight.

> The aerial machine was brought into position at the west end of the track, specially prepared for the aviators, and after tires and engine had been carefully inspected, Ely took his seat, the attendants started the engine and at a word from the pilot cast off the bonds. The machine, after traversing

> the length of the starting track, soared gracefully into the air. . . . Ely brought the machine to the earth after soaring in a long curve to the south, it being his intention to swing back to the starting track, but on account of a sudden breeze tilting the machine at a critical moment, making it difficult to maneuver, no time was lost in bringing the machine to earth in the open, rather than to attempt the descent among the buildings near the track.[17]

Ely's own report of his maiden public flight provides a more prosaic account. In a postcard sent the next day to Mabel, who had stayed in Portland, he wrote,

> *Little One:*
>
> *Had wreck yesterday after two successful flights around field. Have only made one little flight today but will make another at sundown. Too much wind now.*
>
> *Love from*
> *Gene*[18]

Ely had significantly less success on the meet's final day, as reported in the local paper: "After rising to a considerable height, Ely attempted to soar in a circle back to the starting point. It appeared from the ground that he could not control the machine for just an instant. It tilted and then began to fall." Ely landed in the open, breaking several of the machine's ribs and battering the propeller. He was uninjured, but it would take a few days to repair the airplane.[19]

Ely's first exhibition was over. Sixteen hundred people had watched him over the three days. But the promoters, claiming that the flights had been failures, refused to pay a dime, and Ely had to engage local lawyers to attempt to collect his share of the receipts. Newspapers headlined stories with the promoters' position: "COULD NOT FLY OVER THE FENCE." It was a rude introduction to the financial risks of exhibition flying and the importance of defining contractually what constituted a "successful" flight.[20]

Ely then headed for Medford, in southwest Oregon, for an exhibition that was a fundraiser to build a road to Crater Lake. As the date for the exhibition drew closer, newspapers regaled the public with stories of Ely's "many beautiful flights with the Curtiss machine, which he operates, and with which he has broken many records."[21]

News of the arrival of the "young 'man bird'" appeared in a local paper, along with photographs of a Curtiss biplane. (Ely was careful to point out that, though he flew a Curtiss machine, he was not employed by Curtiss.) Readers were told that in Sutherlin, Ely had had some "trouble with his motor," which they were immediately reassured had "now been eradicated."[22]

But just as in Sutherlin, there were problems. During a trial flight on the scheduled first day, "Ely, after flying 150 yards at an elevation of from 10 to 20 feet, suddenly was hurled to the ground by a rift in the wind." The damage to the machine kept the mechanics busy. Skittish promoters announced their intention to refund all admissions "unless a genuine flight is made." And when adverse weather conditions prevented any flights in Medford on both May 28 and 29, Ely agreed to postpone his exhibition to the following weekend.[23]

While Ely struggled in southern Oregon, Curtiss was making headlines on the East Coast. His focus had turned to the design of a "hydroaeroplane" for takeoffs and landings on the water, including successful taxi experiments with a flying machine mounted on a single pontoon made from a sealed canoe. His interest in water-based flight was more than theoretical: Joseph Pulitzer had remained focused on the possibility of a flight between Albany and New York, and Curtiss recognized that such a flight might require the aviator to ditch in the Hudson River.

In the spring of 1910, Pulitzer's *New York World* refined its offer: $10,000 to the first person who covered the 150-mile distance in under twenty-four hours, flying in either direction, with a maximum of two landings along the way. Perhaps still stinging from his ignominious performance at Governors Island in the fall, Curtiss made plans to seek the prize. In secret he began building a special airplane with a 50-hp V-8 engine and underwing pontoons. It got its first public tests at the exhibition in Memphis and at another in San Antonio.[24]

On the morning of May 29, Curtiss took off from Albany in calm conditions and reached New York in under three hours, taking advantage of the permitted two landings: one at Poughkeepsie and the other at the northern tip of Manhattan. In the final miles he soared over Grant's Tomb and circled the Statue of Liberty before coming down on Governors Island at noon to win the prize. He later wrote that "it looked as though half of the population was along Riverside Drive or on top of the thousands of apartment houses that stretch for miles along the river."

Curtiss' historic flight was the longest ever made between two cities, rendering Ely's efforts trivial by comparison. Who cared about a brief circuit of a grass field when a man could cover 150 miles in a single morning? The airplane, which had come to be known as the *Hudson Flyer*, also carried the first unofficial "air mail": a letter from the mayor of Albany to the mayor of New York.[25]

In the wake of Curtiss' success, the *St. Louis Post-Dispatch* teamed with Pulitzer's *New York World* to offer a $30,000 prize for the first flight between St. Louis and New York, while the *New York Times* and the *Chicago Evening Post* jointly sponsored a $25,000 prize for the first flight in either direction between their two cities. Either trip, if completed, would cover more than five times the distance of the famous Hudson flight.[26]

Willard thought such flights impossible. He was reported as saying, "No machine ever made would be able to make a continuous flight of that length. . . . It might as well be an offer of a million dollars for a flight to the moon." Nonetheless, as the sponsoring newspapers no doubt intended, the prize announcements further aroused public interest in long-distance flights.[27]

The stark contrast between Ely's struggle simply to get airborne and Curtiss' apparently effortless success made the Medford promoters nervous. On May 30, the day after the flight from Albany to New York, they announced that the following weekend, Medford would hold "the largest airship meet yet held on the [Pacific] coast, excepting only [the one] held last winter in Los Angeles." It was noted that "Whipple Hall, the celebrated aviator, will fly in his Curtiss biplane. . . . In addition, Mr. Ely will also fly in his airship. Two airships at the same time are seldom seen anywhere."[28]

How Hall came to the attention of the Medford organizers is a mystery. He had made his public flying debut on May 1 in Fresno for the city's Raisin Day, having reportedly added five-foot extensions to each end of the upper wing. His hope was that the increased lift they provided would compensate for his weight; nevertheless, he failed to get off the ground the first day. The following day he crashed into a fence, sustaining cuts to his face and reportedly injuring his back severely enough that he could not walk. A later account described the injury as a "slightly fractured skull."[29]

Two weeks later, feeling sufficiently recovered, Hall appeared at San Jose's Rose Carnival. A crowd of eight thousand spectators waited in breezy conditions. But even before he could get his machine warmed up, foreign object damage rendered it unflyable. So when he finally met Ely at Medford in June, despite several attempts he had yet to leave the ground in public and was no more a "celebrated aviator" than Nathan Ely had been a "jolly jack tar."[30]

The Medford public was expecting to see "men birds." What it got were two novices with limited flying hours (in Hall's case, essentially none), operating finicky machines. The front elevator's extensive surface area caused every Curtiss machine to "pitch hunt," leaping up and down through the air like a porpoise, and the slightest downdrafts and turbulence-related upsets could easily force the machine to the ground. And midafternoon was not likely to produce the gentlest wind conditions.

By Saturday afternoon the breezes were quite strong, and although Ely "made a valiant attempt" to fly, "the high wind prevented him from soaring any distance, and a huge crowd went home disappointed." His first flight, at 3:30, covered some two hundred feet at an average of fifteen feet—impressive under the circumstances, but well short of his own expectations.

As for Hall, he "did not attempt a flight until late in the afternoon, and failed to leave the ground." Seven more times he tried to take off, without success. Then Ely made one final effort:

> Mr. Ely, after Mr. Hall's unsuccessful attempt, took his machine out again and succeeded in flying fully 600 feet at an altitude of from 10 to 20 feet. Suddenly he was forced downward, but could not account for it, as his "front control" was set for an upward flight and his engine was running splendidly. But down he came.
>
> Mr. Ely will endeavor to fly today [June 5]. He demonstrated yesterday that he had the nerve.

The promoters agreed to honor the Saturday tickets on Sunday and further promised to refund all tickets if no flight occurred. On Sunday, although Ely "covered a greater distance than on Saturday he did not make a successful flight," an assertion that was open to interpretation because once again the contract had failed to define "success." Hall attempted no flights.[31]

No one in Medford questioned Ely's sincere desire to fly. He was said to have made many friends there, and he "endeavored to make a flight in order not to disappoint local people." But he recognized the exhibition as a failure, and the refund of all admission tickets meant there were no proceeds from which to pay him.[32]

As Ely's fortunes sank, those of the Curtiss fliers continued to rise. Mars had gained sufficient proficiency to exhibit in Arkansas, Kentucky, and Kansas. Hamilton flew the Rheims racer from New York to Philadelphia and back again on June 13, earning $10,000 from the *New York Times*, which splashed the story across more than nine pages of the newspaper. The first leg of his flight alone broke Curtiss' cross-country record by twenty miles.[33]

The next day, a unanimous U.S. Court of Appeals panel vacated Judge Hazel's injunction in the Wright patent case, ruling that "infringement [of the Wrights' patents] was not so clearly established as to justify a preliminary injunction." This meant that Herring-Curtiss could manufacture airplanes and Curtiss could fly. It also freed up the $10,000 bond that the company had posted while the appeal was pending. The case was far from over, though—the decision addressed only whether Curtiss and the company could be prevented from manufacturing and flying while the substantive issue of whether Curtiss and the company were infringing the Wrights' patents continued to be litigated. But for the moment, Curtiss was relieved: "I am glad the decision has been made, as it sustains the position I have maintained and clears away the clouds in the aeronautical sky."[34]

Even Hall seemed at last to be finding success. Touted by his manager, Charles Bryce, as "one of the world's greatest aviators," and despite the Medford debacle, Hall secured a contract to fly in Eugene, Oregon. Although muddy conditions at the Eugene track caused postponement of his exhibition by a week, Hall finally became airborne in public on June 18, covering somewhere between several hundred yards and three-quarters of a mile.[35]

Shortly after returning to Portland from his disappointing showing in Medford, Ely heard from the president of the Baker City Commercial Club. He had signed a contract to fly on July 4 for a minimum $1,000, but when questioned, Ely admitted that his engine had not been strong enough to cope with the winds at Sutherlin or Medford. The Baker City representative withdrew the offer, leaving Ely with no upcoming exhibitions and no prospect of finding any. He would have to try his luck elsewhere.[36]

CHAPTER 7

OUTLAW

BY JUNE 1910, Curtiss was no longer alone in having what could legitimately be called an exhibition flying team. The Wright brothers, evidently intent on competing with him for public approval, had targeted nearby Indianapolis for their first public aviation meet, to be held June 13–18, even though they had only just started training their first student, Walter Brookins. Their manager, Roy Knabenshue, went about recruiting new talent.[1]

Knabenshue knew California automobile racer Archibald "Arch" Hoxsey through their mutual interest in dirigibles. Hoxsey began training at the Wrights' winter location in Montgomery, Alabama, and in April wrote to his mother that he had enjoyed his first ride in an airplane, with Orville Wright as his instructor. A month later, Hoxsey and Brookins reportedly flew together by moonlight, "circling, wheeling and going through all the evolutions customary in daytime."[2]

Knabenshue also recruited Ralph Johnstone, who since 1897 had been booking paid engagements as the "champion trick bicycle rider of the world," touring the East Coast in vaudeville shows before he was twenty. In 1901, Johnstone moved to Europe, where he performed for the next four years. Dubbed "the reckless king of bicyclists," he developed a stunt in which he ascended a flight of stairs while balanced on one wheel and then dropped twelve feet to the stage, still mounted, to ride away unscathed.[3]

When Johnstone returned to the United States in 1905, he continued to amaze crowds, turning front and back somersaults on a bicycle, high in the air. His signature act was called "The

Wheelman's Rest." According to one reviewer, "It consists largely in jumping from one bench to another while mounted on a bicycle. Finally he rides down a ladder and then goes up step by step, still mounted on his wheel, to the top of a house, jumps across the roof and finally to the floor, a distance of probably twenty feet." The reviewer concluded, "The remarkable part about Mr. Johnstone's work is that he does not break his neck."[4]

In the spring of 1910, Johnstone's bicycle performances abruptly ceased, and he began studying flying at Huffman Prairie, outside Dayton, Ohio. Wilbur Wright reportedly called Johnstone "the quickest pupil we had."[5]

From the beginning, the Wrights took a more organized approach to exhibiting than did Curtiss. For two days before the Indianapolis event, the Wright aviators conducted private trial flights, closed to the press. The public performances that followed were carefully scripted. The Wrights clearly wanted the exhibition to be free from unpleasant surprises. Brookins, by far the most experienced of the team, quickly emerged as the star, repeatedly establishing world altitude records at nearly five thousand feet.

A reporter noted, "So far as the flying itself was concerned, the meet proved pretty conclusively that the Wright aeroplane is a very steady and dependable machine. There were about sixty flights during the six days of the exhibition, and there was no suggestion of an accident. In the tranquility of the performances—the invariably successful starts, and quiet, uneventful landings—lay the chief beauty, from the writer's standpoint, of the meet." But, the same reporter conceded, "after a man has loafed around a railroad station thirty-eight minutes waiting for transportation to the field, has quietly sat . . . for three hours waiting for something to happen, and with equal peace of mind finally watched—at a distance of half a mile or more—these great white birds rise gently into the air and sail placidly around the track until fancy moved them to descend, that man is apt to lean toward something more stirring."[6]

Understanding the need for "something more stirring," the Curtiss team's Charles Hamilton, with his famous "glide," had already tapped into the public's desire to see not merely what a machine could do, but how hard a man could push it without losing his life. Brookins, Johnstone, and Hoxsey, in turn, would soon become known more for corkscrews and other aerial stunts than for placid cruising. The three leading Wright fliers intended to give the public what it wanted.

While Curtiss had been preparing to fly from Albany to New York, he had been sending Hamilton, Charles Willard, and Bud Mars to exhibitions. But he was the celebrity, and the public wanted to see him in person. He committed to fly at meets in Louisville and Minneapolis in the second half of June.[7]

Whipple Hall, probably expecting to trade on his association with Hamilton, proposed to intercept Curtiss in Minneapolis. Ely, at home in Portland, had a Curtiss machine that did not reliably fly. He would have known Curtiss' well-publicized exhibition schedule and had nothing to lose by setting out to meet Curtiss in Minneapolis. Perhaps he could learn why he was having such difficulty with the Hudson-Fulton machine after having flown with such ease the first time he sat behind the wheel.

Ely's first stop was Billings, Montana. His publicist, Hartman Price, had convinced the city's chamber of commerce to engage him to fly there on June 18–19. Halfway between Portland and Minneapolis on the railway, Billings was just then hosting the 1910 Montana Good Roads convention, which meant that not only would Ely make the first flight in Montana; he would also, the local paper explained, "go up into space for the benefit of the Good Roads people." Henry Wemme's old airplane would again be raising money for a highway. Ely's reported fee was a modest $400, which he collected in advance, apparently having learned from his Sutherlin experience.[8]

But Ely again fell victim to the puffery of his advance man and the press. Prior to his arrival, the Billings newspapers reported that he had flown successfully in Sacramento, Stockton, El Paso, and

San Antonio—having reached an altitude, it was said, of 550 feet. Reporters speculated, with no basis in fact, that Ely had "probably made more successful flights than any aviator, except the Wrights, Paulhan and Hamilton." And although Billings is 3,200 feet above sea level—an elevation from which no one had ever launched an airplane—one newspaper confidently predicted, "Mr. Ely will soar over the city and valley for several hours to give all a chance to see a wonderful feat of the man-bird."[9]

There had been reports of unsuccessful attempts by others to take off from Denver and Salt Lake City, both of which are at considerably higher elevations than Billings, so the eyes of the scientific community as well may have been on Ely when he arrived on June 17. He is said to have expressed uncertainty about whether the machine would rise from the ground. "I am certainly going to make every effort to fly," Ely reportedly said.[10]

But on the afternoon of June 18, during his first attempt, he once again encountered high winds, and while he rose several feet a number of times, he "sank to the ground again each time." An hour later the wind had increased, and the most he could manage was a run of two hundred feet. Acknowledging that the prevailing winds in Billings tended to pick up in the evenings, the organizers agreed to begin the following day's flying earlier.

The next day, before an "immense throng," Ely was unable to get airborne on his first attempt, despite ideal conditions. Onlookers reported that the propeller did not appear to be working properly, which suggests that he could have been experiencing the same problem with the Hudson-Fulton machine that had plagued Curtiss at its debut on Governors Island the previous fall. On a second try Ely managed to rise briefly to ten feet before sailing "gracefully to the ground" and apparently concluding that the air was simply too thin for a true flight. He was willing to try again if the organizers wished it, he said, but the odds of success were slim.

If his pride suffered, his reputation did not. "It had been generally understood," the local paper now conceded in an unapologetic about-face, "that the chances of a flight were exceedingly slight, for it is said that no aeroplane has ever made one at an altitude so great as that of Billings."[11]

Ely and Hall were professionals, in the sense that they expected to be paid for their performances, but they were far from being the headliners that Curtiss, Hamilton, Willard, and even Mars were. Nevertheless, on June 19, the day he completed exhibitions in Oregon, Hall announced that he was en route to Minneapolis to fly in the meet there and sent a confirming telegram to the promoters. Ely simply appeared in Minneapolis on June 21, apparently unannounced.[12]

Hall may have hoped his friend Hamilton would introduce him to Curtiss, and that Curtiss would help him with his flying. He might also have seen the benefit in teaming up with Ely to exhibit, as they had done in Medford in May; at least one of them might fly successfully. Whether it was planned or not, Hall and Ely came together in Minneapolis with the common goal of meeting Curtiss.

Hamilton, as it turned out, was not in Minneapolis. He was flying instead at a "military tournament" in Nashville, where he had been engaged to drop dummy explosives from the air in a test of the military usefulness of airplanes. Hall and Ely were left to introduce themselves to Curtiss on their own. Curtiss did not know either man personally and was decidedly displeased at their sudden appearance in Minneapolis. He could hardly claim to disapprove of their machines, but he might well not have wanted to risk seeing them destroyed by two unknown aviators, bringing disrepute to the Curtiss name, to say nothing of the threat the interlopers posed to his exhibition business.[13]

Curtiss must have immediately recognized Ely's airplane as the original Hudson-Fulton machine that had been sold to Wemme at Dominguez—an airplane that was, by contract, supposed to stay on the ground. But the only way he could keep Ely from flying would be by starting another lawsuit, and he already had his hands full with Augustus Herring and the Wrights.[14]

Ely disassociated himself from the Curtiss team by referring to himself as an "independent." The Curtiss aviators were similarly at pains during the exhibition to characterize Ely as an "outlaw"—which he was, in the sense that he had no legal right to fly the Wemme machine for money.[15]

Some 17,000 people attended opening day, as temperatures climbed to eighty degrees and winds gusted to 15 mph. The Curtiss aviators, the crowds had read, were "human monarchs of the air, masters of the locomotion secret of birds, dynamiters of distance, annihilators of altitudes . . . the greatest assemblage of men-birds ever brought together." Hall was said to have been recently "enjoying the mountain scenery out in Montana by looking down on the loftiest peaks and into the deepest valleys from the seat in his 'plane," while Ely had supposedly come direct from the Pacific coast, where he had enjoyed "such success in accurate alighting tests that he would like to wager that he can defeat Mars," who was noted for being "particularly expert and clever in starting and alighting."[16]

Curtiss opened the exhibition in the powerful *Hudson Flyer*, climbing to a hundred feet and passing once before the grandstand before he had to touch down, possibly his shortest flight to date. He then took off in the other direction. "Rising fifty feet he attempted to mount over the poles erected to sustain a dirigible," when suddenly "the aeroplane was sent headfirst to the ground." Curtiss escaped uninjured, but it was his first reported crash.[17]

Mars made two attempts to fly but was unable to get more than a few feet off the ground. Ely followed Mars. His machine "flew 50 feet at the altitude a duck would attain, hit the track again, bounded into the air, mounted higher and seemed destined to make a sensational flight" when it "precipitated itself with a thud on the rough ground." The crowd nevertheless gave him a rousing round of applause. Ely reportedly blamed a "down current" and promised to start from a different place on the field the following day, once his machine was repaired. One final unsuccessful attempt took place that day, attributed to Mars by one reporter and to "the intrepid Ely" by another.

Curtiss reportedly called the atmospheric conditions the most dangerous he had ever experienced. "Aeroplanes, like human beings, are affected by heat and air," the *Minneapolis Journal* reported, and the crowd seemed willing to accept his word that the combination of crosscurrents sweeping the field and rough ground made landing unsafe.[18]

On the second day, the four-cylinder engines used by every aviator except Curtiss proved inadequate to generate sufficient lift for a true flight. Mars managed to hop into the air from one end of the track to the other. After completing this "mediocre flight," he returned—narrowly avoiding a collision with some boys who had ventured from the grandstand—and crashed into the fence below the judges' stand. Willard, recovering from an injured foot from a recent crash in Springfield, Missouri, had little better luck, and Hall was unable to get off the ground. Ely's machine had not yet been repaired, and so—"nattily attired in a white flannel suit"—he borrowed Hall's and flew it as far as the upper end of the enclosure, described by one wit as "the aeroplane magnet."

The crowd of ten thousand, sweltering after having waited nearly five hours for a "real flight," began to grow unruly, prompting Curtiss to make a special effort. Managing to get aloft with his eight-cylinder engine, he flew for seven minutes or more at a height he estimated as six or seven hundred feet, covering six miles and "cutting all kinds of capers in the air to show his control." Upon landing, he said once again that conditions were the most adverse in which he had ever attempted to fly. But his triumphant flight saved the day, leaving spectators optimistic that additional wonderful flights would follow—weather permitting.[19]

On the third day, Ely, Hall, and Willard made flights that "would have been rated as superb on the first day of the meet." Ely's and Hall's brief efforts, the latter lasting sixteen seconds, were adjudged "pretty"; but spectators now used Curtiss as a yardstick, and that day it was again he who astonished the crowd, rising into the overcast sky in four separate flights that totaled just over twenty-five minutes. "Like a cyclist on a park pathway, Curtiss seemed to pick his course through the ozone." The crowd was amazed by the ease with which he dropped from three hundred feet to just above the track, "like a kingfisher from a dead limb on the bank of a stream to the water's surface."[20]

The promoters advertised that the "biggest features" had been saved for the final day of the meet, and a large crowd showed up on Saturday with great expectations. Thunderstorms had soaked the parched ground, but the cooler temperatures that followed allowed the aviators to make numerous flights. One writer noted, "The surprise of the program was when Willard, Mars and Ely scooted through the air and did not light like winged birds, as on previous attempts." Willard drew praise for making the "prettiest" flight, other than those of Curtiss. Ely managed to fly far enough that when he landed it was in a potato field outside the exhibition grounds.

The *Minneapolis Tribune* had the final word, under the subhead "Ely Loudly Praised": "The management predicts a brilliant future for Ely as an aviator. They declare that he has the most remarkable nerve and that he was never asked to attempt a flight that he did not do so. That he did not fly earlier in the meet was due solely to the [inability] of his engine to drive him fast enough. He became a favorite with the crowd through his repeated attempts to give them what they wanted to see, a real flight, and each time he failed there was genuine sympathy for him." The "outlaw" only added to the luster of his image by volunteering to judge a model airplane contest held for local children: "Ely had several disciples about him, all of whom he was willing to help."[21]

In addition to charming the crowd, Ely also somehow managed to overcome Curtiss' initial hostility. Perhaps it was his modest and unassuming manner or his measured approach to flying. Ely, like Curtiss, was a cautious flier, and he understood that Curtiss wanted to "exhibit" what his machines could do. Both men held a dim view of stunt flying, summed up by Curtiss as: "I do not believe fancy or trick flying demonstrates anything except an unlimited amount of nerve and skill, and perhaps the possibilities of aerial acrobatics." Or perhaps it was simply the skill that Ely demonstrated, even in the underpowered Hudson-Fulton machine. Whatever the reason, he won Curtiss over.[22]

Ely's timing had been good. Traveling the country to give exhibitions prevented Curtiss from doing what he preferred, which was designing aircraft. By the end of the summer, Curtiss was reportedly charging at least $5,000 per personal appearance, hoping to decrease demand so that he would have more time in Hammondsport.[23]

There was also the fact that, by the spring of 1910, Curtiss' business manager, Jerome Fanciulli, had grown to mistrust Hamilton. "He does not seem to be getting much money for his flights," Fanciulli wrote to Curtiss, "or else he is misinforming us as to what he is getting." The rift grew so wide that Curtiss began to fear that his star flier would simply break his contract and depart one day, taking the Rheims racer with him. Even before Ely appeared, Curtiss must have known that he needed to make a personnel change soon.[24]

Meanwhile, Ely's neighbors back home in Williamsburg, Iowa, were taking note of the former chauffeur who had scarcely been heard from since his marriage three years earlier. As the local paper reported, with more pride than accuracy,

> Among the daring aviators in the Minneapolis meet is the name of 'Gene Ely and one day none flew farther or higher than 'Gene. . . . For the past few years he had been conducting a garage in Oregon. Six months ago he became interested in aerial navigation and in this his cool head and intrepid nerve give him a prominent place. Mr. Ely intends to visit Williamsburg before long and we all may have an opportunity to see a son of York scudding on white wings through the upper air.[25]

CHAPTER 8

ON THE TEAM

ELY STRUCK OUT on his own. He had a new advance man, Arthur M. McGinniss, from Buffalo. The crowd at Minneapolis had included residents of nearby Superior, Wisconsin, and McGinniss was able to negotiate a one-day exhibition for Ely in Superior, with two flights to take place on June 29. "SEE THE BIRD MAN FLY," urged the advertisement. Press reports claimed that Ely would soar to "almost any height" and that he had the ability to steer through the air "as easily as a bird controls its flight." One reporter made this prescient observation: "Ten years from now these machines will not be looked at with the great amount of curiosity with which they are viewed now, but for the present, they are something brand new and may not be seen here again for a long time at least."[1]

Whipple Hall, having no pressing engagements, traveled to Superior on June 28, expecting Ely to follow that evening. A machine, presumably Ely's, was shipped there for the performance. Meanwhile, Charles Willard and Bud Mars arrived in Sioux City, Iowa, both "a little lame from recent accidents" earlier in the month. Apparently feeling poorly from his injuries sustained in Springfield, Willard departed almost immediately.[2]

This left Curtiss in a jam. He had agreed to provide two aviators for the Sioux City meet. Curtiss could not fulfill the contract himself because of an obligation to stage a bomb-dropping exercise for military observers in Hammondsport. Charles Hamilton, seeking a release from his contract, was unlikely to do Curtiss any favors.[3]

Running out of options, Curtiss turned to Ely. Ely's flying in Minneapolis had been every bit as good as that of Mars, and he was a proven crowd-pleaser. He was also from Iowa and could fairly be billed as a hometown boy. At the last minute, Curtiss asked Ely to join Mars in Sioux City.[4]

That left Hall to cover the exhibition at Superior. A reported 250 people turned up for the afternoon performance, but wind conditions were unfavorable, and Hall made no attempt to fly. Angry attendees rejected an offer of free admission to the evening performance and "made threats to smash the machine and to storm the ticket office," leaving the promoters with little choice but to refund the ticket price.

The thousands of spectators who did arrive for the evening performance left in "anything but a joyful mood" when McGinniss and Hall canceled the event. The promoters obtained a legal order preventing shipment of the machine pending repayment of funds previously advanced. McGinniss and Hall returned the advance the next day, freeing Ely's machine but leaving them with nothing at all for the engagement.[5]

Ely and Mars did not fare much better in Sioux City. Ely's nominal debut flying for the Curtiss team, likely in Willard's machine, went much as his solo career had done up to that point. Roughly four thousand spectators turned up on June 29, only to witness flights in strong wind that were "not thrilling. The 'bird men' were unable either to get very high or to stay in the air any great length of time," though not for lack of trying.[6]

The following afternoon they collectively made five unsuccessful attempts that ended after they smashed both machines. Finally, on the last day of the meet, but after the crowd had left, Ely flew a lap of the one-mile track, and Mars made a few longer flights. While the Sioux City meet was not a success, it cemented a mutual respect and friendship between Ely and the older and more experienced Mars.[7]

Jerome Fanciulli's standard offer to promoters was to furnish an exhibition for a set number of days, "to consist of the various competitions usually provided at an aviation meet," in exchange for fifty percent of gross receipts, with a guaranteed minimum, usually not less than $5,000. The contract said nothing about what constituted a successful flight, however, nor what excused performance. It was a recipe for dispute.[8]

Sioux City residents proved less forgiving than the spectators at Minneapolis. The press branded Mars and Ely as "wretched failures," and the promoters decided to withhold a second payment of $2,000 that was due for the exhibition. Mars threatened that Curtiss would sue the promoters for it, and Fanciulli's records reflect that the fliers ultimately collected a total of $3,000. Ely had no formal arrangement with Curtiss, but under the standard Curtiss contract he would have been entitled to nearly $1,000.[9]

Aeronautics magazine reported that as of the Sioux City meet, Ely was "flying now for Curtiss, using the machine sold [to] Henry Wemme. As far as the press was concerned, Ely was a member of the Curtiss team; but in fact he was a freelancer, still flying on his own. And the machine was no longer Wemme's. It now belonged to the Portland Aeroplane Company, which was entitled to the proceeds of Ely's exhibitions in it.[10]

Reports of the "fiasco" in Sioux City failed to dampen the general enthusiasm for exhibitions over the summer of 1910. As one observer noted: "No state or county affair is considered up to date now unless it announces as a part of its list of attractions aerial flights by one or more of the world's fliers. Of course the fliers come high—no pun intended—but the fairs must have them or be considered hopelessly behind the times. The old-fashioned balloon ascension cannot draw a crowd nowadays, so the fair authorities are falling over one another in their endeavors to get the aviators."[11]

Ely, Mars, and Mars' wife, Marie, took the train from Sioux City to the Hawthorne speedway in Cicero, outside Chicago, for an "aero-auto congress" that was predicted to draw fifteen aviators. Despite significant wind on July 3, Ely and Mars both made flights long enough that "the crowd in the grandstand was satisfied that the skeletons of bamboo and silk oilcloth could really fly." After suffering through two more days of strong winds, Mars at last succeeded in circling the racetrack "at will," about a hundred feet off the ground, though Ely reportedly was unable to make any flights approaching that performance.[12]

The next appearance of the Curtiss team, and of the "outlaw" Ely, would logically have been an Omaha meet scheduled for July 9–14. But because those dates conflicted with an important meet in Atlantic City, Curtiss postponed the Omaha engagement to July 23–27. As a result, when Hall required hospitalization for an unspecified illness or injury and could not make a scheduled exhibition in Winnipeg on July 13–19, Ely had time to travel north to take his place. It marked Ely's first time outside the United States.[13]

Mabel Ely, with her husband's flying career apparently established, traveled east, and had perhaps planned to join Ely before the Omaha meet. She arrived in Williamsburg, Iowa, around July 11, where she stayed at the family farm with Maidie and Emma for two weeks. Ely may have traveled with her there between his engagements in Chicago and Winnipeg. Around this same time, his mechanic Walter Kaufman returned to Oregon, and Ely's cousin Orson Harrington took over the position. Their hometown paper related on July 14 that Harrington, now married and accompanied by his wife and young daughter, "left this week to join Eugene Ely who is giving aeroplane exhibitions in the principal cities of the country," including Louisville, Rock Island (just across the Mississippi River from Davenport), Des Moines, "and several other places." The paper expected "to hear of 'Gene Ely crowding Curtiss and the Wright boys for first honors as aerial navigators."[14]

Ely reached Winnipeg on July 13. He and Hall, the papers puffed, "have performed in the Far East, where millions of Chinese have watched their flights. At Hong Kong alone 72,000 paid for admission to the pavilion where the machine was on view. These two men are among the most celebrated aeroplanists in the world. . . . Ely is a well-known man in the western states, his father being a representative of Iowa congress." The only sliver of truth was that the absent Hall had at one time traveled in China. The press further promised readers that Ely would attempt to collect a $6,000 prize offered for the first round-trip flight between Winnipeg and Portage la Prairie, sixty miles to the west. He would fly out on Friday, July 15, the papers said, and return on the following day with a signed receipt from the mayor. Whether or not that was ever a possibility, it is not what happened.[15]

Again the weather proved daunting. Ely had apparently warned the promoters not to expect "spectacular flights" unless the air was dead calm, and that in winds above 15 mph he would attempt nothing beyond short flights. On Thursday evening he had his airplane taken out onto the open prairie west of the cramped and dangerous exhibition grounds, but gusty winds prevented him from making any attempts at flight. Conditions were no better on Friday afternoon, and faced with a 25-mph wind, he declined to fly. He told reporters that he hoped to go up at sunset, when he expected the wind to lessen.

One paper described Ely as "a slim, deliberate figure in gray coat and white duck trousers." A rather poetic reporter wrote, "He is an unassuming mortal, deliberate of voice and movement, deliberate even in his smiling. His eyes have an odd, far-away look, something of what [Kipling] has called 'that brooding, sheathed glance, characteristic of eagles and aeronauts.' He knows the trick of the wind as a trainer his animal, and can light his thick Egyptian cigarettes in the most boisterous breeze."[16]

The wind was still blowing on Friday evening, and the temperature was eighty degrees; but Ely once more took his machine to the open prairie, intending to fly from there to the grandstand. He succeeded in getting aloft at dusk for three short flights, "the first two of which resembled a bird with a broken wing." One report had him covering six hundred yards at around twenty feet on the first attempt and no better than that on the second, at the end of which he crashed violently enough to damage a wooden stay. Another report estimated the heights he reached as eighty and sixty feet, respectively.

Ely concluded that repairs were unnecessary and took off for a third flight. He completed a circle of perhaps two miles over the unpopulated prairie at a reported height of forty to eighty feet, hailed (incorrectly) as the first airplane flight in western Canada. (Hamilton had flown near Vancouver, British Columbia, on March 25, 1910.) As he headed toward the waiting crowd in the distant grandstand, "the machine struck the ground very heavily at an angle and jarred it sufficiently to wreck some of the stays and braces. Eugene Ely, calm and collected, stepped from his seat and gave directions for hauling the biplane back to the [exhibition] grounds." His only injury was a bruised knee. Hall's manager, Charles Bryce, who had booked the engagement, announced that further flights would depend entirely on the weather.[17]

An overeager wire stringer filed the following report, almost every detail of which is incorrect: "The first serious aeroplane accident in Canada took place today. Eugene Ely, who had contracted to fly between Winnipeg and Portage la Prairie, made his third attempt early today. Before he had traveled far his engine went wrong and his aeroplane fell a distance of more than five hundred feet. Ely was picked out of the wreckage in a dying condition." The story ran across the United States, and Mabel read it. A somewhat less alarming version reported that Ely had been rendered unconscious and had sustained "a mass of bruises," and that four mechanics were at work repairing the airship.[18]

In Davenport, Ely's father contacted Winnipeg's chief of police, who had no information regarding the accident. Nathan was accordingly "inclined to think that the reports of the injury have been greatly exaggerated and that his son met with a mishap in his machine and that some excited person sent out word that he was fatally injured." But Curtiss was concerned enough to wire from Hammondsport, one among the dozen or so telegrams sent to Winnipeg exhibition directors asking about Ely. Mabel, in Williamsburg, took the extraordinary step of placing a midnight long-distance telephone call to receive reassurance that her husband was well. By the middle of the week, with the gravity of the accident still wildly overstated, Ely's grandfather had received word that his grandson would live.[19]

On Saturday evening, with winds too strong for a real flight, Ely brought his airplane into the exhibition grounds and made two straight demonstration dashes across the infield, reaching reported heights of fifty and ten feet. But the crowd of 18,000 had only a partial view of the low flights, due to scenery for a dramatic spectacle—a recreation of the 1880 Battle of Kandahar—that occupied the field.

Ely reportedly drove out to Portage la Prairie to inspect the route on Sunday, and supposedly announced his intention to try for the $6,000 prize as soon as the weather allowed. But Monday's winds were again too strong. On Tuesday, despite continuing high winds, he took his airplane promptly at 8 p.m. to the open prairie, where a crowd was waiting. "Mounting his machine, amidst a great cheer from the spectators who had gathered around him, Ely started his engine and rose from the ground to a height of nearly eighty feet. The aeroplane obeyed her helm with unerring precision and manoeuvred with exactitude. Still gliding through the air like a bird the aeroplane's progress was being keenly followed by the crowd, up to this stage being about two miles from where he started." Ely headed toward the exhibition grounds but had to descend to make an adjustment to the machine's tail. He crashed on the rough ground, damaging the machine and ending all prospects of further flying in Winnipeg.[20]

The Canadian exhibition was decidedly not a success. Although Ely did achieve flight, hardly anyone witnessed it up close. According to newspaper reports, he received $500 in advance and was to receive $200 for each day of actual flights. But while the promotors paid him $400 for the first two days, they claimed that on Tuesday Ely had violated his contract by not flying directly in front of the grandstand. The aviator countered that he had seen the grandstand crowds clearly from the air, so they must have seen him. The local newspaper reported that he threatened to sue, "refused to take his machine out of its tent," and wired Bryce, who was now in Chicago, for further instructions. Eventually Ely was allowed to move his tent into the heart of the fairgrounds and to charge twenty-five cents for the opportunity to inspect his airplane on the ground. He quit Winnipeg on July 22, leaving Bryce to work out a final settlement.[21]

The apparent safety of aviation was beginning to draw comment around this time. An article in *Aeronautics* about the Atlantic City meet in July 1910 noted: "It is a strange fact, but during the entire week there was not a single accident of any kind, except the first day, when Curtiss landed in deep sand and ran into a hole, breaking one post. Outside of that not a wire, nut or any part of the machines had to be altered from the first day of 'setting up.'" When a Wright biplane flown by Rolls-Royce cofounder Charles Rolls failed and crashed on July 12 in England, he was the first Briton to die in an aviation accident. Rolls' was only the eleventh airplane death worldwide. There had not been an American fatality in the nearly two years since Selfridge's death during Orville Wright's Fort Myer demonstration. In the eyes of the general public, if an aviator refused to go up, he did so because he was incompetent.[22]

Hamilton, not unexpectedly, severed his connection with Curtiss in early July 1910 and returned the Rheims racer. Curtiss then brought legal action against him for payments due. Hamilton's departure left the team short-handed, creating an opportunity for Ely. Curtiss and Fanciulli decided that, if nothing else, they could count him as one of their aviators for contracts that required a minimum number of fliers. By the time Ely reunited with Mabel at the meet in Omaha, he was an outlaw no longer.[23]

Ely must have recognized that the financial benefits of sharing the Curtiss appearance fee would outweigh whatever he might command on his own. Mabel's scrapbook annotation calls Omaha his "first work with Curtiss team." Still, the arrangement was likely on a trial basis; there was no contract yet.[24]

Ely and Mars were billed at Omaha as "two of the most daring and venturesome aviators in America today." But it was unclear whether Ely actually would fly. The contract, which called for three aviators, could be satisfied by Curtiss, Mars, and Douglas McCurdy, Curtiss' comrade from the Aerial Experiment Association (AEA). McCurdy, a Canadian, had been trying to interest the government of Canada in military aircraft but had abandoned the attempt and turned to exhibiting on his own. Curtiss was glad to bring him into the Curtiss Exhibition Company, an entity he and Fanciulli were in the process of organizing. Ely first met McCurdy at the Omaha meet, and while both men did ultimately fly, neither did anything of note there. The headlines instead went to Curtiss and Mars. Mabel, for her part, first met Marie Mars at Omaha, and the two women attracted attention from the press when the organizers presented them with pearl fans.[25]

During the Omaha meet, Ely's name became associated with a planned exhibition in Rochester, New York, on August 5–6. It was being called a "meet" because a second aviator—Hall—would also appear. Bryce, acting as the front man for both aviators, was even more exuberant in his fabrications than usual: "Eugene Ely, the California sky pilot, who was the first to fly an aeroplane before the astonished gaze of the Mikado and his subjects and has been decorated for his feats there and in Australia, is announced as the feature sky-scraper of the meet."[26]

En route to Rochester, Ely and Mabel traveled to Hammondsport and stayed for several days as guests of the Curtisses. Ely acquired a new machine from Curtiss, which "behaved beautifully." It had a motor capable of delivering roughly a third more power than any he had flown with before.

From that time on, Ely was an official member of the Curtiss team. It seems likely that Curtiss offered him the standard airplane lease contract for Curtiss Exhibition Company aviators, which would have required him to make exhibition flights, to compete for prizes whenever and wherever Curtiss or his representatives designated, and to pay as rent up to seventy-five percent of all exhibition earnings and prizes, less expenses, which included fuel, maintenance, repairs, and transportation for the machine, aviator, and mechanics. The arrangement required detailed accounting, and disagreements often arose.[27]

Bryce, whom Fanciulli had just hired as advance man for the Curtiss Exhibition Company, continued to give free rein to his imagination, asserting that Ely called his machine *Valkyrie* and that Hall referred to his as *Falcon.* Whatever the name of Ely's new machine, if indeed it had one, its differences from the Hudson-Fulton machine were obvious. On opening day at Rochester, weather conditions kept the airplanes on the ground, but the next day Ely flew for nearly a full mile, notwithstanding "conditions which would have daunted the average aeronaut," including a 17-mph wind. He landed to make a repair and returned to the sky without incident. The meet was extended, and two days later he made a pair of "very successful flights" that covered nearly three miles each and were deemed "as pretty a sight as has been seen in this city in many a day."[28]

No airplane races could take place, though, because Hall did not even attempt to fly. On August 7, which happened to be the Elys' third wedding anniversary, Hall was taken "seriously ill" with what was described as the result of "a slight fracture of the skull" suffered in May. He headed home, quitting his career as an exhibition flier for good.[29]

Nor did Ely attempt what a newspaper had said would be a near-vertical glide, "shooting toward the surface at a hair-raising angle and speed" before pulling up with twenty feet to spare. But the spectators, having seen a working flying machine, were satisfied "that aeroplanes are more than a dream of the future." Mabel was said to have been happy the flights had been successful because "she didn't like to have people disappointed and she herself took pride in her husband's achievements."[30]

The Elys proceeded to New York City and then joined Curtiss and his wife, Lena, for an automobile trip from there to Buffalo via Albany. The *New York Times* and the *Chicago Evening Post* were offering a $25,000 prize for the first flight between New York and Chicago, and Ely "intimated that Mr. Curtiss would probably enter two machines," one to be operated by Ely. Asked by a reporter whether he enjoyed automobiling, Curtiss is said to have declared that he would "just as soon travel over an air route if he had proper places to make landings"; indeed, the purpose of this trip was to "take a view of the country" over which the proposed flight would be made and to scout potential landing spots along the way.[31]

Barely six weeks had passed since Ely, operating an old, underpowered airplane and with not a single wholly successful public flight to his name, had found himself the focus of Curtiss' ire in Minneapolis. Having persevered through the hot winds of a Midwest summer and the unreasonable expectations of the crowds who came to watch him, he was now flying a brand-new machine and was an accepted member of the Curtiss team.

CHAPTER 9

LOFTIER GOALS

THROUGHOUT THE SUMMER of 1910, Curtiss kept an eye on developing plans for the international aviation tournament at which he was expected to defend the Gordon Bennett Cup. The meet would be held in October 1910, near New York City, at the Belmont Park racetrack in Elmont, on Long Island.

Curtiss was deeply unhappy about a rumored arrangement for the Wrights to share in the tournament's gate receipts. No contestant had been paid in 1909 to appear at Rheims; the money the fliers received was based entirely on how they performed. Paying the Wrights in advance while not compensating other aviators was tantamount to conceding the validity of the brothers' patents. One leading aviation columnist, acknowledging "considerable doubt as to the entry of Curtiss in a single event of the meet," explained why: "Presuming upon the possibility of [the Wrights'] obtaining a proportion of all receipts of the meet [Curtiss] will decline to add to their profits, as he believes his entry will do." For some time he refused, on principle, to commit to a defense of the Cup.[1]

But he kept his options open, and in August, Curtiss let it slip that he was building a machine specifically designed to compete at Belmont. "I can't say whether or not I shall fly it myself," he was reported as saying. "All I can tell you now is that I have developed a Curtiss machine, with some alterations from the machine I am now flying, which will be fast.[2]

The brothers, for their part, were busy challenging Curtiss' monopoly on exhibition flights. Five Wright aviators appeared in a meet hosted by the city of Asbury Park, New Jersey, before an audience of some 50,000; no Curtiss machines participated. But things did not go well. On opening day, August 10, the Wrights' star flier, Walter Brookins, swerved to avoid spectators who had run onto the track. He crashed into the grandstand, destroying his machine and injuring himself and seven spectators. Ralph Johnstone collided with an automobile, luckily without injury. And news arrived that the world's record for altitude, recently set by Johnstone, had been eclipsed in Europe by J. Armstrong Drexel, a Philadelphian operating a Blériot monoplane.[3]

As Brookins' replacement machine, the Wrights introduced their Model B Flyer at Asbury Park. It featured a 35-hp engine with a speed of 45 mph and wheels beneath the skids (previous Wright Flyers had been launched from a track), and the front elevator had been removed to create a "headless" configuration. The real revelation, though, was that immediately following Brookins' crash, ticket sales doubled. Spectators wanted something sensational, even if that something was the thrill of potential carnage.[4]

The Wrights were not the only ones challenging Curtiss for the Gordon Bennett Cup. John Bevins Moisant, an American born in Illinois who had spent much of his life overseas, was also a contender. A colorful story had it that he had traveled to Salvador in Central America (now El Salvador), where his brothers operated a sugar plantation. When the brothers were imprisoned by the country's despotic president in 1907, Moisant supposedly organized a cadre of Nicaraguan troops, led them into Salvador, and effectively started a revolution.

Whatever the truth of his origin story, Moisant learned to fly a Blériot in Europe and, in a series of flights that began with what he claimed was only his fifth time in an airplane, flew himself and a mechanic from Paris to London, claiming a $25,000 prize for the first flight between the two cities. In an era when aviators depended entirely on ground features to stay oriented, Moisant's innovation was to use a map and compass to navigate. His "cometlike appearance in the aviation firmament" made him an attractive addition to the upcoming international race.[5]

Just as the Wrights' Asbury Park meet was concluding, Curtiss held an exhibition of his own a few miles to the northeast, billed as New York's first air show. To secure the Aero Club of America's sanction, which was necessary for any records set at the show to be official, the meet had to be open to all aviators. But as a practical matter, it was a Curtiss-only event.

Curtiss believed that the best way to make significant money in the exhibition business was with an "air carnival." In a departure from his earlier approach, he had his team practice prior to the public exhibition, just as the Wrights had done in Indianapolis.[6]

The meet was staged at the Sheepshead Bay thoroughbred racetrack in Brooklyn, which had become available when antibetting legislation in New York essentially killed horse racing. A United Press wire story, noting the transformation of the racetrack into an airfield, foresaw that "the sport of kings will give way to the sport of science." The program listed twenty-five events, including contests of speed, distance, endurance, climbing, and gliding.[7]

Fanciulli gathered seven functioning airplanes in one place, the largest collection yet seen in the United States. Curtiss, Ely, Mars, Willard, and McCurdy were there to fly them. Mars was so intent on practicing in what the press called *Skylark II*—actually the Rheims racer, recovered recently from Hamilton—that he risked taking off in the face of "a wind that made the few spectators frantically clutch their straw hats." Ely, it was said, expected soon to fly with an "eight-cylinder Curtiss engine" (actually, it was the four-cylinder he had acquired in Hammondsport). When asked the name of the machine that spectators at the Rochester meet in early August knew as *Valkyrie*, Ely responded, "Just plain aeroplane."[8]

On the final day of practice, Ely took off into the wind and at fifty feet "was tipped and tossed, raised and dropped as the gusts played with his light machine." He then tried an even trickier flight with the wind at his back. "Just as he was landing, with his motor throttled [down], a quick puff of wind caught the [wings], tilting them to one side. The wheels had touched the ground and the machine seemed about to turn over when Ely accelerated his motor, making a leap which barely cleared the fence around the infield, and landed safely in the turf course." It was a significant advance over his struggles to control the Wemme machine four months earlier.[9]

Mars' reason for making practice flights in the Rheims racer soon became apparent: "Announcement is made by the managers that one of the features of the meet will be a number of passenger flights with women as the passengers." The Rheims racer had an engine powerful enough to lift an aviator and a passenger seated to his left, legs dangling. The day before the meet, Mars made successive trial flights with Augustus Post, secretary of the Aero Club of America, and Frank Tillman from the Curtiss publicity team.[10]

The meet opened the afternoon of August 19 with the promised rides for women. With his wife, Marie, perched on the passenger seat, Mars flew for some two hundred yards before the grandstand at a reported altitude of forty feet, while Marie "waved her hand gayly." His next passenger was "a small brunette whose black eyes were snapping with excitement": barely four months behind her husband, Mabel was airborne. It was an experience she would soon put to good use.[11]

Fanciulli had also arranged for Mars and Curtiss to give rides to "a representative from each of the big newspapers." These produced effusive accounts that suggested that the newsmen were hundreds of feet high, but the passenger flights were actually an exercise in caution. Mars barely lifted off the ground, proceeded straight down the track, and alighted at the far end. He then generally flew back solo for his next passenger without giving his passengers the thrill of a midair turn. The unimpressed spectators, impatient to see "real" flying, grumbled that passenger airplanes were hardly better than trolley cars.[12]

Contrary to popular legend, Mabel was not her husband's business manager. To the extent the Portland Aeroplane Company had a manager, it was advance man Hartman Price, while the Curtiss team was formally directed by Fanciulli. Arthur McGinniss promoted Ely for a time, and the person Ely considered his manager, from Omaha onward, was Charles Bryce.

But, starting with the Sheepshead Bay meet, Mabel served critical functions on the Curtiss team, namely media darling and chief Ely promoter. A reporter who interviewed her many years later explained, “Ely, although a popular man, well-liked by his associates and the public, was modest, not a publicity-seeker. Consequently, his wife took over his public relations. It was she who dealt with the inevitable reporter when they hit a new town. And the young, good-looking, personable Mrs. Ely, who liked to meet people, could charm any newsman.” A reporter approaching Ely for quotes would be met by Mabel “rattling off reams of Ely history and encomiums” with her “Parisian vivacity.”[13]

Mabel was happy to speak authoritatively about what it felt like to fly. For the rest of Ely’s career, she told reporters that she regularly rode as a passenger with her husband, which was almost certainly not true.

Ely once reportedly referred to his wife jokingly as “my press agent.” Many of the quotes attributed in print to Ely were furnished by Mabel, who enthusiastically and unabashedly fabricated stories about his plans and accomplishments. Like Bryce, she knew they would be good publicity.[14]

At sunset on opening day, August 19, Curtiss won a short race against Ely. Then Mars and McCurdy joined them in the air, and with “almost the precision of a military maneuver,” the four machines circled the track at speeds estimated to have approached 45 mph. As the “aerial parade” passed the grandstands, “hats, handkerchiefs, and walking sticks were waved at the aviators, and some who had none of these things handy just waved their hands and yelled.” The normally taciturn Curtiss remarked to a reporter afterward, “I guess that was something worthwhile.” According to one report, Ely landed after the others, having made eight complete laps around the track. “On his last [circuit] he swept far out of the track boundaries, high above a fringe of trees in the distance, until his machine seemed to become a mere speck. Then he came swinging around in a long, graceful curve, swept on past the grandstand and descended amid a storm of applause.”[15]

An estimated 20,000 spectators watched at sunset the next day when Willard joined Curtiss, Ely, Mars, and McCurdy in the air at the wheel of *Banshee*, a powerful new machine that he and Curtiss had designed. The aviators made "dips and turns in the air with the greatest ease" in what was billed as "the first time in the history of American aviation" that five machines were in the air at once.[16]

The U.S. Army at the time owned a single aircraft: an obsolete 1909 Wright Flyer. Maj. Samuel Reber, chief signal officer of the Signal Corps, came to Sheepshead Bay to see a promised demonstration of the airplane's military usefulness.

Curtiss took aloft sharpshooter Lt. Jacob Fickel, armed with a Springfield rifle. From a height of a hundred feet—sometimes reported as three times that—Fickel scored several hits on a target variously reported to have been 18 inches in diameter or three feet by five. Fickel reported that the vibrations from the motor had no effect on his aim, nor did the recoil of the weapon have an effect on the airplane, both of which had been the subject of debate. The flight represented the first step in the development of aerial gunnery.[17]

The meet was extended to the following weekend, and during the intervening week Ely became the center of a story—largely fabricated—that laid the foundation for what would become his most famous accomplishment to date. His involvement started simply enough. The Manhattan Beach Hotel was "Headquarters for Great Aviation Meet, Sheepshead Bay"—was a mile south of the racetrack and across the bay. On August 23, the *Brooklyn Daily Eagle* reported that Mars and Ely would be "dropping in" every afternoon that week via airplane "to have afternoon tea with their wives before completing their daily flights at the Sheepshead Bay Racetrack."[18]

The next day, the story transformed into a formal invitation from the hotel manager for Mars and Ely to fly over from the track and dine with him and some newspapermen, thereby accomplishing "the novel and strictly up-to-date feat of keeping a dinner engagement by aeroplane." Public anticipation grew for three straight days, while high winds repeatedly delayed any flying. On

Friday the *Daily Eagle* reported that Ely alone had tried to fly to the hotel on Thursday at 6:00 p.m. but had been driven back by the wind.[19]

Then on Saturday, two hours into a well-received exhibition attended by eight thousand, Ely suddenly turned southeastward and flew off toward the hotel. The exhibition announcer bellowed to the crowd through his megaphone that Ely had "gone away to dine." The following day's *New York Times* elaborated:

> It was 6:22 o'clock when Ely told Mrs. Ely [at the track] it was dinner time and he was dining out.
>
> "If I find the air lanes open," he said, "you'll see me to the left of the [Coney Island] Dreamland towers," and with that he was up and off, cutting into the eastern horizon at 40 miles an hour. Mrs. Ely . . . ran for the taxi station. . . .
>
> Over Manhattan Beach way some 3,000 people were bathing and lounging about on the piazzas at 6:25 o'clock, but at 6:25½ they were out of the water and off the porches and gazing skyward, while an aeroplane's propeller hummed and chugged and finally came to rest as the visitor from aloft settled down right beside a sign: "Keep off the Grass."
>
> Mrs. Ely was at his side almost before the crowd had turned away from him to his plane to put their autographs upon it.
>
> "Let's go in and eat," he said.

As the *Times* story had it, Mabel replied that she was too excited to eat, and so "Ely reappeared to the grandstand crowds at 6:42 o'clock and landed after circling the field four times, at 6:47."[20]

Mabel's scrapbook has a photo captioned "Gene starting on trip from Sheepshead to hotel Man[hattan]." Clearly, he flew over to the hotel and back, passing over the water, which was remarkable enough. It is even possible that he touched down briefly.

It was a good story, and Fanciulli and the Curtiss marketing team embraced and embellished it. Publicist Tillman's summary of the meet in *Aeronautics* claimed that Ely had won "the trophy given by the Manhattan Beach Hotel for being the only aviator to fly over the bay to the hotel and alight on the beach, go in for his dinner and return to the field late in the evening." The account conveniently ignored the *Times* chronology, according to which Ely was absent for only twenty minutes.[21]

Sheepshead Bay marked a turning point in Ely's flying career: he was now a celebrity, a legitimate member of the Curtiss team, and his flying proved it. The story of his flight across the bay, complete with dinner at the hotel, was romantic and charming. Whether it was true or not was beside the point.

Throughout the meet, Ely's "high flights and graceful glides . . . delighted the crowds." But at one point while in the air he found himself overcome with dizziness. After he landed safely, newspapers were quick to coin a phrase: "air sickness." Ely recovered quickly, but his experience suggested, significantly, that dangers in the air were not limited to mechanical malfunctions.[22]

At the close of the meet, the Aero Club of America contest committee formally invited Curtiss to defend the Gordon Bennett Cup. His written response shows the extent of his displeasure with the Wrights' involvement in the Belmont Park event: "Owing to the fact that I am entirely ignorant of the conditions which would govern my participation in the international aviation meet at Belmont Park I request the privilege of reserving my decision in this matter until I shall have had an opportunity to meet your committee and to confer with my attorneys regarding the legal phases which might possibly be involved in the matter."[23]

In the interim, Curtiss traveled to Cleveland, where on August 31 he set a new overwater record, flying over Lake Erie from Euclid Beach (some five miles northeast of Cleveland) to Cedar Point on Sandusky Bay, some sixty miles to the west. During the seventy-eight-minute flight, Curtiss wore partially inflated bicycle inner tubes wound around his body as a rudimentary flotation device. The next day he made the return flight while Mars and Ely rode with Lena Curtiss in the eastbound Lake Shore mail train, which the aviator quickly outdistanced.[24]

Now having complete faith in Ely, Curtiss dispatched him, accompanied by Mabel, to headline a string of exhibitions in September. Speculation abounded about Ely's exhibition schedule, just as rumors had once circulated that Curtiss or Hamilton might appear at a particular town. He was flying with confidence and pleasing crowds. Ely had developed a reputation not for daredeviltry but for coolly calculated daring.[25]

The day after a successful engagement on September 6–7 in Kalamazoo, Michigan, Ely and Mabel arrived in Rock Island, Illinois, just across the Mississippi River from Davenport. Because he was not scheduled to fly there until the 14th, he and Mabel were able to attend the Harrington family reunion in Williamsburg on September 10, where they saw his mother, sister, and brother. Afterward, Maidie accompanied her brother and sister-in-law back to Rock Island, while Nathan Ely joined them from Davenport, bringing with him Mabel von Schaezler Ely and her son, Paul.[26]

Ely was hailed in Rock Island as "the most daring of the Glenn H. Curtiss corps of aviators," and was erroneously said to have reached 4,200 feet at Sheepshead Bay. This time, barely three months after disappointing the Oregon crowds who had read similar exaggerations, Ely was prepared to live up to the hype.[27]

The Rock Island public had expected at least two flights a day by the Curtiss fliers. What they got was Ely alone, initially grounded by winds far too strong for flying. Fortunately, he had been quoted in advance saying that wind might be a problem. In the meantime, he charged spectators a dime to pose at the wheel of the flying machine.

On September 14, having failed in his first attempt, he rose before a crowd of five thousand and flew for some eight minutes. The effect was electric—similar to what Hamilton had produced in Portland six months earlier:

> Each individual became an aviator for the time being, rising as Ely rose, soaring as he soared, tipping and dipping as he did and finally coming back to earth in one grand sweeping swoop.

> . . . Like a streak, with a slight undulating motion, the aircraft fell till within a few feet of the ground. Then Ely turned his [elevator] slightly upward and finally met the earth so gently that there was not a jar.[28]

Asked afterward how he could succeed at one time and not another, Ely blamed variable atmospheric conditions and air currents close to the ground. "Nobody feels as badly as the aviator himself when he fails," he was quoted as saying. "When we fail we are always condemned, told that our airships won't fly and that we are afraid to go up, anyhow. When we succeed we are the heroes of the hour and nobody can do enough for us. . . . To charge that an aviator is afraid to go up is folly. All he wants is a chance to get up. The danger does not lie in going up, but in coming down." The language is likely the reporter's, but the sentiment rings true as Ely's.[29]

For the rest of his Rock Island exhibition, Ely could do no wrong. On the second evening he outdid his first flight, remaining airborne for twelve minutes while a crowd of seven thousand "craned and strained, held their breath and then cheered madly." On that flight, Ely had evidently brought along a barograph or similar altitude-measuring device; it was said to have told him at a glance that he was climbing past 2,300 feet. He headed northwest, toward the Mississippi River, and "rose till the setting sun appeared under him and he seemed to be traveling on the top of a gold lined cloud that lay low on the horizon." When he landed, the crowd seized him and "carried him on their shoulders to his tent."

Ely made a "brilliant" flight the following day, and on the meet's closing day he agreed to fly in a stiff wind. He managed to get airborne despite a crowd that nearly blocked his way, and he produced what the press reported as the most thrilling of all his ascents: "It was man against elements in a fight for life." The exhibition was in every way a triumph.[30]

It was also a reunion of sorts for Ely. His one-time Davenport mechanical mentor, Pete Petersen, posed at the wheel of the parked airplane for photographs. So did Mabel, with Maidie seated beside her as though in a passenger seat. "New aspirants for stellar honors in aviation circles are Mrs. J. C. (Bud) Mars and Mrs. Eugene Ely," the local paper gushed over the publicity stunt. "Each is now experimenting with her own machine, and it is only a question of a short time when a women's class will be added to the programs of the meets scheduled for early presentation in the East." While the prediction regarding a women's class soon proved true, Mabel told a reporter years later that she "never had any intention of learning to handle a plane."[31]

Ely's whirlwind tour continued with an appearance at the Roanoke Fair in the Blue Ridge Mountains. He was a featured attraction on "Old Soldiers Day," when Civil War veterans, both Union and Confederate, were given free admission. A record crowd turned out to witness one of Virginia's first public airplane flights. But Ely had determined that he would be unable to rise safely from the cramped infield of the fairground racetrack and refused to make the attempt. The local paper did not blame the aviator, instead reminding readers that the average citizen "knows nothing about the machine or its conditions. He has to reflect that the man who rides the machine takes the risk and must be the judge of what the risk is and whether he can afford to take it."

Fortunately, the natural topography provided a solution. Ely had his machine loaded onto the flatcar of an electric-steam train and hauled, fully assembled, up a hill in South Roanoke near Virginia College. At 5:40 p.m., "the graceful machine commenced to move down the slope and rose gradually into the air." He soared across the Roanoke River and over the fairgrounds, landing in the center of the infield as the crowd "shrieked with delight."[32]

Next, Ely was off to Poughkeepsie, New York, for a county fair where attendance peaked at a record-breaking 30,000 spectators, his father, Nathan, among them. On the second day, Ely was racing against an automobile when one of his rudder wires snapped.

Fortunately, he was at an altitude of several hundred feet, giving him time to land safely in a nearby field.

While in Poughkeepsie, Ely took the opportunity to visit the meadow where Curtiss had touched down to refuel during his Hudson flight. He was evidently scouting landing spots for the upcoming race from Chicago to New York.[33]

CHAPTER 10

ENDURANCE

THE MOST-ANTICIPATED airplane spectacle over the summer of 1910 was the Chicago to New York race, first proposed amid the euphoria that had greeted Curtiss' flight down the Hudson River. Visions of reliable long-distance flight tantalized the American public, with Alexander Graham Bell predicting that the "aerial motor car" was just around the corner. There were also concerns that the nation that "gave birth to the aeroplane" was beginning to lag behind England and France; achieving long-distance air travel would put the United States back at the forefront of aviation development.[1]

The *Chicago Evening Post* and the *New York Times*, joint sponsors of the race, outlined the rules. At least three competitors had to start on the same date, no later than October 15. There would be no limit to the number of stops permitted, but the winner had to complete the trip within 168 hours (exactly seven days), using the same machine with which he started. (Given the frequency with which a machine's parts needed to be replaced, this rule potentially raised the paradox of Theseus' ship: If an airplane has had all its components replaced, is it still the same airplane?) Should a flight of equal or greater distance be made earlier anywhere in the United States, the prize would be withdrawn.[2]

The prize of $30,000—with $25,000 put up by the papers plus an additional $5,000 later pledged by millionaire amateur aviator Clifford Harmon—was calculated to attract the best aviators and aircraft in the country. It worked: within ten days Bud Mars, Douglas McCurdy, Charles Hamilton, Tom Baldwin, and Curtiss had all entered.[3]

An aviation meet was to be held at the Hawthorne track in Cicero, Illinois, just outside Chicago, and the Chicago–New York race would be the centerpiece. (While the prize was offered for a flight in either direction, prevailing winds effectively dictated a start in Chicago.) The newspaper descriptions were effusive, with Charles Willard quoted as calling the challenge "the most difficult yet that has confronted any aviator." Hamilton, according to the *New York Times*, said a successful flight would be "the greatest achievement of the age" and "the most important event in the aviation world."[4]

On September 30, Wright aviator Walter Brookins flew half the length of Illinois, from Chicago to Springfield, stopping only twice. In so doing he broke two distance records: the longest nonstop fight by an American (previously set by Hamilton between New York and Philadelphia), and the longest continuous flight by anyone, stops included (previously set by Curtiss along the Hudson). A flight in a Curtiss machine between Chicago and New York would reestablish the superiority of the Curtiss design over that of the Wrights. There was speculation that the Wrights would enter an aviator, but they were the sons of a minister and had never permitted their aviators to fly on Sundays, which effectively ruled out any Wright flier's participation in a race that might last a week.[5]

The race was hailed as "the culmination of a year's remarkable progress in aviation with heavier than air machines." A year earlier, the only public flights in America had belonged to Curtiss, Willard, and the Wrights, while the world's distance record had been twenty-five continuous miles. Now, operating essentially the same machines, the aviators proposed to fly nearly forty times that far in under a week.

Even more astonishing was that most people believed the fliers could do it. "An air trip of 1,000 miles today, with occasional stops," wrote one journalist, "does not look so phenomenal now as Glenn Curtiss' run down the Hudson seemed before he made it." The flying machine had grown in the public eye "from an experimental and dangerous toy to a popular and accepted means of ordinarily reliable transportation." Brookins' record-breaking flight to their state capital had left Chicagoans "agog with excitement" and ready to see aviators succeed in reaching New York City. The run-up week of exhibitions was well calculated to whet an already keen public appetite.[6]

Ely's name was a late addition to the list of entrants, which included his Curtiss teammates Willard and McCurdy. Although gusty winds delayed flights on October 1, the day Ely arrived, around five o'clock Willard, McCurdy, and Curtiss flew simultaneously, thrilling the crowd at the Hawthorne track. The next day, Ely and the three other expert "cloud craft pilots" made virtually continuous flights from 4 p.m. until "long after dark . . . following each other in rapid succession" above a crowd estimated at some 20,000. Dense smoke drifting from the adjacent railroad yard "hung over the field like a tornado cloud," but the aviators flew blithely through it. Curtiss capped his brief Chicago appearance by covering three miles in three and a quarter minutes at a height of a hundred feet. The only mishap occurred when Ely landed in a rough spot and smashed a wheel, but he avoided injury by jumping nimbly to the ground.[7]

A key question for the aviators was which course to follow. To minimize ground turbulence, a level and open route was required. Because they carried no navigational instruments, the aviators would have to fly with constant reference to land features. They also needed reliable spaces where they could touch down. Their tanks held only enough gasoline for a hundred-mile flight, so twice a day they would have to land near a town to refuel. Identifying emergency landing spots was particularly difficult. Unlike modern highways, which today may serve as emergency runways, the roads of 1910 were narrow, winding, and rutted. Fields that were otherwise open could be rendered unusable by a single tree. Even tall grasses could prove hazardous to a fragile propeller.

The proposed course followed railroad tracks from Chicago eastward through Indiana and Ohio, hugged Lake Erie to avoid choppy air over Pennsylvania's Allegheny Mountains, crossed New York to Albany, and then turned down the Hudson to Manhattan.

The total distance was roughly 975 miles, which the newspapers rounded up to a more satisfying thousand. The New York Central railroad ran advertisements in Chicago's *Inter Ocean*, trumpeting the fact that in avoiding sudden changes in elevation, the route logically followed the railroad tracks: "THE WATER LEVEL ROUTE defines the course of the Aviator, as it once did the path of the Indian, the Trader, the Immigrant, and now the Traveling Public."[8]

On Tuesday, October 4, journalists reported that race officials, in a late-night conference, had designated a series of "controls"—landing spots—roughly every fifty miles. A "pathfinding automobile," to be occupied by Fanciulli and representatives from the sponsoring newspapers, would blaze a daily trail for the aviators. Among the methods suggested by which the public could assist the competitors in identifying landing spots were smoke fires, daytime rockets, sheets spread on rooftops, captive balloons, and kites, although McCurdy pointed out the uselessness of kites in the event of little or no wind.[9]

For the moment, the aviators were experiencing the opposite problem. Winds of close to 40 mph that day collapsed the tent that housed the airplanes; one source said Ely had been struck on the head by a falling pole. He and Willard attempted a few takeoffs, but in the end no one ascended that day. "It is as much as a man's life is worth," Ely was quoted as saying. "The trials we have made near the ground show what would happen to a man in a machine if he rose far enough to get the force of the wind."[10]

On Wednesday, October 5, although gusts were again too strong to allow for extended flying, Willard showed "both skill and nerve" by making a brief flight "in spite of ominous skies and treacherous winds" that ultimately brought a rainstorm and nearly resulted in his crashing. The "pathfinding" automobile was reported to have reached South Bend "after traveling for 100 miles over roads which at times were hub deep with sand and again resembled morasses more than roadways." And a new issue arose: smudge fires proved useless as signals because of burning taking place on farms along the route, while white-marked roofs had popped up all over, "owing to everyone wanting to slick up the top of his barn in hopes of coaxing the racers near their place."[11]

On Thursday, October 6, the skies finally cleared, and the aviators flew in the late afternoon. Ely, nicknamed "the Pacific swallow" by one newsman, reportedly operated the eight-cylinder *Hudson Flyer* for what was evidently the first time, possibly testing it for use during the race. He circled the mile track three times at 60 mph, easily beating the mark set by Curtiss earlier that week. At one point he was seen "diving suddenly toward the heart-shaped pond in the center of the grounds," but that may have been a case of mistaken identity: Ely and McCurdy were aloft when Willard thrilled the crowd by diving his powerful *Banshee* from a great height to within a few feet of the ground. "Women screamed and men looked as though they would like to run. One or two men did run." For four long minutes "the three great biplanes wheeled in the sky together, the crowd being moved to rounds of applause as in turn they swept past the grandstand at dazzling speed."[12]

Even novice flier Augustus Post managed to get aloft. It was reported that the "handsome dilettante" was up for only a "short spurt," followed by a near miss of the fence, but as Post himself later recalled,

> Circling the track I was just passing the grandstand when Willard swooped down in front of me having passed right over my head.
>
> I clung on to the steering post and held the wheel as firmly as I could while to my great consternation the machine rocked and swayed fearfully in the backdraft from Willard's propeller. He kept doing the Dutch Roll and the Coney Island Dip right in front of me, which made it all the worse, as the wash of the propeller wake would strike above and below my machine as he pitched up and down in front of me. I stood it as best I could, hardly daring to breathe but holding my course and balancing with all my might, until Willard turned off, and then after a bit I made a good landing. When Willard came down he rushed up to me and grabbed me by the hand

> and said, "Oh, Post! will you ever forgive me for that? I ought to have known better than to back-wash you but you know I thought you were Ely, and I wanted to scare him!"[13]

Post's anecdote highlights the team's camaraderie and the assurance with which the three experienced Curtiss aviators were flying by then. It also shows how difficult the spectators must have found it to distinguish among them. To the extent there was a favorite, it was Willard, "but with engine troubles repaired," noted one article, "Ely will prove a competitor hard to lose."[14]

A crowd turned out in Chicago to watch the final practice flights. Although Ely made only brief trials, he, Willard, and McCurdy did not disappoint. Willard was again the star, climbing to an estimated four thousand feet and flying so far from the track that spectators lost sight of him. Meanwhile McCurdy made a series of climbs and dips, drawing prolonged cheers.[15]

But on Friday, October 7, the day before the race's scheduled start, the Curtiss team made a dramatic announcement: only one Curtiss aviator would attempt the flight. The reason given was that the Curtiss spare parts on hand were insufficient to equip all three machines for a serious race. Never before had a lightweight Curtiss engine been put to seven consecutive days of strain, and many parts would need to be replaced along the route.

Though the team may have been planning for some time to support only a single flier, the story given to the public was that the decision had been made that very morning, after which the fliers had drawn lots, with Ely emerging the winner. "They got me up out of bed and we discussed the thing until daylight," Ely is reported to have said. "We could only see one chance to get a man through, and that was by starting one man and having the others give their machines to help him through."[16]

The announcement presented a dilemma. One by one, all the other competitors had dropped out due to ill health, logistical difficulties, or conflicting obligations. Some simply failed to show up. Now the three remaining aviators were reduced to one—two fewer than the minimum the race rules required.

The promoters were floored. This was not at all what had been proposed. "Would One Man Make a Race?" asked a subhead in the *Chicago Tribune*. The *New York Times* and the *Chicago Evening Post* were unwilling to alter the stated conditions, while the Curtiss aviators took the position that each of them was perfectly willing to fly against all comers, and it was hardly their fault that no one else had come. While both sides pondered, they agreed to postpone the start to Sunday, October 9.[17]

By Saturday morning, someone had consulted the published race rules. The condition was simple: "At least three competitors must start, or no race." The term "start" was undefined, and the rules were also silent about how long a competitor had to continue after starting. Very well, announced Augustus Post on behalf of the aviators: all three would take off from Chicago. What might happen after that, they were not prepared to say. The sponsoring newspapers refused to accept the charade, and the race was in danger of being called off.[18]

But if, as originally proposed, the point was not to conduct a race but to test whether an airplane could fly from Chicago to New York within a week, then whether more than one machine succeeded was immaterial. And even if only one flier made the attempt, the newspapers would hardly lose money.

A story breaking that day underscored the fliers' argument. Newspaper tycoon William Randolph Hearst announced that he was prepared to pay the eye-popping sum of $50,000 for a successful transcontinental flight. No "race" was involved; the prize would go outright to the first aviator who, within the year, flew from coast to coast—New York (or Boston) to Los Angeles (or San Francisco), or vice versa—via Chicago, in thirty days or less. Ely's proposed flight from Chicago, it became apparent, would serve as a test for the Hearst prize. The public was manifestly eager to see him try.[19]

The same day, Arch Hoxsey of the Wright team flew nonstop from Springfield, Illinois, to St. Louis, Missouri, a distance he estimated at 104 miles. His accomplishment was initially lauded as the longest nonstop flight by an American, until it was recalculated at only eighty-five miles. Against this latest show of endurance by a Wright machine, Curtiss needed Ely to make a definitive demonstration.[20]

The newspapers gave in. The *New York Times* wired the *Chicago Evening Post*, and the papers agreed to stop advertising a true "race"; instead, it would label the attempt one man's "endurance run," a "race against time."[21]

Ely anticipated a total of twenty-two hours in the air, at a comfortable average of 45 mph. With departure planned for Sunday afternoon, October 9, he expected to cross the designated finish line at 125th Street in Manhattan by Friday morning, October 14. He would put in about four hours of flying each day, he figured, most likely broken into two sessions of two hours each, with a refueling stop in the middle. A special train would follow his course to the extent possible, carrying among its passengers Mabel, Fanciulli, and Curtiss team mechanics with spare parts.

People across the country waited eagerly to hear the local Chicago weather forecast. October 9 brought a cold, strong wind from the north to speed Ely on his way. As the *Washington Times* reported, "Everything is ready for Eugene Ely, the premier flier of the Curtiss aviation school, to take the air this afternoon." The eyes of the world were upon him.[22]

Which particular machine Ely left Chicago in is the subject of some speculation. The press dubbed it the *Boston Flyer* or *Boston Racer*, two fabricated names dropped into various wire reports and subsequently repeated indiscriminately, but photographs taken at the start show a V-8-powered machine that is evidently *Banshee.* (One possible clue to the origin of the *Boston* moniker is that *Banshee* had made its debut at the Harvard-Boston meet in September.)[23]

A cheering crowd braved the cold wind to see Ely off. His reported destination was South Bend, Indiana, roughly ninety-five miles away, a distance he could expect to cover in approximately two hours of flying. Telephone messages to Chicago promised 50,000 people awaiting Ely at his planned interim stop of LaPorte and another 75,000 in South Bend. News of the anticipated start was reported as far away as England. Chicago's *Inter Ocean* stated,

"He looked for all the world like some old Viking setting sail on a voyage into waters far beyond the ken of man." Ely, "garbed from head to foot in light brown leather," reportedly took off with "a dash through the clouds and smoke of a dying day."[24]

The most believable account came from the *New York Times*: "Ely smiled at his friends. His smile combines modesty with quiet self-assurance. He glanced a tacit inquiry at Curtiss, who stood by, attentive to every circumstance. Curtiss nodded slightly. Then without more ado the young aviator took his seat, adjusted his position to the requirements of various means of control, pulled the steering wheel once toward him to assure freedom of action, then waved his hand to the assistants who were holding the impatient craft to the ground." That wave was the signal to release the wings. The press reported: "The start of the run was made at 4:12 and at 4:17½ Ely was out of sight to the south."[25]

Willard and McCurdy were expected to accompany Ely for as much as the first twenty or thirty miles, but the pair merely circled the field once or twice to effect a technical "start" and then descended so their machines could be disassembled and shipped ahead. Ely, once he climbed to the sky and pointed his airplane south along the lakeshore, was on his own. Without landing, he had no way to communicate his intentions or difficulties, nor to ask directions. Success was a matter of endurance, for both man and machine.

At 4:21 he was back on the ground, "shipwrecked" well within city limits. His engine was misfiring, according to reports. Identifying the fault as a stuck carburetor needle valve, easy to correct on the ground, he touched down in a convenient field and fixed the problem before passersby could reach him. He then, it was said, performed the tricky feat of restarting the motor without assistance, accelerated, rolled across the field, and struck a hidden rock hard enough to destroy his front wheel. Curtiss and a handful of mechanics met him with "an automobile full of tools and bamboo rods," but by the time they had begun repairing the airplane, falling darkness made it pointless to continue.[26]

The smashed wheel was relatively minor; it put Ely barely two hours behind schedule, with ample time to make up the deficit over the next six days. The *Washington Herald* called the start "somewhat of a fizzle," and misidentified the problem as a broken propeller. The *New York Times* called the setback "trivial" and said Ely would certainly have reached LaPorte within the first hour as scheduled, had not the "unfortunate accident" occurred.[27]

On Monday morning, October 10, after a thick fog had lifted, Ely took off at 8:30 a.m. Almost at once he heard the motor misfire again—some reports had it dying completely—and had to touch down in a field barely half a mile away. Before he could stop the machine, it plunged into a muddy ditch concealed by weeds; the front end sustained significant damage that rendered the forward elevator inoperable. One account stated that Ely was "flung from his seat and sent rolling over the ground a dozen feet ahead of his machine." He emerged uninjured.[28]

Curtiss had addressed the problem of treacherous ground conditions in a magazine article published a month earlier, in which he advised the reader: "The next time you are on a train . . . shut your eyes a few moments and then, opening them suddenly, see how few spots you will be able to pick out for a suitable landing place—for you have to choose a landing place in a very short time, if your motor should stop in the air. . . . As for circling around, it is very difficult to turn while gliding to the earth." Ely's ditch, in other words, though an unfortunate development, was hardly unexpected.[29]

Ely discovered that the feed pipe from the gas tank had shaken loose. Once again, the fix would have been a quick one, but due to the significant structural damage Ely could not take off. He was said to have been "both optimistic and determined." The initial delay estimate was five hours, but the repairs took more than eight. What was required, if the report can be believed, was this: "Soldered up engine; put new tire on front wheel; put six-foot splice with bamboo splints on 'push rod,' which guides airship up and down; put three-foot splice on right-hand brace of guiding plane [front elevator]; tied an old mop handle to guiding plane to attach push rod; repaired torn canvas of lower [wing]; put in new lateral brace to replace broken one, and made innumerable minor repairs and splices in the wire guys." Repairs were said to have required 180 yards of "tire tape," the duct tape of 1910. And then Ely was in the air again, "off like an arrow" in perfect weather conditions and crossing the Indiana state line with the city of Gary in sight.[30]

He covered no more than eleven additional miles before the engine acted up again. At 4:30 p.m. he had to descend, touching down in a swamp near East Chicago, Indiana. Muck yanked the machine to a halt, "the front control for the second time in the day having been wrecked and almost torn from the rest of the biplane." Ely, unharmed, walked into town and telephoned for his mechanics. He was variously described as "imperturbable," "worn looking," and "disgusted with the luck that had pursued him."

The *New York Times* remained optimistic, running the story on the front page of Tuesday morning's edition under the headline "ELY, UNDAUNTED, WILL FLY ON TO-DAY." But other journalists, without a stake in the flight, had lost confidence. Newspapers across the country dropped the story from their front pages and, at best, commented on Ely's bad luck. "COVERS 11 MILES, LANDS IN SWAMP," said the *Chicago Daily Tribune* in a story that ridiculed Ely's machine, rechristened it the "mud hen," and described the repair list as being longer than the flight.[31]

The aviator and his mechanics spent Tuesday morning making structural repairs, but the source of the engine trouble remained a mystery. A report circulated that Curtiss had returned to Chicago in search of parts, but later in the day he wired to Ely: "No parts here for repairs. Boxes shipped, Wells Fargo, tonight." The boxes were crates for packing up the airplane—and with it Ely's dreams of reaching New York City. The cross-country flight had officially been abandoned.[32]

It is possible that the repeated clogging of a pinhole air vent in the fuel tank disabled Ely's engine, as was widely reported. Had that been the only problem the flight could have resumed at once. But even with perfect luck, at a hugely optimistic 150 miles per tank he would have to land at least six more times before reaching Manhattan. Those landing spots, assuming he could even locate them without ground communication, would again be mainly in rough fields and swamps. It would be impossible to protect the machine against the shock of half a dozen or more hard landings.[33]

And even supposing repairs could have been made instantaneously, the supply of spare parts was woefully inadequate. At the rate established over the first three days of the attempt, Curtiss would have had to cannibalize all four of his exhibition airplanes on the eve of the big international meet at Belmont Park. It made no sense to press onward.

Curtiss did not blame Ely. He had noted that regular air transportation between distant places would not become practical until "a course is open over which a man can fly from city to city, and be sure of having a good place to alight at any moment." When recounting the race two years later, Curtiss deemed it "a very ambitious undertaking" and concluded, "Mr. Ely made a good attempt, but there was not sufficient time to complete the trip."[34]

But newspapers reported that the aviators had "bungled." After a monumental buildup, Ely had managed to fly all of twenty-two miles in three days. That would have been laudable five months earlier, but it was by then an embarrassment. Worse, on the final day of the attempt, Wright aviator Arthur Welsh set a new American endurance record at St. Louis, remaining aloft for more than three hours "apparently without effort."[35]

"AEROPLANE CRIPPLED, ELY GIVES UP FLIGHT," the *New York Times* announced on Wednesday, October 12, throwing in the towel. The article noted that Chicagoans had "realized for days that no proper preparations had been made for Ely's effort" and reported the aviator's supposed vow to complete the flight and win the prize in the spring of 1911—utterly disregarding the newspaper's own requirement that competitors start no later than October 15. But even that story ran on page two. The front page carried the remarkable news that, around the time Ely found himself stuck in an Indiana swamp, Wright aviator Hoxsey was taking former president Roosevelt for a thrilling ride in St. Louis. By Thursday, with the Hoxsey-Roosevelt flight still occupying page one of the *Times*, Ely's name appeared nowhere. The last word by the *Chicago Evening Post* on Ely's attempt was that "the young aviator appeared to have received more than his share of hard luck."[36]

Still, being overlooked was preferable to the treatment Ely received in other quarters. Editorial comments around the country grew sarcastic. Even the *Washington Post*, reporting Ely's abandonment of the attempt, placed the word *race* in quotation marks. The Indiana newspapers were especially hostile. For days they had promised readers the sight of a flying machine overhead, and the public now suspected that reporters had fabricated the story. The newspapers in turn blamed the aviators and the fact that despite the wide publicity given the attempt, often "no information was obtainable." Beneath the front-page headline "ELY A QUITTER" ran this short piece in Indiana's *Waterloo Press*: "After several attempts to 'fly' by Eugene Ely in his biplane and as many failures, he at last gave up . . . and the so-called race has been indefinitely postponed. The manner in which the whole matter was manipulated was very unsatisfactory to the public, and hereafter it would be well not to advertise such an event until the ships are well on the way."[37]

For Ely, the experience must have been a painful regression to the repeated suggestions in June that he was a fraud, unable to fly. Meanwhile, Wright aviators Brookins, Hoxsey, Ralph Johnstone, and Welsh continued to make spectacular flights while experiencing none of the struggles Ely had undergone. The implication was clear: Curtiss aviators, if not Curtiss airplanes, were inferior to those of the Wrights.

After this blow to Ely's public standing, he returned to the exhibition performances of which he knew he was capable. His first chance came the next day, when he was sent to perform in place of Curtiss at a benefit for a proposed hospital in Youngstown, Ohio. The contract had been signed in September, by which time Fanciulli had learned from experience to define "successful flight" as "the aeroplane travelling above the ground for a period of three minutes." The Youngstown contract promised that a Curtiss aviator would make at least three successful flights unless prevented by "wind, accident, or other unavoidable cause."[38]

The exhibition started inauspiciously. In front of an estimated 20,000 spectators, only half of whom had bothered to pay for entry, Ely tried four times to ascend in the face of a stiff breeze. He never got higher than thirty feet or remained in the air more than half a minute. All his flights were brief, straight runs to a field a couple of thousand feet away—failures, according to the terms of the contract. Promoters promised angry spectators free admission for the following day, assuring them that Ely would deliver all three flights, as advertised.

On his first attempt on the second day, a gust of wind caught and tipped the airplane, causing one of its wings to strike the ground. An hour later, the repaired airplane finally "rose easily from the ground under perfect control and reached an altitude of 135 feet." Excited spectators swarmed over the field and left no clear landing space. Ely somehow narrowly missed a woman and two small children. Back on the ground and reportedly "trembling like an aspen leaf," he was quoted as declaring that he would not fly in Youngstown again. Indeed, he attempted no further flights.[39]

That single flight was insufficient to repair Ely's damaged reputation, and the *Waterloo Press* published the following dark threat: "Eugene Ely packed his little flying machine last week and passed through Waterloo on a night train. He has been heard from again as he tried last Thursday to 'make a fly' at Youngstown, Ohio, but only rose about twenty feet in the air. He will have to do better than this or else it will not be safe for him to attempt to travel from Chicago to New York in any manner." Having endured repeated physical and emotional beatings on his journey eastward, Ely finally arrived in New York City the conventional way: via train.[40]

CHAPTER 11

THE WAR IN THE AIR

FLYING EXHIBITIONS swept the country, and audiences thrilled at the remarkable sight of multiple machines in the air simultaneously. But there was also a darker side to the aviation demonstrations: they suggested the destructive potential of the new technology and raised the question of "what airships could do in the event of war."

In July 1908 Rudolf Martin, the German author of *The Coming War in the Air* and a pamphlet, "Is a World-War Imminent?", granted an eye-opening interview to London's *Daily Mail.* His reported comments included the blunt assessment that England's insular identity was being eroded by the development of airships and airplanes. The "landing of a large German army in England," he asserted, "is a mere matter of money."

By October Martin had formed a German Motor-Airship League and was mounting a campaign to create a German airplane fleet. He reportedly encouraged Wilbur Wright to demonstrate that flight across the English Channel was possible, assuring him that "public opinion in Germany will forthwith demand the acquisition of an enormous number of Wright aeroplanes for military purposes." For fifty million pounds sterling, he calculated, Germany could acquire or build enough machines to carry 100,000 soldiers past the English coast.[1]

Also in October 1908, the American edition of *The War in the Air* was released. This serialized novel, by English writer H. G. Wells, imagines a scenario in which hordes of German *Drachenflieger* (dragon-flier) airplanes, having been towed across the Atlantic by dirigibles, easily annihilate the American fleet from above. New York is sacked in a single night—"one of the most cold-blooded slaughters in the world's history, in which [air]men who were neither excited nor, except for the remotest chance of a bullet, in any danger, poured death and destruction upon homes and crowds below." Full-scale world war ensues, followed by global economic collapse and a return to a preindustrial state. This, as Wells presented it, was to be the legacy of the flying machine.[2]

At the time of the 1908 presidential election, the vaunted U.S. "Great White Fleet" of sixteen battleships was circling the globe, demonstrating the strength of American sea power. Two years later the United States, seeking to keep up with the growing fleets of Britain and Germany, launched its first two larger "all-big-gun" dreadnought-type battleships, USS *South Carolina* and USS *Michigan.* But apart from Roosevelt's enthusiasm for Langley's Aerodrome, all that the U.S. Navy had done by that point to develop the airplane was to send two observers, Lt. George C. Sweet and Naval Constructor Lt. William McEntee, to the Wrights' Army Aeronautical Board tests at Fort Myer in September 1908.

Both observers were deeply impressed by the potential of the airplane. Having discussed with Orville Wright the possibility of flying off a ship, Sweet recommended that the Navy pursue development of an amphibious machine capable of carrying more than one person, "with the possibility of hovering, if such can be accomplished." The machine he envisioned could carry dispatches, spot hidden enemy artillery batteries, and detect submarines and floating mines. It would be stored on board the ship and launched from there, but also could land on water. Sweet also recommended that the Navy buy a number of airplanes and adapt them to naval use. But the Navy's General Board, responsible for planning and acquisition, took no action.[3]

Sweet was undeterred. In August 1909, his Bureau of Equipment sought "authority to advertise for construction of two heavier than air flying machines" as well as approval for him to attend aeronautical exhibitions in Europe. Both requests were denied; it was felt that airplane development had not progressed sufficiently to warrant a purchase, and naval attachés in Europe could more economically attend the expositions. Cdr. Frederick L. Chapin, stationed at the American embassy in Paris, was sent to observe at Rheims, where he saw Curtiss win the inaugural Gordon Bennett Cup in 1909. Shortly afterward, he submitted a report that echoed Sweet's, recommending deployment of airplanes on existing battleships and proposing the construction of new ships with flight decks. His recommendation was ignored and his proposal denied. The closest Chapin's airplane proposal came to fruition was in November 1909, when Sweet became the first naval officer to take to the air, riding in a Wright machine piloted by the Army's first aviator, Frank P. Lahm.[4]

The man who rejected Chapin's proposal was the Secretary of the Navy, George von Lengerke Meyer. Appointed by newly elected president William Howard Taft in 1909, Meyer was a conservative Republican politician from Boston whom the press described as "not a man of mirth." While Meyer had no experience in naval operations, he was a smart, tireless worker and a skilled bureaucrat. Having concluded that the Navy Department would function better under military direction than civilian, he reorganized it into four divisions, each to be headed by a high-ranking military aide. Of those four assistants, responsibility for building and equipping ships fell to the office of the Aide for Materiel, who oversaw four technical "bureaus": Construction and Repair, Ordnance (weapons), Steam Engineering (engines), and Equipment. Any Navy involvement with airplanes would fall within the jurisdiction of the Aide for Materiel.[5]

When Adm. William H. Swift was appointed to that position, he specifically requested as his assistant an 1876 Naval Academy graduate who had finally been promoted to captain more than three decades later. Capt. Washington Irving Chambers, commanding the battleship USS *Louisiana*, had not sought a land-based position, but with his forward-thinking ideas about torpedoes and the designs of "all-big-gun" battleships, he was a logical choice.[6]

Chambers had written in 1904 that the United States should plan for a specific war against its "most probable enemy," Germany. His ideas did not gain wide traction. Many dismissed "invasion literature" as unrealistic. Secretary Meyer believed that Kaiser Wilhelm II, a personal friend, had no interest in war. "No nation," Meyer wrote in 1906, "will go blindly into attacking another in these days." Yet just around the time Chambers was writing his paper, the Kaiser was contemplating using conventional naval forces to launch an attack on the United States.[7]

Following Selfridge's death, the Wrights had received a nine-month extension on their Army acceptance tests. In July 1909, Meyer was present at Fort Myer when they successfully demonstrated the Flyer. He wrote in his diary, "It is the beginning of a new mode of transportation and the aeroplane of the future, twenty-five years from now, will be as different from what we saw to-day as is the present transatlantic steamer from the Fulton steamer that first plied on the Hudson." But while he recognized that aircraft could be used for scouting, he underestimated both their military value and the willingness of nations to use them in an offensive capacity. "That they will ever be used as fighting machines is very doubtful," he told an interviewer. "It has been suggested that they could drop explosives on war vessels and forts. There are some barbarities, however, that are even prohibited in war."[8]

The public did not share his doubt. "A great city cannot be defended from aerial attack, and war in the air means the inevitable destruction of such cities," maintained one 1909 newspaper editorial. Meyer was deluged with letters asking how the Navy planned to defend the nation against foreign air attacks and proposing elaborate schemes for mounting such defenses. For political and bureaucratic expediency, he tended to respond to such unsolicited inquiries tersely and without elaboration, along the following lines: "I have to thank you for your interest in the Navy and to inform you that you have gained a wrong impression from the newspapers in regard to the existence of any apprehension in this matter on the part of the Navy department."[9]

The Navy had no airplanes and no plans to acquire them. But someone needed to reassure Americans that the Navy was keeping abreast of developments in aviation. That responsibility was assigned to Captain Chambers. He later recalled, "I was simply detailed . . . to look after the aviation correspondence for the Secretary's office, in addition to my other duties . . . but I soon found I was in it up to my neck and something more was needed." Chambers arranged to have his responsibilities expanded to include "observing everything that will be of use in the study of aviation and its influence upon the problems of naval warfare." Those orders allowed him to satisfy his technological curiosity and to immerse himself in aviation literature. What began as an administrative task quickly swept Chambers up in the American popular fascination with practical military aviation.[10]

Wells was not alone in predicting that the airplane would revolutionize warfare. Hudson Maxim, the inventor of smokeless gunpowder, observed that airplanes carrying bombs could be used on "baggage trains of armies, upon storehouses and magazines. Large explosive bombs dropped into the smokestacks of warships might prove very destructive." He calculated that ten thousand flying machines could be built for the cost of a single battleship.[11]

In May 1910, as Curtiss flew down the Hudson, with ships and buildings passing beneath him, he had an epiphany: "All the great battles of the future will be fought in the air. . . . Take my word for it, the days for big warships are numbered." He determined to resume his efforts to design "an aeroplane that would be available for starting or landing on water."[12]

Following the June 1910 exhibition at which he met Ely, Curtiss returned to Hammondsport to test the practicality of airplanes for use in aerial bombardment. On June 29–30 he staged a mock bombing run on a 500-by-90-foot dummy battleship floating on Keuka Lake. Armed with chunks of lead pipe to which red, white, and blue streamers had been attached for visibility, he took five practice shots and then began circling at altitudes of a few hundred feet. Even with no bombsights, no firing mechanism, and no ability to observe where his missiles were landing, he hit the target ten out of fourteen times. Then he rose higher, flew lengthwise along the "ship," and scored hits with three out of four shots, including one from "easily nine hundred feet."[13]

The experiment had been devised by the *New York World*, the newspaper whose prize Curtiss had claimed one month earlier with his Hudson River flight. Army and Navy observers were on hand, and Maj. Samuel Reber of the Army Signal Corps commented, "The Army at large is naturally much interested in ascertaining the possibilities of the aeroplane as a weapon of offense in time of war." Curtiss concluded that once a bombardier with a missile launcher was added, the airplane was bound to come into general use, "sooner or later," by both the Army and the Navy.[14]

One week later, Curtiss brought his canoe-mounted hydroairplane to an Atlantic City meet and exhibited it in a static display. At that same event, he took to the air and lobbed half a dozen oranges onto a privately owned sailing yacht that stood in for a battleship. (The Navy was to provide a ship but withdrew the offer, evidently due to concern that foreign agents could be watching.) It was rumored that some Army and Navy officials were so impressed that they predicted Congress would eventually vote not to spend any money fortifying the Panama Canal, given how easily airplanes would clearly be able to destroy any fortifications built to protect it.[15]

Country Life in America magazine was offering a prize for the first flight across Long Island Sound, and Clifford Harmon had widely declared his intention to win it. The Aeronautic Society of New York had the use of a large field at Mineola on Long Island, from which Harmon launched his Farman biplane on July 30. Having decided that the weather was too poor for overwater flying but not for target practice, he circled the field at heights varying between three and eight hundred feet and hurled oranges down at a pair of volunteers who stood before the crowded grandstand. He scored two painful direct hits, and all six oranges landed "close enough to the human targets to spatter them thoroughly." The next day, an even larger crowd turned out, estimated at 15,000. Harmon again judged that the weather would not permit a cross-sound attempt, but a reprise of his mock aerial assault made the front page of the *New York Times*.

Harmon had made his "bombing" runs at the request of retired Lt. Gen. Nelson A. Miles, who had apparently spoken to him after reading about Curtiss' experiment at Atlantic City. Miles, a Civil War veteran who had gone on to command all U.S. forces in the Spanish-American War, reportedly indicated that he found the demonstration "convincing of what might be done with a thousand aeroplanes over a hostile force in actual war."[16]

Harmon's friend John Barry Ryan, a wealthy New York socialite, pushed the exercise further. Ryan arranged to have the outline of a four-hundred-foot battleship painted on the grass of the aviation field at Mineola, along with the outlines of two mock submarines being towed behind the ship. Three-dimensional cylinders representing the battleship's funnels were reportedly covered with "air-tight papers" that would create the sound of an explosion when struck. Newspapers nationwide trumpeted the story, and Army and Navy officers, including Lieutenant General Miles, planned to witness the test.[17]

By August 2, all was ready for a "mimic battle between [Harmon's] aeroplane and a fleet of imaginary war vessels." Poor weather intervened, but on August 6, Harmon flew at a height of 100 to 150 feet and scored hits with nine of sixteen "confetti balls" thrown at the target—including one direct hit on a stack. The crowd witnessing this new form of aerial entertainment "cheered itself hoarse." On the following day Harmon dropped oranges and hit the target eight times.[18]

Some found the demonstration inconclusive. "Naval officers have held that it would be impossible to drop bombs with accuracy from a height at which the aeroplanes would be out of rifle [range]," said one reporter, but "Harmon never got high enough to prove or disprove this contention." Even Hudson Maxim now thought aerial bombardment "a mere layman's fiction."[19]

Curtiss had a different view. Acknowledging the problems presented by wind, he maintained that, from a height of eight hundred to a thousand feet, "if we had a tube from which to shoot . . . we might have a good chance to hit a target as large as the deck of a battleship." He estimated that his machine could carry 150 pounds of explosives.[20]

One of the most important matters to consider in naval aviation, according to Curtiss, was whether to land on the deck of a ship or in the sand on the seashore. Notwithstanding the difficulties posed by turbulent offshore winds, he felt that beach landings were feasible. "As for landing on the deck of a ship, that I have never tried, but I should think it would be quite possible. You could do it only when you could head into the wind, following over the ship with the deck right below you, and then drop on the afterdeck." Curtiss concluded that the biggest problem of all was starting an airplane from the water, and that solving it would open up a "great new field."[21]

Whatever the merits of Harmon's demonstrations, he finally succeeded in his quest to make the first flight across Long Island Sound, claiming the prize on August 20.[22]

Meanwhile, plans were materializing for an international aviation meet in Boston. It was organized by the Harvard Aeronautical Society, whose founding president, Professor A. Lawrence Rotch, was known worldwide not only as a leading meteorologist but also as a premier balloonist. He led the society's efforts to promote aerial navigation as a science.[23]

Rotch offered a startling calculation of the money spent by foreign governments on military aviation experiments in 1908: Austria and England had each invested about $27,000, France $280,000, and Germany a staggering $670,000. In contrast, as of September 1910 the sum total of the investment in airplanes by the U.S. government was the purchase of a single 1909 Wright Flyer that was already obsolete.[24]

The Harvard-Boston Aero Meet, held on the Squantum Peninsula extending into Boston Harbor, was scheduled for September 3–13, 1910, and was ultimately extended two days due to its popularity. Ely's other engagements prevented him from participating, but Curtiss and Charles Willard appeared. Rotch knew the Wrights personally and persuaded Wilbur to compete, along with Walter Brookins and Ralph Johnstone.

The meet was a high-society affair as well as a flying exhibition: President Taft watched events with his family, and Secretary Meyer motored down from his vacation home on the North Shore. A young Harvard alumnus in the audience, Franklin D. Roosevelt, would later serve as assistant secretary of the Navy during World War I and as commander in chief during World War II. Estimates put the total number of spectators at over one million, counting both those who paid for the privilege and those who watched from boats in the harbor or from their own front yards. *Scientific American* deemed the meet "the most important thus far held in the United States."[25]

Harmon participated, as did Britain's best aviator, Claude Grahame-White. On the meet's opening day Harmon made a brief flight while a band played "The Star-Spangled Banner." He then lent his machine to Grahame-White, who flew to the strains of "God Save the King."

Watching the proceedings, Ryan found himself envisioning a standing association of amateur and professional aviators, ready to be mobilized in time of war for the aerial defense of the United States. That same day, he sent a telegram to the Aero Club, notifying members that soon "an organization would be formed in this country, which would be known as the United States Aeronautical Reserves" (later the U.S. Aeronautical Reserve). His idea quickly gained the support of the contestants at the meet, including Curtiss, who was one of the first to join.[26]

Grahame-White dominated the meet, winning more events than anyone else. A prize of $5,000 was to be awarded for bomb-throwing at a battleship's outline. He took the early lead, scoring thirty-seven out of a possible fifty points, and seemed to be comfortably ahead—until Wilbur Wright put his marksmanship on display. Wright racked up a score "so promising" that Grahame-White felt compelled to devote "practically an entire afternoon to bomb-dropping," ultimately winning the contest handily. Curtiss registered hits on seventeen of his eighteen shots, including a bull's-eye on the funnel.[27]

But the demonstration did not convince everyone. A *New York Times* headline a week later read, "Secretary Meyer Thinks [Battleships] Have Little to Fear from Aeroplanes." In Meyer's view, "The aviator would have to go up several thousand feet to be out of rifle range, and the size of the bomb he would be able to carry would not seriously hurt any battleship unless it went down the funnel, and that would be a pretty remote danger," like "trying to hit a ten-cent piece on the ground from the top of the Washington Monument."[28]

John Moisant, the American who had made the first flight from Paris to London, and who was in New York for the coming Belmont meet, disagreed. "People talk of shooting at flying machines from the ground," he reportedly said, "and warding off an attack that way. We can travel 70 miles an hour, and more than that soon, and go up 5,000 feet or more. Can they hit us under those conditions? Of course not." Meyer did concede that airplanes might play one important military role, noting that they would "prove of great service to the country in time of war as observers."[29]

Ryan, the self-styled "Commodore" of the U.S. Aeronautical Reserve, appointed Harmon chief of staff; Wilbur Wright and Glenn Curtiss were on the board. Annual dues were two dollars for established aviators and half that for "apprentices" (enthusiasts). With public acceptance immediate and nearly universal, Ryan aimed to organize formal units in each state. The massive recruiting effort that ensued resulted, within a few weeks, in a reported membership of 3,500—more than a hundred times the total number of aviators in America.[30]

Eager to gain government support for his Reserve, Ryan met with Gen. James Allen, chief of the Signal Corps, the sole U.S. military unit that had an airplane. The news report that followed their September 22 meeting in Washington, D.C., probably originated with

Ryan, who "did not ask a dollar of government money in return for the creation of a reserve of 1,000 aeroplanes. . . . What he did want was the moral support of the [War and Navy] departments. This was given him with hearty good will." That final sentence was a bit of a stretch, and where he expected to find a thousand airplanes was a mystery. Nevertheless, encouraged by General Allen, Ryan sent letters to Secretary of War Dickinson and Secretary of the Navy Meyer, "requesting an officer . . . be designated, with whom the United States Aeronautical Reserve may consult and correspond."[31]

Within a few days he received affirmative replies. The officer designated by the War Department was General Allen; the one for the Navy Department was Captain Chambers. Although the Navy Department's letter to Ryan was signed by Asst. Sec. Beekman Winthrop as Acting Secretary of the Navy, initials in an upper corner reflect that it had been dictated by Chambers himself. Ryan's letter did, after all, qualify as "aviation correspondence," and therefore Chambers was responsible for addressing it.

Because Chambers had no office, no staff, and no budget, his appointment as liaison to the Reserve was without practical effect. Ryan was nevertheless delighted. He immediately sent Chambers copies of all the literature he possessed on aviation.

Chambers may have thought he had found a simple way to deflect some of the burdensome aviation mail: in a letter to Ryan, he mentioned that he was referring one such letter to the Reserve (and, implicitly, that he would be referring others in the future). But Ryan's response turned the conversation in another direction. "As I understand that there is to be a very interesting Aero Meet in Washington about the middle of this month," Ryan wrote on October 4, "I trust I shall have the pleasure of a talk with you on Naval Aeronautics at that time." Chambers, who had missed out on the Harvard-Boston meet, began seriously to consider attending flying exhibitions.[32]

Secretary Meyer left Washington on September 30 for a five-week tour of navy yards and training facilities without having given instructions regarding naval aviation. The likelihood of the Navy acquiring airplanes seemed remote. But with Meyer traveling, responsibility for the Navy Department fell to Assistant Secretary Winthrop. Winthrop's regular duties as Meyer's assistant were essentially limited to oversight of the various navy yards. But he, unlike Meyer, was extremely interested in military aviation experiments. The coincidence of Meyer's absence from Washington with the formation of the Reserve was fortunate for the development of naval aviation. Things began to happen rapidly.[33]

The day after Meyer left Washington, the Navy's General Board issued its specification for the design of new scout cruiser ships: "Recognizing the great advances which have been made in the science of aviation and the advantages which may accrue from its use in this class of vessel, the General Board recommends that the subject of providing space for a dirigible or aeroplane (whichever is deemed most advisable), as well as the means for [flying] them be taken up by the technical bureaus." Winthrop promptly directed the technical bureaus under Capt. Frank F. Fletcher, who succeeded Admiral Swift as the Aide for Materiel, to take up that question.[34]

On October 7, Capt. Hutchinson I. Cone, chief of the Bureau of Steam Engineering, sent Acting Secretary Winthrop a memorandum headed "CHESTER: Aeroplane," lauding the value of flying machines for scouting purposes. The subject of that memo, the scout cruiser USS *Chester,* was being repaired at Boston Navy Yard:

> The rapid improvement in the design and manipulation of aeroplanes, and the important role which they will probably play as adjuncts to a fleet for scouting and signal purposes, make it desirable that our Scouts be each provided with one. With this end in view, authority is requested to make requisition for one aeroplane for the CHESTER, the requisition to cover delivery at such navy yard as may hereafter be determined, and also the services of a skilled operator to instruct one or more officers in its operation. The cost will probably

not exceed $10,000, and will be chargeable to appropriation "Equipment of Vessels."

Winthrop referred the Cone memo to Chambers.[35]

Assuming the suggestion was even legal, Chambers was uncertain how to charge the appropriation. Any funds Congress had appropriated the previous year for "equipment of vessels" surely had not been intended to include money for airplanes. Without taking a position on the proposed purchase, he prepared a memorandum titled "Aeroplanes in Warfare." In it, he observed that "the present state of the art will limit the use of the aeroplane in the immediate future to reconaissance or scouting duty," but that an "ability to rise from or light upon the deck of a large ship" could reasonably be expected at some point in the future, and concluded merely that the Bureau of Steam Engineering had adequate facilities available to it at Annapolis for experimental work directed toward increasing maximum aviation speed.[36]

Chambers sent the memo to the Aide for Personnel and the Aide for Operations for their comments. Adm. William P. Potter in Personnel deemed it "desirable to defer action until a more perfect machine is developed," but Adm. Richard Wainwright in Operations recommended that "the Navy should enter actively into the subject of securing satisfactory aeroplanes or kites for observation purposes at sea." Wainwright's response evidently satisfied Chambers, who persuaded Winthrop to forward the *Chester* request to the General Board the next day.[37]

Wainwright's belief, shared with Meyer, that international law precluded the use of airplanes as offensive weapons, had caused Chambers to see him as the "principal stumbling block" to the establishment of a formal Office of Aeronautics. Perhaps for this reason, in his memoranda regarding airplanes in warfare Chambers was careful not to mention their offensive capabilities. As far as Wainwright was concerned, the hypothetical *Chester* flying machine would be limited to scouting.[38]

On October 12, Grahame-White, Harmon, Ryan, and General Miles addressed a dinner meeting of the National Press Club of

Washington. All four reportedly "expressed confidence that when the possibilities of the aeroplane become generally recognized the nations of the world will settle their differences by other means than war." At the same time, Grahame-White commented, "The future of the aeroplane is closely interwoven with both branches of the military service. It already has been demonstrated that the aeroplane is useful in war." Rather ominously, mention was made of "how easy it would be for Mr. Grahame-White to fly over this city and destroy the Capitol, the White House and the Treasury."[39]

Secretly, Ryan was planning a compelling demonstration of that very possibility. On October 14, Grahame-White flew unannounced from the Benning track on the east side of Washington, D.C., where he had been exhibiting. He circled the Capitol dome, went into a glide, and landed his Farman biplane neatly on Executive Avenue between the White House and the State, War, and Navy Building—directly outside the office of the Secretary of the Navy. It was a feat hailed as "the most remarkable and daring landing ever made from such a height by an aviator."

The dashing Englishman's charm and panache made him a welcome invader, and the enthusiastic officials who swarmed outdoors to congratulate him included General Allen and Assistant Secretary Winthrop. Given that Ryan and Harmon were on hand to greet Grahame-White when he landed and lunched with him before he flew back to the Benning track, it was clear that the Reserve was behind the stunt.[40]

That same day, the General Board acted on the *Chester* request, concluding that "the value of aeroplanes for use in naval warfare should be investigated without delay" and recommending "that the Department approve the request of the Engineer-in-Chief" to acquire a flying machine for the Navy.[41]

CHAPTER 12

BELMONT STAKES

FOLLOWING THE CHICAGO-TO-NEW YORK debacle and his undistinguished performance in Youngstown, Ely traveled to Cleveland with other members of the Curtiss team to perform on October 10–15 for an "aviation week" held in conjunction with the centennial celebration of Cuyahoga County. The Wright fliers and Clifford Harmon were expected as well, and the organizing committee reportedly sought Claude Grahame-White as "the star of the occasion." But he was busy dazzling Washington, and the Wright team was concluding an exhibition in St. Louis, so only Bud Mars, Douglas McCurdy, and Ely appeared.

Ely engaged in a brief mock race with McCurdy and later won an impromptu precision-landing contest, stopping with his rear wheels directly on a tape mark on the ground. He also had the distinction of making the first flight over downtown Cleveland ("the sensation of the afternoon"), and it was reported that "the circular glide to the field with which he finished the flight was as thrilling as the journey itself."[1]

The Cleveland flights seem to have reaffirmed Curtiss' faith in Ely, whom he now invited to join the other three fliers at the upcoming Belmont Park meet in New York. At the meet, the Aero Club of America would be conducting elimination trials to determine the makeup of the American team that would compete in the Gordon Bennett Cup race. Curtiss, who still had not responded to the Club's invitation to defend the Cup, finally announced that he would leave that honor to his pupils. Ely, Mars, and Charles Willard would enter the trials at Belmont. (McCurdy, a Canadian, was ineligible.)

Pragmatism may have been a key factor in Curtiss' decision. At Rheims a year earlier, he had nipped Louis Blériot by less than six seconds. This year, with the likes of Britain's Grahame-White expected to be competing in a powerful 100-hp Blériot monoplane, he would almost certainly lose.[2]

After the Navy's Bureau of Steam Engineering proposed the purchase of an airplane for USS *Chester*, Rear Adm. Richard M. Watt, chief of the Bureau of Construction and Repair, sent a memo to Secretary of the Navy Meyer. Watt recommended designating one of his own officers and an officer from Steam Engineering "to investigate and follow the subject of aviation with a view to gaining a technical knowledge of such apparatus and enabl[ing] the Department to make use of such advantages for naval purposes as the development of dirigibles or aeroplanes may offer."[3]

Assistant Secretary Winthrop had not acted on the General Board's recommendation to buy an airplane; Secretary Meyer had to make that decision when he returned. But Winthrop would follow the board's original recommendation that "the value of aeroplanes for use in naval warfare . . . be investigated without delay." He approved Watt's request, ordering each of the two bureaus to assign an officer to follow the subject of aviation for naval purposes, and to "treat all discoveries or advances . . . as confidential information." By October 21, 1910, the Navy had an "aeroplane investigation" team: Lieutenant McEntee from Construction and Repair, and Lt. Nathaniel H. Wright from Steam Engineering.[4]

The timing was perfect: the Belmont Park meet would begin on October 22. While Belmont would not showcase any demonstrations of the military capabilities of airplanes—bomb-dropping or otherwise—it would feature marquee events: a race to the Statue of Liberty and back for a $10,000 prize, and the long-awaited Gordon Bennett Cup race. Captain Chambers, recognizing the significance of the meet, arranged to receive orders to attend, as did Army liaison General Allen and Lieutenants McEntee and Wright. With Chambers, they planned to assess the relative strengths of biplanes and monoplanes, and of American machines against those of other nations.[5]

Three days before the opening of the Belmont meet, surprising news broke from Hammondsport: the new Curtiss racer was not a biplane but a monoplane. In a revolutionary departure from earlier Curtiss designs, in place of an upper wing it had a small surface resembling an awning, above and behind the pilot.[6]

The "single-surface" racer had evolved from a comment by Willard to Curtiss that he preferred a machine with more power and less head resistance. Curtiss understood that biplanes were structurally stronger than monoplanes, but he also knew from experience at Rheims that monoplanes achieved superior speeds. With its relatively light weight and its eight-cylinder 51-hp engine, the untested racer offered the team's only chance of beating Grahame-White's Blériot monoplane.[7]

"The Curtiss racer," wrote a *New York Herald* reporter, "looks like a handkerchief just out of the shop. It is perfectly clean and without a spot or stain of any sort. It never has been flown and is wholly an experiment. The new 'single surface' machine looks like a racer, however. It is stripped to the bone and looks naked and bare when compared with the other machines. It has something of the appearance of a [rowing] racing shell in its bold bareness." Willard considered the machine too flimsy and refused to fly it, but Ely was reportedly game to compete in it at Belmont.[8]

Curtiss was not the only one with a new machine: the Wrights also unveiled a new racer at Belmont. Formally known as the Model R but dubbed the *Baby Grand*, it had reportedly achieved a speed of over 70 mph when Orville took it for a test flight. The 60-hp biplane, like the Model B that the Wrights had introduced at Asbury Park in August, used a "headless" configuration with no forward elevator. The high-speed airflow created by the propellers, it turned out, magnified the up-down sensitivity of a rear elevator placed in their wake, rendering the forward elevator superfluous.

The new configuration created new challenges, though. Captain Chambers reported afterward, "The aviators of both the Wright and Curtiss schools seem to think this [headless configuration] is logical progress, but the performances of the Wright biplanes in comparison with the Curtiss and Farman biplanes, both of which had the front control, at these meets, indicate that if this is so, the new [rear] position of the elevator planes requires more skill, as in the monoplanes, to handle the machines while landing."[9]

In spite of the new designs, the *New York Times* reported "a moody apprehension on the part of some" that the Gordon Bennett Cup would be "feebly defended." Curtiss' approach to Belmont seems to have been more to endure than to dominate it—with good reason. The Wrights were publicly guaranteed $10,000 in exchange for not interfering with the meet by raising their patent claims. Curtiss and Jerome Fanciulli further suspected, correctly, that there was a secret agreement to pay the brothers an additional $15,000 from the meet's proceeds. Curtiss presumably had no wish to add to the Wrights' earnings.[10]

Even if he had chosen to compete, it was clear from the start that all glory would go to others. Curtiss machines were not designed to achieve altitude records, and in order to preserve their airplanes for the American elimination trials, the team would attempt no distance flights. As for speed, former Curtiss flier Charles Hamilton appeared with his own 110-hp "Hamiltonian" machine, while Americans John Moisant and J. Armstrong Drexel both proposed to use Blériots in the elimination trials. Curtiss knew the theoretical capabilities of his single-surface machine, and may have realized that it could not outdo the Wrights' *Baby Grand* and the other American machines, let alone French or British ones.[11]

For Ely, Belmont Park offered a return to the national spotlight and a chance at redemption after the Chicago–to–New York fiasco ten days earlier. For the first time in his six-month career, he would compete directly against the Wrights' exhibition team and against foreign aviators.

On opening day, Saturday, October 22—the day after Ely's twenty-fourth birthday—the weather was miserable. No records were broken; a reporter declared that "it was sufficient triumph to fly at all." Hardly two thousand spectators showed up, and only six of the twenty-four listed aviators take to the sky. Ely was the only Curtiss flier to appear, but he did not risk flying the new single-surface machine. During the first in a series of hourly altitude competitions, he had ascended to 404 feet when "a stream of yellow smoke" poured from his engine, causing him to descend in "a pretty steep swoop." Ely reached barely half the height Arch Hoxsey reached that hour, but because they were the only two to go up, Ely's flight was good enough for a $100 second prize. He went up again briefly during the second hourly competition, but engine trouble again forced him to the ground. His 206-foot climb left him in a distant fourth place and out of the money.[12]

John Moisant completed, and therefore won, a twenty-mile cross-country event, which no one else attempted. Fog obscured the ground and he had to navigate by compass, as he had done on his celebrated Paris–to–London flight, and he averaged only 30 mph. But Chambers was astonished by the feat, and immediately understood its application to the Navy. "The air man," wrote Chambers, "although greatly handicapped by the difficulty of calculating his leeway [drift], has the advantage over the seaman in being able to rise above the fog, as the usual fogs rarely extend to high altitudes." Moisant's method, as described by Chambers, was to mark out the legs of the course on a map beforehand and, at the start of each leg, use the compass to orient the aircraft and then maintain that bearing by means of landmarks—high ones, if there was fog. Chambers perceived the inherent problem for the naval aviator: "Up to the present time, although there have been several flights across the English Channel, and other large bodies of water, no flight has been made in which the aviator has been independent of landmarks for guidance. The problem of accurate flying for distances out of sight of land, or a base ship, presents greater difficulties in navigation but these difficulties are not prohibitive."[13]

It is reasonable to suppose that Chambers met Ely at Belmont, although there is no record of such a meeting. With orders directing him to observe "everything that will be of use in the study of aviation and its influence upon the problems of naval warfare," Chambers tried to inspect as many airplanes as he could. His chief interest lay in examining French makes not previously seen in America, but his report on the meet also made mention of the machine that Ely intended to try out: "A new model Curtiss machine attracted much interest. It was a small high-power biplane, or rather a monoplane with a small upper plane over the [aviator]."[14]

On Monday, October 24, the meet's third day, ten machines rose into the air simultaneously—a sight never seen before in the United States. Ely was in one of the machines, but it was not the single-surface racer, which, like the Wrights' *Baby Grand*, had yet to make an official appearance. Curtiss and the Wrights seemed to be protecting their respective speedy machines, each daring the other to make the first move.[15]

The concluding event of the meet would be a "grand speed contest" between the fastest biplane and the fastest monoplane. McCurdy and Mars participated in the biplane elimination heat; Ely, formally announced as the "tentative driver" of the single-surface machine, did not. McCurdy won with a respectable time of just under twenty minutes for twenty-five kilometers. Willard and Ely each took another stab at an altitude prize, but with their combined heights barely topping a thousand feet, it was apparent that Curtiss biplanes were simply not meant for climbing.[16]

The *Baby Grand* made its first appearance on Tuesday, October 25, when Orville Wright steered it around the course at speeds approaching 70 mph—half a minute faster than McCurdy's average lap time. It was by far the fastest flying that had been seen at the meet. At that pace, the Wright racer would finish the Gordon Bennett hundred-kilometer race some twenty minutes ahead of any Curtiss biplane. As for the new single-surface machine, Curtiss evidently concluded that its improved features, whatever they were (and assuming it was even airworthy), would not make it competitive with the *Baby Grand*.[17]

It is not known whether the new machine ever left the ground at Belmont. Ely went on a tune-up flight in advance of the elimination trials, but the machine he flew was not reported. New York's *Sun* ran a front-page photograph of Ely at the wheel of the single-surface racer, and Mabel's scrapbook holds a number of similar photographs, but none shows the machine in flight.[18]

The Curtiss aviators, having given up all attempts at altitude flights, watched along with everyone else as Hoxsey climbed to 5,796 feet, a personal best, and Ralph Johnstone established a new American record by reaching 7,313 feet. The next day, the two Wright fliers ascended simultaneously at twilight, in what a *New York Times* reporter saw as "a duel of endurance." An enthralled crowd watched as the pair "guided their Wright biplanes to altitudes of 6,000-odd feet . . . and remained there until darkness had settled over the field and the stars had come out in the heavens." Other poet-journalists would muse that the two aviators had "gone up to light the stars" and dubbed them the "heavenly twins," or the "Star-Dust Twins." Johnstone and Hoxsey vanished into darkness, lost to sight for more than ten minutes. Concerned about their safety, the Wrights had gasoline poured onto the grass and set ablaze "as signal lights for the men in the sky," dramatically illuminating the track. The flaming beacons brought the fliers safely back to earth.[19]

Strong winds had wreaked havoc with the planned elimination trials for the Gordon Bennett Cup. Three days before race day, the Aero Club of America faced a dilemma: the American team would have to be chosen from among several hopeful aviators on the ground rather than by performance in the air.[20]

With Curtiss unable to guarantee that the single-surface racer would fly, Ely was out of the running to compete. In the end, the Americans chosen were Wright flier Walter Brookins, who could pilot the demonstrably swift *Baby Grand*; Drexel, who had won an hourly endurance contest on Monday in his Blériot; and Hamilton, who had barely flown all week, but whose 110-hp Hamiltonian was the most powerful machine available to the Americans. Mars, Moisant, and Hoxsey were reserves, while Willard and Ely were shut out.[21]

The weather cleared at last, just in time for the race on Saturday, October 29. Grahame-White got into the air first and had already made five laps of the five-kilometer course at 60 mph when Alfred LeBlanc, chief pilot for the Blériot company and the French favorite, rose and began steadily chasing—and then passing—him. LeBlanc, through more efficient turns, maintained a speed of nearly 70 mph. He seemed assured of besting Grahame-White, until he ran out of gas on the final lap, lost control, and crashed straight through a twelve-inch-thick telephone pole as if it were a toothpick. Miraculously, he survived. Brookins took to the air in the *Baby Grand* but crashed during a pre-race trial run when four of his eight cylinders failed. Drexel descended after seven unimpressive laps, and Hamilton was disqualified for making a late start.

The chances of an American defending the Cup had all but evaporated. But Brookins had not technically made a start, which meant there was a place for one more American flier. Mars was first in line as a substitute, but when he was approached thirty minutes before the deadline, he declined. The *Washington Herald* speculated perceptively that the members of the Curtiss team "weren't too anxious to put a man into what was probably a losing race." With mere seconds before the time cutoff, Moisant, the second alternate, scrambled to get his Blériot aloft. Even with one stop for a mechanical adjustment, he turned in the second-best finish time of the day behind Grahame-White, and transformed himself into America's latest aviation hero.[22]

There remained the second marquee event: the Statue of Liberty race on Sunday, October 30, featuring Grahame-White, Count Jacques de Lesseps, and Moisant, all flying Blériots. The new American hero had another shot at glory. But, as Mabel Ely recorded in a pair of photographs shortly after the event, Moisant crashed into Clifford Harmon's parked machine and could not manage to get his own repaired by the time the other two aviators left, one at a time.[23]

Grahame-White's time beat that of de Lesseps. But at the very last instant, Moisant's brother Alfred bought one of LeBlanc's Blériots on the spot, and John Moisant jumped into the seat of an airplane he had never flown before. By using his compass and taking a more direct route, he beat Grahame-White's time by forty-three seconds.[24]

The enthusiasm that had greeted Moisant's second-place finish in the Gordon Bennett Cup race the day before was nothing next to the jubilation attending his Statue of Liberty victory. Never mind that he had a foreign name, flew a French machine, had spent much of the past decade in Salvador, and had achieved his greatest previous fame in Europe with his flight from Paris to London. At Belmont he was an American hero.[25]

On Monday, October 31, the final day of the meet, McCurdy gamely raced Grahame-White, biplane against monoplane, in the "grand speed contest," but the outcome was a foregone conclusion. Grahame-White circled the course nearly twice as quickly in his Blériot and won by eleven minutes. The day also offered up one final heroic American aviation feat: Johnstone ascended to 9,714 feet, a new world's record—so high that he was completely lost to sight until his wings glinted in the sunlight.[26]

But for the Curtiss team there was little glory. The fastest machines in the Cup race were, far and away, the 100-hp Blériots of Grahame-White and LeBlanc, and Moisant's 50-hp Blériot. The Wright machines excelled at "high flights," while the Curtiss machines "did not particularly distinguish themselves."[27]

The Curtiss team's winnings were equally dismal. McCurdy, by finishing second in the two-man race with Grahame-White, took home $1,000, bringing his Belmont total to $1,100. Mars and Willard each ended up with $100 for the week. Ely, too, won only $100, from his 404-foot-high flight on the first day. Adding insult to injury, a typographical error on the meet's printed report omitted even that small amount from the final tally of winnings published in American newspapers.[28]

Licking their wounds following Belmont, Ely and Willard entered a Baltimore Aero Club meet at Halethorpe, Maryland, from November 2–8. Cash prizes totaling $50,000 would be awarded for distance, speed, and altitude events. Adding to the excitement, the outline of a battleship had been painted on the field for a bomb-throwing competition. Promoters, who had selected the venue with input from Curtiss, hoped the Halethorpe meet would be a repeat of Belmont on a slightly smaller scale. Chambers once again arranged to receive orders to attend.[29]

Shortly after Ely arrived at the aviation grounds, he made a complaint to officials about the automobiles parked on the infield of the track, which was also cluttered with several canvas hangars and a hospital tent. Evidently the organizers thought an aviation tournament was like an automobile race and were oblivious to the need for a space to land if a machine developed trouble.[30]

By the time the meet opened, further logistic difficulties had arisen. The lateness of the season meant that the aviators had to contend with strong, cold winds. Spectators shivered as they awaited the delayed firing of the bomb signaling the start of competition. Several aviators were unable to fly at all, their machines having been held up between New York and Baltimore by a railway expressmen's strike.

The promoters decided that any flights made on opening day "were only exhibitions," and ineligible for prizes. Willard and English aviator James Radley, who made a dramatic entrance by assembling his Blériot at the train station and flying in from there, simulated attempts at an hourly "distance" prize by circling above the track; some reports put Ely in the air with them. Drexel may likewise have made a mock "altitude" flight, and Ely was expected to travel cross-country later in the afternoon.[31]

While the aviators struggled with the challenges, the newspapers covered a report by General Allen of the U.S. Army to the secretary of war. Noting how quickly the Spanish-American War had started a dozen years earlier, Allen observed that "experienced military airmen cannot be created after war is declared, and the demands of this new service will undoubtedly require higher qualities of training, judgment and courage than any other branch of the military service." He suggested that the Army should have at least twenty airplanes for practice work. There was no such sense of urgency in the Navy.[32]

At Halethorpe it began to rain heavily. On November 3, a storm forced postponement of all scheduled events, and it appeared there would be nothing that day to excite the aviation-mad public.[33]

But the New York and Washington papers ran a dramatic story. A front-page headline in the *New York Times* read, "TO FLY AEROPLANE FROM OCEAN LINER."[34]

CHAPTER 13

THE RACE WITH THE FLOATING ZOO

THE FRONT-PAGE STORY was electrifying:

> New York, Nov. 2—J. A. D. McCurdy, of Glenn H. Curtiss' staff, will attempt to fly by aeroplane from the deck of a vessel fifty miles at sea . . . next Saturday [November 5]. The *Kaiserin Auguste Victoria*, of the Hamburg-American Line, . . . will carry McCurdy and his Curtiss biplane.[1]

Reports promising "a flight such as the world never saw before" were, for once, not mere hyperbole. Douglas McCurdy would attempt to fly an airplane from a ship—a first in history—and not from just any ship, but from a German ocean liner. The purpose, ostensibly, was non-military: to "demonstrate the feasibility of equipping the new liner [*Europa*], the largest ship in the world . . . with a regular aeroplane service for transferring mail at sea." For the demonstration, the airplane would be launched from Europa's sister ship *Kaiserin Auguste Victoria* off a a temporary platform built on the ship's forward deck. The aviator would carry a small mailbag containing letters from the passengers, for delivery at the New York post office.[2]

But the test would also be "observed by a party of navy and army officers, and a flotilla of torpedo boats will patrol the course." Capt. Frank Fletcher, the Secretary of the Navy's Aide for Material (and Captain Chambers' superior), was indirectly quoted as observing that a successful flight "would demonstrate that for scouting purposes an aeroplane costing from $5,000 to $10,000 was considerably cheaper and more economical than an armored cruiser costing $5,000,000."[3]

Curtiss later laconically recalled the events that led to the astonishing announcement: "It was suggested to me by the *New York World* to launch an aeroplane from the deck of a ship at sea and have it fly back to shore carrying messages. The Hamburg-American Steamship Company offered [an ocean liner] for this test, and I sent a standard Curtiss biplane to be operated by J. A. D. McCurdy."[4]

The relatively modern *Kaiserin Auguste Victoria* was the largest operational Hamburg-American steamship and the fastest in crossing the ocean; she was therefore a logical selection for the flight experiment. Competition was intense among steamship lines for government contracts to carry transatlantic mail, and Hamburg-American would gain the inside track if it could demonstrate a reliable way to speed mail delivery by even half a day. The *New York World*'s own announcement of the flight said nothing about mail, but once the test flight was announced, Postmaster General Frank Hitchcock reportedly told Hamburg-American he did not object, provided all senders of "air mail" letters were notified of the patently insecure manner of the proposed delivery.[5]

Any airplane test "at sea" would present two major challenges to the aviator: getting clear of the ship without hitting the water—which had never before even been attempted—and flying over water to land. Having McCurdy start a full fifty miles from shore was consistent with the stated purpose of the Hamburg-American test, even if it increased the danger should he encounter the sort of engine problems that had plagued Ely in Chicago.

There was likely another reason for holding the test at sea: the *New York World*'s reporter and photographer on board would be the only journalists to witness it, thereby ensuring an exclusive story. But those journalists needed a way to return to New York after the launch while *Kaiserin Auguste Victoria* and her passengers continued on their transatlantic crossing. This logistic problem may have been one of the motivations that led the *New York World* to contact Acting Secretary Winthrop, who "evinced keen interest" and requested "full details of the plan."

The proposed Hamburg-American flight was certainly a way to conduct a close study of aviation, as the General Board had recommended, without much risk or cost to the Navy. Accordingly, on November 2, following "telegraphic correspondence" with the *New York World,* Winthrop sent an order to the commander of the Atlantic Torpedo Fleet, directing that two destroyers accompany *Kaiserin Auguste Victoria* out to sea, "render any assistance necessary in case of accident," and return to New York. Winthrop expressly authorized passage for "one or two representatives of the World who may desire to go aboard the destroyers," thus solving the paper's problem of enabling its journalists to witness the launch and afterward return to Manhattan. Finally, he instructed the naval officers to "report fully on the flight of the aeroplane with particular reference to the value of the experiment in its bearing on the possibilities of employing aeroplanes for scouting purposes at sea." As to logistics: "You will confer with representatives of the New York World and arrange the details of this matter."[6]

But Winthrop had miscalculated. German steamships in 1910 were official auxiliaries to their own country's navy. The prospect of "an air journey toward American soil" launched from a German military vessel—particularly one named for the wife of Kaiser Wilhelm II—brought vividly to life the horrors detailed by H. G. Wells in *The War in the Air.* It also echoed what Chambers had written in 1904 about preparing for war against America's most probable enemy.[7]

President Taft overruled Winthrop two days later and canceled the orders for the destroyers, his reasoning being that "it would be inconsistent with previous refusals to permit such use of naval vessels." Perhaps he was concerned that the kaiser might interpret the American destroyers as threats to his merchant vessel. More ominously, if the idea of the test had originated with Hamburg-American, Taft might have worried that the Navy's assistance could be seen as aiding the kaiser in his military experiments.[8]

Winthrop was obliged to send the commander of the Atlantic Torpedo Fleet a telegram annulling his earlier instructions, followed by orders stating, "You will not participate in any way in the proposed aeroplane test." The *New York World* staffers would have to find some other means of viewing the launch and getting ashore.[9]

During the flurry of activity in New York and Washington, Chambers was confined by the terms of his orders to rainy Baltimore, where the Halethorpe meet was becoming a complete waste of his time. November 4 had been designated "Army and Navy Day," but the rain turned to snow overnight and collapsed the canvas tents serving as airplane hangars. Five or six machines were severely damaged, including those of Charles Willard and Ely.

In search of operational machines, Ely wired to Hammondsport and Willard wired to Norfolk, where McCurdy and Bud Mars were flying in an exhibition. But both of their airplanes—one of which was the *Hudson Flyer*, which Mars had been using since mid-October—had been damaged in the storm as well. With the Norfolk event effectively halted, Mars left for Edgefield, South Carolina, just across the Savannah River from Augusta, Georgia, where he was scheduled to spend the following week at the Georgia-Carolina Fair, flying every day.[10]

In Hoboken, meanwhile, Hamburg-American's "German carpenters" were said to have been "on hand with the lumber to build the special platform to be used in launching the aeroplane from the steamship." But the stormy weather that had damaged machines at Halethorpe and Norfolk was forecast to continue through the planned launch date of November 5. On the evening of November 4, the news came that the flight off the German ship had been delayed: "After a consultation between Glenn H. Curtiss, representing Mr. McCurdy, and the Hamburg-American Line officials it was declared to postpone the trial until Nov. 24, when the *Amerika* [a sister ship to *Kaiserin Auguste Victoria*] will be substituted for the experiment."[11]

In the absence of Navy destroyers, the *New York World* chartered a "fleet of fast tugboats" to ferry reporters and photographers, as well as a yacht to carry its guests—including Army and Navy officers—to watch the planned flight from *Amerika*. The *Kaiserin Auguste Victoria* sailed east on November 5, disappointing any passengers who had hoped to post a letter by airplane.[12]

While the cancellation of Winthrop's orders meant that the Navy would not play an active role in the experiment, the boldness of the plan sparked the imagination of some of its officers. "Since the announcement Thursday last that the flight would be made, officers of the several branches of the navy have been keenly interested," the *New York World* reported, "and all interviewed declared that not only was the plan suggested by the *World* feasible, but an idea the Navy Department should consider sooner or later."[13]

Captain Chambers clearly agreed: the U.S. Navy, and not a newspaper in collaboration with a German steamship company, should be conducting the experiments. With McCurdy not due to fly for another three weeks, Chambers saw a window of opportunity. Moreover, the General Board's recommended purchase of an airplane for USS *Chester* gave him a way to justify the Navy's involvement in the experiment. If a successful launch could be made from a Navy ship, the United States would have beaten Germany, and the world—not merely in implementing an aerial postal service, but in demonstrating the possibility of naval aviation. All he needed was a ship, an aircraft, and a willing aviator.

Chambers was still stuck in Halethorpe, where the only American fliers were J. Armstrong Drexel, Willard, Ely, and Arch Hoxsey. Drexel operated a French-made Blériot, which was less than ideal politically, and Willard and Ely were still without machines. Hoxsey had made far and away the best showing of the four at Belmont Park in October, and his machine was intact.

Chambers found Hoxsey "willing and very enthusiastic" about making the attempt, "but Wilbur Wright strenuously objected." According to Chambers, "The only response that could be obtained from the director of [Hoxsey's] company was the disappointing word, 'Impossible.'" (This passage appears in Chambers' draft of a speech he made before the Aeronautical Society in April 1911, but the sentence is crossed out. Evidently, he had second thoughts about speaking negatively of Wilbur Wright in public.) Wright was not merely unwilling; he believed an airplane could not safely take off from a ship, and he refused to risk his aviator's life in the attempt.[14]

Running out of options, Chambers approached Ely—who, to his delight, accepted. Chambers later recalled that, after Wilbur Wright objected, "the Curtiss Company . . . readily acquiesced, and to its able representative, Mr. Eugene Ely . . . is due the credit of arousing a worldwide interest in Naval Aviation." Evidently Curtiss, in contrast to Wilbur Wright, had confidence that, with the right aviator and an appropriate platform, the proposed flight was feasible. Ely was quoted as saying, "I am not going to do this for a prize and will carry nothing in the machine. Curtiss was requested recently by the government to let them see what his machine could do, and he selected me to give the demonstration. I expect to make the distance all right, and I will not even ask for some swift [water]craft to follow me."[15]

The Halethorpe meet had been extended through November 12, and Ely was expected in Raleigh three days later. This meant that the flight would have to take place between November 13 and 15, somewhere along the coast between Baltimore and Raleigh. A platform would have to be constructed on the deck of a ship and an airplane brought aboard. That work would be performed at Norfolk Navy Yard, midway between the two cities.

As luck would have it, Norfolk was where the *Hudson Flyer* idly sat, storm-damaged but reparable in time to make the flight. Now Chambers had an aviator and an aircraft. All he needed was a ship.

On November 4, USS *Birmingham*, a scout cruiser, having concluded five days of torpedo practice off the coast of Rhode Island, made routine anchorage at the Newport Torpedo Station. She lay at anchor for two days.

Given Taft's refusal to permit the use of Navy ships for the Hamburg-American attempt, it was prudent, possibly mandatory, to get his explicit approval for the new experiment. Secretary Meyer returned to Washington from his two-month inspection tour on the morning of November 6 and left that afternoon to vote in the midterm elections in his hometown of Boston. Taft planned to leave Washington on November 7 to vote in Cincinnati. Winthrop may have deliberately engineered the approval to occur during the brief window between their respective departures in order to bypass Meyer and go directly to the president.[16]

A popular myth, recounted decades later by Rear Adm. George van Deurs (Ret.) but unsupported by any available contemporary sources, has Ely, at Chambers' request, traveling to Washington on November 6 and attempting to convince Meyer to approve the Navy's flight. When Meyer turned him down, so the imaginative story goes, John Barry Ryan came to the rescue, threatening to use his political clout against Meyer, who ultimately secured approval from the White House.[17]

However it was arranged, on November 6 *Birmingham*'s commander, Capt. William B. Fletcher, received a telegram from the Navy Department ordering him to proceed to Norfolk, Virginia. The message may have arrived too late in the day for the ship to leave port. But early the following morning, Fletcher—no relation to Chambers' superior officer—lost no time covering the nearly four hundred miles to Norfolk. The ship arrived November 8, and her crew spent the next few days, as the ship's log reveals, "fitting ship for aeroplane experiments." Despite the Navy's documented reluctance to pursue naval aviation beyond the passive observation of developments, less than a week after the postponement of McCurdy's flight, it was hastening to perform its own shipboard launch.[18]

The plan was straightforward: as soon as the wooden platform was completed and the *Hudson Flyer* loaded aboard, *Birmingham* would steam into the harbor at Hampton Roads and then out to sea, whereupon Ely would launch himself from the bow of the ship and fly, if all went well, back to Norfolk Navy Yard. Chambers may have felt confident that the Navy was in position to claim the world's first ship-to-shore flight, and in the process to lay the groundwork for naval aviation in the United States.

On Monday, November 7—the day *Birmingham* sailed from Newport, and well before Chambers' plan became publicly known—word arrived that McCurdy's rescheduled flight would now take place not on November 24 from *Amerika*, as had been announced only forty-eight hours earlier, but rather on November 12 from Hamburg-American's *Pennsylvania*. McCurdy would be flying at an exhibition in Charlotte, North Carolina, on November 10 and could get to Hoboken just barely in time to make the attempt two days later.[19]

The reason for the change of plans is obscure. Perhaps it was merely a conflict in McCurdy's schedule, discovered only after the initial announcement. "After it had been decided to postpone the event until Nov. 24," according to the *New York World*, "Glenn H. Curtiss consulted his manager as to the dates at his disposal, and it was found that McCurdy is under contract to fly elsewhere on that day." (McCurdy did, in fact, fly in Mobile, Alabama, on the 24th.) Or perhaps the newspaper had learned of Chambers' plan and arranged an earlier date in order to beat the Navy to it.[20]

Curtiss and Fanciulli were privy to the Navy's efforts and may have shared them with the *New York World*. Curtiss had a financial interest in the success of McCurdy's flight, but he knew that an attempt from the constricted space of an ocean liner's deck could easily end in disaster. He also had an incentive to cooperate with the Navy, which represented a potential market. Others were aware of Chambers' plan and could have leaked the information. Evidence suggests that it was important to someone—the newspaper, the kaiser, the steamship line, or the Curtiss company—that the historic flight be made off a Hamburg-American ship.[21]

Pennsylvania had docked in Hoboken the day before the original McCurdy announcement, carrying along with her human passengers a veritable floating zoo: seventy apes, eight polar bears, four dogs, a hippopotamus, an elephant, and more than seven thousand birds. The vessel seemed an odd choice: an aging, second-tier ship with just one engine, she was a hundred feet shorter and three days slower in crossing the Atlantic than the prides of the Hamburg-American fleet, *Kaiserin Auguste Victoria* and *Amerika*. The floating zoo also did not normally carry mail. Nevertheless, special "air mail" envelopes and postcards were printed, and on November 9 carpenters set to work constructing a platform above the cramped stern.[22]

Some three hundred miles to the south, Lieutenant McEntee was supervising a crew of Norfolk Navy Yard shipwrights in building a launch platform on *Birmingham*'s foredeck. Lieutenant Wright's later report states the following:

> On the bow was erected a platform eighty-three feet long by twenty-six feet wide, rising . . . at about a five degree angle. From the forward end of this platform to the water was a drop of thirty-seven feet. As the distance from the end of the [airplane's] rear control to the front wheel was about twenty-six feet, there was a clear runway of fifty-seven feet. No guide rail was built, the width of the platform giving a sufficient margin of safety. Down the center line of the platform was painted a dark guide line.[23]

McEntee expected to complete his platform by Saturday morning, November 12. Hamburg-American's *Pennsylvania* had been scheduled to sail at two o'clock that same day, and McCurdy would take off about three hours later. On Monday her sailing time was moved up to noon, ostensibly so that McCurdy could be certain of making the entire flight by daylight, but perhaps also—considering that the trip would take less than an hour—to reduce Ely's opportunity of getting an earlier start. McEntee assured Chambers that if Ely could get himself and his airplane to Norfolk Navy Yard by Friday night, a flight could take place the following morning—just hours ahead of Hamburg-American's attempt.[24]

As planning and construction proceeded on the competing platforms, the weather at Halethorpe finally improved enough for exhibitions to resume on Sunday afternoon, November 6. Senior military officials, including General Allen and General Miles, arrived on Thursday, the rescheduled Army and Navy Day, to watch bomb-throwing and sharpshooting exhibitions. Ely attempted a bombing run but had to land before completing his first lap; the problem was said to have been resolved by an adjustment of his steering wires. On Friday,

November 11, gusty winds of 20–30 mph kept him on the ground. Ely's paternal grandfather and namesake died that day, but a pressing exhibition schedule and the upcoming *Birmingham* flight made a detour to Iowa for the funeral out of the question.[25]

Flying also resumed at Norfolk, where on Tuesday, November 15, Mars set an altitude record. He had been scheduled to appear at the Georgia-Carolina Fair, but having arrived at the fairgrounds ahead of schedule, he purportedly declared the weather to be unsuitable for flying. He retrieved the airplane that had been sent there for him and returned immediately with it to Norfolk. Deprived of one of their featured attractions, the fair directors sued Curtiss. He declined to settle.

On Friday, November 11, Curtiss arrived in New York City from Hammondsport, bringing with him what was evidently a standard Curtiss biplane, though equipped with an eight-cylinder engine. But high winds were still keeping McCurdy on the ground at Charlotte. He reportedly told the crowd, "I came here to fly and I am going to stay here until I do fly." Abandonment would have meant bad publicity and the forfeiture of the exhibition fee.[26]

Because McCurdy could not make it to New York by the next day for the Hamburg-American flight, newspapers reported a last-minute change: Bud Mars, previously mentioned in passing as McCurdy's assistant, would make the flight from *Pennsylvania*. The "nervy" Mars agreed to make the attempt—but it was one for which he had not volunteered, for which he had not been the first choice, and on which he had probably never been consulted.[27]

Lieutenant McEntee's platform may have been ready for a flight off *Birmingham* on Saturday morning, November 19, but Ely and the *Hudson Flyer* were not. The Halethorpe meet closed that day, and Ely would not have been able to reach Norfolk until Sunday. He and Chambers had to wait in Baltimore for the result of the Hamburg-American test. With fair weather forecast for New York, the stage appeared set for Mars to make a historic flight off *Pennsylvania*.[28]

CHAPTER 14

SHIP TO SHORE

FESTIVE FLAGS AND BANNERS hung from the German steamship where "the band was playing spiritedly," while passengers placed their souvenir postcards and letters into a special mailbag, to be postmarked with the date: November 12, 1910. The *New York World* had arranged for the private yacht *Wild Duck* and a pair of chartered tugboats to follow the aviator—and to ferry the paper's reporters—back to shore. Bud Mars arrived from Virginia at 10:30 a.m.

Just before the ship was to sail, Mars and Curtiss went aboard and climbed the ladder to the platform. One or the other suggested testing the engine; if the motor did not work when Mars tried to fire it at sea, both machine and aviator would spend the next twelve days crossing the ocean to Hamburg. The propeller was cranked by hand and the engine sprang to life. "Curtiss nodded to his men as if to say, 'It's all right; she'll do.'"[1]

What happened next sealed the fate of Mars' attempt. Some reports described the entire airplane as having been thrown by the wind against an iron pipe; others maintained that an "L-shaped piece of pipe" used for oiling the engine had been sucked into the propeller, or that "an oil can, carelessly left on one of the [wings] by a mechanic, was knocked off and fell into the whirling propeller," or that a "piece of rubber tubing" that had been left on the lower wing did the damage. Whatever the details, the propeller sustained irreparable damage, and no spare was immediately available. The machine was unflyable, and the experiment could not proceed. *Pennsylvania* signaled to *Wild Duck* the mournful message: "HAS FLOWN."[2]

The mishap was dismissed as an accident. Curtiss and Mars supervised as the damaged machine was offloaded to the dock. The special "air mail" letters were delivered by ground transport to a regular post office, and the *New York World* bemoaned the lost opportunity to "show the possibility of launching scouting ships at sea and of sending out aeroplanes armed with bombs to hurl upon enemies' ships." *Pennsylvania* steamed away, and when she reached open ocean, her crew dismantled the temporary platform and tossed the lumber into the Atlantic.

Captain Chambers, now with a fresh chance, acted quickly. The Navy Department announced that Ely's USS *Birmingham* flight would take place on November 14, "weather conditions permitting," and Chambers arranged to receive orders directing him to report for "special temporary duty" aboard *Birmingham* "in connection with experimental work designed to demonstrate the practicability of using aeroplanes from vessels in connection with scouting duty." Naval Constructor Lt. William McEntee and Lt. Nathaniel Wright would join him on the ship.

Ely and Mabel boarded a six o'clock steamer the evening of November 12 to arrive in Norfolk the next morning. Ely's four-cylinder motor was sent from Baltimore to Norfolk that same night, while the *Hudson Flyer* was transported to Norfolk Navy Yard the next day and fitted with under-wing pontoons.

The platform McEntee's crew had created on *Birmingham* sloped down toward the stem at a uniform angle of roughly five degrees. Ely would not actually start fifty miles out at sea. The revised plan was for *Birmingham* to leave the Navy Yard, steam downriver to Hampton Roads, and turn north into the Chesapeake Bay for twenty to thirty miles. With the ship underway, Ely would launch into the wind and turn south, retracing the ship's outbound route until he landed in a cleared space back at the Navy Yard. He could thus stay within sight of land for the entire flight, although finding an emergency landing spot might be challenging if things did not go smoothly.[3]

The morning of November 14 brought drizzle, fog, and 8–10 mph winds, but the experiment could not wait. The circumstances that had combined to furnish the Navy with a ship and an aviator were not likely soon to recur. Ely had exhibition dates to keep, *Birmingham* would be ordered to other stations, and Secretary of the Navy Meyer's long absence from Washington was over.

It is impossible to overstate Ely's courage in attempting the flight. He had never practiced with the *Hudson Flyer*, and its controls were still adjusted for the shorter Bud Mars, who had been flying it for several weeks. Nor had Ely ever had the opportunity to simulate the launch by tasking off down a ramp that ended in a significant drop. The last flying machine launched from a watercraft had been Samuel Langley's 1903 Aerodrome, which had crashed spectacularly. Still, having just experienced a full month of failure to meet public expectations at Chicago, Youngstown, Belmont Park, and Halethorpe, Ely was reportedly "determined to prove . . . that he could accomplish more than had been expected of him."[4]

He was by then an experienced aviator, intimately familiar with the mechanics of flight. To generate sufficient airspeed, he would need to dive off the end of the remarkably short platform toward the water. Once he was going fast enough, he would be able to pull out of the dive. It was a matter of precise timing. The *Hudson Flyer*'s old-style two-planed front elevator, "although it gives a less steady machine, gives quicker control in rising from the dip than the newer machines of the Curtiss and the Wright types," Lieutenant Wright reported to Meyer.[5]

But if Ely miscalculated, there was a real risk of plunging into the bay. Chambers, concerned for Ely's safety, arranged to borrow a pneumatic life preserver from the commander of the torpedo boat USS *Bailey*. No provision was made to protect the aviator from being run down by the moving warship, however.[6]

Captain Chambers, Lieutenant Wright, and Assistant Constructor A. W. Chantry came aboard *Birmingham* in the morning, along with Ely, Curtiss publicity man Frank Tillman, and three assistants: Cy Perkins, A. D. Cook, and William H. Hoff, the last of whom had recently replaced Ely's cousin Orson Harrington as his chief mechanic. Also aboard was a reporter from the *New York*

World's Washington office, apparently in a nod to the paper's role in bringing about the experiment. At 11:30 a.m., while Ely and his team worked to install the motor sent from Baltimore, *Birmingham* pulled away from the dock, followed by two destroyers, USS *Roe* and USS *Terry*, and torpedo boats *Bailey* and USS *Stringham*.

When *Birmingham* and her escort reached Point Comfort at the mouth of Hampton Roads at 12:35 p.m., Capt. William Fletcher gave the order to drop anchor to wait out a rainstorm. At 2:48 p.m. the ship was moving once more, and preparations began for the flight; but the persistent rain was too heavy. Seven minutes later, Fletcher gave the order to drop anchor again.[7]

Ely climbed onto the seat of the *Hudson Flyer* to test the motor while *Birmingham* lay at anchor. The plan was to make the flight while the ship was underway, but when Ely spun the motor up to full speed the powerful backdraft blew directly in the face of the helmsman, and it was doubtful whether he would be able to steer the ship while the airplane's motor was running. Conditions were unlikely to improve, and the ship was unlikely to move. Ely concluded that his only option was to try the experiment from the ship at anchor. "Without previous warning," wrote Chambers, "Mr. Ely gave the signal to let go and at 3:16 p.m., he quickly flew off the platform without having any assistance from the ship whatever in the matter of speed, or lifting power."[8]

Lieutenant Wright's report picks up the narrative: "The engine was tuned up and gave a pull which eight men [holding onto the wings] could hardly resist. When the signal was given [by Ely] to let go, the machine darted down the incline in a perfectly straight line, the front wheel not going six inches from the [painted] center line." Ely was airborne.[9]

As expected, the moment he passed the platform's edge he plummeted toward the water. As he picked up speed, he pulled back on the wheel to rise. Ely elevated his front planes almost from the start; yet he kept hurtling downward.

Multiple factors were to blame. The aircraft was heading into the wind, roughly northeast, but without the benefit of the additional lift from the airflow that the ship's forward motion would have imparted. The bamboo rod on which Ely was pulling had been lengthened to accommodate the shorter arms of Bud Mars, and the unaccustomed life preserver made operating the machine awkward.

The airplane, continuing to drop, began to nose upward. But there was no more room to maneuver. According to Wright, "The propeller touched the water as the machine started to lift, splintering the end and leading edge of one blade for a distance of about two inches, and just catching the end of the other blade."[10]

Remarkably, the machine now rose, "very similar to the swoop of a gull," Wright reported. Ely could no longer see clearly through his rain- and spray-covered goggles and had become disoriented, so with a curving sweep southward he headed for the first land he spotted: Willoughby Spit, about two miles distant, on the southern side of the entrance to Hampton Roads. Within five minutes he had made a safe landing on a sandy beach.[11]

As the *New York World* reporter described it, "When it was seen that Ely had really flown away from the deck of the big slate-colored war dog, the whistles of the craft in the roads let loose shrill after shrill and the sailors sent up a cheer."[12]

Chambers, accompanied by the Curtiss mechanics, set out at once in a motor launch to retrieve Ely. They found him unhurt and took him in the launch back to *Birmingham*, arriving at 4:15, and transferring later to the *Roe*, which took them back to Norfolk Navy Yard.[13]

The wire story that ran across the country exulted: "Aerial navigation proved today that it is a factor which must be dealt with in the naval tactics of the future." The *New York World* sent a telegram to its correspondent aboard *Birmingham*, instructing him: "In your story tonight give credit to *World* Aero [for] the idea of the flight adopted by the Navy." The newspaper indeed took credit for the success—its page-two headline read "*WORLD* PLAN TO FLY FROM SHIP TO LAND WINS IN NAVY TEST"—but to Ely went the glory, as front pages across the country reported the "epoch-marking event."[14]

For Chambers, Ely's flight was "more than he had anticipated," and he was "confident that the time is near when all scout cruisers will be equipped with a number of aeroplanes." Lieutenant Wright's official report concluded that Ely's experiment could not truly be considered successful as a "practical naval flight," given the inadvertent contact with the water and the risk that such contact posed to future flights. Nevertheless, said Wright, given that public interest had been aroused and "the aviator got away and made a landing safely . . . the flight was a success." Wright further believed that, absent a general call for marine aviation, the Navy needed to assume responsibility for developing naval aeronautics. He recommended the purchase of two each of the current Curtiss and Wright airplanes, assignment of a pair of officers to each type of machine, "and that the services of experienced [civilian] aviators be obtained to instruct the officers detailed for that duty."[15]

Chambers, in his own preliminary report, reached the same conclusion. The first step had been taken toward proving the practical value of airplanes to the Navy. Secretary Meyer could not continue to turn a jaundiced eye. The USS *Chester* plan could proceed.[16]

Curtiss was not present to witness Ely's pioneering flight. He was in Hammondsport that day, worn down by fifteen months of patent litigation. The dispute with the Wright brothers still dragged on, with all efforts at settlement unsuccessful.[17]

The day after the historic *Birmingham* flight, a *Washington Times* reporter wrote that, "wonderful achievement" though it was, Ely's flight solved only "half of the problem, in that the aviator did not return to the ship from which he started." The following week Ely made the front page again. In a story that ran nationally, the *New York Times* reported that he had received a letter from Secretary Meyer congratulating him on the flight from USS *Birmingham*, and inquiring whether he might "attempt a flight from the deck of a war vessel and return, landing again on the deck." Ely, the story continued, announced that he would make just such a trial "at San Diego in about two months."[18]

In fact, Meyer's letter, which Chambers had drafted, said nothing about further experiments, and Ely had no immediate plans to travel west. The letter read, in its entirety, as follows:

Sir:

On behalf of the Navy, I desire to thank you for the services you have performed, gratuitously, in demonstrating the possibility of using an aeroplane, from a ship, in connection with the problem of naval scouting.

So far as is now known at this Department, you are the first aviator in the world to have accomplished this feat, and I congratulate you upon your successful flight from the U.S.S. "BIRMINGHAM" on November 14, 1910. The fact that you made this flight under adverse conditions of weather, with a comparatively old aeroplane, and while the ship was not underway, increases the information sought and the satisfaction of the Department with your efforts.

Your achievement, which was actuated by purely zealous and patriotic motives, is much appreciated. A copy of this letter will be sent to the headquarters of the United States Aeronautical Reserve.

Respectfully,
(signed) G. v L. MEYER,
Secretary of the Navy[19]

The shipboard landing proposal reported in the *New York Times* was sheer invention, likely by Jerome Fanciulli. But Chambers clearly believed such a feat was possible. Following the *Birmingham* flight, he wrote that it "would be comparatively easy, in smooth water, for a scout to steam head to wind at the proper speed to allow for the gradual approach and descent of an aeroplane to a platform located aft."[20]

And Ely was willing to try it. Immediately after the *Birmingham* flight, he reportedly said that he was confident that he could "alight on a warship, either standing still, or under way," and that a platform with a similar five-degree grade would be sufficient "to take up the momentum of the machine, and bring it to a gentle stop." Chambers, who recognized the unique opportunity presented by the anticipated congressional appropriations to secure funding for "aviation experiments," let Ely keep the pneumatic life preserver for use in a future flight onto a ship.[21]

CHAPTER 15

STAR-DUST FALLING

RALPH JOHNSTONE, the trick bicyclist, had spent his entire adult life as a paid performer. Impressing crowds was what he did. For the first two months of his employment with the Wrights he was as cautious as they directed him to be. But when Walter Brookins crashed at Asbury Park on August 10, 1910, and attendance immediately doubled, anyone could see what spectators really wanted. Johnstone and Arch Hoxsey began staging "a thrilling aerial duel of sensational performances" and "flirted gaily with death in order that no one might be able to say that one was more skillful than the other."[1]

Wilbur Wright cautioned his fliers against reckless performances, but Johnstone and Hoxsey continued to take increasingly greater risks—including flights in the rain and at night. Hoxsey claimed that he sought only to show how safe and reliable Wright airplanes were, but what the Star-Dust Twins and Brookins were doing on a routine basis was clearly "stunt" flying.[2]

At the Harvard-Boston meet in September 1910, Johnstone and Brookins crossed a line. Johnstone, knowing President Taft was on the ground, threw in several "graceful dips and tip-tilted air turns" as a salute. Five days later he and Brookins engaged in some "fancy aeroplaning": "Johnstone's favorite act was to indulge in steep slides, shutting his engine almost off, then suddenly shooting down until he almost touched the ground, then sweeping up like a bird in flight." Brookins performed a maneuver in which he made a series of short turns, standing his biplane almost on edge and descending steeply as he made a complete circle within a few seconds. Hoxsey and Johnstone copied Brookins' signature stunt, which came to be known as the "spiral glide." Crowds showed up demanding it.[3]

Evidently none of the fliers understood the tremendous stress placed on the fragile wings by such tight turns. Wilbur Wright fully realized the danger, though. He "feared for their safety and ordered them to desist." But Wright's warnings went unheeded.[4]

In Europe, during the week of the Belmont meet in New York, four aviators died in crashes within five days. By the time of Ely's USS *Birmingham* flight, close to seven years of professional powered flight in the United States had resulted in only one death: Tom Selfridge's in September 1908 as Orville Wright's passenger at Fort Myer. All the Curtiss and Wright aviators had survived falls, some quite serious, but with only minor injuries at worst.[5]

At an exhibition in Denver, Johnstone was said to have promised to attempt no "stunts" in the thin air. Indeed, on November 16, the first day of flying, Brookins and Johnstone made no sensational flights. Johnstone explained afterward that he "could not get his machine off the ground until he had increased the power much more than is necessary in lower altitudes." (Due to the reduced atmospheric density at higher elevations, an aircraft requires a higher airspeed to achieve as much lift as at sea level.) On one landing he collided with a fence, breaking a wing; but the damage was apparently soon repaired.

During his first flight the next day, Johnstone went through "his usual program of dips and glides." As he prepared to take off for his second flight, the crowd was reportedly amused to see a small dog challenging his machine, barking furiously. Johnstone avoided the dog, rose to a height estimated at five hundred to eight hundred feet, and went into a spiral glide. "With his [wings banked] at an angle of almost 90 degrees," the papers reported, "he swooped down in a narrow circle, the aeroplane seeming to turn almost in its own length." As he started the second circle a wing support, perhaps weakened from the previous day's collision, gave way, and his wings "folded up as though they had been hinged." The airplane swerved "like a wounded bird" and plunged toward the earth. Less than six months after learning to fly, Ralph Johnstone became the first American professional aviator to die while piloting an airplane.[6]

On the day of Johnstone's death, Ely, his star still on the rise, was flying at an exhibition in Raleigh. From there he traveled to Birmingham, Alabama, where for possibly the first time in his flying career he gave a ride to a passenger, which suggests that he had the Rheims racer or the eight-cylinder engine from the *Hudson Flyer.* It was not a spur-of-the-moment offer; arrangements had reportedly been made a day or two earlier for Mary Corner Evans Sullivan to ride with either Ely or James "Jimmie" Ward, who was making his first major flights for Curtiss. Mrs. Sullivan, the newlywed daughter of a local rector, became the first woman in the South to fly.[7]

In late November 1910, Curtiss and Jerome Fanciulli announced plans to establish a winter camp and training school in southern California. They hoped that the publicity would increase their chances of selling airplanes to the government the following spring. Fanciulli wrote to Captain Chambers on November 29 that Curtiss, on his way to the West Coast, was "arranging to give a great number of experiments which he believes will be of interest to military experts and of value in demonstrating to Congress the necessity for appropriations for aviation purposes." He further reported that Curtiss had that day "written to the Secretary of the Navy"—and similarly to the secretary of war—"formally offering to instruct an officer in the operation of the Curtiss machine. If an officer is assigned for such instruction, he would be actively identified with the experiments Mr. Curtiss proposes to make in the vicinity of Los Angeles" and would receive "wide publicity" regarding his "progress and activity." In his letter to Secretary of the Navy Meyer, Curtiss wrote that he was making the offer "with the understanding that it involves no expense for the Navy Department."[8]

The next day, Meyer issued the Secretary of the Navy's annual report. Chambers had apparently convinced him to suggest that Congress appropriate $25,000 for airplane experiments.[9]

Chambers advised Curtiss on December 19 that the commander-in-chief of the Pacific Fleet, Rear Adm. Edward B. Barry, had been authorized to detail a ship to cooperate in airplane experiments during a San Francisco meet in January. The only function such a ship could conceivably serve was as an aviation platform. Curtiss and Fanciulli now had an opportunity to show Congress the practicality of shipboard landings.[10]

The aviation committee for the January 1911 San Francisco meet invited local son Bud Mars to inaugurate the event by flying over the city and landing in Union Square. Mars accepted. He was also reported to have "volunteered to undertake the experiment of landing on the deck of a warship." Mars, it was further stated, "will probably be chosen for the most 'scary' experiments." But although virtually no one knew it, Mars had just concluded his final flight for Curtiss, ending an association that had lasted for less than nine months.[11]

Mars and his old friend, pioneering balloonist Tom Baldwin, had secretly decided to embark on an around-the-world exhibition, beginning in Honolulu and focusing on the Far East. Despite fabricated tales of earlier performances in Asia by the "man-dragons" Ely and Whipple Hall, airplanes were essentially unknown across the Pacific. As of December 16, the first day of a Fresno exhibition at which Mars was flying for Curtiss, Hawaiians understood that Mars and Baldwin would "usher in the New Year in Honolulu by going after some altitude records." On December 21, Mars sailed west.[12]

It is unclear exactly when Mars told Curtiss he was leaving, if indeed he ever did. The news did not break until Christmas Eve, at which point the story was that Mars felt no compulsion to honor engagements made for him by Curtiss, from whom he merely leased a machine, as opposed to contracts made by "his agent, who had his power of attorney."

Curtiss, who valued loyalty above all else, was furious. Feeling that Mars had "cast discredit upon the Curtiss camp," Curtiss announced in a formal statement to the press that "Mars, whom

I taught to fly, will no longer be connected with the Curtiss camp. . . . I will fulfill all the contracts made by me for Mars with the San Francisco aviation board. More daring and possibly more competent men will do all the things Mars promised to do, and there is no doubt but that all world's records will be broken in January." He later wrote to Fanciulli, "Mars got away, owing us considerable."[13]

Ely, unaware of the impending drama involving Mars on the West Coast, continued to give exhibitions without incident throughout the Southeast. After performing in Mississippi, he, Douglas McCurdy, and Jimmie Ward were scheduled to fly in New Orleans for three days. High winds kept them on the ground on all but Friday, December 2, when the three "gave some splendid flights," including a "graceful glide" by Ely from a reported height of a thousand feet.

On Monday, December 5, Ely left for Columbia, South Carolina, where two days later, in "almost ideal" conditions, he made what was reported to be the state's first exhibition flight. McCurdy joined him there, as did a representative of the Georgia-Carolina Fair Association, still seeking damages in connection with Mars' failure to appear the previous month. A writ of attachment was served on both their airplanes, released only after the meet directors posted a $1,000 bond.[14]

By Sunday, December 11, conditions in New Orleans had improved enough for McCurdy to return and demonstrate aerial target practice using oranges. Ward, who also flew, reported that conditions aloft were "excellent."[15]

On Monday, December 12, Ely and Mabel arrived in Atlanta; McCurdy and Ward reunited with them the following day. With winds on Thursday, December 15, approaching 30 mph, only Ward, the least experienced of the aviators, attempted to fly. On his second attempt he reached a height of fifty feet, his machine "bucking like a newly saddled bronco."[16]

In the course of a test flight on Saturday, the closing day of the exhibition, a piece of pipe broke loose from Ely's machine and damaged the propeller. He glided the airplane to a smooth landing "without injury to either himself or further damage to his machine," then switched to another machine with a 60-hp motor to race an automobile and "swept over the finish lines a few feet ahead of the auto."[17]

Fanciulli traveled to Atlanta, where he "settled up with the boys." He reported to Curtiss that "Ely was prepared to do a lot of kicking, but when he found out that our records gave his figures a more rosy look, he was very well satisfied. He put in a plug for more commission, but I told him that was a matter we [Curtiss and Fanciulli] had not decided upon although we had discussed it. . . . Should you decide to give him any increase you better have him agree in writing that all expenses incident to filling a contract should be included in the amount deducted from the gross, prior to the division of the net."[18]

Looking ahead to 1911, Fanciulli expected that the price Curtiss could charge for exhibitions would drop by 50 percent. To generate interest, Fanciulli proposed "putting a monoplane and biplane in competition"; presumably he anticipated that Ely, who had been asking to fly the Curtiss monoplane, would pilot the single-surface machine in those races.[19]

Had Mars not abandoned the team, Curtiss might have kept Ely flying exhibitions in the Southeast for the winter. But with Mars gone, Curtiss summoned Ely west to fly the new Model D-III biplane at the big meets in Los Angeles and San Francisco.

Ely jumped at the chance. He and Mabel arrived in Los Angeles on December 23, six days after the Atlanta exhibition ended. He was quoted as calling the new Curtiss machine "a dandy." Curtiss had told Fanciulli that "the old type controls are not as easy to handle, in any way, as the new," and that difficulty might be experienced only "by those who have always flown the old ones," but Ely apparently did not take long to master the new controls.[20]

In a Christmas Eve letter to Curtiss, Fanciulli reported: "Recent developments in aviation circles here [in New York] indicate that the Wrights have become even more unpopular. . . . We have received publicity almost every day from [Ely's] Naval stunt and we have our lines out for next year's business in splendid shape. . . . I hope that Ely's trip to the coast will pay for itself." Fanciulli had told Ely "to send one of his mechanics to Hammondsport, in order to cut down expenses," but Ely had taken the man along to California anyway. "I believe Ely would pay his expenses if you put it up to him, because he said as much to me in Atlanta."[21]

Meanwhile in Washington, news broke in mid-December that the Navy had accepted Curtiss' offer to provide complimentary flying lessons for one officer, effectively beginning a public-private partnership that would become a hallmark of military aviation. On December 13, with Meyer again out of town, Assistant Secretary Winthrop formally authorized Chambers to identify a volunteer student.

Lt. Theodore G. "Spuds" Ellyson, a 1905 Annapolis graduate and former submarine commander, was desperate to escape his monotonous posting at the Newport News Naval Shipyard. With fortuitous timing, Ellyson had written to Meyer on December 16 requesting assignment to duty in connection with aviation. He learned of his acceptance on Christmas Eve, and on December 27, he received formal orders to rendezvous with Curtiss at Dominguez Field, and then to confer with the aviation meet committee in San Francisco. According to Chambers, Ellyson was selected as "a well balanced man who would be able to assist in building up a system of aviation training in the Navy."[22]

The second Dominguez Field meet opened on December 24, 1910, with altitude and speed demonstrations. Ely placed second in the hourly duration contest and the quick-start competition. In the latter, he required more than two hundred feet to get off the ground, highlighting how critical his dive from the *Birmingham* platform had been in order to generate speed. Yet, in a good omen for any future attempt to land on the confined deck of a ship, Ely won the precision landing contest when he rolled to a stop exactly on the start/finish line, thirteen feet to one side of the center mark. Given that his airplane lacked any brakes to speak of, this was no small feat.[23]

On Christmas Day, Ely finished third in the bomb-throwing contest, close behind Charles Willard and Frenchman Hubert Latham. But it was Hoxsey who drew the attention. Defying the Wrights' proscription against Sunday performances, he flew to just under eight thousand feet with ease and then descended so rapidly that he "seemed to be falling." He remained in the air for over two hours in all, performing stunts "while the crowd went wild in its appreciation of his efforts."[24]

The following day, before a crowd of 75,000, Hoxsey flew to a jaw-dropping 11,474 feet, well over two miles high, claiming a world record for the Wrights by nearly a thousand feet. There was not much else for the crowd to cheer that day: winds of 40 mph wrecked Latham's Antoinette monoplane and caused Willard to suffer a small crash, while Ely experienced engine trouble.[25]

On December 27, Ely, fighting winds estimated at 30 mph, had his first head-to-head race against a Wright aviator. He defeated Phil Parmelee in a five-lap contest by thirty-two seconds, and then again in a one-lap contest by six. Englishman James Radley, flying shortly afterward in his Blériot, unsurprisingly turned in a time faster than either of the biplanes.

Ely also set what was probably a personal altitude record of an estimated two thousand feet, well below Hoxsey's 6,800 that afternoon. And Hoxsey for the first time participated in a bomb-throwing contest, featuring California oranges as projectiles. Rising two hundred feet higher than Willard or Parmelee, he cavalierly ate one of his orange-bombs in mid-flight. Even with a three-point penalty for "willful and malicious waste of ammunition," he came in just six points behind Willard, the winner.[26]

The following day, Ely competed once more against Radley and Parmelee. All three flew the five-lap course faster than they had the day before, but the results were the same: Radley first, Ely second, and Parmelee third.[27]

On December 30, Hoxsey, in another foray into the rarified air of high altitude, flew to ten thousand feet and circled Mount Wilson, some forty miles away. Radley, Ely, and Parmelee repeated their "air derby," with identical results. Afterward, in a new 80-hp "racing machine," Curtiss flew a single lap slightly faster than Ely's average time. But the pecking order remained unchanged: Blériot monoplane, 60-hp Curtiss biplane, 30-hp Wright.[28]

Parmelee and Brookins flew over the grandstand scattering red carnations, while Ely finished third in a special contest for crossing the finish line in front of the grandstand as close to the spectators as possible. He also took the new Curtiss "racer" for a spin, clocking a time roughly one second faster than Curtiss' the day before.[29]

Hoxsey set a new American endurance mark, staying up for three and a quarter hours, as he sought unsuccessfully to break his own altitude record. He fought his way through "air holes" that caused his engine almost to stop. When he landed, he told newsmen that he had found it difficult to breathe even at the relatively unexceptional height of seven thousand feet.

December 31 ended the most spectacular year in aviation's short history. The mayor declared it Los Angeles Aviation Day and urged everyone to come see the birdmen perform experiments that would "result in making navigation of the air practical." Half an ocean away, Bud Mars made the first airplane flight in the Hawaiian Islands. But in the end, it was not a day for celebration.[30]

As the year drew to a close, John Moisant, the winner of the Statue of Liberty race, had set his sights on the 1910 Michelin Cup, a $4,000 prize for the year's longest flight over a closed circuit. He was in New Orleans on December 30 when Frenchman Maurice Tabuteau moved into the lead by covering more than 363 consecutive miles, spending nearly eight hours circling a field in Pau, France. With scarcely a day left to best Tabuteau, Moisant borrowed a powerful Blériot and planned to spend all day December 31 circling in the air.[31]

The winds were fairly strong when Moisant went up shortly after nine o'clock in the morning. Just before landing to make the official start, he was blown sideways. Perhaps because the auxiliary gasoline tank that had been added for the long flight altered the balance Moisant was used to, or because the machine itself was unfamiliar to him, the airplane suddenly "turned head downward." The spectators "saw the aviator pitch clear of the machine, falling like a plummet fully 100 feet, lighting on his head." Two months and a day after winning the Statue of Liberty race, America's hero died on a field outside New Orleans.[32]

The Dominguez Field aviators learned of Moisant's death well before their one o'clock start. While some of the others began a desultory exhibition within sight of the grandstand, Hoxsey rose once more into the sky, reaching for the undiscovered country beyond 12,000 feet. He had been gone over an hour when spectators spotted him spiraling downward to about two thousand feet and then going into a nosedive. The Wrights' manager, Roy Knabenshue, who was in front of the grandstand, described to the Wrights what happened:

> About 800 feet the machine commenced to turn over, that is, the left wing came down [and] the right wing rose higher and higher until it was upside-down, and continuing to turn in this manner, came again into a normal position at about 75 feet from the ground. . . . [Hoxsey] could have very easily . . . saved himself, but I firmly believe the poor boy had been either dead in his seat or in some manner beyond control, for the machine continued to turn, striking head-on—the left wing first, and of course the whole apparatus was a complete wreck.[33]

Curtiss saw the crash. It was the first time he had witnessed an aviation fatality. He is said to have ordered his crew to tear down the bunting and lower the flags on their hangars.[34]

Hoxsey had not been engaged in stunt flying when he died, as Johnstone had been. And although his crash during the altitude attempt was at first attributed to unusual atmospheric conditions, the intact barograph revealed that he had climbed to barely seven thousand feet before inexplicably descending. Ely, who witnessed the crash, reportedly believed that it was due to "heart failure or 'mountain sickness,' caused by the high altitude." He had reportedly experienced such sickness himself at Sheepshead Bay, at a much lower elevation.[35]

Crashes of powered, heavier-than-air machines resulted in more than thirty deaths in 1910. Although only three were in the United States, the aviators who died—Johnstone, Moisant, and Hoxsey—were among the best known in the world.[36]

In 1908, under the guidance of managing editor John Trevor Custis, the *Philadelphia Inquirer* had launched "Birdman," the country's first newspaper aviation column. Three days after Ralph Johnstone died, the pseudonymous columnist declared: "There is too much commercialism in aviation today. There is too much risking of life for the sake of giving a good show." Following the deaths of Moisant and Hoxsey, he wrote: "The year just ended has been marked by a reign of folly in American aviation." Calling for an immediate end to acrobatic flying, he added: "Show the world that aviation, while still a dangerous sport, is not a system of suicide, and thousands will fly, where now [only] a handful, other than paid professionals, dare more than look on."[37]

Over the final eight months of 1910, Ely appeared at exhibitions in eighteen states. The more frequently he flew, no matter how cautiously, the greater the likelihood that something would go wrong. America's hero and the Star-Dust Twins, gods in machines, had all died within two months of achieving their greatest fame. Johnstone's death could be ascribed to sheer recklessness, but Moisant and Hoxsey had not been attempting sensational stunts.

Ely could hardly help sensing his own mortality.

Eugene Ely and sister Maidie, ca. 1889 *Collection of Lois G. Durr*

The extended Harrington family. Gene kneels third from the right, in front of the fence; Maidie sits in the front row, second from right; Julia stands behind her, holding the hand of their mother, Emma. Orson Harrington Jr. stands at the far left. Williamsburg, Iowa, ca. 1895. *Williamsburg (Iowa) Historical Society*

Eugene Ely, 1910

Eugene B. Ely Scrapbooks, Naval History and Heritage Command, S–005, NH #77598

The Lakeview-Likely Auto Stage service, with Ely at the wheel, Lakeview, Oregon, fall 1908 *Eugene B. Ely Scrapbooks, Naval History and Heritage Command, S–005*

Ely and his mechanic finishing the California Grand Prize Auto Race, Santa Rosa, California, May 9, 1909 *Eugene B. Ely Scrapbooks, Naval History and Heritage Command, S–005*

Glenn Curtiss, aviator, and Jerome Fanciulli, passenger, Dominguez Field, Los Angeles, California, January 11, 1910 *Jerome S. Fanciulli Collection, McDermott Library, Special Collections, University of Texas at Dallas*

One of Ely's early attempts to fly. To the right, Whipple Hall looks on, dressed in a dark suit and standing next to an unidentified man in a white shirt. Medford, Oregon, June 1910. *Southern Oregon Historical Society (Medford, Ore.)*

Ely in his new four-cylinder Curtiss machine, Hammondsport, New York, August 1910 *Eugene B. Ely Scrapbooks, Naval History and Heritage Command, S–005*

Mabel Ely's first flight, with Bud Mars, Sheepshead Bay, Brooklyn, New York, August 19, 1910 *Eugene B. Ely Scrapbooks, Naval History and Heritage Command, S–005*

Mabel poses at the wheel of Ely's airplane, with Maidie as her "passenger." Rock Island, September 1910. *Eugene B. Ely Scrapbooks, Naval History and Heritage Command, S–005*

Ely (*left*) and his father, Nathan Dana Ely, Rock Island, Illinois, ca. September 13–18, 1910 *Eugene B. Ely Scrapbooks, Naval History and Heritage Command, S–005*

Mabel and Eugene Ely, Rock Island, September 18, 1910 *Eugene B. Ely Scrapbooks, Naval History and Heritage Command, S–005*

"Hauling machine up the mountain to jump off" (Mabel's annotation). Roanoke, Virginia, September 22, 1910. *Eugene B. Ely Scrapbooks, Naval History and Heritage Command, S–005*

Mabel, Ely, and Glenn Curtiss just before the Chicago to New York "race," October 9, 1910 *Eugene B. Ely Scrapbooks, Naval History and Heritage Command, S–005*

Ely with Curtiss, preparing to take off. The trailing edge ailerons and the fabric under the upper wing's outer sections indicate that the machine is *Banshee*. Chicago, October 9, 1910. *Eugene B. Ely Scrapbooks, Naval History and Heritage Command, S–005, NH #77547*

America's Famous Aviators: The Curtiss Exhibition Team, Chicago, October 1910

Estate of Whipple S. Hall

Ely flying the Curtiss single-surface machine, Belmont Park, New York, October 1910 *Naval History and Heritage Command, NH #77558*

Bud Mars (*left*) and Ely demonstrate the use of the anemometer to gauge wind speed. Belmont Park racetrack, Elmont, New York, October 1910. *George Grantham Bain Collection, Library of Congress, Prints and Photographs Division, 2014688523*

Ely at Halethorpe, Baltimore, Maryland, November, 1910

Eugene B. Ely Scrapbooks, Naval History and Heritage Command, S-005

Hamburg-America's SS *Pennsylvania*, with Curtiss biplane and the temporary flight deck that was never used, New York City, ca. November 11, 1910 *George Grantham Bain Collection, Library of Congress, Prints and Photographs Division, 2014688723*

Floating crane lifts the *Hudson Flyer* onto the foredeck platform of USS *Birmingham*. Norfolk Navy Yard, Virginia, November 14, 1910. *Eugene B. Ely Scrapbooks, Naval History and Heritage Command, S–005, NH #77550*

USS *Birmingham*, with the *Hudson Flyer* poised on the platform, November 14, 1910 *Eugene B. Ely Scrapbooks, Naval History and Heritage Command, S–005, NH #1831*

World's first flight off a ship: Ely departs USS *Birmingham*. Hampton Roads, Virginia, 3:17 p.m., November 14, 1910. *Eugene B. Ely Scrapbooks, Naval History and Heritage Command, S–005, NH #77601*

Ely stands on board USS *Roe* after completing his flight off USS *Birmingham*. Hampton Roads, Virginia, November 14, 1910. *Eugene B. Ely Scrapbooks, Naval History and Heritage Command, S–005, NH #77555*

Ely and Mabel, Birmingham, Alabama, ca. November 21–22, 1910 *Eugene B. Ely Scrapbooks, Naval History and Heritage Command, S–005, NH #77491*

Curtiss and Ely (*center*) inspect the platform on USS *Pennsylvania* with Captain Pond (*far left*) and officers. One of the center guide rails is clearly visible. San Francisco, California, January 9, 1911. *Keith-McHenry-Pond Family Papers, BANC MSS C-B 595, The Bancroft Library, University of California–Berkeley*

World's first shipboard landing: Ely on final approach to the stern deck of USS *Pennsylvania*. San Francisco Bay, 11:01 a.m., January 18, 1911. *Eugene B. Ely Scrapbooks, Naval History and Heritage Command, S–005, NH #76510*

Ely in the final seconds before landing on USS *Pennsylvania*. San Francisco Bay, 11:01 a.m., January 18, 1911. *Naval History and Heritage Command, NH #1385*

Ely about to touch down on the stern deck of USS *Pennsylvania*. The guide rails and sandbag braking system are clearly visible. San Francisco Bay, 11:01 a.m., January 18, 1911. *NHHC, S-005, Eugene B. Ely Scrapbooks, Naval History and Heritage Command, S-005, NH #82737*

Ely shortly after landing on USS *Pennsylvania*. Three of the five braking hooks are visible under the central skid. Pontoons are visible under the lower wing, and a splash board to buoy the nose is attached behind the front wheel. Ely is wearing partially inflated bicycle inner tubes as a simple flotation device. San Francisco Bay, January 18, 1911. *Eugene B. Ely Scrapbooks, Naval History and Heritage Command, S–005, NH #77588*

Ely takes off from USS *Pennsylvania*. The crosswind is evident from the smoke. San Francisco Bay, 11:58 a.m., January 18, 1911. *Eugene B. Ely Collection, Naval History and Heritage Command, UA 450.07*

A hero's welcome. Still wearing the rudimentary flotation device, Ely shakes hands with Lieutenant Walker, already slated to become one of Curtiss' first students at North Island. Selfridge Field, San Francisco, January 18, 1911. *Eugene B. Ely Scrapbooks, Naval History and Heritage Command, S–005, NH #77567*

Ely shakes hands with Major O'Neil as Charles Willard looks on. The USS *Pennsylvania* sailor's cap ribbon is visible on Ely's left arm. Selfridge Field, San Francisco, January 18, 1911. *Eugene B. Ely Scrapbooks, Naval History and Heritage Command, S–005, NH #77566*

Mabel examines the medal commemorating Ely's USS *Pennsylvania* flight. San Francisco, California, January 1911. *Eugene B. Ely Scrapbooks , Naval History and Heritage Command, S–005, NH #77529*

Curtiss and Ely race. San Diego, California, January 1911. *Eugene B. Ely Scrapbooks, Naval History and Heritage Command, S–005*

Left to right: Ely, Lieutenant Walker, Captain Beck, Lieutenant Kelly, and Major Squier at Fort Sam Houston, San Antonio, Texas, April 1911 *Von Schaezler/Ely Scrapbooks, Collection of William and Paul Henderson and Ann Stamets*

A mustachioed Ely arrives in Eureka, California. *Left to right*: Norman DeVaux, mechanics P. J. Rooney and William Hoff, Ely, Mabel, and Mabel's sister Mercedes ("Mercy"). May 26, 1911 *Eugene B. Ely Scrapbooks, Naval History and Heritage Command, S–005*

The wreckage of Ely's airplane, Macon, Georgia, October 19, 1911 *Eugene B. Ely Scrapbooks, Naval History and Heritage Command, S–005, NH #77605*

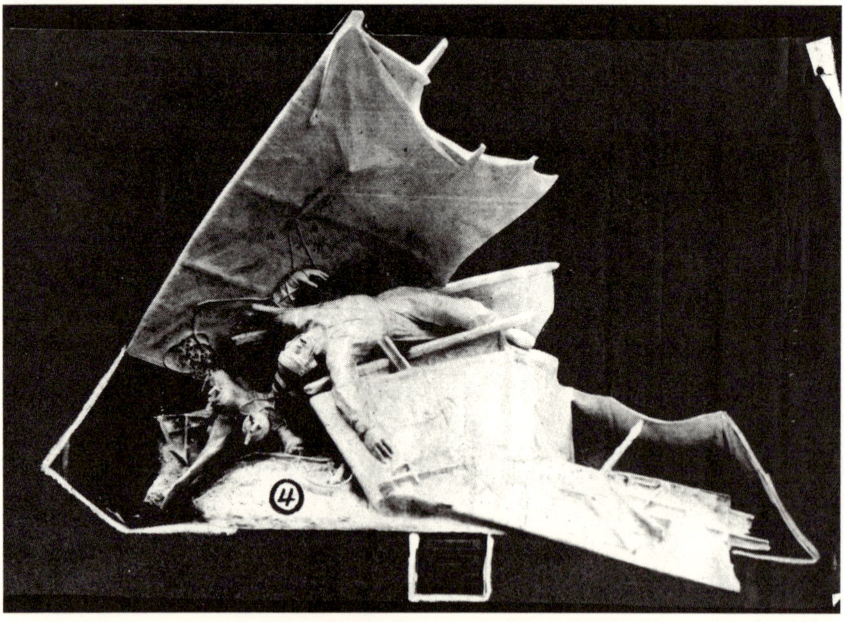

Paul Roger-Bloche, *Monument aux aviateurs*
Eugene B. Ely Scrapbooks, Naval History and Heritage Command, S–005

President Herbert Hoover presents Col. Nathan D. Ely, USA (Ret.), with the Distinguished Flying Cross, posthumously awarded to Ely's son. Washington, D.C., February 16, 1933. *Von Schaezler/Ely Scrapbooks, Collection of William and Paul Henderson and Ann Stamets*

“Nothing but the world before him.” San Diego, California, January 1911.
Eugene B. Ely Scrapbooks, Naval History and Heritage Command, S–005, NH #77532

CHAPTER 16

THE DOVE TO THE ARK

WHEN THE *New York World* first announced that Douglas McCurdy would fly off *Kaiserin Auguste Victoria* in November 1910, the plan ignited controversy. Skeptics doubted that flying machines could ever be useful in naval warfare. Even if the experiment succeeded, some still saw an obstacle: "the difficulty, or rather impossibility, of landing on a war vessel after the aeronaut has once soared from the deck." But Secretary Meyer's official report at the beginning of December proposed otherwise, and Assistant Secretary Winthrop authorized the use of a Navy ship for experiments to be conducted under Curtiss' guidance in San Francisco Bay.[1]

The experiment would take place during the San Francisco international aviation meet, scheduled to begin on January 7, 1911. Lt. Paul W. Beck of the Army Signal Corps, who had been in charge of the Army's dirigible at the first Dominguez Field meet, was the meet's secretary. Second Lt. John C. Walker Jr. of the 8th U.S. Infantry, stationed at the Presidio, was detailed as Beck's assistant. The organizing committee guaranteed ten days of flying, even if that meant extending past the scheduled closing date of January 16.

The meet's principal stated aim was to demonstrate the airplane's military capabilities—in other words, to catch the eye of Congress. With a program boasting bomb-dropping "using real explosives," wireless sending and receiving, airplane reconnaissance, "special military and naval events," including fence-scaling and two military bands, and the centerpiece—landing on the deck of a warship—the meet would shatter attendance records.[2]

"Either Eugene Ely or Glenn Curtiss will make the flight," reported the *San Francisco Chronicle*. The *Tacoma Times* elaborated, saying that an aviator would take off from and land back on a vessel, which would "be in motion all the time." Years later, Charles Willard maintained that he would have been selected to make the attempt, had his machine not "had a French Gnome engine—and Curtiss wanted [a Curtiss] plane and engine to do the test."[3]

On December 31, 1910, the San Francisco committee received a telegram from the Curtiss Company formally designating Ely as the aviator to attempt the ship landing and takeoff. Lieutenant Beck, in his capacity as military liaison, called on Rear Admiral Barry to finalize arrangements for the flight.[4]

The armored cruiser USS *Pennsylvania* (not to be confused with the Hamburg-American "floating zoo" steamship of the same name), at anchor at San Francisco with the rest of the fleet, was identified as the most suitable vessel for the experiment. Under the command of Capt. Charles F. ("Frog") Pond, "a peppery and valiant little man," *Pennsylvania* sailed to nearby Mare Island Naval Shipyard on January 4 to be fitted with a landing platform.[5]

Meanwhile, Lieutenant Ellyson had arrived in Los Angeles to meet Curtiss, as ordered. The two traveled together to San Diego to inspect North Island, a sand flat in San Diego Bay, as a possible venue for flying instruction. They then went on to San Francisco, arriving on January 5. Willard, whose contract with Curtiss was due to expire in roughly two weeks, arrived the following day.[6]

Ely had arrived one day before Curtiss, and the San Francisco papers gushed over his first return to the Bay Area since his 1909 driving days, when he had held "first rank among the level headed, iron nerved auto drivers of the city." Whenever the "former San Franciscan" and "hero of the great fire" flew, old friends were said to accord a "honking" ovation from a temporary auto row set up at the Tanforan racetrack just south of the city, where Ely had raced automobiles a year and a half earlier.[7]

Ely was "one of the best liked of the aviators," admired for his calm demeanor. "He never appears to use a word too much in his speech, and he gives his orders to 'let go' . . . with a single wave of the hand. Seated at his lever [*sic*], he begins to soar with the nonchalance of a man seated at the wheel of an automobile." Asked about his intentions for the San Francisco meet, Ely expressed confidence that he could land on the ship. "I would not attempt the flight," a newspaper story reported him saying, "if I did not think that it was practical." He felt it was "only a matter of practice in accuracy landing."[8]

"Most difficult of all aviation feats heretofore attempted is the one which Eugene B. Ely proposes to try," the national press trumpeted. "He is not a spectacular"—that is, risky—"flier. He exercises extreme care and attempts none of the daring feats which caused the deaths of Johnstone, Moisant and Hoxsey." The ship landing would nevertheless present its own risks and would require much more skill than the USS *Birmingham* launch.[9]

Ely would fly the powerful Curtiss Model D-IV military machine, a prototype for the "war machine" (so called because it was being designed for the War Department). He had flown it before, but he needed time to practice his precision landings. He set up his airplane at the temporary aviation field that had been created for the meet adjacent to Tanforan. For the duration of the exhibition, it was designated "Selfridge Field," in honor of Lt. Tom Selfridge.[10]

On the grounds of the field, the 2nd Battalion of the 30th U.S. Infantry, under the command of Maj. Joseph P. O'Neil, set up camp in four tidy company rows of twelve tents each, while a machine-gun platoon occupied tents on the right flank of the main body. All was "in readiness" for the "reconnaissance tests" to be made by "officers from biplanes."[11]

Assistant Naval Constructor Lt. (jg) Richard D. Gatewood, in charge of building the *Pennsylvania* platform, had a budget of $500, nearly twice the cost of the lumber used on *Birmingham*. In an autobiography published nearly four decades later, Rear Adm. Rufus F. Zogbaum Jr. included a colorful, if perhaps exaggerated, account of the construction of the aviation platform. Captain Pond, according to Zogbaum, was livid at the noise caused by the sawing and hammering directly over his cabin. "'Is it necessary,' he wanted to know, his round face getting redder, 'to make so much god-damn noise over my head when I have work to do? letters to write? ship's business to attend to? Is it necessary to mar the snowy planking of my quarter-deck—above all to drive *nails* into it? Can't you think up some other way to fasten this god-damn thing down?'" Wanting "nothing to do with the silly experiment," Pond placed Lieutenant Zogbaum, his young gunnery officer, in charge of logistics for the "damned flying-machine."[12]

The 119-foot platform was thirty feet longer than the one used on *Birmingham*, had half as steep a slope, and was situated aft rather than forward, meaning that Ely would land on the stern of the ship. It ended in a fourteen-foot fantail, sloping down at a thirty-degree angle. The fantail would act as a ramp to protect him from being slammed against the stern on approach by any sudden gust of wind. It would also give him more speed on takeoff.

The real innovation lay in the design of an arresting device. Surprisingly, that key feature was not a part of the original design. Ely, who had triumphed in precision-landing contests, evidently expected simply to coast to a stop without crashing into the ship's superstructure.

Captain Pond's report explains the original concept:

> The platform bore at its forward end a canvas screen . . . intended to catch the aviator and his machine should all other means fail, and ten feet from its forward end, a two-inch by twelve-inch plank extending across the face of the platform. These . . . were very crude devices, and had they come into use would probably only have caused serious if not fatal injury. . . . Abaft [that is, closer to the stern than] the solid plank stop and spaced about 6 feet apart were fitted two canvas screens about twenty inches in height. These, together with the slight slope of the platform, were the only means provided in the original construction to check or stop the flight of the machine.[13]

With the platform effectively shortened twenty feet by these barriers, Ely would scarcely be able to stop in time unless he killed his engine in flight and glided in. If he needed to abort the landing, he would have no time to restart the engine.

"It was very evident," the Pond report continues, "that something more was needed, and after several consultations with Messrs. Curtiss and Ely, during which several schemes were considered and rejected, it was finally decided to adopt a system of sandbags such as had been successfully used to check automobiles at racing meets." That system became the forerunner of the modern tailhook system for arresting aircraft on carrier decks.[14]

The ship's deck log reflects that Curtiss and Ely came on board the anchored *Pennsylvania* on January 9, the day after the ship had left Mare Island, and "inspected [the] aviation platform." As is apparent in photographs of that visit, a pair of twelve-inch-high guard rails lined the port and starboard edges of the platform, to prevent the machine from veering off either side. Parallel to those rails, six feet to either side of the center line, ran a pair of four-inch-high "guide" rails, between which the aviator would land. Twenty-two lengths of rope, each secured by a pair of fifty-pound sand-filled bags "accurately weighed to ensure uniformity of action," would be stretched across the guide rails at three-foot intervals. Five metal hooks projecting about four inches downward from the airplane's central skid would engage some or all of the ropes, bringing the machine to a quick stop.[15]

It is unknown who the designer (or, more likely, designers) of the arresting system were; various names, including those of Ellyson and of Curtiss aviators Hugh A. Robinson and Charles Willard, have been associated with the solution. Willard, a skilled engineer, had been working on the problem in the days leading up to Ely's attempt. The meet committee's original proposal had called for up to three separate landing attempts, including one in which a naval officer would ride along as a passenger. Willard, recognizing that Ely had already been selected to make the initial attempt due to "the standing he [had] with the Navy," hoped to make the second or third. Years later, Willard reported that his manager had been negotiating with a San Francisco newspaper publisher to sponsor him to make one of those flights for a fee of $2,500—"enough to motivate me," the aviator said. In the end the additional landings were scrubbed, and Ely, as Willard put it, "made the flight for free."[16]

Willard's design was ingenious. His machine was already equipped with a "fail safe" braking mechanism: a pivoting metal hook that could be lowered to dig into the ground. At Selfridge Field he began experimenting with adapting it to shipboard use. Later he recalled that

> the solution began taking the configuration of a series of rope barriers stretched across the field, and anchored to sand bags. [But w]hen I experimented, I found that as the wheels passed over the ropes they would become depressed, making it difficult for the hook to engage.
>
> This was overcome by improvising two 2 × 4 planks about six inches inside of the tread of the main wheels, running the length of the simulated deck-field. In the span between the 2 × 4's the ropes were raised taut by four inches when the wheels passed over the depressed ropes outside the 2 × 4's. With the inside span of ropes pre-stressed, it was not difficult to engage them with the hooks.[17]

Although Willard's design was similar to the system ultimately employed on *Pennsylvania*, there was an important tradeoff. Willard's system kept the ropes raised and taut, making it easy for his hook to catch them—but only if he landed the machine dead center, with its front wheel inside the guide rails and its rear wheels straddling them. By contrast, the twelve-foot separation between the guide rails on *Pennsylvania* gave the aviator a much wider target—since the rear wheels were only six feet apart—but then the airplane would stop only if the ropes, after the wheels had depressed them, immediately sprang back up into the path of the hooks.[18]

As opening day of the "greatest aviation meet in history" approached, the city rushed to complete construction of a grandstand for 16,000 people. Bidders at auction paid a premium of $540 to select the first twenty-five seating boxes, and a special "automobile grandstand" was constructed opposite the main one, allowing owners who wished to watch from their vehicles to "secure reserved space for their machine" by purchasing a numbered ticket for one of the six hundred parking stalls. A "picked platoon of city police and a squad of plainclothesmen" would be on hand to "preserve order."[19]

Frenchman Hubert Latham thrilled spectators on opening day with a flight over Golden Gate Park. Englishman James Radley buzzed the warships at anchor in the bay, and Ely, Willard, and the Wright fliers flew circuits of the field. On Sunday a "record-smashing crowd of 200,000" taxed the city's transportation system, but high winds grounded the monoplanes of Latham and Radley. Ely "rose nicely" in his biplane until an object (variously described as a pipe or a nut) broke loose and "mixed in with the propeller," snapping it; he glided to a "clean and light landing." The propeller was replaced in time for Ely to take part in a mock attack on "Camp Selfridge" in the afternoon, "swooping down" and mimicking dropping bombs while soldiers "rushed hither and yon, grabbing their trusty rifles and their trusted blank cartridge boxes." As night fell, "the glow of many campfires could be seen," where tired spectators warmed themselves "while waiting to board something on wheels and ride home."[20]

Stormy weather and continuing "lively" breezes inhibited flying for some days. *Pennsylvania* was anchored in "man-o'-war row"—just northwest of the present-day western end of the San Francisco–Oakland Bay Bridge and very close to the San Francisco waterfront—and the public was eager to know when Ely would make the flight. He was quoted expressing confidence that he could do it, saying that he had prepared carefully, but that the attempt depended entirely on the wind. "I shall not make the attempt until the weather seems to be as near right as possible."[21]

In a front-page "birdmen's wives" feature, a reporter remarked how calm Mabel Ely and Lena Curtiss seemed to be while watching their husbands aloft. Mabel was quoted as admitting that she would be "all stirred up" when Ely finally made the ship flight, although she was quick to clarify that she would not be *afraid*: "Only I am so anxious for him to succeed."[22]

Curtiss later wrote: "I regarded the thing as most difficult of accomplishment. Of course, I had every faith in Ely as an aviator, and knew that he would arrive at the ship without trouble, but I must confess that I had misgivings about his being able to come down on a platform but four feet wider than the width of the planes of the aeroplane, and to bring it to a stop within the hundred feet available for the run."[23]

Meanwhile, Curtiss made arrangements for his winter camp on North Island in San Diego Bay. Called an "aviation school," the camp was designed primarily to instruct the officers the War and Navy Departments had chosen for training. On January 16, originally scheduled as the meet's closing day, with the timing of the ship experiment still uncertain, Curtiss left San Francisco for San Diego, taking Ellyson with him.[24]

That same day, the wind settled enough for Lieutenant Beck to move forward with the first true test of the airplane's usefulness as a scout. An "invading" force (Major O'Neil's battalion) had ostensibly landed at Half Moon Bay, southwest of the aviation field, and was camped at Tanforan, while a "defending" force of cavalry and artillery moved south toward them from the Presidio. The invaders sent out two airborne scouts from Selfridge Field: Walter Brookins and Ely. Army observer 2nd Lt. George E. M. Kelly, riding as Brookins' passenger, took aerial photographs from 1,200 feet, sketched the landscape, and tried in vain to spot the defenders hiding in the Sutro forest. Ely, "the most willing aeroplanist of the meet, nearly turned the trick." He flew due north and came within half a mile of the defenders' position before returning to the field, having assumed that they would have advanced farther from the Presidio than they had. His return flight was "one of the most picturesque sights of the meet." Spectators could estimate his speed "by the rapid increase in the size of the biplane as it came scooting out of the north, like an impersonation of Boreas," the Greek god of the north wind.[25]

Ely's biplane was already on the way to its hangar when the Army requested a mock battle on the field, and he "proved his obliging disposition by asking that his aeroplane be brought back." He rose into the air "from the north end of the field, sailing south toward the camp." On sighting him, Major O'Neil "gave the signal for the call to arms. But before the troops could be aligned and could fire at the flying death, which took forty-seven seconds, Ely had crossed the camp" and could easily have annihilated it. He demonstrated conclusively that an airplane could move fast enough to rout a ground force, even one that expected its arrival.[26]

The favorable weather continued, and on January 17 it was announced that the ship-landing attempt would occur the following day. If all went well, Ely would fly to *Pennsylvania* and return in time for the scheduled afternoon program at Selfridge Field. That same day the House of Representatives passed the 1911 Army appropriations bill. It totaled $93 million, of which a generous $125,000 was provided for airplanes.[27]

There is no record of Ely practicing on land with the rope-and-sandbag arrangement, although Willard's design was certainly available to him. No one knew whether the hooks would grab as they were designed to do. In case of disaster, the machine had been fitted with under-wing pontoons for flotation and, just behind the front wheel, a splash board to jerk the nose up on contact with the water. But Ely's only personal safety equipment was a padded helmet and two partially inflated bicycle tubes crisscrossed around his chest; he had found that the pneumatic life preserver from Chambers overly restricted his movements.[28]

The morning of January 18, Mabel, armed with binoculars and a folding camera, joined a crowd of dignitaries and photographers on board, while crewmen, seeking an unobstructed view, "clung to the sides of the stacks and . . . the military masts and far out onto the lofty signal yards," creating the appearance that "a great swarm of bees had settled on the ship's spars and upperworks."[29]

After some discussion, it was agreed to keep the ship at anchor. *Pennsylvania*'s bow was pointing northwest by north, with USS *Maryland* anchored one thousand yards off her starboard quarter and USS *West Virginia* five hundred yards off her port bow. To either side off *Pennsylvania*'s stern, "a swarm of small boats" jockeyed for position to watch the "conquest of the air," while the crowd along San Francisco's waterfront was estimated variously between 75,000 and over 400,000.[30]

Ely took off from Selfridge Field, about ten miles from the ship's position, at 10:45 a.m. and flew north at 60 mph at an altitude of about 1,500 feet. The wind was behind him from the south, a "good, stiff breeze" once he got up a few hundred feet, and the air was cold but not incapacitating. Making his way through skies described as "cloudy and smoky and hazy," he could not see the ships until he was within about two miles of them. A mile from his target, he veered right and dropped in salute from a thousand to about four hundred feet over *Maryland*—mistaking her for the flagship USS *California*, which had left the harbor days earlier. Then he banked west, passing low over *West Virginia*'s bow, and turned sharply to complete a circle that brought him onto final approach directly off *Pennsylvania*'s stern.[31]

With seconds to go, Ely aligned himself with the guide rails and slowed to about 40 mph. A breeze had kicked up, estimated by Captain Pond as 10–15 knots three points on the starboard quarter (that is, roughly 15 mph from the east-southeast), and as it blew against the stern of the ship, the sloped fantail redirected it upward. This would substantially increase the difficulty of landing: Ely now had the wind coming from behind and below him and slightly to his right, making the airplane unstable at lower ground speeds and pushing it up and toward the left.

Curtiss aviator and engineer Robinson later remembered crouching beside the platform and waving Ely off because of the wind, in the manner of a landing signal officer on a modern carrier. Ely either did not see him or did not agree. He pointed his machine slightly to the right and continued his approach.[32]

Photographs show the airplane coming in nearly dead center, the right wing a bit higher as a result of the updraft. Though Ely corrected quickly, the hooks sailed over the first eleven ropes. But they caught the other eleven, and airplane and aviator came to an abrupt stop within thirty feet, with plenty of room to spare. Ely remarked later that the landing would have been smoother had the sandbags been a little lighter.[33]

Pennsylvania blared its siren, and ships in the bay blasted their horns and whistles in salute. Sailors, reporters, photographers, other aviators, and dozens of invited guests swarmed the platform. The wireless station at Selfridge Field received a telegraph message from the ship: "ELY AT 10:59 LANDED ON THE *PENNSYLVANIA* AS PRETTY AND LIGHT AS A BIRD," and the entry in the ship's deck log read: "Eugene Ely of the Curtiss team alighted upon the aviation platform of this ship at 11:01 a.m., a feat that never before had been successfully accomplished."[34]

By Captain Pond's estimate, less than two minutes had passed between the time the sailors first sighted Ely and the moment he touched down, "and no one had imagined he would make the landing on the first turn." Fifty years later Zogbaum marveled, "He flew down the port side of the ship, banked steeply into a left turn and settled his plane into a 'groove' directly astern, as expertly as any modern carrier pilot does today. He came into his landing without benefit of signal officers to wave him on or off. He . . . made as beautiful a precision landing . . . as has ever been witnessed." Pond reported that, given the size and weight of the machine, the speed of approach and the effect of the wind, "the marvelous skill, accuracy of judgment and quickness of brain of the aviator may be imagined. The slightest error of judgment meant serious, if not fatal, injury to both the aviator and his machine."[35]

"You dear, brave boy!" Mabel reportedly exclaimed as she ran to embrace Ely. The sandbags and crash-protection measures were cleared away, and the airplane was turned around for the return flight. A photograph shows a jubilant Mabel fastening a small bouquet, said to have been a corsage of violets, to the front elevator plane. The party posed for photographs and then adjourned to the wardroom for, as Mabel remembered it, a champagne toast at which Ely drank only ginger ale—a refreshment "which he didn't need," Zogbaum wrote, "for he was as calm and casual as if walking down Market Street." Pond's assessment was much the same; he reported "nothing damaged in the least, not a bolt or a brace started, and Ely the coolest man on board."[36]

Almost exactly an hour after the landing, the party returned to the platform, from which the guide rails had been pried up and discarded. Ely mounted to the seat of his airplane. What happened next is recorded in the deck log: "At 11:58 the Aviator departed from the ship in his flying machine without an accident." As Ely accelerated off the platform, he dipped to increase his speed, but this time he kept clear of the water. By 12:12 p.m. he was back at Selfridge Field.[37]

He dismounted, a USS *Pennsylvania* sailor's cap ribbon tied around his left arm. Soldiers—the same men on whom Ely had pretended to drop bombs days earlier—hoisted him to their shoulders and carried him to commanding officer Major O'Neil's tent. Later that afternoon, Captain Pond, his wife, and a party of civilians arrived by automobile at Selfridge Field, having been ferried back to shore. Ely's flight was "the most important landing of a bird since the dove flew back to the ark," Captain Pond was quoted as saying.[38]

Throughout and afterward, Ely displayed nothing but calm modesty. The grand narratives that appeared later under his byline were mostly, if not entirely, fabricated by others. Reporters seeking sensational quotes from the aviator about his epic flight soon discovered that "you'll not make him talk of it, except as a scientific consideration, if you try for an hour."[39]

Public acclaim for Ely was immediate and universal: the story made newspapers across the country. The *San Francisco Examiner* laid out the military implications of the feat: "EUGENE ELY REVISES WORLD'S NAVAL TACTICS." Ely had demonstrated that a naval squadron could carry an aerial scout, by means of which the squadron could determine the disposition of an enemy fleet that was otherwise out of sight from even the crow's nest. Captain Pond, previously a skeptic, declared himself "on record as positively assured of the importance of the aeroplane in future naval warfare, certainly for scouting purposes."[40]

Ely's demonstration was widely cited as advancing the practical side of aviation. The *New-York Tribune* said, "It has now been finally proved that there are no insurmountable difficulties in utilizing aeroplanes for the Navy in practical work."[41]

The *Philadelphia Inquirer*'s weekly "Birdman" column had devoted its first two installments that year to decrying "the foolish side of aviation." Following the *Pennsylvania* flight, the paper now saluted Ely. "Having considered the wrong kind of flying it is with all the more pleasure that we can emphasize the value of the right kind. Ely's kind is the right kind. His work of the past two weeks has been instructive, constructive and progressive. He has demonstrated that phase of aeroplane development that is attracting the earnest consideration of every great nation in the world, namely, its application to military and naval service."[42]

Less discerning reporters expressed disappointment that "the seeming ease of the whole performance lessened the spectacular effect." But to Ely, the point was to show the "general utility of the machine" by demonstrating that a landing on a ship was practicable. "It was probably the novelty of the performance and not the scientific features that caused such a sensation. I was no doubt given a great deal of credit that I did not deserve," he was reported to have said several months later. He saw no great difficulty in the mechanics of the landing. "It was easy enough," he was widely quoted as having said upon alighting at Selfridge Field. "I think the trick could be successfully turned nine times out of ten." Captain Pond agreed in his formal report: "The extreme accuracy of control, as demonstrated by Ely, while perhaps not always to be expected to the same degree, was certainly not accidental and can be repeated and probably very generally approximated to."[43]

Curtiss, though he had missed the historic event, appreciated as much as anyone what Ely had achieved: "I don't think there has ever been so remarkable a landing made with an aeroplane as Ely's, and probably never so much store put by the mere act of coming down in the right place. A few feet either way, a sudden puff of wind to lift the aeroplane when it should descend, or any one of a dozen other things, might have spelled disaster for the whole undertaking, deprived the daring aviator of a well earned success, and the world of a remarkable spectacular demonstration of practical aviation."[44]

CHAPTER 17

WATER AND AIR

FOR THE REST of the San Francisco exhibition, Ely was a genuine, if unwilling, celebrity. "Ely's performance commanded the world's attention not less than the passage of Halley's Comet or the discovery of the North Pole," declared the *San Francisco Call*. Newspaper stories, breathless with exaggeration, recounted his heroism during the Great Fire; schoolchildren wrote essays about him; amateur poets ground out doggerel about the historic landing. When he was discovered in the audience at a motion-picture screening of the USS *Pennsylvania* flight, the crowd was said to have "cheered for several minutes until he rose and bowed." One editorial marveled at how radically Ely's life had changed since his chauffeuring days a few years earlier: "Now he's a world hero. The clubs are open to him. So are many homes. He is feted and toasted and medals are proposed for him." Soldiers at Camp Selfridge chipped in, along with *Pennsylvania*'s sailors and the San Francisco aviation committee, to order a commemorative medal depicting the moment of landing. It was presented to Ely four days after the flight, at a Selfridge Field ceremony that also featured the unusual sight of a military squad "presenting arms" to a civilian. Ely was said, characteristically, to have appeared extremely uncomfortable with the attention.[1]

On January 25, the San Francisco meet's last day, winds reportedly gusted at 25–35 mph. Wright fliers Walter Brookins and Phil Parmelee went up for short flights in front of a small crowd, after which Brookins reportedly declared it the most dangerous flying he had ever done. Ely and Charles Willard flatly refused to fly and left directly for a meet in San Diego.[2]

During December, Jerome Fanciulli had kept Douglas McCurdy and Jimmie Ward busy appearing at exhibitions throughout the Southeast. By January McCurdy had set his sights farther south: the *Havana Post* was offering a $5,000 prize to the first aviator to fly nonstop from Key West to Cuba. At nearly 110 miles, this was double the greatest distance ever flown over water and nearly five times the length of Louis Blériot's 1909 Channel crossing.

Fanciulli contacted Captain Chambers, who had long been interested in the question of reliable aerial navigation, to request Navy cooperation in safeguarding any aviator who made the attempt. Chambers notified Lt. Commander Yates Stirling Jr., captain of the destroyer USS *Paulding*, which was then stationed with the Atlantic Torpedo Fleet, that the commander's duties might soon include rendering assistance in the Key West–Havana flight.

As Chambers explained to Stirling: "The great difficulty in such a flight is to steer a straight compass course in the air, the leeway or drift being the uncertain quantity. Improved compasses and other instruments will soon simplify the problem, but I don't think that those who will be at Havana will be provided with them. [The aviators] will be all right on a clear day if they have a line of torpedo boats to sight on, for their horizon is very much extended while aloft and your boats should be amply supplied with distinguishing bunting."[3]

McCurdy, who had announced his intention to make the Key West attempt as soon as weather permitted, envisioned another purpose for a naval escort. He had arranged to have pontoons attached to the wings of his machine for safety, enabling it to land on the water in the event he had to ditch. This made it, in effect, a crude hydroairplane, although not one that could take off again from the water. He suggested to Stirling that a hinged platform be fitted to *Paulding*'s stern. McCurdy's plan was to land not on the ground but in Havana harbor, where he would have the airplane hoisted onto the ship. He would then fly off the ship and land on shore, as Ely had now done twice. It was the next step in proving how useful airplanes could be to the Navy.[4]

The day after Ely's historic San Francisco flight, the Army selected the officers Curtiss would train in San Diego: Lieutenant Beck, secretary of the San Francisco meet, and Lieutenant Walker, Beck's assistant. Lieutenant Kelly, who had ridden with Brookins in the troop-scouting experiment in San Francisco and been hailed as the "first aerial scout," soon followed them. Because the Army had sought—and received—five times the appropriation for aviation that the Navy had, it could assign more men for aviation training.[5]

But before Curtiss set about instructing anyone, he took some time to revisit the problem of designing a true hydroairplane. Such a machine, he had written for the Aerial Experiment Association (AEA) in 1908, would be "indispensable for war purposes." At that time, he and McCurdy had tinkered with a catamaran design and with hydrofoils, but those designs met with equal lack of success. Now he proposed to repurpose the body of an existing machine and give it a boatlike hull to replace the wheels employed on land.[6]

Curtiss, Lieutenant Ellyson, and the newly arrived Army flight students took up the problem. Over the course of ten days, they considered and rejected some fifty designs, all employing multiple hydroplaning surfaces in place of wheels. Finally, Curtiss started over. He sketched a single narrow, shallow pontoon with the front curved upward, which a local fabricator constructed out of light spruce. On January 26, 1911, making his first trial flight, Curtiss lifted clear of the water for fully five seconds. He repeated the test successfully, returned to his starting point, and landed without incident. "I have succeeded in solving the one problem the Secretary of the Navy regarded as the most difficult," journalists quoted him saying, "and the one necessary to make the aeroplane of value to the Navy."[7]

Captain Pond said he considered the Curtiss "feat" an illustration of how rapidly the technology for naval warfare was developing. An editorial assessment appeared in the *Oakland Tribune*: "Curtiss' achievement at San Diego was a material advance in naval aviation over that of Ely, for he proved that the ship's deck was not an essential factor to success in aerial scouting at sea under favorable conditions." An article in *Aeronautics* agreed, calling the hydroairplane "a still greater step" than Ely's flight.[8]

Chambers had shown rather less enthusiasm for Ely's *Pennsylvania* landing than he had for the more scientific *Birmingham* test; he regarded the *Pennsylvania* flight as having been "arranged for the spectacular." The situation at San Francisco had been different: there was no looming race involving Germany, and no pressure to establish the basic value of airplanes to the Navy. Chambers' recommended $25,000 item was already part of the appropriations bill, on track to be approved. He did not need Ely to succeed, as he had a couple of months earlier; he did not witness the flight—his work prevented him from traveling to California—and he sent no letter of commendation.[9]

For Chambers, airplanes were "equipage," analogous to a battleship's small motorboats—in effect, flying boats. He noted that Curtiss had "already made some independent experiments with aeroplanes fitted to rise from and land on the surface of the water." Boats were hoisted out of the water using winches and davits; airplanes could be handled in the same way. So while it was possible to land an airplane on the aft deck of a ship, it might not, Chambers thought, be either practical or necessary. "If the condition of the wind and sea should render such a landing inadvisable," he wrote, "the aviator could land in the water under the lee of the ship and be picked up by a boat's crew." Evidently Chambers, like the rest of the world, could not envision the flattop design of a ship dedicated exclusively to carrying aircraft.[10]

Two days after Curtiss' successful hydroairplane test, he and Ely flew in the San Diego meet, at which Ely reportedly executed a reckless stunt:

> Flying at great speed, the biplane reached a point about 500 feet above the field. There it appeared to pause. Then one side deflected dangerously toward the earth, but the machine did not lose poise. Once again it swept around in short circles,

> nearing the ground. Just when it seemed that another sweep would dash the machine down upon the heads of the spectators, the pilot righted the craft, and with one long, graceful sweep settled to the ground. Ely had added to his laurels by the thrilling "spiral dip" that has made the Wrights famous.[11]

The daredevil maneuver seems so out of character that it would be tempting to dismiss the description as mere journalistic invention, had not Ellyson written to Chambers, "Ely gave the prettiest exhibition of flying that I have ever seen, but if he keeps on taking the same chances he won't last six months."[12]

The next day, Ely reportedly did it again: "Aviator Ely gave several exhibitions of the death-defying dip and executed spiral glides as thrilling and dangerous as the one which resulted in the death of Arch Hoxsey." (The reporter evidently confused Hoxsey with Johnstone.)[13]

The explanation may be that Ely was not executing the dangerous spiral glide at all—rather, that he was merely landing in a way that, to spectators, *looked* like a spiral glide. A later reporter described him performing what was certainly a landing maneuver:

> Dropping a couple of hundred feet as he approached the starting course . . . Ely, when almost over the heads of the spectators, suddenly threw the rudder of his machine, warped the transverse stability planes [ailerons] and like a gull about to alight swung around a narrow circle with his control planes so elevated that the aeroplane was robbed of much of its onward energy. Dropping lower as he again swung around toward the starting course he glided swiftly to earth, shutting off the power as the wheels of the machine touched the ground and elevating the front plane as though to rise again, thus bringing the [machine] to a stop without breaking a wire or tearing an inch of cloth of the supporting planes.[14]

In both this maneuver and the spiral glide, the aviator banked the machine into a tight descending spiral. In the "gull" method described by the reporter, the aviator pointed the machine's nose up to shed momentum; in the spiral glide, the aviator pointed the nose down, causing the machine to accelerate. The spiral glide was a spectacular and dangerous trick; the "gull" method was an effective technique to slow the airplane for landing.[15]

Both maneuvers could appear dangerous to spectators—and to reporters. Ely was later quoted as saying: "If it were not for the fact that flights are made much more spectacular by the evolutions which are necessary in alighting, I would simply rise into the air and amuse myself for an hour or more five or six hundred feet above the earth and out of danger. It is in alighting that the aviator's skill is tested and the spectacular features of aviation witnessed."[16]

By late January, no other aviator had indicated a desire to fly across the Straits of Florida to Cuba, which made McCurdy, like Ely in Chicago, the sole entrant in a "race." Still, his attempt at a seemingly impossible challenge made front-page news. By the time the winds at Key West and Havana had calmed sufficiently, the prize had reportedly grown to $8,000.[17]

McCurdy launched at 7:22 a.m. on January 30. Chambers had sent him the pneumatic life preserver that Ely had declined to wear for the *Pennsylvania* flight. Gaining the open ocean under a cloudless sky, McCurdy became the first aviator ever to fly out of sight of land. There, in the absence of any fixed object to use as a point of reference, the sea appeared to him as a "huge vertical picture," and he experienced a "strangely beautiful" mirage: ships just beyond the horizon appeared "suspended upside-down in midair."[18]

At 9:17 a.m. McCurdy passed over USS *Terry* and came in sight of *Paulding*, the last of the six ships that had been positioned at intervals between Key West and Havana, when the lubricating oil in his motor ran out. The bearings burned up, the motor stopped, and he had no choice but to ditch. At 9:33 a.m., twelve miles from his goal, his airplane alighted on the water. The underwing pontoons or the gas tank kept it afloat, but the tail had been damaged in the landing and the machine was badly unbalanced. The motor went underwater, tipping the front elevator planes high into the air.

McCurdy, unhurt, barely got wet. As sharks began circling him *Terry* came to the rescue, and *Paulding* arrived a few minutes later. The hinged platform on *Paulding* proved ineffective, and the airplane had to be skidded vertically up the side of the ship, sustaining further damage in the process.

Nevertheless, Stirling, impressed by McCurdy's ability to steer a compass course over open ocean, concluded his report: "To alight in the ocean, as he did, unhurt, and his machine only slightly damaged, was more wonderful than if he had safely landed [in Havana]." The *New York Times* expressed the prevailing view: "McCurdy will presumably receive a medal, the general sentiment being that his performance is just as meritorious as if he had made the remaining ten miles."[19]

The value of McCurdy's flight to the Navy was obvious. A lubricating-oil issue could be dealt with, and a machine equipped with Curtiss' hydroairplane pontoon could rise again from the water after repairs were made. A winch system could be devised for lifting machines from the water onto the deck of any number of ships. There would be no need in the future, so the thinking went, for specialized hinged platforms or the sort of "false deck" Ely had required.

Within the span of ninety days, naval aviation had become a practical reality.

CHAPTER 18

TWISTS AND CORKSCREWS

THE NATIONAL PRESS had lauded Ely as "the bright particular star of the San Francisco aviation meet." What he might choose to do for an encore soon became a matter of intense speculation.[1]

In January 1911 he was halfway through his one-year contract with Curtiss and looking to his future. On the day of Douglas McCurdy's celebrated Havana flight, Ely wrote to Captain Chambers:

> *Dear Sir:*
>
> *According to the newspapers, the Army has an appropriation for aeroplanes and if the Navy has none, it will get one soon I suppose. There will probably be an experimental station and someone who is competent will be needed to carry on the work.*
>
> *If you will let me know how to go about it, I shall try to be the one selected. Mr. Curtiss has proved that an aeroplane can rise from the water and we knew before that one could alight without trouble. I have proved that a machine can leave a ship and return to it, and others have proved that an aeroplane can remain in the air for a long time, so I guess the value of the aeroplane for the Navy is unquestioned.*
>
> *Let me hear from you soon and oblige,*
>
> *Yours Sincerely,*
> *Eugene*[2]

Ely was incorrect in one respect: while the House had passed the Army appropriations bill, the Senate would not do so for another week. But even if the Navy received the entire $25,000 it had requested—and spent none of it on machines—that would be nowhere near enough to compensate Ely for a year of supervising experimental work instead of flying at exhibitions. Lieutenant Ellyson reported to Chambers that Ely was "very anxious to get the head of the Navy experimental station and told me that he was going to write to you about it. He would be a fine man for the job but I think that he expects a salary about four times as much as the government would ever give him." Chambers responded promptly: "Will try to arrange for Ely's employment but I'm afraid it cannot be done on terms satisfactory to the Department."[3]

The Navy was sending officers to learn from Curtiss at no charge. Those officers would eventually be able to pass on their acquired knowledge at no additional cost to the government. And even supposing Chambers had been looking for a civilian candidate to run experiments, he might not have been impressed with Ely following Ellyson's report of his recent flying.

Chambers was deluged with requests from Naval Academy midshipmen, officers, enlisted men, and other civilians to be assigned to the Navy's "Aerial Corps." He responded along these lines: "We do not anticipate the formation of a separate aerial corps any more than a submarine corps or an ordnance corps. There are so many officers and enlisted men carried away by the present craze for aviation that if all were encouraged to form a separate corps we would have difficulty in finding people to run the more important thing—the Navy itself."[4]

Curtiss continued to question whether to remain in the exhibition business. He wrote to Jerome Fanciulli in February 1911: "The Wrights have gone out of the exhibition business, notwithstanding that they made big money." (In fact, the Wright Exhibition Company was not dissolved until November 1911.) "While I do not say it outright," Curtiss continued, "still I believe we can make more money selling machines and granting licenses to customers to use them at $150 per day of flights, than we can trying to monopolize the exhibition business." Ultimately, Curtiss deferred to Fanciulli as to whether the exhibition company should remain operational, while emphasizing his desire to avoid litigation "and also keeping in mind the worry connected with giving exhibitions. You can imagine," he wrote, "how the Wrights felt after the loss" of Ralph Johnstone and Arch Hoxsey.[5]

Remarkably, after more than fifteen months of exhibitions, no Curtiss aviator had yet been seriously injured. Chambers remarked on that safety record in the official Navy report he published in March 1911. But Curtiss understood that he might well lose one of his fliers at any time, and he would not allow the company's advertising to suggest a level of safety it could not deliver. "Don't brag [about having] no fatalities," he wrote to Fanciulli. "I am in constant dread & fear of something of this sort." He instructed Fanciulli to remove from all printed exhibition programs a claim suggesting that Curtiss machines were fundamentally safer than those of the Wrights.[6]

Fanciulli was therefore understandably surprised when he read in the *New York Herald* that Curtiss had said, "I have always impressed upon Curtiss machine aviators the necessity for extreme cautiousness, and we have a record of not a single death and no serious accidents with our machines." Stung by the perceived inconsistency between Curtiss' words and his instructions, Fanciulli clipped the *Herald* article and sent it to Curtiss, along with a curt note to the effect that, given this change in policy, he had canceled the order to eliminate the offending text from the company's exhibition programs. An irritated Curtiss returned the clipping, denying that he had made any such statement to the press and questioning how Fanciulli, himself a newspaper man, could reverse course on such an important matter based on what he read in the papers.[7]

The incident exposed twenty-three-year-old Fanciulli's insecurity and his perception that Curtiss was critical of his management skills. Fanciulli was suspicious that an unnamed "confidential informer" in the New York office was "knocking" him to Curtiss, and he complained about being "left out" of the manufacturing side of the business. Instead of apologizing for the overreaction, he offered his resignation.[8]

Curtiss declined the offer, denying any secret activity or distrust: "I don't know what you mean by being left out of the Aeroplane Co. Nothing has been done except to incorporate." His goal, he said, was to realize proceeds sufficient to pay for new airplanes, repairs, Fanciulli's New York office expenses, lawyers' fees, "and enough more to cover the possible judgments in the patent suit or other damage suits which may result from [an] accident." Following up a few days later, he reiterated that the exhibition business entailed so much risk that unless it "pays and pays big, we do not want it."[9]

But he evidently valued Fanciulli's acumen and began taking greater care not to offend him, having learned how sensitive his business manager could be to perceived slights. In a note to Fanciulli written a few months later, Curtiss quipped: "I'll bet you have a new stenographer, maybe a lady. I never saw so many letters from you in so short a time." He then felt compelled to scrawl an explanatory note in the margin: "Joke—don't take it as a reflection on you."[10]

While Ely waited for Chambers' reply, he returned to the exhibition circuit, beginning with a Sacramento engagement with Charles Willard scheduled for February 4–6. Willard made headlines with an opening-day flight in which he circled the dome of the state capitol in gale-force winds. The airplane was said to "roll and pitch like a ship at sea," and the aviator reportedly described the flight as the "most troubled" he had ever made. With conditions no better the following day, Willard nevertheless made two short flights, while Ely made one "long and fairly brilliant flight," ending with a landing in thick mud.

But there would be no third day of flying. According to the aviators, the promoters were contractually required to place $7,000 in escrow—$3,500 for each aviator for the three days—but the funds were not there, and they received only $1,000 each. The promoters argued that the aviators had not fulfilled their commitments and claimed to have paid Willard $5,000 for his flight around the state capitol. Willard, according to the local newspaper, responded that he "didn't receive 5000 cents for it." With no resolution to the dispute, the aviators unilaterally terminated the exhibition.[11]

Their next scheduled engagement was in Salt Lake City at Utah's first air show, beginning Saturday, February 11. In June 1910, Ely had faced strong winds in Billings, Montana, at an elevation of 3,200 feet above sea level, and had been unable to fly. At Salt Lake City, a thousand feet higher, Ely and Willard initially had the same problem. On opening day, strong winds made flying impossible. But the next day the two "raced through the air at great speed, turning and twisting" like "great birds," and "proved conclusively that aeroplanes [at this elevation] can be flown with great success."[12]

Ely was asked to comment on a rumor that he had been "engaged by the government to take charge of a school of aeronautics for army and navy officials." He said the story was news to him but conceded that "he was interested in the proposed government schools in aeronautics and hoped some day to be associated with these institutions."[13]

What he did not tell the reporter was that while he was in San Francisco he had met with Lt. John McHenry, Captain Pond's nephew, whom he had apparently met in January in connection with the USS *Pennsylvania* flight, and with Col. George A. Schastey, commander of the Coast Artillery Corps of the California National Guard. McHenry and Schastey had been developing the idea of a dedicated National Guard aviation squadron—to be instructed by Ely. On February 13 the news broke nationwide that the first aviation squad ever organized by a militia unit would have Ely at its head.[14]

Evidently caught by surprise when a Salt Lake City reporter showed him the announcement, Ely reportedly "said that he had received no notice of the completion of such arrangements," though he had expected "some action to be taken in the matter." Apparently recovering his balance, he was then quoted as calling the proposed squadron "a step in the right direction for the advancement of the science of aviation" and was said to be "heartily in favor of such squads." The *San Francisco Chronicle* correctly observed that in order to accept command of the squad, Ely would have to "enlist as a private and receive his promotion." Six weeks later Ely reportedly contributed a thousand dollars to a fund established for the coast artillery corps to obtain airplanes and wireless equipment.[15]

Before Ely left Salt Lake City, a discouraging reply arrived from Chambers. After offering belated congratulations on the *Pennsylvania* flight and regretting that he had been "unable to be there to grasp your hand and that of Mrs. Ely on that occasion," Chambers explained that the Navy's requested $25,000 would be used exclusively to buy "practice machines." Further appropriations were not anticipated. The new hydroairplanes would likely be assigned to the scout cruisers; each ship would use them "for instructional purposes whenever she gets in smooth water." Chambers went on to say that "it is valuable to us if we can demonstrate that smooth water is a good and sufficient aerodrome. I suppose they can readily be fitted so as to be hoisted out and in."

He said he foresaw no "independent experimental work for a long time," aside from small models or laboratory work. Perhaps some instruction stations would need a trained aviator, Chambers wrote, "but it will probably be a year before the entire scheme can be perfected and you may rest assured that we will keep you in mind for any opportunity that may arise." If, Chambers added, Ely had specific ideas about "how . . . the scheme should be organized," he would be happy to discuss those ideas and advise Ely "concerning the best thing to apply for."

In closing, Chambers wrote,

> *I understand you made some very risky flights out there at San Diego and I want to give you the advice of a friend to cut out the sensational features. I don't want to hear of your meeting the fate of those other fine fellows, Johnstone, Hoxsey and Moisant.*

> *Please remember me most cordially to Mrs. Ely and say that I shall expect her to continue keeping her eye on you for our sake and for the sake of the noble art of aviation.*[16]

The rebuke was clear. Chambers thought Ely had lost sight of the importance of demonstrating the capabilities of the airplane and was instead debasing the "noble art" with stunt flying and what Chambers disparagingly called "the hippodrome part of the business." A reporter who witnessed the performances of Ely and Willard at Salt Lake City saw in their "dips, glides, twists, [and] corkscrew turns" a demonstration of the aviator's "absolute control of the biplanes and the present practicability and future possibilities of the air craft." Chambers, who understood how substantially naval aviation could be set back by a fatal crash, saw a darker side.[17]

The aviators were under contract in Salt Lake City until Thursday, February 16. Snow and winds over 40–50 mph prevented an exhibition on Monday, while Tuesday was so cold that the promoters canceled rather than face poor attendance. Despite more snow and cold on Wednesday, the aviators flew. One highlight of the day was an "aerial promenade," in which Ely maintained a position just a few feet above Willard. Heading out over the Great Salt Lake, he reached 5,700 feet above sea level—a personal best.

But when he set out the following day to soar over the city on a cross-country flight to Fort Douglas, a wire on his machine snapped. That in itself was not a major problem, but its aftermath was unfortunate, as described by the *Salt Lake Tribune*:

> Ely turned back and alighted at the usual place in the middle of the field. The brake on the front wheel of his machine refused to work properly, however, and the machine did not stop as quickly as it should have stopped. He turned out to avoid a collision with the machine of [an amateur flier] and found that a large crowd of spectators was directly in front of his machine. They had not time to flee and a serious accident appeared inevitable. Without hesitation, Ely steered his machine into a large post.

Although he was uninjured and "appeared unconcerned at the narrow escape from a serious accident," the airplane could not be repaired in time to fly again that day.[18]

Because the exhibition contract obligated the two Curtiss aviators to fly for a combined daily total of one hour, the promoters refused to pay them their $2,500 for Thursday's flights unless they stayed over the following weekend. Ely and Willard adopted a "no money, no more flights" position and threatened to sue. But before quitting Utah, they signed a new contract with several Salt Lake "capitalists" to return in April for a joint exhibition with the Wright aviators.[19]

On the day Ely had flown over the Great Salt Lake, Fanciulli wrote to Curtiss, "The Navy will buy a machine as soon as the matter can be put through the red tape. There seems to be no ifs or ands about this." But both of them were aware that the red tape might be eased considerably if Curtiss could make the demonstration that Chambers was keen to see. In a letter to Ellyson, Chambers referred to the problem as "the aerodrome question": whether it was possible to develop a machine that was "able to rise from and land on both land and water." Ships could then deploy such a machine by simply hoisting it over the side, without needing specialized platforms.[20]

Curtiss and his team had been working since early February on a hydroairplane with a "tractor" configuration in which the propeller was in front of the engine, the engine in front of the aviator, and the forward elevator eliminated. But Congress had not yet made the appropriation, and Curtiss knew from Ellyson that Chambers was interested in a demonstration. He also knew that the warships then anchored in San Diego Harbor were due to leave shortly.[21]

Ellyson reported to Chambers on February 14: "I spoke to Mr. Curtiss today regarding your suggestion that an aeroplane be so developed that it could land alongside a ship and be hoisted aboard. He says that he has done this and tomorrow or the day after, if the necessary arrangements can be made with one of the ships now in the harbor, he will fly from the hangar, land alongside the ship, and be hoisted aboard, then be hoisted overboard again." *Pennsylvania* was anchored at San Diego; on February 17 Curtiss sent a message to Captain Pond asking permission to fly out to the ship and come on board. Pond readily agreed.[22]

Without fanfare, Curtiss skimmed the hydroairplane across the bay, stopped it beside the ship, and hooked it onto a boat crane. "In five minutes from the time I landed on the water alongside the ship," Curtiss reported, the hydroairplane was on board. "It had been the easiest sort of work to land it there, and thus one more of the problems that stood in the way of a successful naval aeroplane was overcome." The machine was lowered to the water again, and two minutes later, Curtiss was back at North Island.[23]

Only eight days after Chambers had written to Ely about the need to demonstrate that calm water would make "a good and sufficient aerodrome," Curtiss informed Fanciulli: "I made the trip to the battleship and they hoisted the machine aboard today, before they left the harbor. Think this stunt may help in the sale." Ellyson's telegram to Chambers was more definitive: "EXPERIMENT PROVED AEROPLANE ADAPTABLE USE NAVY."[24]

Returning to San Francisco, Ely met with Colonel Schastey on February 20 and enlisted as a private in the California National Guard. He may have expected to take command, ultimately, of the aero squadron; perhaps he also thought a military rank might help his standing with the government.[25]

He may also have consulted with his father. On February 24, Nathan wrote to Secretary Meyer: "Will you kindly advise me whether or not there is now in existence or contemplated such a position as superintendent of aeronautics or some position for such purpose in the navy, and whether or not there has been any provision made for the payment of expenses involved. I make this inquiry for the reason that my son has been doing the flying on and off the battleships at Hampton Roads and at San Francisco, and I am very anxious to connect him, if possible, in some way with the navy or army in his line of business."[26]

Nathan had no way of knowing that, barely two weeks earlier, Chambers had drafted a memorandum proposing an Office of Naval Aeronautics, "to keep the Department fully informed of the general progress of aeronautical development, to encourage the manufacture in this country of air craft specially equipped for effective use with the fleet, to inaugurate an efficient system of training in the use of air craft and to maintain the aeronautical equipment of the Fleet in the highest state of efficiency for naval purposes." The senior member Chambers proposed was himself.[27]

In early March 1911, Nathan Ely received a reply to his letter to the Secretary of the Navy. The letter, signed by Assistant Secretary Winthrop but drafted by Chambers, was blunt: the Navy did not "contemplate the establishment of such a position in the near future."

"In regard to your son," the letter went on, "the Department considers that his exceptional skill as an aviator was demonstrated by his [ship flights], which flights have added to his prestige throughout the world; but while appreciating his services in thus demonstrating the possible uses of aeroplanes in naval services, the Department regrets that it cannot contract for his employment at present." The Navy had no budget to bring in an outsider, however skilled.[28]

In fact, Chambers was struggling to keep his own position. Admiral Wainwright, the Aide for Operations, had rejected his suggested Office of Naval Aeronautics, which Chambers later ascribed to Wainwright's belief that "aerial warfare would be prohibited by international agreement." Chambers himself held no such illusions. In a pointed letter to the editor of *Aeronautics*, he recalled that during the Revolutionary War an American admiral had made a similarly naive declaration about torpedo warfare; namely, that it was "inhuman and ought to be suppressed by international agreement."[29]

Though history would shortly prove Chambers right, to Ellyson he said only, "I met with an obstruction to my pet scheme of an Office of Aeronautics, but I am headed now in a slightly different direction because I am determined to see the aviation business started off right if possible."[30]

And indeed, shortly after the naval appropriations bill passed in early March 1911, Chambers obtained Secretary Meyer's signoff on something not far from his pet scheme: "You are hereby directed to keep informed of the progress of aeronautics, especially in this country, and of the development of aircraft generally, with a view to advising the Department concerning the adaptability of such material for naval warfare, especially for purposes of naval scouting and the steps required, from time to time, to gradually provide the Navy with suitable equipment for aerial navigation and to instruct the Navy personnel in its use."[31]

While Ely looked for gainful employment that was less risky than exhibition flying, his activities continued to make the papers in San Francisco. During a gap in his schedule before an exhibition in San Jose on March 18–19, he posed in an advertising photo at the wheel of a new Buick "Forty" and was initiated into the Professional Chauffeurs' Association at a "rally" in the group's "clubrooms" at Bush and Van Ness.

It was perhaps at that event that Ely again crossed paths with Norman DeVaux, the one-time cross-country bicycle racing champion and Auburn automobile dealer and racer. DeVaux had played a role in Ely's move to Portland when DeVaux had left the Oregon Auburn dealership to work for Buick and his replacement, Robert Simpson, had hired Ely. Now back in San Francisco as the West Coast representative for Reo automobiles, DeVaux apparently believed that automobiles and airplanes would soon be manufactured and marketed jointly. He proposed that he could take the West Coast Curtiss franchise, while Ely, the chauffeur-turned-aviation star, could appear in Reo cars in connection with flying exhibitions, the two of them to split all airplane sales profits.

It was not the semipermanent position Ely sought, but it was financially attractive and would keep the Elys near Mabel's parents. All Ely had to do was to sell Curtiss on the idea.[32]

CHAPTER 19

WAR MACHINE

THE CURTISS "war machine," designed for the War Department, arrived in Washington, D.C., on March 12, 1911, and was put on static display at a local air show. This newest version could be broken down into small sections for ease of transportation. On March 17, Douglas McCurdy successfully demonstrated its abilities, but to Curtiss' surprise the Army refused to accept the airplane until it had been demonstrated again at San Antonio—at his expense. The machine was duly shipped, and the three Army lieutenants learning to fly at North Island—Lt. Paul Beck, 2nd Lt. John Walker, and 2nd Lt. George Kelly—were ordered to report to Fort Sam Houston in San Antonio around March 20. They would join Lt. Benjamin D. Foulois, already posted there with a Wright machine.[1]

Curtiss privately expressed dismay at the Army's decision to relocate his students before they were competent. He wrote to Jerome Fanciulli,

> *San Antonio is one of the worst places in the country to fly. It is wicked to send inexperienced men there. Foulois has had three years. In a few weeks Beck will be pretty good, if he can practice here [in San Diego], but to go there now is the biggest mistake that could be made.*
>
> *Kelly and Walker are not cut out for aviators, although they may get along. . . . None of these men have made a turn [in the air] yet or gotten more than 10 feet high. . . . I cannot understand it, ordering these men out there and expecting them to do real flying.*[2]

Beck, the senior lieutenant among the four, was promoted to captain and named flight instructor of the newly created "Provisional Aero Company." But, as with the other two Curtiss students, his training had been minimal. When he enthusiastically suggested a test run of two hundred miles, Curtiss declared long cross-country flights "unnecessarily dangerous for aviator and machine" and asserted that the war machine's capabilities could "be proven without risk" by other means.

The Army, apparently aware of the limitations of its budding fliers, requested that a professional aviator be dispatched to Texas, both to fly the war machine for the acceptance tests and to provide instruction. Or, as Navy aviator Lieutenant Ellyson somewhat less charitably put it in a letter to Chambers, it became necessary for the Army "to send an aviator and mechanicians to their [new] aerodrome in order to set up the machine and keep an eye on the [students]."[3]

But this presented Curtiss with a logistic problem. He was still instructing Ellyson in San Diego. And once he was done there, he planned to exhibit the hydroairplane in Salt Lake City in April, and then return home to Hammondsport.

According to Curtiss, Jimmie Ward was "the only aviator who could be spared or who would accept the offer," but he had little experience with the powerful machine. Ely, on the other hand, had mastered the prototype of the war machine for his USS *Pennsylvania* flight and had continued to fly it regularly. Curtiss telegraphed Ely, asking him to give up his previously booked engagements and head to San Antonio. The request immediately became public. Ely, who presumably had hoped to stay in California with Mabel for as long as he could, was quoted as saying that he expected to go to Texas after honoring his exhibition obligations, which ran through mid-April.[4]

Demand for Curtiss' best-known aviator was high, with Edward D. Moore, the Curtiss publicity director on the West Coast, arranging exhibitions for him in the Pacific Northwest and Northern California, at the same time that Fanciulli was lining up a May date for him in Dallas and pursuing additional prospects in Wichita and Kansas City. He could not be everywhere at once.[5]

On March 22, 1911, Ely underwent a physical examination and took the formal oath of enlistment for a three-year term in the Coast Artillery Corps of the California National Guard. While Mabel apparently stayed on at her parents' home in Corte Madera, Ely headed south to participate in an exhibition in the San Joaquin Valley at which he raced a motorcycle and a Pierce automobile around a half-mile dirt track. The land vehicles covered two miles, while Ely flew four: flying at a conservative pace of 40 mph, Ely beat the automobile but lost to the motorcycle.[6]

He continued on to San Diego to meet with Curtiss. "Ely came down [on March 28] and spent the day," Curtiss wrote to Fanciulli, "and we had an opportunity to straighten things out generally." One topic of discussion was Ely's current account with the exhibition company: Ely claimed he was owed close to $1,500, while by Fanciulli's reckoning it was less than $400. Though Fanciulli had not seen Ely in three months, he wrote to Curtiss on March 27 that "some of Ely's actions lead me to believe that he will, sooner or later, give us considerably more trouble than Mars did." Curtiss and Ely apparently worked out the discrepancy, and following the meeting, Curtiss directed Fanciulli to "send Ely's statement at once" so Curtiss could "settle up with him before leaving, so as to get rid of the old [Ely] account." Ely "is all right," he told Fanciulli. "I don't anticipate any trouble with him."[7]

Ely apparently took the opportunity of the meeting to raise Norman DeVaux's proposal, and Curtiss wrote to Fanciulli that he had promised Ely's services on the West Coast for six weeks to DeVaux, beginning with an exhibition in Eureka, California, on May 27. The "coast agent for Reo cars," as Curtiss described DeVaux, was worth perhaps a million and was "a *good* businessman." He elaborated: "The arrangements with DeVaux are that he books [exhibitions and meets] on a 10% basis, and sends reports and remittances from each meet directly to the office and we send him checks for his commissions. If he takes the Coast [sales] agency" and orders fifteen machines, "we will allow him [25 percent] on all [exhibition receipts] over $12,000 per month, which he takes for each man. He is a good man and perfectly responsible." Curtiss reiterated, "I do not anticipate any trouble with Ely."[8]

Whether by agreeing to DeVaux's proposal or otherwise, Curtiss somehow secured his star aviator's pledge to assist in the war machine acceptance tests and in further training of the Army aviators in San Antonio. Meanwhile, Ely still had exhibition engagements to honor. His first stop was Pasadena, where he and Charles Willard flew before a crowd of two thousand "wild with applause." On his first flight Ely reportedly "got a thrill himself" when, while flying at an altitude of two hundred feet, "he struck a strong current of air which turned his machine partially over." At that moment, his engine stopped. But it began running again after a few seconds, and the danger was over. "It looked a little bad for an instant," he was quoted as saying.[9]

Ely and Willard returned to Salt Lake City in April with Wright aviators Walter Brookins and Phil Parmelee for the meet they had agreed to in February. While the Wright aviators thrilled the crowd, Willard and Ely demonstrated "scientific work in the manipulation of aircraft." Ely landed on the outline of a battleship and came to a stop on the "deck" without using a system of ropes and sandbags.

The following day, while the other aviators exhibited their bomb-throwing prowess with sacks of flour and oranges, Ely "sailed over the Great Salt Lake 3000 feet above its waters . . . going higher and higher, until his machine was just a dot in the sky, which finally completely disappeared." The crowd "kept their eyes glued to the place in the sky where Ely was last seen, waiting for him to reappear. He emerged finally from the space that had so completely swallowed him and grew larger rapidly, until he again neared the earth and in a graceful sweep landed directly in front of the grandstand." His barograph had reportedly recorded an altitude of 9,126 above sea level, a record for a Curtiss biplane—as well as a personal record for Ely—and proof that the machine was a strong climber even when starting in the challenging atmospheric conditions four thousand feet above sea level.[10]

Curtiss and Ellyson brought to Salt Lake City a new version of the hydroairplane featuring retractable wheels; Curtiss called it the "Triad" because of its ability to operate in air, on water, and on land. On April 8, he started the Triad's motor on the beach and taxied it into the Great Salt Lake. After skimming along the water, the machine rose into air for several minutes, then lighted on the water again before rising for a second time and finally landing on shore in front of a crowd of some 12,000.[11]

Brookins gave Ellyson a ride in a Wright machine, showing the feasibility of passenger-carrying at higher elevations. And on April 11, Curtiss wrote to Secretary Meyer: "I have the honor to report that Lieutenant Ellyson is now competent to care for and operate Curtiss aeroplanes and instruct others in the operation of these machines." The Navy had its first qualified aviator.[12]

A few days later Curtiss received some long-awaited good news. A year earlier the Herring-Curtiss Company had been forced into bankruptcy and the court had appointed a receiver to hold the company's assets. A decree in bankruptcy was issued in December 1910, and the assets were to be sold at public auction. Curtiss was the high bidder at auctions held in February and March 1911, but Herring successfully contested both results. Finally, on April 15, 1911, with Curtiss the high bidder for a third time, the sale was confirmed without further protest from Herring. The new Curtiss Aeroplane Company was in business.

Curtiss planned to return to Hammondsport as soon as possible to begin manufacturing. Nevertheless, he remained anxious about whether the hoped-for military purchases would materialize, even after receiving a "request for specifications and prices" from Chambers. Ellyson told him confidentially that Chambers had the "money available for buying aeroplanes as equipment for the cruisers," and Fanciulli tried to reassure him in a telegram: "Soon as President signs appropriation bill [Army] will take delivery machine, seven thousand at Washington. Navy bound up with red tape."[13]

Still no order came. Curtiss, worried that Fanciulli had quoted too high a price for a pair of machines, suggested lowering it. Fanciulli tried to dissuade him "from pressing the matter when it required delicate handling."[14]

When weather forced postponements in Salt Lake City, Ely left to keep an engagement in Bakersfield on April 15–16. Mabel traveled from Corte Madera with her parents to see him fly there. The "sprightly Mrs. Ely" reportedly rejected the notion that his flying ever made her anxious: "I have always had absolute, complete confidence in my husband's exceptional understanding of air conditions at all times and under all circumstances."[15]

Ely arrived in San Antonio on April 19, 1911, and Frank T. Coffyn, a member of the Wright team who was there to demonstrate the Wright B machine, turned up the following morning. The war machine had been assembled under the direction of James Henning, a Curtiss mechanic who had worked with Ely in Winnipeg the previous summer. Like the Wright machine, it was a two-seater, but with the passenger riding directly behind the pilot, rather than at his side.[16]

The Curtiss and Wright machines that had been shipped to Fort Sam Houston had never been flown before, and Ely and Coffyn made trial flights before the formal tests began. Both also made instructional flights with their students as passengers: Ely twice took Kelly up on April 20, while Coffyn gave a ride to Foulois, the only Army aviator designated for the Wright B machine.[17]

The grounds of Fort Sam Houston were not well configured for aviation. The only place takeoffs and landings could be made was on a street that ran directly through the camp, lined by the tents of 20,000 soldiers. The tight quarters left the student aviators little room for error.

The weather, too, was far from ideal. A heavy rain on Thursday, April 20, turned the grounds of Fort Sam Houston to mud. The conditions did not prevent a military parade on Saturday of "10,000 men in khaki," however, followed by 240 mule-drawn wagons and two hundred pack animals, all before a reported ten thousand spectators at the San Antonio Spring Carnival. Coffyn and Ely flew over the troops before the reviewing stand and dipped their machines in salute. Ely "indulged in several well executed dips and curves" in the new Curtiss airplane, which had clearly been designed for great speed. The crowd loved it; one can only imagine the reaction of the mules and pack animals.[18]

Lieutenants Foulois, Walker, and Kelly had been appointed to a board of officers headed by Captain Beck to determine acceptance of the Wright and Curtiss machines. Other officers expressing interest were detailed to the newly formed aero squad: first to choose which machine they wanted to fly, next to face "elimination tests" by Ely and Coffyn, and finally to be instructed by the three Curtiss pupils and Foulois.

Beck's board devised a practical test: the Southern Pacific Railroad would "theoretically" be blown up somewhere between San Antonio and Galveston, and the aviators would have to find the point of destruction. But on April 26, two days into the tests and before the railway "interruption" exercise could take place, General Allen, evidently in anticipation of making an announcement the following day, sent orders that both machines were to be accepted forthwith.[19]

In New York City the following evening, The Aeronautical Society (which had recently changed its name from The Aeronautic Society of New York) held its first annual dinner, a white tie event attended by a host of dignitaries, including President Taft and William Randolph Hearst. General Allen announced that the Army had bought two aircraft—one Curtiss and one Wright—and that it planned to use the remainder of its $125,000 appropriation to buy "as many aeroplanes as we can. . . . It is very important to have trained aviators in this country if there should be any occasion for the mobilization of any large army for any purpose whatever." Allen believed that the four military aviators in San Antonio would have no difficulty training the officers who followed them. In other words, the Army did not contemplate any position, or any budget, for civilian instructors such as Ely.[20]

Chambers delivered a short speech on the development of naval aviation, in which he struck a far more cautionary note. "To advocate conservatism in aviation now, in the face of its present popularity, will seem almost heretical," he observed, but nevertheless "a certain amount of conservatism is imperative, and as aeroplanes are quickly made," his advice was to "make haste yet a little slowly until the machines are better adapted to our special needs, or at least, until we have a sufficient number of aviators trained to use them." He reflected, "It was only last summer that demonstrations of air flights in this country made it seem probable that aeroplanes could be used from a ship. At that time the principal factor in the general development of aviation seemed to be the stimulus afforded to aviators by substantial money rewards for exhibition flights, and . . . Mr. Eugene Ely deserves special credit for cheerfully and enthusiastically entering into the spirit of naval aviation without the prospect of any reward whatsoever." Ely's work, Chambers declared, was "brilliant"; he was a "pioneer" of naval aviation.[21]

Though Ely had been invited to the Aeronautic Society's dinner, he was not there to acknowledge the tribute, which doubtless would have made him uncomfortable anyway. The morning after the dinner, he and Coffyn reportedly took each other as passengers in the Curtiss and Wright machines in the clouds over San Antonio in order "to show there is such thing as camaraderie of the air."[22]

Beck and Walker had trained with Curtiss in San Diego from late January to mid-March 1911; Kelly had started in February. In Curtiss' estimation, Beck was the only one of the three with any aptitude for aviation. As late as April 26, none of them had yet been certified as competent in a basic four-cylinder airplane, let alone the highly maneuverable eight-cylinder war machine.

Competence in one did not automatically confer competence in the other, as Ellyson learned to his chagrin: "Having successfully flown the four-cylinder machine, which was slow and sluggish in movement, I did not realize the sensitiveness of the eight-cylinder machine, even after repeated warnings. . . . In attempting to land I found difficulty in keeping the machine on the ground, and only landed after having made a succession of bumps."[23]

Ellyson had written to Chambers from San Diego that the "Army crowd" at North Island was impatient with the pace of instruction. He observed in February that Beck, Kelly, and Walker were "not doing the amount of work which they should. None of them have any idea of engineering or desire to learn the practical side of the care of the machine, which in my opinion are the most important. Their one and only idea seems to be to learn to fly." In Curtiss' view, understanding the machine was the first step: "It is necessary to know every detail of the machine—every bolt, nut and screw, and the purpose each serves in the economy of the whole."[24]

The far more experienced Foulois would later say of the three, "They were still in the 'danger period' which I define as that time in a pilot's life when he *thinks* he knows all there is to know about flying and will take unnecessary risks while trying to prove to himself and his contemporaries that he is God's gift to the aviation world." A reporter noted Kelly's "desire to get into actual service with a biplane as quickly as possible," and his having declared, "There is but slight danger." Curtiss later wrote, "Eagerness to fly too soon is responsible for many of the accidents that befall beginners." In the month before Ely arrived, not one of the Army aviators had a single minute of flight time in a Curtiss machine. And following his arrival, conditions were suitable for flying on only a very few days. Beck "made some fine flights" on April 28, but Kelly had a "very narrow escape in landing" the next day. "It frightened me to watch them operate," Foulois wrote.[25]

The *New York Times* reported on April 30 that the Army's "pupils of aviation," now that the Army had accepted the machines, would "immediately begin to take lessons" from Ely and Coffyn. But Ely left Fort Sam Houston that day for an exhibition in Wichita that Fanciulli had arranged. The *Galveston Daily News* reported that he would "return in a few days," and perhaps he intended to do so—after scheduled exhibition appearances in Kansas City and Dallas.[26]

The Army aviators whom Ely left behind struggled to master the war machine. On May 2, Walker, having obtained Beck's approval to solo, stayed up for ten minutes, but his flying was erratic, reportedly because his foot kept slipping off the pedal that controlled the throttle. Apparently seeing thunderheads ahead of him, he made a sharp turn at 60 mph and the machine went into a near-cartwheel, tumbling two hundred vertical feet. Walker managed to save himself, but the machine hit the ground with enough force to sustain damage.

The following day Beck was flying the war machine when the engine stopped at three hundred feet. He landed safely but "ended up in a heap" short of the field, among the mesquite and cactus. The crash wrecked both wings and damaged the front wheel. Beck was reportedly knocked unconscious and came to his senses "walking around through the brush with the control wheel in his hands."[27]

Repairs took several days, during which Beck apparently considered whether the Army aviators could operate on their own. President Taft, the Secretary of War, and other dignitaries were to visit Fort Sam Houston on May 20; Beck was not confident that his team could make a respectable showing. He asked Curtiss to send someone to help.[28]

Foulois, who observed the repairs being made to the war machine, later wrote: "What I saw I didn't like. One of the two wooden forks was knotty, cross-grained, and of inferior quality as compared to the knotless, straight-grained quality of wood used in the Wright planes. I also saw where an unnecessary bolt hole had been drilled in the same fork, probably because the mechanics made a mistake in measurement." Foulois recalled that he pointed out the evident hazard, but that Beck "shrugged it off."[29]

From May 4 to 6 Ely, along with fellow Curtiss fliers Jimmie Ward and Charles C. "C. C." Witmer, delighted the crowds in Wichita. The riskiest trick Ely attempted was the "Ely glide," Charles Hamilton's original stunt, in which he throttled back while still several hundred feet high and glided to a landing with the engine off.[30]

On May 5, the first anniversary of the formal launch of his aviation career, it was reported that Ely had been made a major in the Army. Officers in San Antonio promptly discredited the story—a civilian could receive such a commission only by an act of Congress—but the rumor continued to circulate. Nathan suggested that the newspapers had perhaps mistaken his son for Nathan's brother, Capt. Hanson E. Ely, who was stationed in the Philippines and was in line for a promotion to the rank of major.

On the final day of the Wichita meet, with the wind picking up, Ely made a preliminary flight to test conditions. "His plane had barely lifted from the ground when quick, vicious gusts began to hammer it," and the crowd could see he was fighting for his life. Upon landing, he was quoted as saying it had been the most dangerous flight of his career and that no more flying would happen in Wichita unless the wind abated. When Ward and Witmer attempted short hops anyway, Witmer's machine sustained damage. The meet was over.[31]

Ely's next scheduled exhibition was in Kansas City, May 12–14. With a gap in his schedule and finding himself relatively close to Iowa, he traveled directly from Wichita to Williamsburg, arriving at his boyhood home the night of May 7. Orson Harrington and a friend with an automobile met him at the train station in Ottumwa and "made a record run": six hours from Williamsburg to the station and back. Ely had not seen his mother, Maidie, or Hubert since the Harrington family reunion eight months earlier, and it was his first time home without Mabel since 1905. "The delight of Mr. Ely to be again at home," gushed the local society page, "was only equaled by the delight of his mother, sister and brother and his many other relatives in the neighborhood." Three days later he was on his way to Kansas City, with a tentative plan to return in a few months.[32]

On May 8, 1911, Chambers finally completed the requisition process for three aircraft for experimental use: one from the Wrights, and from Curtiss a conventional machine plus a Triad hydroairplane. That event is now considered to mark the birthdate of U.S. naval aviation.[33]

By May 10, with the damage inflicted by Walker and then Beck repaired, the war machine was once again ready for flight. Despite the doubts that had led Beck to ask Curtiss for assistance, he permitted Kelly—the least experienced of the students—to go up on his own. Kelly failed to conduct a ground test to verify the repairs and launched into an uneventful flight that lasted about five minutes. He circled the field several times, then tried to land on the narrow camp road. But he came in "hot and high." At too steep a gliding angle, and with the engine racing, he "smacked into the ground on the nose wheel, then the main wheels, and bounced back up into the air again." He circled and made another attempt, but this time the machine struck the ground with "a sickening, wrenching sound." The machine vaulted into the air and careened toward the camp tents.

Kelly tried to bank hard left, but he was only thirty feet up. His left wing struck the ground, throwing him out in a violent somersault as the machine spun to a stop just short of the tents. The aircraft was reduced to "a chaotic collection of splintered wood, torn canvas, tangled wires and twisted tubing." Kelly suffered a fractured skull and a broken neck. A large wooden splinter pierced his chest. He died within the hour—the first fatality in a Curtiss machine.[34]

Ely learned of Kelly's death the day it occurred. He sent his condolences and wired Norman DeVaux, who was arranging his exhibition in Eureka: "Lieutenant Kelly of Army killed today in Curtiss biplane at San Antonio, my pet pupil, am all knocked out."[35]

Division commander Maj. Gen. William H. Carter promptly forbade any further flights at Fort Sam Houston and ordered the training program to relocate elsewhere. And with that, Ely's association with the Army came to a sudden end.[36]

CHAPTER 20

FULL CIRCLE

CURTISS ALSO LEARNED of Lt. George Kelly's death on the day it occurred and sent his condolences. He telegraphed Capt. Paul Beck, asking for information, but Beck wrote back that neither he nor Lt. John Walker had been present. As Beck understood it, "the accident was due to the breaking of the seat fork when poor Kelly struck the ground the first time." He acknowledged that the wiring to the hand-throttle switch had been discovered intact, which meant Kelly, had he thought to do so, "could have used it to kill the power." When Lieutenant Ellyson received a copy of Beck's letter, he wrote to Chambers, "If Kelly had closed the hand switch when he first landed, as a skilled operator would have done, there would have been no accident."[1]

Ely, along with Curtiss fliers Jimmie Ward and C. C. Witmer, was scheduled to appear in Dallas from May 17 to 19. "I have a letter from Beck, written before the accident," Curtiss wrote to Jerome Fanciulli on May 14, "in which he says it is necessary for some one of us to come down there. I don't know how this matter stands now, but Ely might go the last day of Dallas if they still want him." Curtiss knew that he had not promptly responded to Beck's request for someone to be sent to San Antonio before Kelly's crash.[2]

Fanciulli reached Dallas on May 20. "I found that the boys had had mighty hard luck with the weather and that they had quite a number of wind checks outstanding," he wrote Curtiss. By arranging for one extra day of flying on Sunday, he was able to increase gross receipts from scarcely $1,000 to over $3,900.

Curtiss had given him the task of "making settlements with the boys," but Fanciulli reported that he had no luck with Ely, who was "very evasive at Dallas and sidestepped all my efforts to get a settlement. He was very anxious to find out whether you wouldn't place him in charge of the factory and just what interest in the aeroplane [manufacturing] company you were going to give him." (The reference here is unclear. There is no record of Curtiss' ever having considered putting Ely in charge of the factory or giving him an interest in the company.) Fanciulli continued, "He is more alive to his tremendous value and indispensability than anyone we have yet had associated with us. While I did not dampen his hopes, I made no promises."[3]

Continuing south, Fanciulli arrived in San Antonio late on May 23, where he found things "in very bad shape." He initially met with Maj. George Squier, the officer responsible for the Army's acquisition of its first airplane, who "was very apparently affected by the accident and altogether prejudiced against us. . . . He saw Kelly's accident and now he doesn't want anything to do with a fast machine. He also intimated very strongly that there was a defect in the machine."[4]

Fanciulli next spoke with the three remaining Army aviators, and separately with James Henning, the on-site Curtiss mechanic. He had a long private talk with Beck, who, though he largely blamed himself for the accident, stated emphatically that Ely had been "of little benefit to the officers." In the wake of Kelly's death, with the program terminated and the visit by President Taft and General Allen canceled, Beck felt that no aviator "could be of much value to them."[5]

After the near disaster on May 2, Walker, who Beck believed had "no business flying," indeed never flew again. Beck himself was seeking leave in hopes of joining the Curtiss team, "both for the experience and the money." Foulois flew only Wright machines. With no pupils left, there was no longer any need for a Curtiss instructor at Fort Sam Houston.[6]

The board of officers that was subsequently convened to determine the cause of Kelly's death consisted of Beck and Walker, both of whom had a conflict of interest due to their supervision of the front wheel assembly repairs, and Foulois. No other officers had sufficient aviation experience to reach meaningful conclusions. In the end, the board determined that Kelly had not landed with abnormal force, and that the front wheel must have struck "an abrupt depression in the ground or some obstacle, causing the strain which resulted in the break." Kelly's death, the board concluded, was the direct result of a heroic effort to avoid crashing his damaged machine into the tents of the camp. The reputations of Kelly, Walker, and Beck, as well as that of the Curtiss brand, all survived intact.[7]

On May 25, Assistant Secretary Winthrop approved Chambers' requisition for two Curtiss machines and one Wright machine. "The foundation of Uncle Sam's aerial navy was laid today," said the Associated Press story. At the same time, news broke that Annapolis had been selected as the site for a naval aviation school to be opened in the summer under Chambers' supervision. It was the job that Ely had written to ask about four months earlier.[8]

Ely did not return to San Antonio. Instead, he boarded a train for San Francisco on May 21, reuniting four days later with Mabel, her ten-year-old sister, Mercedes (known as "Mercy"), mechanics William Hoff and P. J. Rooney, and Norman DeVaux. This was the beginning of the six weeks of Ely's services that Curtiss had promised to DeVaux. Now identified by the press as Ely's manager, DeVaux had arranged for the party to make a twenty-four-hour voyage up the coast aboard a mail steamer from San Francisco to Eureka, California, for Ely's next exhibition. The vessel was to have sailed the evening of May 24, but the promoters arranged to have it held for Ely's arrival the morning of May 25.

Six days after leaving Dallas, Ely arrived in Eureka—tired, recovering from seasickness, and still shaken by Kelly's death. When the steamer crossed the bar into the harbor, a welcome committee set out in a launch to intercept it. But in spite of Ely's widespread fame, "there was not one man in the welcoming party" who recognized him on the passenger deck. He was a hero and they expected him to be larger than life, but in the one year he had been flying he had lost twenty pounds or more, and "the slightness of his figure was a matter of surprise to those who welcomed him." At a reported weight of "almost 140 pounds," he was now affirmatively gaunt. The bushy mustache he had grown during the trip compounded the difficulty in recognizing him. He shaved it off at the hotel.[9]

The press described him as charming, accommodating, and unaffected. "Ely is a modest man if ever there was one," observed one article. He "does not talk a great deal about himself," said another, "for he leaves that to his genial manager, Norman DeVaux."[10]

The prototype war machine that Ely had used in the *Pennsylvania* flight made the voyage with him. He was to fly from an amusement park on an exposed, sandy peninsula prone to both high winds and dense fog, with the ocean on one side and a bay on the other. The day after his arrival, facing a stiff wind, Ely rose to a height estimated at between 1,000 and 1,500 feet and spent fifteen minutes or so making four simple circles over the bay and the ocean breakers, alighting in a depression among the sand dunes from which he had arisen. "His flight was even and steady and he faced the fair breeze blowing, steadying himself with the poise of an immense bird," one newspaper reported.

The lack of spectacular dips and spiral glides did not seem to bother spectators, particularly since Ely was quoted as saying that the swirling winds above the dunes had made the flight one of the most dangerous of his career. The next day he completed two flights, attempting little in the morning due to heavy fog but executing "some beautiful curves and dips" in the afternoon.[11]

Ely reportedly told journalists he expected to retire from exhibition flying and afterward to manufacture machines "for the coming generation of bird-men." In a separate interview, Mabel was quoted as saying that by year's end "Mr. Ely is going to devote himself to the business instead of making flights." The couple planned to move to New York, the newspaper reported, where there was "more interest and business in aviation."[12]

The following day, Ely's machine was sent north by steamer on the first leg of its journey to Oregon's capital, Salem, for an engagement in June. Ely himself, apparently not keen to make another coastal passage, departed with Mabel, Mercy, and DeVaux to return to San Francisco in a Reo touring car—presumably supplied by DeVaux—that had arrived that morning on a steamer from San Francisco. They would return Mercy Hall to the care of her parents and journey north again by train to Ely's next engagement, at Medford, in southern Oregon.[13]

Fanciulli's unhappiness concerning his own situation with Curtiss had been deepening. In a petulant letter written en route to Dallas, he professed to Curtiss that he was "amazed recently to find that outsiders were more familiar with your plans than I have been," and he expressed concern that "several people who seem for the present to have much influence with you" were "openly hostile" to him. He wanted a 1 percent commission on airplane and motor sales in addition to his salary and commission on the exhibition business, and he insisted that he be given responsibility for the "entire business management of your exhibition and aeroplane manufacture and sale businesses." Curtiss wired back from Hammondsport: "YOUR LETTER FROM DALLAS SATISFACTORY. COME HERE IMMEDIATELY UPON RETURN."[14]

Jealousy seems to have colored Fanciulli's subsequent reports of Ely's behavior. Suspicious of the new arrangement with DeVaux, which had not yet been reduced to writing, he obtained Curtiss' authorization to sound out DeVaux himself.[15]

DeVaux announced that his Reo Pacific Company had secured the West Coast agency for Curtiss airplanes: "The men who have operated motor cars are taking the lead in the sport of the aeroplanes and the salesmen who have sold automobiles will undoubtedly be called upon to sell aeroplanes in the near future."[16]

In reality, DeVaux had not "secured" anything beyond the promise of Ely's services for six weeks. That promise may have justified

DeVaux's telegrams to the promoters of various West Coast exhibitions, signed by him on behalf of the Curtiss Exhibition Company. But as to the agency arrangement, though there had been discussions with Curtiss and Fanciulli was coming west to California to offer DeVaux a contract, the deal was not yet final.[17]

Fanciulli arrived in San Francisco at the end of May, expecting to resolve the outstanding balance with Ely and to reach agreement with DeVaux on a two-year West Coast Curtiss agency. He would have to wait; Ely and DeVaux were still motoring down the coast from Eureka.

When they did arrive, neither of them seemed to trust Fanciulli, who reported to Curtiss,

> Ely continued to fight shy of a settlement at Frisco and DeVaux also did a lot of sidestepping. Almost the first thing [DeVaux] did was to inform me that you had made a net price of $4000 to him on the eight-cylinder machines. Ely later stated that you said this before him. It was soon apparent to me that Ely and DeVaux have got a working arrangement and Ely advised me . . . that he was to demonstrate for DeVaux and to share equally in the profits from sales. Of course he will stand by DeVaux on the $4,000 proposition as that means one thousand to him instead of five hundred.[18]

Learning that the Elys and DeVaux were to take the 375-mile train trip north to Medford, Fanciulli booked a berth on the same train. He expected to "sign up the contracts and arrange details" for the coast agency during the long ride and then to continue another 275 miles to Portland. But to Fanciulli's annoyance, DeVaux "locked himself up in a drawing room and didn't show up until a few minutes before the train reached Medford" on the evening of June 2. Fanciulli quickly changed his plans and left the train with him. "I think it was DeVaux's idea that I would go on and let the contract matter remain open for a time," he wrote to Curtiss.[19]

When Ely and Whipple Hall had failed to make even one successful flight at Medford the year before and all tickets had to be refunded, the locals had seemed to recognize the twenty-three-year-old's small-town sincerity. The press had described his efforts as a "valiant attempt" that the "high wind" had thwarted. A year later, and now a national figure, Ely could do no wrong The story spread that he had requested the return engagement specifically to make good his disastrous showing the previous year. Ely had come back to Medford, according to one paper, "to demonstrate to local people that he has the nerve and the ability to fly." And although Ely had lived in Oregon for only a few months before embarking on his peripatetic flying career, the locals viewed him as one of their own. "His aerial flights are sensational," gushed the promoters in the advance advertising. "In one short year Ely, the Oregon boy, has eclipsed all aviators."[20]

A brand-new Curtiss airplane was waiting for him at Medford. Curtiss had originally shipped it to Chico, California, 175 miles northeast of San Francisco, for Ely to use at an appearance scheduled for May 30. When the Chico exhibition was postponed, the machine was sent on to Medford, where it arrived a few days early. On Saturday, June 3, Ely flew it for the first time.[21]

"Manbird Ely Makes Good on Aviation Field Where He Failed One Year Ago," the headline read. "Ely the Silent," as the press dubbed him, a "little man dressed in unpretentious citizens clothing," dipped, wheeled, and flew "as gracefully as any bird," and his three flights "could not be improved upon." The crowd, it was said, remained spellbound until he touched down; then they tendered a tremendous ovation. "Where there was criticism a year ago, today is only praise."[22]

Up to this time, Ely had never given Mabel a ride in an airplane, notwithstanding fabricated reports (some of them hers) claiming otherwise. Until he started flying the war machine, he did not have an airplane with enough power for a passenger, and then for the first five months of 1911 there had not been an opportunity. In Medford, Mabel reportedly asked him to take her up. He explained that it was too windy, whereupon she supposedly told a reporter, "He simply refuses to take me when there is any risk. If he ever does fall, though, I want to be with him in the machine. It would be better to 'go' together." The same reporter quoted her as saying, "I am his good luck. Things go wrong when I am not around. He says so himself."[23]

In between Ely's exhibition flights in Medford, Fanciulli sought to close the deal that he had expected to make on the train. "I have suggested to both [DeVaux] and Ely," he wrote to Curtiss in a lengthy report, "that we might entertain a proposition for the coast agency for two years, carrying with it the exclusive exhibition privilege in so far as we could control the exhibition business, provided a certain number of sales were guaranteed, and we received a percentage of the gross exhibition business" or a fixed monthly fee. But in the end no contract was signed, and Fanciulli was left "greatly disappointed" in DeVaux. "I am satisfied that he is not to be trusted and that it will be difficult to hold him in line," he warned. "I think it was a mighty good thing that I went to the coast. DeVaux now knows with whom he is dealing and I also know pretty well what I will have to guard against."[24]

Aware of the boss's desire to keep his star aviator happy, Fanciulli claimed to have "handled Ely very diplomatically and encouraged him to unburden his ideas as to the future," though he was unable to settle all of Ely's compensation claims. "There are a number of items on which we did not agree," he acknowledged. "I am enclosing a memorandum of the disputed items and would like . . . your decision regarding them." Fanciulli seems to have viewed Ely as a competitor for Curtiss' trust, and his own actions appear to have been designed to undermine that trust:

> That he can stand a good deal of watching was made apparent by a number of things he said at unguarded moments. For instance, he said that he could clean up $30,000 on a proposition that is open to him, but which would involve using you in a way not altogether square, yet legitimate, as he put it. My opinion is that he and DeVaux want to get ahold of a number of machines and run the business along the [flying] circus idea.[25]

Curtiss had already experienced his share of deceit. The perceived backstabbing by Bud Mars was still a fresh wound. Surely the thought of now being used "in a way not altogether square"—assuming Ely had ever said or even considered such a thing—raised for him the specter of Herring, an association that a Curtiss biographer described as "the classic mistake of his life."[26]

"I am sorry to get your reports of Ely and DeVaux," Curtiss wrote Fanciulli. But he apparently never confronted Ely regarding the matter, and Ely would never have a chance to explain.[27]

From Medford, Fanciulli headed directly to Seattle, forgoing the planned stop in Portland altogether, while the Elys proceeded north to Salem. As for DeVaux, Ely's relationship with him appears to have ended not long afterward. DeVaux is identified in the press as Ely's manager for the last time on June 4, offering Ely up for a repeat performance in Medford on July 2 for the price of $1,000, to precede dates already booked for Ely in Chico on July 3, and in Reno on July 4. But the Medford return engagement did not materialize, and by early July the promised six weeks were at an end. By the fall, DeVaux was still identified in the press as the Pacific coast representative for the Curtiss Company, but he was booking dates for another flier "under the management of the DeVaux aviators."[28]

In Salem, Ely caught up with his tried and true machine from the USS *Pennsylvania* flight, which had been shipped from Eureka. A year earlier, the chance to see an airplane on the ground in Salem had drawn almost no one. Now, promoters scrambled to put on a true flying exhibition by the world-famous Ely. After a "pretty exhibition" he raced a car, swooped down in the home stretch, "and passed the auto as though standing still." He gave a motorcycle the same treatment. But the highlight of the day was a six-minute dash out and around the state capitol building dome; on his return, "as he circled the track, he was greeted with cheering."[29]

On June 6, Ely was back in Portland, closing the countrywide circle of travel he had begun thirteen months earlier. One newspaper breathlessly claimed that he would attempt the "tragic spiral glide," which was almost certainly not true. His recent flying had been controlled and careful. The same newspaper also asserted that Arch Hoxsey had died while attempting the spiral glide (which was not true; he was attempting an altitude record), that Ely had helped to clear away the wreckage from Hoxsey's body (of which there is no record), and that Ely would attempt to fly a mile high over Portland (he did not do so). Another newspaper spread the rumor that Ely would offer a ride to Henry Wemme, who was still hard at work on his pet project, the Mount Hood highway. Wemme, who had never expressed any definite interest in an airplane ride and did not receive one, had stepped down from presidency of the Portland Automobile Club a year earlier, shortly after selling his airplane to Ely's investors.[30]

With Ely back in town, the officers and directors of the Portland Aeroplane Company met one last time and voted to dissolve the corporation. Given that Ely was no longer flying the Wemme machine, the company had "entirely ceased to do the business for which it was formed and operated." The investors had likely realized a return far beyond their May 1910 dreams.[31]

The Portland exhibition coincided with the 1911 Rose Festival, for which the city expected thousands of visitors. From a makeshift aviation field established five miles east of the city, Ely made three flights on June 6 in the *Pennsylvania* machine, soaring both east and west over the city, including a trip over the downtown business district. Throughout the city, "men, women and children stood with their mouths agape at the spectacle." It was said that each time he landed, Mabel "would rush to him laughing and try to drag him away so she could talk to him." Ely reportedly set new Portland records for both distance and flight time.[32]

Ely was at the top of his profession. He had come home a hero three times: to his family at the exhibition at Rock Island, to San Francisco, and now to the city that had launched his aviation career. "It was by far the prettiest exhibition of aviation seen in Portland," raved the *Morning Oregonian*. "The crowd cheered for several minutes upon his return from the last flight."[33]

CHAPTER 21

SPIRAL GLIDE

THE EXHIBITION ERA as Curtiss knew it was drawing to a close, and the man most responsible for its demise was one of his own aviators: Lincoln Beachey.

Beachey, the former dirigible pilot, joined the Curtiss team in the fall of 1910. He had struggled for months to get the feel of heavier-than-air machines, crashing repeatedly, but by March 1911, descriptions of his flying reflected a newfound mastery: "Instead of the large audience being excited or fearful that Beachey would fall, the majority of them watched with eager eyes" his "graceful flights and perfect control of the machine."[1]

Early in May 1911, during the Benning racetrack meet in Washington, D.C., Beachey flew his Curtiss biplane around the dome of the Capitol, as he had done with his dirigible in 1906. Had the winds not been too strong, he would have continued to the end of the National Mall.[2]

Later that month *Aeronautics* described Beachey's flying as "most sensational. He shoots down at fast speed toward a scampering crowd, then slants up at a 45-degree angle and straightens out. Some day he may not level in time and then—"

Beachey "made his aeroplane do every antic known in the world of the air." The day he earned his pilot's license, he bested Douglas McCurdy in a race and then, "driving his aeroplane to a height of 600 or more feet, glided in a spiral fashion almost to the earth, and as the machine was about to touch the ground he pointed its nose upward, and a few minutes later was again near the clouds. This was done repeatedly." Beachey was apparently doing spiral glides.[3]

When he crashed into a fence in early June at a meet in Wilkes-Barre, Pennsylvania, and damaged the front elevator, he simply removed it, anticipating that the tail elevator alone would provide more than sufficient maneuverability. The next day he flew "without any front canvas surface," and on the following day he flew with only a small front control. This was not an innovation; the Model B the Wrights had debuted the previous summer was a "headless" machine, as was the Model R *Baby Grand* that flew at Belmont in October 1910. Lieutenant Ellyson had already anticipated removing the front control of the Curtiss hydroairplane for experiments. But it was Beachey who became best known for "flying headless."[4]

All spring, he and McCurdy flew together in exhibitions throughout the Northeast. Like Ely, both were now twenty-four years old, but their styles and goals were markedly different. Beachey, like Ralph Johnstone, approached flying as pure performance. In mid-June he appeared unannounced at a meet in Waltham, Massachusetts, nonchalantly flying over from his own nearby exhibition. He descended "in a spiral curve, with his machine dangerously near the perpendicular, banking right and left, and shutting off his power at just the right moment, when the machine seemed to straighten out and land on the field like a feather." Beachey's flying "made people fairly hold their breaths and caused some to scream." It worried Curtiss. "So far, we have been extremely fortunate in not having any accidents happen to the men or spectators," he wrote to Jerome Fanciulli on June 12, "but we cannot hope for this good luck to continue long when we consider how Beachey is flying."[5]

In contrast, McCurdy, an original Aerial Experiment Association (AEA) member, saw aviation as a field for scientific experimentation. His background included an engineering degree from the University of Toronto and a wealth of experience gained working alongside Alexander Graham Bell and Curtiss, "two of the most eminent scientists of the age." And he was by this time one of the most experienced aviators alive. His January flight from Miami to Havana had demonstrated a world of possibilities for naval aviation and navigation. "Anybody who talks with him," one reporter noted, "must feel convinced that the science with him has a more worthy end than the plaudits of the grandstand." It was now time for McCurdy to put that expertise to use on his own terms. He made his final flights for Curtiss at Wilkes-Barre before leaving to join Charles Willard in the business of airplane design, manufacturing, and exhibition. Their first designs would be headless biplanes.[6]

Ely, like McCurdy, viewed flying as a scientific endeavor. A journalist reported, "Unlike some aviators, Mr. Ely does not seek to risk his neck. According to his view of flying there are all manner of 'stunts' that thrill and please spectators, that can be performed in safety. There are others, however, which are foolhardy. Ely believes in scientific aviation. He believes he can fly without great risk, and perform such evolutions as to give spectators the greatest amount of pleasure, without making a corpse of himself."[7]

In June, Ely headed from Portland to Montana, just as he had done a year earlier. He spent the month crisscrossing the state by train, back and forth over the Rocky Mountains. In 1910, he had struggled to get aloft in the thin air at elevation; this year he was bringing greater experience and a more powerful machine. But trouble awaited him nonetheless.

Ely and Hugh Robinson were to fly in Butte, a mining town on the western slope of the Continental Divide, under a contract that required two aviators. The promoters of the Butte meet, possibly aware of Ely's inability to fly in Billings a year earlier, were determined to see that spectators got "the worth of their money. It will be 'no fly, no pay' with the Butte men." But Robinson was booked into engagements in Kansas, and covering for him would have required canceling an engagement in Bismarck, North Dakota, that Curtiss aviator Robert St. Henry was scheduled to fly. "I wired Ely repeatedly to re-arrange the contract for one man," Curtiss wrote to Fanciulli. "He could do it if he would, I am satisfied." But telephone and telegraph lines were down, and the contract remained unchanged.[8]

Butte newspapers reported the fiction that Ely was heading a party of "three more aviators and a dozen mechanicians, hangar attendants, watchmen, etc." He was said to have promised spiral glides, altitude flights, and an attempt to cross the Continental Divide.[9]

"The birdman is here," announced the *Anaconda Standard* when Ely arrived on June 9 with Mabel, three mechanics, and Samuel G. Rayl "of the Curtiss Exhibition Company," identified as Ely's manager. Rayl had been an automobile dealer in San Francisco when Ely raced there in 1909, and he had been active in the Northwest on behalf of Curtiss since at least early May.[10]

A reporter found the "foremost aviator in the world" to be "a young man of slim build, quiet and unassuming," who appeared to be "a little bit reticent in discussing some of his famous aerial evolutions." Ely's "charming young wife" was, as usual, far more loquacious, and she reportedly revealed that Ely would retire from flying after the Chicago International Aviation Meet in mid-August. "Of course he will in all probability stay in the aviation business," Mabel was quoted as saying, "but he will not do any more flying."[11]

On Sunday afternoon, opening day of the Butte meet, Ely ascended before a crowd estimated at ten thousand and circled seven times before descending with "ease and grace." Some spectators "were disappointed at not witnessing the spiral glide, but the weather conditions, although perfect on the surface, were not favorable overhead." On his second flight, Ely raced an automobile for three miles, then flew to a reported 7,800 feet in what was hailed, improbably, as an attempt to cross the Continental Divide. It changed the crowd's mood and converted the skeptics. The press reported that Ely was hailed "as the greatest of his day and everywhere he is greeted with applause as he is recognized while passing along the streets."[12]

Ely had supposedly planned a circular route for that Tuesday that would have enabled him to cross the Divide. His success on Sunday had led thousands of visitors to pour into Butte from neighboring counties. But the afternoon began inauspiciously with a thunderstorm, forcing a one-hour delay. By the time the rain and wind had subsided, a crowd of "miners and [cow]punchers were becoming restless." Seeing the airplane being wheeled onto the track, they surged forward and pressed closer, physically threatening the machine, until the police and players from the Boise Irrigators and the Butte Mountmen baseball clubs—scheduled to face each other in a series at the nearby ballpark—formed an impromptu protective cordon around it. When Ely finally gave the signal and started down the track, the crowd failed to make way, and he was forced to turn out to avoid them. He rose "only 30 feet off the ground, when a puff of wind caught him and he dropped to the ground, damaging the machine so badly that further attempts were out of the question." Ely reportedly "was thrown from his seat as if shot from a catapult." Remarkably, he was not badly injured.[13]

Though Ely's failure to fly was no fault of his own, the promoters nevertheless proposed to withhold $1,000 of his $5,000 exhibition fee. Their stated reason was that the "contract called for three machines and three [*sic*] aviators, and he came here by himself and brought but one machine." Ely disputed this impromptu "fine," but rather than precipitate a lawsuit, he offered them, in exchange for the full fee, his personal check for $1,000, to be donated to the city's fund for a tuberculosis hospital for miners. It was an elegant gesture, until the promoters torpedoed it by rejecting his check, paying him $4,000 anyway, and pledging $1,000 to the fund themselves.[14]

Butte did have one positive outcome for Ely: it was there that he hired a new chief mechanic. Frank Callan, a local chauffeur and auto mechanic, was known as a "careful and conservative driver" and an "ardent good roads booster."[15]

Ely's next stop, on June 16, was at Great Falls, east of the Continental Divide. Businesses closed for the afternoon in anticipation of his flights. But his challenges continued. He had thought he would be flying from a racetrack, but the promoters decided to stage the exhibition during a baseball game, with Ely expected to take off from, and land again on, the infield. The area was much too small, and the danger to the spectators too great, so he had the machine wheeled outside the ballpark and flew it from there. He made three flights, "but all were devoid of the sensational features anticipated by the crowd." The 2,500 people who had paid a dollar each to watch him rise and descend from up close were outraged. Once again, his pay was docked: Ely would be paid only his guaranteed $1,000. Curtiss representative Rayl hired an attorney, and Ely left town. A local newspaper ran the headline: "BUTTE TOO HAD TROUBLE WITH AVIATOR ELY." He was risking his life with every exhibition flight and yet still had to fight for his fee with people who knew nothing about flying.[16]

Ely's luck finally changed in Kalispell, to the west of the Divide near newly established Glacier National Park, where he drew a crowd of five thousand on June 21. "It was an exhibition such as his watchers had often read about, one such as most of them had never seen, and such as many of them will never see again," wrote one reporter. The exhibition had scarcely finished when "a terrific thunderstorm broke, accompanied by hail." The mechanics, who "were pressed to get the biplane under cover," crated it up and boarded a train with it to Lewiston, east of the Divide again, for an exhibition on June 26. There, Ely "made thrilling dips and the flights were absolutely perfect."[17]

Ely and his entourage crossed once more to the west of the Divide for his final Montana engagement: a June 28 appearance in Missoula, timed to coincide with the second annual convention of the Montana Good Roads Congress. The papers reported that he "gave the crowd a constant succession of thrills in the masterly manner with which he piloted his swift-flying craft through the air." When a local man reportedly offered to buy his machine, Ely was quoted as saying, "I would sell him one like it, but not this one." It was the prototype war machine from the *Pennsylvania* flight that he had been flying since December 1910, and by now it had reportedly flown 109 hours and 20 minutes. "I have flown it so much that I have grown pretty fond of it," he explained. The machine was shipped to Reno, while Mabel and Ely headed to Chico.[18]

Meanwhile, Beachey, seeking to add to his repertoire of aerial acrobatics, announced his intention to fly over Niagara Falls. Even by his standards, the undertaking would be sensational.[19]

On June 27, an estimated 150,000 spectators watched Beachey rise from a baseball diamond on the New York side of the river and cross over the American Falls. He circled and made a dive for the rim of the Horseshoe Falls on the Canadian side but pulled up again. He made two more circles, dropping to an estimated two hundred feet above the river, and suddenly plunged down over the falls and into the gorge. Skimming the turbulent surface, he flew through the mist—one report said he had to shut his eyes against the stinging droplets—and under the span of the Upper Steel Arch Bridge, also known as the Honeymoon Bridge. He continued down the river almost to the whirlpool rapids, "mounted again, and, shaving the wooded cliff, landed safely and unconcerned on the Canadian side."[20]

With a single astonishing flight, Beachey had effectively ended the pure "exhibition" era. Eighteen months earlier, hardly anyone had believed that a man could fly. By mid-1911 it was an accepted fact, and few people cared about the science of flight. One editorial said,

> With all due respect to Glenn Curtiss, the Wrights and other pioneers whose achievements will ever be remembered, the ordinary aeroplane flights such as they now give, even with the new hydroplane device, no longer satisfy the public. And this is no compliment to the public, either. Recent events are demonstrating that the people want thrillers and, in plain terms, this means an extreme risking of human life. The ordinary flights have become so common as no longer to attract crowds. . . .
>
> A press dispatch says Beachey has no fear. Probably true, but it is also evident that he has little common sense.[21]

Another called Beachey's stunt "foolhardy" and noted: "Even after he had accomplished the feat he did not add an iota to human knowledge or human progress." Editorial opinions notwithstanding, the sun had set on Ely's careful exhibition style. It was time to get out of the business—or fly like Beachey.[22]

CHAPTER 22

OFF GUARD

AS THE SUMMER PROGRESSED and temperatures rose, Ely and Mabel wrapped up the long month in Montana and made their way back toward San Francisco. Ely made a brief stop in Chico on July 3, to satisfy the appearance that had originally been scheduled for late May, before rushing off to Reno, arriving on the morning of July 4 to fly at an Independence Day celebration. His USS *Pennsylvania* war machine was waiting for him. The weather in Reno reportedly exceeded ninety degrees, with "air blankets" and crosscurrents creating treacherous conditions. "The great Ely" flew "above the sparkling waters of the Truckee" River before a crowd estimated at 15,000 to 20,000, but a broken wrist pin damaged the engine sufficiently to prevent him from making a second flight.[1]

In booking the engagement, Norman DeVaux and the Reno promoters had agreed that the $2,500 fee would be placed into escrow at a local bank, to be paid out only if Ely gave the people "a satisfying exhibition." There was no question that Ely had met the requirement, but payment was not forthcoming; the contract had explicitly called for payment to DeVaux, who apparently was no longer in the picture. The company instructed the bank "to pay the amount to another person," but that arrangement "did not appear clear to the bank people," who insisted on receiving orders from DeVaux himself. Evidently DeVaux finally wired instructions, and ultimately "the matter was settled without trouble," with payment made to Curtiss representative Edward B. Hine.[2]

On the morning of July 6, traveling from Reno, Ely stopped in Sacramento, where he sat for and passed the examination for a second lieutenancy in the California National Guard. The proceedings were concluded in time for him to catch the 3:30 train to San Francisco. His new rank qualified him to take charge of the Guard's proposed aviation squad, and it was reported that he would "take up his headquarters at San Francisco" and "devote a large part of his time" to teaching the Guard to fly.[3]

Around this time the San Francisco papers reported that Ely had taken delivery of a Stevens-Duryea "Big Six" automobile. Notably, it was not a Reo, which suggests that his business relationship with DeVaux had indeed ended.[4]

Before Ely could participate in any Guard activities, he had more exhibitions to give in the Northwest. The first one, at Baker City in eastern Oregon, closed yet another personal circle: it had been the Baker City Commercial Club's president who, having lost confidence in Ely's ability to fly, had canceled the fledgling aviator's Independence Day engagement in 1910.

Ely and Mabel traveled first to Portland, where they enjoyed a reunion with Bud and Marie Mars. Two weeks earlier, at the conclusion of the six-month global tour for which he had left Curtiss in December 1910, Mars had arrived in Quebec aboard—ironically—Hamburg-American's *Kaiserin Auguste Victoria*. The four traveled together to Baker City. There, notwithstanding "a disastrous first attempt, in which the famous aviator crashed into a fence and damaged his aeroplane considerably," Ely eventually circled the valley for many miles.[5]

While Bud and Marie Mars headed east to Pennsylvania, the Elys traveled north to Canada for an exhibition at Lethbridge, Alberta. It had been a year since the crash in Winnipeg that had spawned reports of Ely's death. This time around, the sole snag was getting the war machine through customs. The day of the performance "had practically been declared a holiday." In Canada, Ely did not need to resort to stunt flying to impress the crowd, for whom "the sight of a man sitting in the frail aeroplane was new and interesting." Advertisements had promised that he would perform the spiral glide and the "ocean dip," but he attempted neither. Instead, in "perhaps the most thrilling moment of the day," he astonished the audience by landing in almost the exact spot from which he had taken off seven minutes earlier. A reporter found him afterward, "calmly smoking in the shade of the great planes, as though he had performed nothing out of the ordinary."[6]

The Coast Artillery Corps of the California National Guard was taking part in war games in San Francisco, and Ely was expected to join the squad to make several demonstration flights. But first, the Elys headed to Seattle for what was intended to be his next-to-last exhibition before his retirement.[7]

Seattle's "Golden Potlatch," the brainchild of civic boosters, was a festival ostensibly commemorating an event fourteen years earlier that had brought "progress and prosperity" to the Pacific Northwest. The arrival in 1897 of SS *Portland*, carrying the first load of gold from the Klondike, had sparked the gold rush in which Henry Wemme had made his fortune selling tents to prospectors. At the 1911 festival, the arrival of "Lieut. Eugene Ely" was highly anticipated: "Ely has been flying scarce two years, yet is as deeply informed upon the science as any man in it. He is looked to confidently to put the air craft far ahead of its present status and those most closely, intimately interested in its development are given to calling upon their gods of luck to keep him whole of limb and 'in the game.' He is counted one of the sort that cannot be replaced."[8]

The Elys arrived in town three days early, giving themselves time to enjoy the festivities. Ely and his mechanics assembled the machine on Harbor Island at the south end of Elliott Bay, and for three days he put it through its paces while Hugh Robinson demonstrated the hydroairplane. When the Potlatch King and Queen arrived on Wednesday, aboard a vessel representing the original "gold ship" *Portland*, Ely flew out over the bay and circled above in greeting, passing as well over USS *Pennsylvania* and USS *West Virginia*, which happened to be anchored in the harbor with the rest of the Pacific Reserve Fleet. (The flight coincided with a seventeen-gun salute to the admiral, which some reporters mistook for a salute to the aviator.) At dusk, he "soared over the skyscrapers," executing what some reporters took to be the so-called fatal dip, "and 150,000 people, packed like sardines in the streets below, howled themselves hoarse."[9]

Ely's mastery of the machine was said to render the efforts of previous birdmen in Seattle "most amateurish if not positively ludicrous"—perhaps a reference to Charles Hamilton's ignominious crash into a pond in 1910. A reporter painted the scene: "From his hangar on Harbor Island, Ely rose for his flights punctually on the minute and drove his machine through the clear sky with the methodical precision of an expert, attempting none of the tricks of the applause-seeking showman, but conducting his flights rather as the practical scientist which he is." Ely, "bathed in golden sunshine," was his usual unflappable self, "sitting serenely at his place, confident, daring and composed."[10]

Meanwhile, Jerome Fanciulli arranged for Gimbel Brothers to sponsor an air race in early August. Three Curtiss machines would race between the firm's New York and Philadelphia department stores for a $5,000 prize. Ely and Robinson left Seattle to rendezvous with Lincoln Beachey for the "epochal event." By the time they reached the East Coast, there was a potential fourth entrant: Hamilton had apparently resolved his differences with Curtiss and returned to the exhibition company.

Ely's participation in the race meant that he would miss the entirety of the California National Guard training exercises, but it could not be helped. Assuming the airplane lease he presumably signed in Hammondsport in August 1910 had a duration of one year, he was still bound for a few more weeks to fly whenever and wherever the Curtiss Aviation Company directed him.[11]

But Ely's plans changed yet again. "Hundreds of young men in the service" were "clamoring for a chance to be sent" to the Army's aviation school at College Park, Maryland, where Army flying was centered following the shutdown at San Antonio. Capt. Paul Beck was to instruct the new class of would-be aviators and was poised to demonstrate the Army's new war machine. But Major Squier, who Fanciulli felt was prejudiced against Curtiss airplanes because of

Lieutenant Kelly's death, refused to allow the test unless Beck made an adjustment that "lessened the speed." Beck made an urgent call to Curtiss, who hastened to College Park to fly the war machine himself. Ely's presence in the Northeast, his familiarity with the war machine, and his history with the Army aviators in San Antonio made him a logical choice to assist Curtiss.[12]

Both men were in College Park by Saturday, July 29, when Curtiss "demonstrated to the army officers that his [four-cylinder] practice machine is satisfactory so far as control is concerned." But he was reportedly "called to Hammondsport," leaving Ely to complete the demonstration. Hamilton, it was announced, would take Ely's place in the Gimbels race.[13]

On Sunday, according to the *Washington Post*, Ely took the Army's new Curtiss machine up briefly and treated the visitors to "one of the most sensational bits of aeroplaning they ever saw." He reportedly first rose to an estimated one thousand feet at 70 mph, then "dropped 600 feet in a beautiful left-hand spiral glide, ending up with the exact opposite, a right-hand spiral," with "one wing almost grazing the ground." In fact, the report appears to describe not a spiral glide but the "gull" landing maneuver.[14]

Ely was scheduled to fly a thirty-minute endurance test with the four-cylinder machine on Monday, July 31, but he was in the air only a few minutes before a rain and windstorm "tossed the small plane about," threatening to "capsize" it several times before he was able to land it safely. He emerged from the airplane "soaked to the skin," but unscathed. The following day he too departed for Hammondsport, on "official business." By Friday, August 4, both he and Curtiss were in New York City.[15]

The Gimbels race was scheduled to start at noon the next day from Governors Island just south of the island of Manhattan, the scene of Curtiss' poor showing at the Hudson-Fulton celebration in the fall of 1909 and of his triumphant finish to the Albany–New York flight in May 1910. The start was postponed for nearly three hours, purportedly due to marginal weather. The greater issue was Hamilton's last-minute refusal to fly. He cited the weather and his unfamiliarity with the new Curtiss controls, but it is also possible that he and Fanciulli had been unable to agree on terms for his rejoining the Curtiss team. Ely was present at the start, and in one more change of plans, Curtiss publicity man Edward Moore asked him to fly. Although he had not prepared to race, after a brief test flight he agreed.

The aviators were all required to follow the same general course: taking off from Governors Island, flying uptown to make an official start directly above the New York Gimbel Brothers store, crossing the Hudson, following the tracks of the Pennsylvania Railroad to Trenton, New Jersey, then following the course of the Delaware River, making an official finish above the Philadelphia Gimbel Brothers store, and finally landing in Philadelphia's Fairmount Park.

One at a time, beginning at 2:40 p.m., the airplanes took off to the south from Governors Island, heading into the wind, before banking around north and disappearing into thick haze. They passed over the Gimbel Brothers store at Herald Square in Manhattan about ninety seconds apart, with Beachey leading, Ely second, and Robinson trailing. Some accounts had Ely taking a substantial lead over Beachey before they were a third of the way to Philadelphia; another had the two men flying abreast at Rahway, New Jersey.

Gasoline was available to all three competitors at Trenton, but at 3:27 p.m. Ely realized his tank was leaking, and he landed at New Brunswick, New Jersey, some twenty-five miles northeast of Trenton, for a repair that consumed nearly eighty minutes. By the time Ely took off again, Beachey was crossing over the Gimbel Brothers store in Philadelphia at Ninth and Market Streets with an elapsed time of 2:01, including the scheduled stop for fuel in Trenton. A few minutes later, as Beachey landed before a crowd estimated at 100,000, a clogged fuel line forced Ely to touch down again, in a haunting echo of his Chicago to New York attempt. Robinson reached Fairmount Park about an hour after Beachey. Ely did not finish.[16]

Two days later, Ely and Mabel, on their fourth wedding anniversary, arrived in Chicago for the international aviation meet. The press was giddy with hyperbole. Ely was quoted, in what was almost certainly a fabrication, as seeking redemption for his failure in Chicago ten months earlier: "I am in Chicago with blood in my eye." One paper reported that, when asked whether his wife objected to his flying, he responded, "Mrs. Ely lets me fly all I want to." In fact, he supposedly added, "The more flying I do, the better she is satisfied."

On the same day another paper printed a story under Mabel's byline that asserted, "'Gene is never going to fly in exhibitions again. . . . He has proven his genius as an aviator and he terminated his contract with Glenn Curtiss with his flight last night." This was obviously untrue, and three days later, on opening day of the Chicago meet, he placed third in an over-water race, besting all other biplanes in the race.[17]

Bud Mars was in Chicago, too, ready to compete and regaling newsmen with stories of his adventures in the Orient. A month earlier, while flying in Erie, Pennsylvania, Mars had crashed badly, and several papers declared his injuries fatal. His reported demise came a year to the day after the crash that had prompted reports of Ely's death at Winnipeg.[18]

Chicago again established Mabel as the darling of the press: "'I have become so accustomed to this thing,' said Mrs. Ely, 'that I am not a bit nervous. I take it as a matter of course. But I have to keep close to Mrs. Mars, or she would go to pieces. I suppose I would be just as nervous as she is if my husband had been picked out of a wreck of sticks and canvas only a short time ago. I don't see how she manages to watch the flights at all after such an experience.'"[19]

Orville Wright was also in Chicago, demanding that the meet organizers set aside 20 percent of the receipts to satisfy his claims for royalties on his patents, which he maintained all of the airplanes in the meet were infringing. He threatened to pull his fliers out of the meet, but the promoters nevertheless refused his demands. Shortly before the meet's opening, the Wrights entered their fliers after all, and within a week had filed suit against the organizers.[20]

Opening day, August 12, was billed as the largest gathering ever in the history of Chicago: "From the edge of the lake front to State

Street was one solid, seething mass of humanity." The following day more than 600,000 spectators reportedly thronged Grant Park and Michigan Avenue to get a vantage point from which to see more than thirty fliers from five countries.[21]

Beachey's stunts were "declared by experts never to have been equaled in the history of air sport." Even Lieutenant Ellyson reported to Chambers: "Beachey's flying was the most wonderful that I have ever seen."[22]

From the start, the meet was plagued by a number of "narrow escapes from death." Several collisions and accidents occurring on opening day were shrugged off as minor. But two days later Douglas McCurdy had engine trouble and crashed his headless biplane through high-tension electric wires running from the Chicago Yacht Club. The machine flipped upside down. McCurdy jumped clear and landed on his feet, but sparks ignited the spilled gasoline, and the machine was reduced to charred wood.[23]

At one point, Pittsburgh native and affable "young millionaire aviator" William R. Badger got caught in the "air wash" of another airplane's propeller dangerously close to the ground and briefly lost control. "That was the nearest to dying that I ever came," said the former automobile racer.[24]

Badger, in his mid-twenties, had become enamored of flying the previous summer and had just earned his license in June. Friends had nicknamed the "little auburn-haired flier" and his brightly painted "Red Devil" Baldwin biplane "Red and his Red." The day after his close call, he was about ten minutes into a flight when his machine suddenly plunged to earth. Ellyson, who witnessed the accident, reported that Badger was evidently "trying to imitate Beachey's steep dives" by coming down at a near-vertical angle and then attempting to "shoot the machine up again when he was about 30 feet from the ground." The machine, Ellyson wrote, "seemed to fly all to pieces with a report like a gun, and smashed into the ground with terrific force, the radiator striking him in the back of the head." Badger's skull was fractured, and his back was broken in "several places." He died soon afterward.[25]

The meet went on. Ely was reportedly incensed and asked that the rest of the day's program be canceled. Frank X. Mudd, chair of the contest committee, refused, reportedly because there was "$30,000 in the grandstand." Ely was quoted as responding, "What can we think of a man like that? . . . What can the public think of a man who refuses to show even common respect to the dead and declines to make an effort to save more lives for a reason like that?" It was said that he and several other aviators had signed a petition seeking Mudd's removal as chairman.[26]

Ninety minutes after Badger's crash, twenty-four-year-old local flier St. Croix Johnstone (no relation to Ralph) was performing an endurance flight in a Moisant monoplane above Lake Michigan when his airplane suddenly shot downward. Alfred Moisant, brother of John, was quoted as reporting, "Then it dropped to the water, turning around in the air with a corkscrew motion." It struck about a mile offshore. Robinson, who had been demonstrating his Curtiss hydroairplane nearby, sped to the spot, but the wreck had already gone under, with the aviator trapped beneath it. By the time rescue boats arrived, Johnstone was dead.[27]

Even after this second catastrophe, the meet was not called off. Chicago Aviation Meet Association officials issued a clutch of statements, remarkable in their callousness, that "deeply deplore[d] the deaths" of Badger and Johnstone while emphasizing the association's "obligations to the public, thousands of whom have come great distances and at great personal sacrifice." Association president James E. Plew declared simply, "The meet must go on."[28]

Resistance from the fliers and their families was intense. Mabel, who had witnessed Arch Hoxsey's death in December, reportedly declared herself "thoroughly disgusted" with the organizers for treating the aviators and their wives "as if we amounted to nothing" and allowing events to continue after the two deaths. She and Marie Mars issued public statements of opprobrium. On Thursday, while their husbands served as pallbearers at Johnstone's funeral, flying was suspended for fifteen minutes as a "tribute."[29]

No one could explain Johnstone's crash; he was a relatively experienced aviator with no history of sensational flights. As for Badger, the *Tribune*'s aviation expert attributed his death to "trying to do something for which his machine was not designed and which no machine made at the present time could safely attempt." The commentator thought Badger had been trying to copy the far more experienced Beachey, who routinely used his machine "to the limit of capacity" and who had been "doing tricks successfully so far. . . . But all men fail sometime."[30]

The next day saw one of the largest crowds of the meet. Just as the Wrights had learned at Asbury Park following Walter Brookins' accident, crashes provoked even greater interest in flying. Spectators jammed the aviation field, streets, and roofs, "in the morbid hope that the spectacular accidents of Tuesday would be duplicated." On that Wednesday

> they came to see live men, daring young aviators, hurtling to their death through space. They were disappointed, for only once did they rise to their feet and utter groans—half delight, half horror—as Lincoln Beachey shot from a height of nearly 3,000 feet and seemed to be rushing to his death with the speed of an express train.
>
> Then when he settled easily with the wind a few feet above the ground and landed gracefully, cheer after cheer rang out. Exclamations of relief and sighs of satisfaction were heard on all sides. Every one was pleased, having witnessed a man shooting to earth and [having] experienced all the thrills of a great catastrophe without the toll of human life.[31]

A high wind limited events that day—Ely flew for less than twelve minutes—and after Beachey's spectacular plunge, many spectators "concluded that they had witnessed the most exciting event of the day and departed."[32]

Over the next days Ely and Beachey competed directly against each other. Ely lost a distance race by six seconds when Beachey "cut down his time by daring banking at the turns," but Ely won two others by eight and fifteen seconds, respectively, and took first place in a quick-climbing contest. The final day, he established the meet speed record for an eight-mile flight by a biplane, while Beachey climbed to 11,642 feet—until his gasoline ran out—to establish what was hailed as a new world's record. His achievement was seen as "the climax of a series of spectacular and thrilling 'circus stunts' Beachey has been performing during the nine days of the meet."[33]

Professional aviators, for obvious reasons, could not obtain traditional life insurance. Six days after the Badger and Johnstone crashes, a one-day benefit event was held in which the aviators agreed to fly without compensation and donate all admission proceeds to St. Croix Johnstone's widow (Badger had been single). But high winds made it impossible for any monoplanes to get aloft, and Johnstone's father sent a message begging the aviators not to fly recklessly. Ely did not go up, but Beachey, Jimmie Ward, and two others performed. The benefit was estimated to have netted $10,000 to $12,000.[34]

Ely had now been flying for the Curtiss Exhibition Company for a full year. Mabel had been quoted two months earlier, whether accurately or not, as saying that he would "make his last flights" at Chicago around August 20 and would then cease exhibition flying.[35]

But if he was indeed thinking of retiring from exhibition flying, his options were limited. There was no realistic possibility that he would fit into the Army's or Navy's instructional budget. The arrangement between Curtiss and DeVaux for the West Coast agency had never materialized. While he had a new role with the California National Guard, any anticipated financial rewards could not have touched what he earned from exhibitions. And as for a position in Curtiss' manufacturing business, it is not clear what discussions Ely and Curtiss ever had, or what, if anything, Curtiss might have promised.

In fact, Curtiss himself was looking to make a change, as he confided in a letter to Chicago Aviation Meet Association president James Plew, who had purchased Herring-Curtiss machine No. 4 nearly two years earlier. Having pondered the matter for months,

Curtiss had concluded that his time was better spent in designing and developing new machines "for pleasure, for racing, and . . . for commercial purposes" than in continuing to run the exhibition and manufacturing businesses. With demand continuing to grow, he had "no one who was capable of coping with the great volume of business which is in sight." For approximately $100,000, therefore, he was willing to sell a controlling interest in both businesses—including the factory that Ely might have harbored hopes of managing.

In the end, Curtiss did not sell. Nor did he offer Ely a position in the manufacturing business. August was coming to a close, and still Ely pursued the "conquest of the air," in which, according to the Chicago Aviation Meet Association, "it is regrettable that . . . the sacrifice of human life is not infrequent."[36]

CHAPTER 23

FULL MEASURE

ENGLISH AVIATOR Claude Grahame-White had dominated the inaugural Harvard-Boston meet one year earlier, in 1910. Ely, a relative unknown, had not been included. Now he was a headliner.[1]

"The fast work of Eugene Ely, the Curtiss flier, in a shortened biplane, was one of the features" of the second Harvard-Boston aviation meet, ran a wire service story. If accurate, the story would suggest that Ely was flying a machine in a "headless" configuration. Another possible explanation is that the reporter misidentified the flier, as commonly happened, and that the aviator in the "shortened biplane" was Lincoln Beachey.[2]

On opening day, August 26, Ely raced for the first time against Grahame-White. The two went head-to-head in a speed contest, with Grahame-White in an inherently swifter monoplane. Ely, predictably, finished second, as he did to Beachey the following day in a new type of altitude contest: rising to two thousand feet in the shortest time.[3]

On September 1, Grahame-White's countryman Thomas Sopwith won one of a series of races out over the harbor and around Boston Light. Ely, forced to touch down on the return leg because of what was said to have been a radiator leak, did not finish.

Two days later, Boston experienced "the first flying ever seen in this vicinity on a Sunday" when a couple of aviators took their machines up for a test run. Just before dusk, when the wind had "died down to almost a calm," Sopwith seized the moment to give Mabel Ely a ride in his two-seater Wright machine. She had told many enthusiastic stories about her past flights, and the press had been only too happy to print them. But the brief sunset flight on the Squantum Peninsula with Sopwith was likely her second experience in the air, preceded only by her ride with Bud Mars at Sheepshead Bay a year earlier. "Just grand," she reportedly exclaimed.[4]

The meet's marquee event, held on Monday, was a 160-mile, three-state cross-country race with designated checkpoints: Boston to Nashua, New Hampshire; to Worcester, Massachusetts; to Providence, Rhode Island; and back to Boston. Grahame-White, Sopwith, and Ely, among others, refused to compete after unsuccessfully arguing for a safer course that would avoid highly populated areas. Ely instead took part in a figure-eight flying contest. He "could bank around a pylon closer than any of the contestants," including second-place finisher Grahame-White, but he failed to round the course at the finish and was disqualified. Reportedly taking this as the latest in a series of perceived slights against the Curtiss team by the contest committee, he at once withdrew from the meet, under the instructions of team manager M. L. Nolan.

In the end, Ely's winnings at Boston totaled a mere $150, while Beachey won over $3,000, Grahame-White over $5,000, and Sopwith over $6,000. The winner of the cross-country race, American Earle L. Ovington, earned nearly $12,000.[5]

A news story had been circulating that Ely was "planning an exhibition tour of the world" during the winter. Jerome Fanciulli had persuaded Curtiss that the European market was ripe for sales. The Russian government had purchased a hydroairplane, to be followed by eleven more pending a successful demonstration, and Fanciulli proposed to take a few aviators on a European tour to give sales demonstrations. He certainly had Hugh Robinson in mind, and perhaps Ely as well.[6]

From Boston, the exhibition treadmill took Ely to Hillsgrove, Rhode Island, for "a series of very successful flights" at the state fair beginning September 5. Following that, the "Wizard of the Air" was one of a handful of aviators who appeared at New York City's Brighton Beach racetrack, barely half a mile west of the Manhattan Beach Hotel where he had supposedly taken dinner during the

Sheepshead Bay exhibition a year earlier. His flights this time were "characterized by dash and brilliancy." Despite favorable conditions, almost all the other fliers suffered crashes.[7]

When Jimmie Ward, who had been scheduled to appear at St. Johnsbury, Vermont, bowed out in order to attempt a transcontinental flight, Fanciulli asked Ely to fill in. Ely obligingly did so, soaring to one thousand feet in strong winds on the first day. A "freaky wind" kept him on the ground the next day; his three flights on the third day were adjudged "gilt-edged."[8]

During Ely's brief New England detour, the Brighton Beach meet had been extended. On September 16, novice aviator George W. Beatty, who seemed to be making a specialty of giving rides to young women there, took both Mabel Ely and Marie Mars aloft together in his Wright Flyer. The two women pronounced it "the most delightful excursion ever experienced." Ely flew the following day, landing with his signature "gull" maneuver that the press insisted on characterizing as a "spiral dip." From Brighton Beach he traveled upstate to two more exhibitions: Oneonta on September 21, and Corning the following day.[9]

The final international meet of 1911 was scheduled for September 23–30 at Nassau Boulevard Field on Long Island. Opening day was designated "Army and Navy Day," and Ely, with Captain Beck as his passenger, took part in a scouting exercise to spot a squad of soldiers known to be hiding within three miles of the aviation field. There was "keen disappointment" when their team failed to find the men, who had been crouching in a cornfield.[10]

On the second day Ely won a quick-starting contest and later bested a crowded field in a speed race for biplanes. "Helmeted like a gridiron warrior," he "proved to be the proper sort of a favorite, never leaving the result in question at any stage of the contest after the first minute of flying." He was also teamed with Army Lt. Henry H. "Hap" Arnold, a Wright-trained aviator, in a novel two-man relay race. One aviator reported to the judges' stand, where he was given a handwritten message. He ran with it to his airplane, flew four laps (a total of five miles), then handed off the slip of paper to his teammate, who took it up for another four laps and then delivered it on foot back to the judges. This required a good deal of sprinting by men who were not necessarily sprinters. Grahame-White was "puffing badly" when he arrived at the judges' stand. Although he and his teammate, Sopwith, were the only team with two monoplanes, Ely and Arnold lost to them by scarcely forty-five seconds.[11]

The sheriff of Nassau County decided to enforce a local prohibition against Sunday competitions for money, so Ely collected no prizes on September 24. His overall winnings were nonetheless a respectable $1,400.[12]

Next, Ely headed to Canton, Ohio, while Mabel stayed on in New York City in an apartment with Marie Mars. On September 27, his first day in Canton, the man who had been touted as the "Curtiss Comet" could not fly because his machine had not yet arrived. Flying the next day in a "treacherous wind," Ely was turning in "a rather short curve" about a hundred feet above the ground when a gust caught his machine, which wobbled and then "shot to earth." Some reports had his machine brushing another on the way down; others said it disappeared behind a small hill and then "bounded into the air like a rubber ball." Mechanics running to his aid found him on his feet, "cut about the head and bruised about the body," which was later magnified into his having been "almost scalped" by the front control plane as he was thrown from his seat. He reportedly "smiled, however, as he helped push his machine back to the hangars" and remarked that he had simply overcorrected.[13]

Curtiss had experienced a similar injury in May, when his head struck the front elevator of his hydroairplane during a test flight. Aware of the success Beachey was having with a headless configuration, Curtiss determined to do away with the canard in future designs. The 1912 Curtiss Headless D hydroairplane would have no front control surfaces at all.[14]

Ely did no more flying at Canton, returning instead to Nassau Boulevard Field. On September 30, he took a passenger up for ten minutes and also took fourth place in a bomb-throwing competition and second place in a mail-carrying event, both won by Sopwith.

All events were canceled on the final day of the meet due to "pelting rain," but several of the aviators went up anyway, which "pleased the few spectators remaining on the field," and Ely "flew and flew and flew and flew."[15]

The newest member of the Curtiss team was nineteen-year-old dirigible prodigy Cromwell Dixon, who had received his aviator's license on August 31. The day before the Nassau meet ended, Dixon became the first person to fly across the Continental Divide. On October 2, flying in Spokane, he had just "banked his [wings] for a turn when a sudden gust of wind tipped them." The machine crashed to the ground and Dixon was killed.[16]

Public sentiment was beginning to turn against aviation exhibitions. *Outing* magazine, decrying the deaths of Bill Badger and St. Croix Johnstone in Chicago, called for an end to aviation meets, and in mid-October *Scientific American* magazine reported that exhibition flying "has begun to decline."[17]

On October 17, Curtiss wrote to Fanciulli, "I am going to sell out the exhibition and aeroplane [manufacturing] business to [a] new company, or reorganize the system so as to minimize our responsibility in connection with exhibitions." The "new company" would be the Curtiss Motor Company, Inc., which was formed two months later.[18]

Ely had been searching without success for alternatives to the exhibition circuit—and his options were dwindling. One potential solution was to learn to operate the Curtiss hydroairplane and demonstrate it in Europe over the winter. But first, he and Mabel headed west again to another exhibition, this time in his hometown of Davenport.

A gap in Ely's schedule permitted him to visit his mother and siblings in Williamsburg, as well as his father, stepmother, and stepbrother Paul in Davenport. He likely did not anticipate the reception awaiting him on October 6 as he stepped off the 1:45 p.m. train. His father was reportedly the first to greet him, followed by a crowd of "old school chums," businessmen, and his old mentor, Pete Petersen. Ely did not know about the brass band waiting to parade the hero of the USS *Birmingham* and *Pennsylvania* flights into town, and if he had, "he probably would have got off the train at Rock Island," Nathan supposedly quipped. In the midst of the parade, according to the local paper, he "took the wheel in Pete Petersen's car, in which he was riding, perhaps to detract attention which might be centered on him." Ely, the paper beamed, "is a modest young man, without a show of one spoiled by the gaze of the public eye."[19]

That night he was feted with a seven-course banquet reportedly organized by Petersen, featuring a floral biplane suspended above the table and the presentation of a gold watch inscribed "From Friends at Home." In accepting it, Ely was said to have "feelingly responded, assuring those present that his heart was ever with Davenport and his host of friends here."[20]

The hometown crowd at the exhibition on Suburban Island that weekend swelled to an estimated ten thousand. They were treated to about a dozen ascents, of which "every trip proved a thriller." On Sunday, October 8, Ely made two trips with passengers: one with Pete Petersen, and one, at long last, with Mabel.[21]

Filled with the well-wishes of his family and friends, Ely departed the next day for an exhibition in Georgia, while Mabel returned to New York. Fanciulli had also committed Ely to perform in Charlotte, North Carolina, over the weekend of October 26–27, but after that he had no further flights scheduled in the United States. He would be back in New York City with Mabel by the end of the month.[22]

The 1911 Georgia State Fair opened at Macon on Tuesday, October 10. Officials had specifically requested Ely; their second choice was Beachey. Ely agreed to fly almost every afternoon from October 12 to 19, weather permitting. He would skip only Sunday, when the fair would be closed, and another day when the infield would be occupied by Buffalo Bill's Wild West show, the immensely popular variety attraction created by fellow Iowan William F. Cody. On October 12, Ely flew twice, first swinging past downtown Macon at an estimated height of four hundred feet, and later soaring at perhaps five hundred feet over the fairground area.[23]

A reporter found Ely "an exceedingly modest chap, and he would never be singled out as a daring aviator. He would rather talk about almost anything else than his personal achievements and the great records that he has made."[24]

Ely did not fly on Friday the 13th—but not because of superstition. In landing on the rough field the previous day, his machine had sustained damage. As a result, to meet his contractual obligation he would have to add an extra day. On Saturday, he telegraphed Mabel: "Having lots of bad luck but think the run is over. Did not fly yesterday so won't leave here till the nineteenth [*sic*]. Your letter very welcome. Write some more."[25]

On the day Ely sent that telegram, a Swiss flier's gas tank exploded at 150 feet, killing him, and a Frenchman fell 250 feet at Rheims. He died two days later. According to the *New York Times*, the number of aviator deaths worldwide, beginning with Tom Selfridge's death three years earlier, now totaled an even hundred. From January to December 1910, thirty-two people had lost their lives in airplanes; the toll for the first three-quarters of 1911 was already nearly twice that number. As the newspaper noted soberly, "The progress in the science of aviation has been costly in human life."[26]

Ely's flights on Saturday, reportedly a series of circuits of the field with some thrilling swoops toward the crowd, "were the best that have ever been seen in Macon." Monday's program featured flights and motorcycle races, which were deemed "classy in the highest degree," but rain and a soggy track precluded both entertainments on Tuesday.[27]

Wednesday's Buffalo Bill's Wild West performance began with a "Grand Parade" through town. Before a record crowd of 20,000 Ely made up for his missed day the previous Friday with a few unscheduled flights. "Ely gave his best," the local paper lauded him, "and gave full measure and running over."[28]

Thursday, October 19, was Ely's final day of contractually required flying. Around noon, in weather conditions described as favorable, he went aloft and rose to a reported 3,100 feet without incident. Shortly before the day's second scheduled performance time of 3:00 p.m. he rose again and made a single circle of the track. It was later reported that Ely's chief mechanic, Frank Callan, saw him signal that he was preparing to land and that "everything was O.K. The motor was shut off and on its customary angle the machine swept to the ground; but the biplane was tilted and instead of alighting on its wheels the lower end of the cross frame struck the ground and the impact threw the young driver from his seat."

Mechanic Edgar Turner immediately sent a telegram to Mabel: "ELY HAS FALLEN. COME AT ONCE." He followed soon afterward with a brutally blunt message: "ELY IS DEAD. MEET THE BODY AT DAVENPORT, IOWA."

Eyewitnesses disagreed about what had happened. A police lieutenant remembered realizing, just before the crash, that "something was wrong with the machine." Some people were sure a cable had snapped. Others remembered seeing Ely struggling with the controls or leaning out of the seat.[29]

Fanciulli learned of the crash within hours and dashed off a letter to the aviation editor of the *New York Herald*, emphasizing that Ely was an exceptionally cautious aviator: "His accident cannot be chargeable to any unusual dangers in aviation. . . . He has made many great flights, had rare judgement and ability and was in no way sensational. . . . His accident can be compared to those accidents which occur so frequently with automobiles, such as skidding, running into a telegraph pole or similar accidents."[30]

But, as in the case of Lieutenant Kelly, Fanciulli must have been aware that to exonerate the aviator could call into question the integrity of the machine. Mid-letter, he raised the possibility of pilot error: "While I do not care to say this for publication until we have received details from Macon, it is very probable that the accident to Ely was caused either by some miscalculation on his part in respect to the height at which he was flying or from the fact that he has been experimenting recently in flying without the front elevator on his machine, as Beachey has been flying for the past six months."[31]

The *New York Herald* printed a portion of Fanciulli's message, identifying him only as a "representative of the Curtiss Company," and concluded with an evidently unsubstantiated quote: "Mr. Ely . . . enjoyed the confidence of Glenn H. Curtiss as a conservative aviator. Mr. Curtiss himself, being the most conservative of men, always urged caution to all of the aviators who were associated with him. The only reasonable surmise is that Mr. Ely in some unaccountable way lost control at a critical moment."[32]

If Fanciulli was correct that Ely had been experimenting with flying headless, the extent of those experiments remains unknown. He had certainly been flying with a front elevator in recent weeks; photographs clearly show the canard in place on the day his machine "almost scalped him" in Canton and on the day he gave Petersen a ride at Davenport. But no such structure is visible in any of the known photographs of Ely's crumpled machine. (Newsreel footage of Ely in flight at Macon was later released as part of a Pathé weekly series, but it has been lost to time.)[33]

The day after Ely's death, the *Macon Daily Telegraph* quoted Curtiss mechanic Turner as saying that Thursday was the third day on which Ely had flown without the front elevator, "He told me yesterday he had tried out the ship and thought it would work all right." Just before the crash, he reportedly saw Ely "working with the gearing" and was not sure "whether he was trying to make a dip or whether the machine wouldn't work as he expected it to without the front plane."[34]

Ultimately, whether Ely was flying with or without a front elevator proves little regarding his caution or recklessness. The headless configuration was not inherently a more dangerous one. True, it had been popularized by the undisputedly reckless Beachey, but the Wrights had begun making headless machines in 1910, and within seven months Curtiss would introduce his Headless D Racer. Indeed, soon all exhibition machines would be headless. If Ely was in fact flying headless in Macon, the most that can be said is that he might have been unaccustomed to the altered balance and responsiveness of the machine.

Being an aviator during the infancy of heavier-than-air flight was a dangerous and all-too-often deadly business, with little margin for error. "I have been with flying men for quite a while, know most of them, and like them," Turner reportedly said, "but Ely was the best of them all in my opinion. He simply made the mistake that the others have made—flew once too often."[35]

The wire service story out of Macon opened: "Eugene Ely, noted aviator and the first bird-man to alight on the deck of a man-of-war in a heavier-than-air machine, was fatally injured at the fair grounds here shortly after 3 o'clock this afternoon, when his biplane failed to rise from a sensational dip and fell fifty feet to the ground." The aviator's seeming intention, said the story, was "to startle the thousands beneath him."[36]

Many newspapers and magazines jumped to similar conclusions about what Ely had been attempting, and why. The Macon paper, which had earlier promoted Ely's upcoming appearance by trumpeting as "hazardous in the extreme" the feats of the man "styled the most daredevil flier in the country," now chose to blame his death on "an exhibition 'stunt.'" Had he but been engaged in "some practical use" for the airplane, the paper editorialized, "he would not have fallen. The . . . rocking of the boat, so to speak, to produce thrills, caused the accident."[37]

"Poor Mr. Ely!" wrote Captain Pond to his wife. "I was greatly shocked this morning when I picked up the paper. Only to think that after all his wonderful feats he should be killed so foolishly flying [at] only fifty feet. It only emphasizes the danger they all run."[38]

An unsigned article titled "Death of Eugene Ely," reminiscent of Fanciulli's letter in both style and substance, appeared in the November issue of *Aeronautics*. While acknowledging him as "one of the very best American fliers," the author equivocated: "He had always been known as a very conservative flier and only lately had taken up sensational 'stunts.'" The piece speculated that "it is possible either that Ely waited too long before straightening out or that the wind velocity changed close to the ground and he dropped further than he expected," but it simultaneously damned Ely with the summary observation that "aviators will get reckless." *Scientific American* concurred, bemoaning "the loss [of an aviator] which was most keenly felt in America," but identifying its cause as "the performing of foolhardy tricks."[39]

Such stories did a disservice to the man and his legacy. A defect, a structural failure, wind shear (that is, a sudden wind shift), or an unanticipated crosswind—all are possible explanations for Ely's crash, and all are more plausible than that he inexplicably decided to perform a risky stunt at an impossibly low altitude. For even the most conservative aviator, the dangers inherent in coaxing a fragile, winged machine upward toward the sun were legion.

If a defect did cause the final plunge, forensic analysis might have identified it. Accordingly, what remained of Ely's airplane was carefully crated for shipment back to Hammondsport and carted to the Macon train station in the morning, where the local sheriff intercepted it.

It had been nearly a year since Bud Mars had brazenly reclaimed the machine he was to use at Augusta, Georgia, and had instead brought it to Norfolk, just in time for his attempt to fly off Hamburg-American's *Pennsylvania*. Now the Georgia-Carolina Fair Association, in its ongoing lawsuit alleging breach of contract, had obtained yet another writ of attachment against the Curtiss company. This time, they were demanding payment out of any Curtiss assets still in the hands of the (Macon) Georgia State Fair Association—which included the wreckage.

In July 1912, the Macon officials finally made a settlement payment, and the attachment was released. But there is no evidence of what had happened to Ely's machine in the meantime, and its fate remains a mystery.

The day after Ely's death, a reporter declared, "The cause of the accident has not been ascertained," before adding prophetically, "and it is hardly probable that it ever will."[40]

Given the reams of sensationalist fiction that reporters and front men had concocted about Ely, it is hardly surprising that many dismissed him as a daredevil who threw the dice one time too many. But the remembrances of some journalists saw through the fictions to the modest man who thoughtfully weighed the ever-shifting elements of risk each time he took to the air. The *Atlanta Georgian and News* pronounced that Ely "had done as much perhaps as any other man to develop the art [of flying], particularly in applying it to the practical uses of the Army and Navy," while the *New Orleans Item* asserted: "Ely was one of the most scientific of all air men . . . always careful and by no means a showman in the air." Under the apt headline "Passing of a Student of Aviation," the *Seattle Daily Times* eulogized him as

> more than a "birdman." He was an adventurer of a cautious and far-seeing type that set new marks far in advance of the army of progress.
>
> His work demonstrated the availability of the airship for marine work. It proved conclusively that the new scientific toy could be used with success in new ways of which the world previously had been only dimly aware. . . .
>
> Men who met him here were impressed with Ely's consistent caution. He was not a man to take needless chances. His courage was unquestioned; but while his iron will scorned the prospect of danger, he did not overlook any chance by which his life might be imperiled. . . .
>
> Whatever the circumstances [of his death], the new science has lost one of its ablest exponents—a man who had just commenced to demonstrate the wider applicability of the flying machine.[41]

The *Philadelphia Inquirer*'s "Birdman" distinguished Ely from Ralph Johnstone, who had "used an aeroplane merely as he once used a bicycle—to amuse crowds and make money." Ely, by contrast,

> was in an entirely different class from Johnstone. . . . His flights to and from the decks of government cruisers, together with his scouting experiments for the Army, in Texas, showed him to be a pilot of rare ability, . . . well fitted for constructive work, . . . too good a man to be flying at county fairs, or any place where fancy or trick flying is at a premium.
>
> . . . There are plenty of men anxious to buck the game, but they are not equally equipped, physically and temperamentally. Let the second best men fly for gate receipts, but hold on to the Elys—this is Birdman's advice.[42]

Among the many messages of condolence to Mabel was a telegram from Captain Chambers. Having struggled between "daring" and "gallant" as the best way to describe Ely, in the end he simply wrote: "Please accept assurances of my heartfelt sympathy for you in your bereavement."[43]

The Georgia State Fair directors sent Mabel a letter expressing their sympathy and itemizing her husband's personal effects. Those included a "watch chain, ladies, with gold cross," and a "gold watch, chain and medal"—tokens of love and respect from his wife and hometown. The directors also enclosed copies of local news coverage of the crash, along with a postal card photograph of the wreck.[44]

Mabel may have seen an image strikingly similar to the postal card five months before, when a wire service ran an illustrated story about a large sculpture commissioned by the French government in tribute to the martyrs to aviation. *Monument aux aviateurs* had been introduced at the 1911 Salon des Artistes Français in Paris. Described as conveying "a pathos almost gruesome," the sculpture depicted an Icarus-like figure in a flying helmet much like Ely's, sprawled dead on his back amid the wreckage of the mechanical wings he had strapped to himself.[45]

She located a photograph of the sculpture and pasted it into the final page of her scrapbook, along with a pair of images of the splintered, tangled machine that, in the end, had betrayed her "dear, brave boy"—the "man-bird" who had briefly brushed the sky with his wings.[46]

CHAPTER 24

THE WORLD BEFORE HIM

ELY'S BODY WAS SENT north by train, with Frank Callan accompanying the casket. Nathan and his wife traveled east from Davenport to meet the train in Chicago, while Mabel came west from New York. They all rode together from Chicago to Davenport. On Saturday night, October 21, 1911, Eugene Ely's twenty-fifth birthday, his remains reached Williamsburg.[1]

The Presbyterian service was held the following afternoon at Ely's boyhood home, his mother's farm in York Center. The coffin was reportedly banked with magnificent floral tributes from around the country, among them "strikingly beautiful pieces" from Buffalo Bill Cody and Glenn Curtiss. Pete Petersen, Curtiss manager M. L. Nolan, and four Harrington cousins shouldered the coffin. Marie Mars had taken a train from Michigan, where her husband was exhibiting, but an unspecified "serious illness" kept her from attending.

The burial took place just up the hill, in the Harrington family cemetery. The cortege was said to have stretched for nearly a mile, many mourners having driven long distances through a cold rain to "pay their last respects to the boy who gave his life in his conquest of the air."[2]

On a blustery afternoon in October 1911, American "bird man" Eugene Ely was laid to rest beside his sister Julia, less than half a mile from where he had spent his boyhood. "Sad, beyond telling was the scene," said his hometown newspaper.[3]

Mabel moved back to Corte Madera to live with her parents. Despite having earned considerable sums in eighteen months of flying, Ely apparently left her with little more than the cash he had on him in Macon. Family lore holds that $75,000 or more lies in a long-forgotten bank account somewhere in the Midwest, but it has never been found.

In February 1912, Bud Mars organized a six-day aviation meet in Oakland. February 23 was "Ely Day," and Mabel was to receive half of the day's proceeds. She had planned to ride as a passenger with Blanche Scott, one of the first women aviators in the United States, now a member of the Curtiss team, and to sprinkle violets, her favorite flower, over the crowd. But high winds kept the pair on the ground that day and the next. Only a few daring souls managed to get aloft, including Lincoln Beachey—flying in drag as a "Parisienne aviatrix"—and Wright aviator Phil Parmelee. The six days grossed $22,000, of which the fliers shared $14,300; Mabel may have received a few thousand.[4]

Vivacious, charming, and still very much in the public eye, the twenty-one-year-old widow did not lack for suitors. Six months after the "Ely Day" benefit, her elopement with Philip B. Cross, the manager of a hotel in Marin County, made national headlines. Cross later became wealthy through real estate transactions, and by 1918 he and Mabel were said to be living in a "beautiful Oakland home." But she divorced him later that year, initially alleging that he had fraudulently deceived her into deeding to him her community property interest in valuable real estate. Ultimately, she settled for a payment of $45,000.[5]

In late 1920 she was in the news again following her midnight marriage to Wilfred Meloche (or de Meloche), a mining engineer who claimed to be a Belgian nobleman. The following March the society pages chronicled the couple's visit to San Diego and their plans to build a home in Pebble Beach, but within a month they had separated. Mrs. Meloche, still "one of the most attractive young matrons in San Francisco," obtained her second divorce in November 1922, on the basis of desertion.[6]

Fourteen years later, deep in the Great Depression, she married Richard Pierce, the operator of a chicken ranch in Sonoma County. During World War II she was active in county civil-defense efforts and worked as a teletype operator for the Army intelligence office at Fort Mason in San Francisco.

Around 1951 Mabel returned to San Rafael alone and worked for the Marin County Taxpayers' Association for the rest of the decade. She spent her last years trying to ensure that Ely's legacy endured. In the 1950s she lobbied heavily for a commemorative stamp, but in 1961 the U.S. Post Office celebrated fifty years of naval aviation with a stamp depicting not Ely, but the Curtiss A-1 hydroairplane that had been delivered to the Navy in July 1911.[7]

Mabel died after an illness in March 1960, just short of her seventieth birthday. Her final resting place in Colma, California, is less than ten miles from the site of Ely's historic landing on USS *Pennsylvania.* Sadly, she did not live to see Ely inducted into the National Aviation Hall of Fame in 1965, nor did she witness the placement of a plaque honoring him at the site of Selfridge Field ten years later.[8]

In 1913 Captain Chambers was placed, against his wishes, on the Navy's "retired list." Responding to "expressions of regret and sympathy" from a host of well-wishers, he wrote, "Aviation has its martyrs in more ways than one, and to me it seems that the crash which results in oblivion and glory to the aviator is preferable to some other results that come to the enthusiast who is laboring to make flying safe and who believes in its future usefulness to the country."[9]

That same year Beachey, declaring himself "a bad influence" on impressionable young aviators, announced his retirement from exhibition flying. Scarcely six months later he changed his mind and went back to pushing the envelope. On March 14, 1915, flying a brand new monoplane, he went into a steep dive over San Francisco Bay. The airplane's wings crumpled, and it plunged into the water. Two hours later, divers recovered Beachey's body. He had survived the crash but had become entangled in the machine and drowned. He was twenty-eight.[10]

Bud Mars, erroneously reported to have died in a crash in July 1911, lived another thirty-three years, to the age of sixty-eight.[11]

Nathan Ely, the one-time sailor, in 1918 received a commission at age fifty-two as a major in the Judge Advocate General's Corps, the U.S. Army's legal department. He rose to the rank of colonel and in 1919 was assigned to duty in the nation's capital, where he remained for most of the rest of his life. Through his Washington, D.C., connections he was able to advocate for recognition of his son's achievements.

The Distinguished Flying Cross medal was established by an Act of Congress in 1926; one of the earliest recipients was Charles Lindbergh, in 1927. In 1929, the award would go to the Wrights, and another to Curtiss four years later. In 1932, Adm. William A. Moffett, the "architect of naval aviation," who had been stationed in San Francisco at the time of Ely's *Pennsylvania* flight and who was an acquaintance of Nathan's, put forth Ely's name. On February 16, 1933, President Herbert Hoover held a Rose Garden ceremony at which Nathan accepted the medal on behalf of his son. The citation reflects a posthumous commendation to Eugene Burton Ely "for extraordinary achievement as a pioneer civilian aviator and for his significant contribution to the development of aviation in the United States Navy."[12]

Nathan kept his son's Distinguished Flying Cross for five years before donating it to the U.S. Naval Academy. On his suggestion it was placed on display, along with official photos of the *Pennsylvania* landing, for the edification of the Corps of Midshipmen. The six photographs can be found in the archives at Annapolis, but the medal itself has disappeared.[13]

Ely's candle burned briefly but brightly. At the time of his death, just shy of age twenty-five, he had been flying for a mere eighteen months and yet had become one of the most famous aviators in the world. That he accomplished so much in aviation at such a young age is not by itself surprising—Charles Lindbergh was twenty-five when he made the first solo nonstop transatlantic flight, and Chuck Yeager was twenty-four when he became the first pilot to exceed the speed of sound in level flight. Ely's life was cut short, but his achievement stands the test of time.

Ely's USS *Birmingham* and *Pennsylvania* demonstrations did not immediately change the course of naval warfare, but they did spark a long evolution: from the awkward and dangerous temporary platforms that Ely used to today's modern aircraft carriers. Chambers, so farsighted in other ways, did not envision the utility of dedicated aircraft carriers. He focused instead on hydroairplanes, even though experiments had already shown their impracticality in battle: they could be deployed only on relatively calm water, and not at all while the host ship was underway.

But until a number of practical issues could be addressed, on-deck flight operations would remain equally unrealistic. On a battleship of any class, a fore-mounted flight deck (as on *Birmingham*) blocked the view from the helm, while a stern-mounted one (as on *Pennsylvania*) interfered with the ship's guns. The longest flight deck either configuration could support was still too short for safe operation. Ely had proved that flights could be made, even in the face of adverse wind conditions, but soon a number of aviation mishaps would prove just how skillful—and how lucky—he had been.[14]

Airborne attacks during World War I spurred the next phase of the evolution of the flight deck. The British light battle cruiser HMS *Furious* was fitted with a planked "flying-off" foredeck that sloped downward, and in the summer of 1917, the Royal Navy conducted launching and landing trials with Sopwith Pups (manufactured by Thomas Sopwith, the English aviator-turned-industrialist who had taken Mabel on her second flight). Squadron Commander Edwin H. Dunning made the first successful landing on a ship underway (*Pennsylvania* had been at anchor) on August 2, but he was killed five days later during an attempt to land on the foredeck when an updraft caught a wing and threw his machine overboard. *Furious* was reconfigured a few months later with a separate landing deck at the stern, outfitted with a sandbag arresting system similar to the one used on *Pennsylvania*. The ship launched aircraft against Zeppelin sheds in 1918, but deck landings were never attempted once the ship began operational cruises.[15]

By the end of the war, the generally accepted approach involved "through-deck" carriers, in which the flight deck spanned the full length of the ship. Hulls of carriers rapidly lengthened to accommodate the greater runway required by larger aircraft and heavier payloads. For expediency, carriers were initially built on repurposed hulls, such as that of *Furious*, but eventually they would be purpose-designed, enhancing safety and functionality. But it was not until 1933, more than two decades after Ely had demonstrated the feasibility of aircraft operations at sea, that the U.S. Navy finally launched USS *Ranger* (CV 4), its first ship designed specifically as an aircraft carrier.[16]

Although it would be a fitting tribute to Ely, no aircraft carrier has been named after him. The first U.S. carrier, converted from the collier *Jupiter* in 1922, was rechristened USS *Langley* (CV 1), after the inventor of the "Aerodrome" that crashed into the Potomac in 1903. The seaplane tender USS *Wright* (AZ 1/AV 1) was commissioned in 1921, followed by the carrier USS *Wright* (CVL 49), commissioned in 1947, and the aviation logistics support ship USNS *Wright* (T-AVB 3), commissioned in 1986. The first of these three was named for Orville alone; the other two also honor Wilbur, who had been so quick to dismiss naval aviation as "impossible."[17]

And yet Ely lives on: the dates of his famous flights are committed to memory by midshipmen at Annapolis, and modern historians regard his landing on *Pennsylvania* as "epic." Ely was inducted into the First Flight Society at a 1994 ceremony at Kill Devil Hills in North Carolina, and he is enshrined in the Naval Aviation Hall of Honor at the National Naval Aviation Museum in Pensacola, Florida. His statue graces the Naval Aviation Monument in Virginia Beach, while one of the bronze reliefs at the Navy Memorial in Washington, D.C., depicts the *Birmingham* flight. In 2010 and 2011, newspaper and magazine articles commemorated the centennials of his ship flights, and the centennial of his burial was marked with a graveside ceremony.[18]

Other aviators might possibly have done what he did, but Ely was the first, acting "cheerfully and enthusiastically," as Chambers put it, "without the prospect of any reward whatever"—a true "pioneer" of naval aviation.[19]

Two decades after Ely's *Birmingham* flight, Nathan Ely wrote to the Smithsonian Institution: "I have here in my possession the propeller used in the flight from the ship. The plane came so close to the water that the tip of the propeller just touched the top of a wave and was somewhat splintered. If your institution desires the propeller I will be glad to arrange to turn it over to you." The Smithsonian gratefully accepted the donation, one of the few surviving artifacts from Ely's flying career. The propeller remains today in the Smithsonian's National Air and Space Museum collection.[20]

The letter Nathan wrote to accompany the propeller effectively summarized his son's brief life with a simplicity that Ely would have appreciated: "The plane was a 'Curtiss' with front controls, and the pilot sat out on the front edge with nothing but the world before him."

He was sitting out on that front edge on a hazy afternoon in January 1911. It had been barely an hour since he had made the world's first shipboard landing, barely two months since he had made the world's first shipboard launch. Now he prepared to fly into history once more.

An eyewitness described what happened next:

> Ely left the cruiser with the dispatch of an automobile on the ground. Ascending as soon as he left the platform, he dipped down until he was within ten feet of the surface of the bay. Then he shot upward. . . .
>
> There was another chorus of screeching sirens from the harbor craft, and Ely was on his way over the hills. . . .
>
> In a few minutes he had melted into the gray sky.[21]

AFTERWORD

FROM HIS YOUTH, my eldest son, John H. Zobel, found fascination in the sea; the Boston Red Sox; hiking in the White Mountains and other places worldwide; the English language; acting; and wit: oral, written, and musical.

Earning a Harvard degree in 1981 (English language and literature, cum laude), he anticipated law school. In 1982, Stanford Law School accepted him. Following a solid three years there, with particular brilliance in Evidence, he entered a clerkship with the late Harold M. Fong in the U.S. District Court in Honolulu. Then, rejecting offers from Los Angeles and San Francisco firms, he began practice as a litigator with Davis Wright & Jones, a large Seattle law firm now known as Davis Wright Tremaine, where he met LaVerne Woods. The two would marry a few years later and eventually have a son, Eric.

The courtroom turned out to be John's natural stage. His seniors (soon to be his law partners) recognized his perceptive, thorough trial preparation. My judicial friends in the King County Superior Court have told me how calmly and effectively he conducted himself, an evaluation with which, after seeing him in action, I (dispassionately) concurred.

Meanwhile, John was working himself into another career: as an author. He eventually left the firm to devote himself full time to the roles of father and writer-in-residence.

In 2011, for the one hundredth anniversary of Eugene Ely's historic landing on USS *Pennsylvania,* John and I collaborated on a piece in *American Heritage*. For John, it was only the beginning of years of internet scouring, hands-on archival digging, and personal interviews, in search of the real Eugene Ely.

The result, in John's direct, precise writing style, is this book—which he never saw in its finished form.

At age fifty-six, atop Aconcagua, highest peak in the Southern and Western Hemispheres, he died of cardiac failure—not lack of heart.

—HON. HILLER B. ZOBEL

ACKNOWLEDGMENTS

IN JANUARY 2017, my husband, John H. Zobel, received an email of the sort that writers dream about: the Naval Institute Press was considering his biography of early aviator Eugene Ely for publication. But the manuscript's word count was twice what the Press could publish. Could he produce a trimmed version by the end of May, for further review? John replied that he would do his utmost.

A few days later, we left for Argentina to meet our dear friend Alexander ("Sasha") Alexievich Tokarev, a top Russian climber, who had been my teammate on Mount Everest in 1990. The three of us had climbed together in the Tavan Bogd mountains of Western Mongolia and the Sayan Mountains near Sasha's home in Siberia. Our trip to Aconcagua was to have been a last hurrah, our final high-altitude climb. At just under 23,000 feet, Aconcagua is the highest peak in the Southern and Western Hemispheres: formidable in height but not technically difficult, making it a perfect objective for three "mature" climbers. On January 30, as an afternoon storm began to gather, we reached the summit, where John quite suddenly died.

For some time, I did nothing with his manuscript. The project was too massive. While the core of the book was the Ely biography, it was wrapped in a scholarly history of the evolution of transportation at the turn of the twentieth century and adorned with fascinating digressions. Ely's story—the book's heart—needed to be set free. Little by little, I began to release it. I can only hope that the result honors John's memory and that he would have been pleased with it.

The emergence of this book from the chrysalis of the original manuscript would not have been possible without the partnership of the author's brother Dave Zobel in every aspect of the process. For all his many roles and thousands of hours of work, I cannot thank him enough. Hiller B. Zobel, the author's father, worked closely with the author on the development of the original manuscript and first suggested the Naval Institute Press. The author's brother Thomas Calder served as *chercheur* in all matters concerning early aviation in France.

This work would not exist were it not for the patience beyond measure of acquisitions editors Laura Davulis and Susan Brook, who were my gracious guides through the process. Project editor Jane Lincoln Taylor hewed the manuscript to a size that allowed me to begin the work of fashioning it into its present shape. Auburn University professor emeritus William Trimble, the preeminent scholar of Glenn Curtiss' life and work, generously lent his careful eye and provided comments on two drafts of the manuscript. Kathy Svitil was merciless in the rigor of her fact-checking and unstinting with her humor. Cdr. Robert Coolbaugh, USN (Ret.), was a source of extensive technical information about the Glenn Curtiss pusher biplane and gave the author much enthusiasm and encouragement, for which I thank him profusely.

Anna Durr, Lois Gene Durr, and James R. Austin; Ann Stamets, Janis Henderson, and Paul and William T. Henderson III; Daniel Ely Farr III and Barbara McVeigh; and Elaine Hall, family members of Eugene Ely and Mabel Hall, honored us with their trust, shared their family albums, and provided invaluable information about Ely's life. Jackie and Elizabeth Manning, family members of Whipple Hall, were generous with their time and their collection; and John Pond shared information on his great-grandfather, Capt. Charles F. Pond.

If the author were here, I know he would have expressed his gratitude to Donald Lamm for his wisdom and consistent encouragement on this and many other projects over the years; and to Stephen Surko for his contributions to the research for this book and his decades of friendship. Many thanks to Steve Cottrell for his insights regarding Ely's days as an auto stage driver; Martina Fähnemann of Hapag-Lloyd AG for information regarding the Hamburg-American Line; Martin Mitchell for sharing the artifacts of his friend Jerome Fanciulli; John Sippel for multifaceted assistance and encouragement; and Gary Yelle for background regarding Ely's driving career.

So many dedicated historians, librarians, curators, archivists, museum and historical society staff, and others provided crucial assistance, among them Thomas Allen, Julia Blum, Lisa Crunk, Scott Daniels, David D'Onofrio, Peter Drummey, Susan Falknor, Carroll Gray, John Hattendorf, William Heitshusen, Jessica Herrick, Lygia Ionnitiu, Christina Kastell, Giacinta Koontz, Dave Lam, Ryan Leichenauer, Rick Leisenring, Mary Miller, Paul Oelkrug, Sinclair Powell, Claudia Reeder, Michael Rhodes, John Ross, Alex Spencer, Chris Stanton, Stephen Stein, Joshua Stoff, Dean Veremakis, and Katherine Williams.

Finally, my deep appreciation to Katharine Wroth, Sarah Zobel, and Libby Zobel for their moral support; and to Dee Wroth for bringing them, Thomas Calder, Dave Zobel, and the author into this world, and forever changing my life.

—LaVerne Woods

NOTES

AUTHOR'S NOTE

1. For example, Mills, "When Aviators Are Up in the Air"; Eugene B. Ely biography, Morehouse Collection, National Air and Space Museum, Smithsonian Institution, Washington, D.C. (hereafter Ely biography, NASM); Aviation Biography Collection: Eugene Burton Ely, Naval History and Heritage Command, Washington, D.C.; *Evening Sun* (Baltimore, Md.), 11/7/1910, supp., 2.
2. *Circleville (Ohio) Herald*, 12/6/1926, 7.
3. Glenn Curtiss, letter to Lincoln Beachey, March 26, 1914, Glenn H. Curtiss Museum, Hammondsport, N.Y.
4. *Independent-Journal* (San Rafael, Calif.), 9/6/1958, M3; *Evening Sun* (Baltimore, Md.), 11/7/1910, supp., 2; *Rock Island (Ill.) Argus*, 10/9/1911, 8.
5. McCullough, *Wright Brothers*, 107, 109–10.
6. Casey, *Curtiss*, 39, 71.

INTRODUCTION

1. Corn, *Winged Gospel*, 48; Bulfinch, *Bulfinch's Mythology*, 124–26, 156–57; Olcott, *Star Lore of All Ages*, 295; Goss, *Life and Death of Llewellynn Jewitt*, 46–47.
2. Paine, *Sea and Civilization*, 546.
3. *Morning Oregonian* (Portland), 3/6/1910, 8.
4. *Williamsburg (Iowa) Journal-Tribune*, 6/30/1910, 2.

CHAPTER 1. SON OF YORK

1. Bradford, *[History] Of Plimoth Plantation*, 2nd page following 270; Ely, *Records of the Descendants of Nathaniel Ely*, viii–ix, 1–5; Weis, *Early Generations*, 7–8; Abbott, "Cambridge," 305–6.
2. Ely, *Records of the Descendants of Nathaniel Ely*, 59, 131–32, 268; Warner, *History of Portage County, Ohio*, 416; Union Historical Company, *History of Iowa County*, 696.
3. Ely, *Records of the Descendants of Nathaniel Ely*, 412; *Iowa State Register* (Iowa City, Iowa), 12/4/1885, 7; 12/16/1885, 6; *Vidette-Reporter* (Iowa City, Iowa), 1/31/1885, 4; 3/21/1885, 4; 10/23/1886, 4.
4. *Iowa State Register* (Iowa City, Iowa), 12/29/1885, 6; *Vidette-Reporter* (Iowa City, Iowa), 1/16/1886, 4; *Williamsburg (Iowa) Journal-Tribune*, 9/7/1939, 1; Iowa County, Certificate of Live Birth 1/166-11 (11/6/1886) for "Eugene H. Eally," Lois G. Durr, private collection. (The birth certificate misspells Ely's

name and gives his birth date as October 21, 1886, although the date written in the family bible, in Emma's handwriting, is October 22.)

5. Iowa County Atlas: York Township, 1886; *Williamsburgh (Iowa) Journal*, 2/26/1886, 2.
6. Iowa Legislature, 34 GA (1911), 1757–58, http://www.legis.iowa.gov/docs/publications/YSJL/855223.pdf#page=1762; *Williamsburg (Iowa) Journal-Tribune*, 1/19/1911, 1; *Daily Citizen* (Iowa City, Iowa), 6/23/1892, 3; *Cedar Rapids (Iowa) Evening Gazette*, 3/15/1906, 6; *Iowa State Register* (Des Moines), 10/14/1891, 8; *Iowa Citizen* (Iowa City), 12/25/1891, 9; *Davenport (Iowa) Daily Leader*, 5/9/1894, 2; *Muscatine (Iowa) Daily News-Tribune*, 5/16/1894, 1; *Iowa State Press* (Iowa City), 1/10/1900, 5; *Williamsburgh (Iowa) Journal*, 5/17/1889, 3.
7. *Williamsburg (Iowa) Journal-Tribune*, 9/7/1939, 1; von Schaezler/Ely Scrapbooks, Collection of William and Paul Henderson and Ann Stamets; Iowa State Census, 1895, Iowa City Township, First Ward, 211; *Daily Times* (Davenport, Iowa), 3/7/1941, 8; *Palimpsest* 23, no. 5 (May 1942): 153.
8. Julia M. Ely, http://FindAGrave.com/memorial/74630941; *Burlington (Iowa) Hawk-Eye*, 7/14/1896, 1.
9. *Maine* I, in Naval History and Heritage Command, *Dictionary of American Naval Fighting Ships*, https://history.navy.mil/research/histories/ship-histories/danfs.html (hereafter *DANFS*); *New-York Tribune*, 2/16/1898, 1; 2/26/1898, 1; 4/23/1898, 1; 4/26/1898, 1; *New York World*, 2/17/1898, 1; 2/28/1898, 4.
10. Enlistment Record and Descriptive List, Nathan Dana Ely, May 26, 1898, National Personnel Records Center (NPRC), National Archives, St. Louis, Mo.; *Davenport (Iowa) Daily Leader*, 5/27/1898, 2.
11. *Davenport (Iowa) Daily Leader*, 5/31/1898, 2; *Lancaster* I, in *DANFS*.
12. *Davenport (Iowa) Daily Leader*, 8/14/1898, 6; 6/13/1898, 6; *Lancaster* I, in *DANFS*.
13. Enlistment Record and Descriptive List, Nathan Dana Ely, May 26, 1898, NPRC.
14. *Age-Herald* (Birmingham, Ala.), 8/11/1898, 5; *Oregon* I, in *DANFS*.
15. *Davenport (Iowa) Weekly Leader*, 8/26/1898, 2; *Davenport (Iowa) Daily Leader*, 8/14/1898, 6; 9/29/1898, 2; 2/28/1899, 14; *Davenport (Iowa) Daily Republican*, 3/22/1901, 6.
16. *Davenport (Iowa) Daily Leader*, 9/29/1899, 2; 10/2/1900, 7; 11/11/1900, 7; *Davenport (Iowa) Democrat*, 7/16/1899, 6; *Davenport (Iowa) Daily Republican*, 11/13/1900, 7; Vital Statistics: Births, Keokuk County–Wright County, 1900, RG 48 Public Health, vol. 163, 336, Iowa State Archives, Des Moines.
17. *Daily Times* (Davenport, Iowa), 1/24/1901, 4.

CHAPTER 2. RISE OF THE WHEELMEN

1. Trimble, *Hero of the Air*, 5–11; Crouch, *Bishop's Boys*, 112–15.
2. *Pall Mall Gazette* (London), 6/23/1881, 10; Goddard, *Colonel Albert Pope*, 67–78.

3. *Times* (London), 10/30/1901, 7.
4. *New York Times*, 6/14/1887, 4; 7/9/1887, 8; *Elyria (Ohio) Democrat*, 6/27/1889, 8; McCullough, *Wright Brothers*, 22.
5. Crouch, *Bishop's Boys*, 94–100, 107–9, 113, 160–61, 167–69, 200; McCullough, *Wright Brothers*, 25.
6. Crouch, *Bishop's Boys*, 143–45, 167–68; McCullough, *Wright Brothers*, 36–39.
7. McCullough, *Wright Brothers*, 55–56, 133; Casey, *Curtiss*, xi–xii; Crouch, *Bishop's Boys*, 246, 276, 300; Crouch, *Wings*, 145–47; Roseberry, *Glenn Curtiss*, 63.
8. Roseberry, *Glenn Curtiss*, 9–12; Trimble, *Hero of the Air*, 3–5.
9. Roseberry, *Glenn Curtiss*, 17, 20–21; Trimble, *Hero of the Air*, 6, 9.
10. *Bryan (Ohio) Democrat*, 7/28/1911, 2; Roseberry, *Glenn Curtiss*, 35–36; Trimble, *Hero of the Air*, 11.
11. *Bryan (Ohio) Democrat*, 7/28/1911, 2; *New York Times*, 7/27/1944, 17; U.S. Census, 1910, San Antonio, Texas; Roseberry, *Glenn Curtiss*, 37, 40; *Engineering* 2, no. 1 (October 1891): 2.
12. Roseberry, *Glenn Curtiss*, 40.
13. A. Roy Knabenshue Collection, 1.1, box 1, folder 2: [biographical sketch], 5, National Air and Space Museum, Smithsonian Institution, Washington, D.C.; *New York Times*, 10/26/1904, 1; 11/6/1904, part 3, 6; *St. Louis (Mo.) Globe-Democrat*, 10/26/1904, 1; 11/2/1904, 1.
14. Trimble, *Hero of the Air*, 13.
15. *Oakland (Calif.) Tribune*, 9/12/1904, 8; *Birmingham News*, 8/19/1905, 2.
16. *Evening Star* (Washington, D.C.), 6/14/1906, 2.
17. Crouch, *Bishop's Boys*, 281, 298–99.
18. Crouch, *Bishop's Boys*, 313–14; Roseberry, *Glenn Curtiss*, 51–53; Trimble, *Hero of the Air*, 14–15.
19. *Rochester (Ind.) Weekly Republican*, 5/26/1898, 6; *Williamsburgh (Iowa) Journal*, 5/17/1895, 4; Downer, *History of Davenport*, vol. 2, 63; *Daily Iowa Capital* (Des Moines), 11/6/1899, 8; *Boston Globe*, 1/22/1900, evening ed., 19; *Buffalo (N.Y.) Courier*, 1/22/1900, 1; *New Bethlehem (Pa.) Vindicator*, 3/23/1900, supp., 2; *Davenport (Iowa) Daily Republican*, 5/2/1900, 8; *Cedar Rapids (Iowa) Republican*, 5/3/1900, 3.
20. *Rochester (Ind.) Weekly Republican*, 5/26/1898, 6; *Kendallville (Ind.) Daily Sun*, 10/1/1898, 1; *New York Times*, 10/2/1898, mag., 6; *Indianapolis Sun*, 2/21/1899.
21. *Goshen (Ind.) Daily News*, 6/1/1899, 4; *Kansas City (Mo.) Star*, 12/29/1898, 4; *Fort Wayne (Ind.) Journal Gazette*, 10/28/1900, 14.
22. *Davenport (Iowa) Daily Republican*, 12/10/1902, 8; 12/16/1902, 7; 2/7/1903, 8; *Iowa State Press* (Iowa City), 1/14/1903, 7; *Williamsburg (Iowa) Journal-Tribune*, 1/22/1903, 6; *Davenport (Iowa) Times*, 3/3/1903, 9.
23. *Williamsburg (Iowa) Journal-Tribune*, 5/7/1903, 3; 7/9/1903, 2; 8/20/1903, 3; *Iowa Citizen* (Iowa City), 9/1/1905, 7.

24. Peter C. Petersen Sr. Collection, Putnam Museum, Davenport, Iowa; *Argus* (Rock Island, Ill.), 8/8/1904, 6; *Motor Age* 15, no. 12 (March 25, 1909): 46 (Petersen misspelled as Peterson).
25. Mahan, "Eugene B. Ely," 74; *Williamsburg (Iowa) Journal-Tribune*, 11/10/1904, 4; *Iowa State Press* (Iowa City), 11/18/1903, 8, citing the *Oxford (Iowa) Messenger*; *Williamsburg (Iowa) Journal-Tribune*, 11/19/1903, 3.
26. *Iowa City Daily Press*, 9/27/1904, 1; *Muscatine (Iowa) Journal*, 9/27/1905, 3; Mahan, "Eugene B. Ely," 75.
27. *Williamsburg (Iowa) Journal-Tribune*, 6/16/1904, 5; *Iowa City Daily Press*, 8/26/1904, 4.
28. Mahan, "Eugene B. Ely," 75–76.
29. Mahan, "Eugene B. Ely," 74–75; *Iowa City Daily Press*, 12/5/1904, 1.
30. Mahan, "Eugene B. Ely," 75; Oath and Enlistment Papers of Eugene Burton Ely, California National Guard, California State Archives, Sacramento.
31. Mahan, "Eugene B. Ely," 75; *Muscatine (Iowa) Journal*, 9/27/1905, 3.

CHAPTER 3. **FIRE AND EARTH**

1. *Williamsburg (Iowa) Journal-Tribune*, 2/4/1904, 1.
2. *Williamsburg (Iowa) Journal-Tribune*, 10/19/1905, 2, 4.
3. "Lost Film from 1906" (San Francisco), YouTube, accessed December 17, 2022, http://YouTu.be/ZdvRNdGlgzY.
4. *San Francisco Call*, 3/8/1900, 5; 8/20/1901, 7; 9/28/1901, 4.
5. *San Francisco News Letter and California Advertiser* 86, no. 25 (Christmas 1913): 64; *Motor Age* 5, no. 16 (April 21, 1904): 9; *Western Field* 7, no. 1 (August 1905): 584; *Automobile* 13, no. 19 (November 9, 1905): 534; *San Francisco Chronicle*, 8/9/1906, 14.
6. *San Francisco Call*, 3/22/1904, 10; *Automobile Topics* 13, no. 13 (January 5, 1907): 1130; *Supplemental List of Owners*, 1906 (1/1/1906–2/1/1906), 5.
7. U.S. Census, 1900, San Francisco, Calif.; *San Francisco Call*, 8/9/1905, 9; 9/27/1905, 13; "San Francisco Blue Book" (1906), 398; *Supplemental List of Owners*, 1906 (3/1/1906–4/1/1906), 4.
8. *Williamsburg (Iowa) Journal-Tribune*, 4/26/1906, 5; 5/10/1906, 1; National Oceanic and Atmospheric Administration (NOAA), "Study of Earthquake Losses," 5, 25; U.S. Census, 1910, English Township, Iowa; *Bismarck (N.D.) Daily Tribune*, 4/25/1906, 1; *Chicago Tribune*, 4/20/1906, 1; *San Francisco Call*, 4/23/1906, 1/9/1911, 5; *Norfolk (Neb.) Weekly News-Journal*, 10/20/1911, 1.
9. *Williamsburg (Iowa) Journal-Tribune*, 5/24/1906, 3; *Iowa City (Iowa) Daily Press*, 3/17/1906, 3; Daily Times (Davenport, Iowa), 9/17/1901, 5.
10. *Williamsburg (Iowa) Journal-Tribune*, 10/11/1906, 1; 10/25/1906, 5; 11/1/1906, 1, 3; 7/11/1907, 1, 4; 9/19/1907, 1; 9/26/1907, 4.
11. *Oakland (Calif.) Tribune*, 1/22/1911, 23; *San Francisco Call*, 5/3/1906, 2; 5/15/1906, 3; *Santa Cruz (Calif.) Sentinel*, 6/26/1907, 5.
12. *San Francisco Call*, 12/31/1906, 6; 1/21/1907, 5; 2/19/1907, 6; 2/23/1907, 5; 2/25/1907, 3.

13. *New York Times*, 4/25/1907, 5; *San Francisco News Letter and California Advertiser* 86, no. 25 (Christmas 1913): 60–64; *Morning Echo* (Bakersfield, Calif.), 4/21/1906, 1.
14. *San Francisco Call*, 4/9/1907, 8; 4/14/1907, 43; 5/5/1907, 21; *San Francisco Chronicle*, 6/16/1907, 43; *Supplemental List of Owners*, 1907 (5/1/1907–6/1/1907), 9.
15. *San Francisco Call*, 3/2/1907, 8.
16. *San Francisco Call*, 5/16/1907, 7; 5/20/1907, 5.
17. *Arkansas City (Kans.) Daily Traveler*, 6/2/1896, 2; *Westfield (N.Y.) Republican*, 6/10/1896, 1; *New York Times*, 7/10/1896, 6; *Philadelphia Times*, 9/26/1896, 8; *Ogden (Utah) Standard-Examiner*, 2/19/1928, B, 2; *Time* 16, no. 26 (December 29, 1930): 31.
18. *Arizona Republic* (Phoenix), 10/29/1958, 13; Jones, "If Only in Another Time," 1; *Inter Ocean* (Chicago, Ill.), 8/15/1906, 5; *Brooklyn (N.Y.) Daily Eagle*, 8/16/1906, 10; *Inter Ocean* (Chicago, Ill.), 8/27/1906, 9; 9/16/1906, 16; *Ogden (Utah) Standard-Examiner*, 2/19/1928, B, 2.
19. *San Francisco Call*, 5/26/1907, 33.
20. *San Francisco Call*, 2/23/1907, 5; 2/25/1907, 3; 7/5/1907, 12; *San Francisco Examiner*, 7/5/1907, 10; *Automobile Topics* 14, no. 15 (July 7, 1920): 1302.
21. *San Jose (Calif.) Herald*, 8/6/1887, 2; *Sausalito (Calif.) News*, 12/4/1926, 1; *Independent-Journal* (San Rafael, Calif.), 9/6/1958, M3; *San Francisco Call*, 7/28/1907, 36.
22. Marin County (Calif.) Recorder's Office (Ely's age incorrectly listed as twenty-seven); *San Francisco Call*, 7/28/1907, 36; *Sausalito (Calif.) News*, 8/10/1907, 3; *Williamsburg (Iowa) Journal-Tribune*, 7/7/1907, 1, 4; 8/29/1907, 10.
23. *San Francisco Call*, 8/6/1907, 8; 10/6/1907, 49; 8/29/1907, 10.
24. *San Francisco Call*, 8/29/1907, 10; 8/26/1907, 9; 8/11/1907, 39.
25. *San Francisco Call*, 9/15/1907, 37; 9/16/1907, 9; 9/17/1907, 10; 9/22/1907, 21; *Automobile* 17, no. 14, October 3, 1907, 471; *San Francisco Call*, 10/6/1907, 49.
26. *Lake County Examiner* (Lakeview, Ore.), 10/15/1908, 5.
27. *Lake County Examiner* (Lakeview, Ore.), 10/15/1908, 8; 11/5/1908, 1, 8; 11/26/1908, 4; 5/20/1909, 1; *San Francisco Chronicle*, 12/2/1907, 6.
28. *Lake County Examiner* (Lakeview, Ore.), 10/29/1908, 8; 5/20/1909, 8.
29. *San Francisco Call*, 12/20/1908, 20; 12/29/1908, 7; *San Francisco Chronicle*, 12/22/1908, 9.
30. *San Francisco Call*, 12/20/1908, 20; 12/29/1908, 7; 1/3/1909, 35; 1/4/1909, 9; 1/5/1909, 10; 1/8/1909, 10; *San Francisco Chronicle*, 12/25/1908, 5; 1/8/1909, 9.
31. *San Francisco Call*, 2/18/1907, 2; 5/25/1907, 8; 9/25/1907, 10; 2/19/1909, 7; *Los Angeles Times*, 5/29/1908, 6; *Oakland (Calif.) Tribune*, 1/7/1909, 12.
32. *San Francisco Call*, 2/20/1909, 11.
33. *San Francisco Examiner*, 3/21/1909, 40; *San Francisco Call*, 3/10/1909, 4; 3/28/1909, 46; 3/29/1909, 9, 10; Eugene B. Ely Scrapbooks, NHHC, S–005, folder B, 49 (photograph of Ely driving the Tourist).
34. *San Francisco Call*, 5/3/1909, 5.

CHAPTER 4. INTO THE AIR

1. *New York Herald*, 6/12/1861, 8; 6/19/1861, 1; *Chicago Tribune*, 9/2/1861, 1; *Philadelphia Inquirer*, 10/14/1861, 8.
2. *Los Angeles Times*, 10/8/1903, 2; *Evening Star* (Independence, Kans.), 10/10/1903, 4; *Chicago Tribune*, 12/9/1903, 1; Anderson, *History of Aerodynamics*, 239–40; Winchester, *Chronology of Aviation*, 21–22; Turnbull and Lord, *History of United States Naval Aviation*, 1; Roseberry, *Glenn Curtiss*, 13, 26, 30–31.
3. Crouch, *Bishop's Boys*, 291–93, 304–12; Roseberry, *Glenn Curtiss*, 63–64.
4. Bonney, "Chiefs of the Army Air Force," 130; *Automobile* 21, no. 7 (August 12, 1909): 282; *Bulletins of the Aerial Experiment Association* 35 (March 8, 1909): 33; Crouch, *Bishop's Boys*, 346–48; Corn, *Winged Gospel*, 37.
5. *National Geographic Magazine* 24, no. 6 (June 1903): 219; Roseberry, *Glenn Curtiss*, 47–49; Crouch, *Bishop's Boys*, 350; Trimble, *Hero of the Air*, 11, 14, 20.
6. Roseberry, *Glenn Curtiss*, 54–57, 58; Trimble, *Hero of the Air*, 15–16, 20–21.
7. *National Geographic Magazine* 24, no. 6 (June 1903): 231; Roseberry, *Glenn Curtiss*, 69–71; Trimble, *Hero of the Air*, 21; Crouch, *Bishop's Boys*, 350–51.
8. *Bulletins of the Aerial Experiment Association* 10 (September 14, 1908): 22; Crouch, *Bishop's Boys*, 351; Roseberry, *Glenn Curtiss*, 72; Trimble, *Hero of the Air*, 21–23.
9. Trimble, *Hero of the Air*, 26–27, 29–31; Bulletins of the Aerial Experiment Association 6 (August 17, 1908): 9.
10. Roseberry, *Glenn Curtiss*, 102–4, 107–11; Trimble, *Hero of the Air*, 31–35.
11. Roseberry, *Glenn Curtiss*, 144; *Bulletins of the Aerial Experiment Association* 9 (September 7, 1908): 4; Trimble, *Hero of the Air*, 43.
12. Roseberry, *Glenn Curtiss*, 87, 124–25, 127; McCullough, *Wright Brothers*, 190.
13. Roseberry, *Glenn Curtiss*, 127–28; Trimble, *Hero of the Air*, 39–40; McCullough, *Wright Brothers*, 191.
14. *San Francisco Chronicle*, 5/7/1909, 9; 5/10/1909, 8.
15. *Motor World* 20, no. 8 (May 20, 1909): 291; *San Francisco Call*, 5/10/1909, 9; *San Francisco Chronicle*, 5/10/1909, 8; *San Francisco Examiner*, 5/10/1909, 9.
16. *Motor Age* 15, no. 20 (May 20, 1909): 18.
17. *San Francisco Call*, 5/4/1909, 11; 5/12/1909, 4; 5/17/1909, 7.
18. *San Francisco Call*, 5/23/1909, 39; 5/24/1909, 5; *San Francisco Chronicle*, 12/22/1908, 9.
19. *San Francisco Call*, 5/24/1909, 1.
20. *San Francisco Call*, 5/24/1909, 5; 6/12/1909, 11.
21. *Morning Union* (Grass Valley, Calif.), 8/1/1909, 6; 8/4/1909, 6; *San Francisco Chronicle*, 9/2/1909, 12; John Daly, E-M-F expert, email correspondence with the author, March 2014.
22. *Morning Union* (Grass Valley, Calif.), 10/22/1909, 6; *San Francisco Examiner*, 10/23/1909, 3; *Oakland (Calif.) Tribune*, 10/24/1909, 13; *San Francisco Call*, 10/24/1909, 37.
23. *San Francisco Call*, 11/24/1909, 10; 11/26/1909, 7; *Oakland (Calif.) Tribune*, 11/27/1909, 3; *San Jose (Calif.) Mercury*, 11/26/1909, 16.

24. *Motor World* 21, no. 11 (December 9, 1909): 523.
25. *San Francisco Examiner*, 11/29/1909, 8; *Hawaiian Star* (Honolulu), 12/7/1909, 6; *Automobile Topics* 19, no. 10 (December 11, 1909): 646 (misidentifying the White as a Buick and giving Turner's name as "Lever"); *San Jose (Calif.) Mercury*, 11/26/1909, 16; 11/29/1909, 8; Eugene B. Ely Scrapbooks, NHHC, S–005, folder B, 37 (photograph caption giving Ely's racing results); *San Francisco Call*, 11/30/1909, 10.
26. *Bulletins of the Aerial Experiment Association* 10 (September 14, 1908): 22; 34 (March 1, 1909): 40–41; Roseberry, *Glenn Curtiss*, 149–51.
27. Thomas, "Question Concerning Patent Law," 45; Trimble, *Hero of the Air*, 48–49; Roseberry, *Glenn Curtiss*, 150–51.
28. *Bulletins of the Aerial Experiment Association* 37 (March 22, 1909): 47; Plaintiff's Brief on Appeal, *Herring-Curtiss Co. v. Curtiss*, 223 App. Div. 101, 227 N.Y.S. 489 (N.Y. App. Div. 1928), 28; *Minutes of the Meetings of the Aerial Experiment Association* (March 31, 1909): 50; Roseberry, *Glenn Curtiss*, 157–60; Trimble, *Hero of the Air*, 50–52.
29. "Epitome of the Work of the Aeronautic Society," 7–8, 19; *Aeronautics* 6, no. 5 (May 1910): 180; *New York Times*, 4/9/1910, 9; Roseberry, *Glenn Curtiss*, 153, 156–58, 177; Casey, *Curtiss*, 38–41.
30. Crouch, *Bishop's Boys*, 179; Crouch, *Wings*, 87; Trimble, *Hero of the Air*, 55–56; Winchester, *Chronology of Aviation*, 30.
31. *New York Times*, 7/19/1909, 1; "Epitome of the Work of the Aeronautic Society," 23, 29; *Automobile* 21, no. 7 (August 12, 1909): 282; Cole and Schreiner, "Charles Willard," 178–79; Trimble, *Hero of the Air*, 56.
32. *Morning Oregonian* (Portland), 8/20/1909, 5; *Automobile* 21, no. 7 (August 12, 1909): 282; Curtiss and Post, *Curtiss Aviation Book*, 65–70; Roseberry, *Glenn Curtiss*, 169, 180, 185–86, 188, 190–92; Casey, *Curtiss*, 46–50.
33. Curtiss and Post, *Curtiss Aviation Book*, 67 (nominally a collaboration among Curtiss, Augustus Post, Lt. Paul Beck, Lt. Theodore "Spuds" Ellyson, and Hugh A. Robinson, although the portions attributed to Curtiss were likely ghostwritten by Post); Roseberry, *Glenn Curtiss*, 188, 193.
34. *Morning Oregonian* (Portland), 8/29/1909, 1; Curtiss and Post, *Curtiss Aviation Book*, 73; Roseberry, *Glenn Curtiss*, 203.
35. *New York Times*, 1/31/1909, sec. 1, 8; *New York Times*, 4/4/1909, mag., 10; Roseberry, *Glenn Curtiss*, 181–82, 208, 211, 215–16; Trimble, *Hero of the Air*, 68–69.
36. Casey, *Curtiss*, 51–52; Trimble, *Hero of the Air*, 69.
37. *New York Times*, 9/30/1909, 1; 10/1/1909, 6; 10/2/1909, 2; Casey, *Curtiss*, 52–53; Roseberry, *Glenn Curtiss*, 207, 218, 221–22; Trimble, *Hero of the Air*, 69.

CHAPTER 5. ROAD TO THE SKY

1. *Morning Oregonian* (Portland), 8/31/1909, 2.
2. Jerome S. Fanciulli Collection, University of Texas at Dallas, McDermott Library, Special Collections, box 2, folder 14: Fanciulli affidavit, 4; folder 18: Curtiss, letter to Fanciulli, October 4, 1909; Record on Appeal [decision on

appeal reported at *Herring-Curtiss Co. v. Curtiss*, 223 App. Div. 101, 227 N.Y.S. 489 (N.Y. App. Div. 1928)], 5983–84, ex. 367 (hereafter RoA); *Bulletins of the Aerial Experiment Association* 34 (March 1, 1909): 40–41; Roseberry, *Glenn Curtiss*, 160; Casey, *Curtiss*, 55.

3. RoA, 2468; Stevens, *St. Louis*, vol. 2, 280, 823; Roseberry, *Glenn Curtiss*, 222–223; Trimble, *Hero of the Air*, 70.
4. *Aeronautics* 5, no. 2 (August 1909): 69; RoA, 6016, ex. 397; Roseberry, *Glenn Curtiss*, 224, 227; Trimble, *Hero of the Air*, 75–76.
5. *New York Times*, 11/2/1909, 5; Roseberry, *Glenn Curtiss*, 228; RoA, 1645–46; 5190; 6016–17, ex. 397; Trimble, *Hero of the Air*, 75.
6. RoA, 5099; Jerome S. Fanciulli Collection, box 2, folder 1: Fanciulli, letter to Larry Sall, November 8, 1983; folder 2: undated biographical sketch; ca. 1932, Record of Jerome Fanciulli; folder 10: Fanciulli Special Honorary Award, May 15, 1974, Aviation/Space Writers Association; Trimble, *Hero of the Air*, 71; Roseberry, *Glenn Curtiss*, 218–19.
7. RoA, 5191; 6021, ex. 397; Roseberry, *Glenn Curtiss*, 228; Trimble, *Hero of the Air*, 71.
8. *Morning Oregonian* (Portland), 11/8/1899, 5; 2/16/1908, sec. 4, 6; 12/18/1914, 9; *Oregon Daily Journal* (Portland), 6/15/1913, sec. 2, 8; Gale Research Company, *Author Lists*, vol. 147, 409; Lockley, *History*, vol. 1, 675–78; Duncan, *Goths and Vandals*, 11, 102, 107.
9. *Morning Oregonian* (Portland), 9/11/1900, 7; 3/7/1909, auto, 2; 12/18/1914, 9; Duncan, *Goths and Vandals*, 108; *Oregon Daily Journal* (Portland), 12/18/1914, 6.
10. *Morning Oregonian* (Portland), 3/12/1909, 10; 4/4/1909, sec. 4, 5; 4/20/1909, 5; 7/11/1909, sec. 1, 10.
11. *San Francisco Call*, 8/15/1909, 29; *Los Angeles Herald*, 9/4/1909, sec. 2, 5; *Medford (Ore.) Mail Tribune*, 12/29/1909, 2; *Auburn (Ind.) Courier*, 10/18/1909, 2.
12. *Independent-Journal* (San Rafael, Calif.), 9/6/1958, M3; *Morning Oregonian* (Portland), 1/25/1910, 1.
13. Roseberry, *Glenn Curtiss*, 231; Trimble, *Hero of the Air*, 76–77.
14. *Aeronautics* 6, no. 3 (March 1910): 80; *Los Angeles Times*, 12/2/1909, ed., 7; *Buffalo (N.Y.) Commercial*, 1/3/1910, 11; *Buffalo (N.Y.) Courier*, 1/4/1910, 7; Roseberry, *Glenn Curtiss*, 231–32, 334–35; Trimble, *Hero of the Air*, 76–77, 79.
15. *Morning Oregonian* (Portland), 8/1/1909, sec. 2, 10; 10/17/1909, sec. 4, 6; 10/24/1909, sec. 4, 4; 12/10/1909, 16; 12/12/1909, sec. 4, 5; 12/19/1909, sec. 4, 7; Hill, *Oregon Trail*, 19.
16. *Morning Oregonian* (Portland), 1/23/1910, auto, 11; RoA, 7007, ex. 1135; Casey, *Curtiss*, 42, 224.
17. *Buffalo (N.Y.) Commercial*, 1/8/1910, 9; *Los Angeles Herald*, 1/11/1910, 2.
18. *San Francisco Call*, 1/15/1910, 11; *Aeronautics* 6, no. 3 (March 1910): 80; *Los Angeles Herald*, 1/10/1910, 2; 1/14/1910, 3.
19. Jerome S. Fanciulli Collection, box 2, folder 3: Undated Fanciulli notes, January 11, 1910, Los Angeles photograph; *Popular Mechanics* 13, no. 3 (March 1910):

328; *Los Angeles Times*, 1/12/1910, ed., 1; 1/20/1910, ed., 1, 8; *Los Angeles Herald*, 1/15/1910, 6; *Salt Lake Tribune* (Salt Lake City, Utah), 1/20/1910, 10.

20. *Los Angeles Herald*, 1/21/1910, 1; *Morning Oregonian* (Portland), 2/26/1910, 8; 3/5/1910, 12.
21. *Buffalo (N.Y.) Commercial*, 1/21/1910, 2; *Los Angeles Herald*, 1/14/1910, 3; *Marion (Ohio) Daily Mirror*, 1/22/1910, sec. 2, 3; A. Roy Knabenshue Collection, NASM, 1.1, box 1, folder 2: [biographical sketch], 19.
22. *Los Angeles Times*, 1/6/1910, ed., 8; U.S. Patent #821,393, 3–7; RoA, 5207–8; *Springfield (Mo.) Leader*, 3/4/1910, 6; Roseberry, *Glenn Curtiss*, 142.
23. Casey, *Curtiss*, 54; *Morning Oregonian* (Portland), 1/16/1910, sec. 1, 3; 1/17/1910, 14; 1/25/1910, 14; RoA, 1483; 3422–23; 5763, ex. 154; 5800, ex. 179; 5958–59, ex. 307; 6003, ex. 384; 6143–44, ex. 472; 6144, ex. 473; 6304–8, ex. 539; 6532, ex. 721; 6746, ex. 808; 6930, ex. 1060; 7007, ex. 1135; *Aérophile* 8, no. 9 (May 1, 1910): 212–13; *Americana* 7, no. 4 (April 1912): 350–51; *Aeronautics* 6, no. 3 (March 1910): 80–81; *Los Angeles Herald*, 1/10/1910, 1.
24. *Oregon Daily Journal* (Portland), 1/16/1910, sec. 6, 6; *Oakland (Calif.) Tribune*, 1/13/1910, 3.
25. *Oakland (Calif.) Tribune*, 1/13/1910, 3; RoA, 7007, ex. 1135; *Morning Oregonian (Portland)*, 1/16/1910, sec. 1, 3; 1/25/1910, 14; *Oregon Daily Journal* (Portland), 1/16/1910, sec. 6, 6.
26. RoA, 3422–23; 5800, ex. 179; 5958–59, ex. 308; 5986–89, ex. 371; 6142–43, ex. 471; 6700, ex. 798; 6930, ex. 1060; 7003–5, ex. 1132; *Morning Oregonian* (Portland), 1/25/1910, 14; *Oregon Daily Journal* (Portland), 1/30/1910, sec. 2, 7; Trimble, *Hero of the Air*, 54; Casey, *Curtiss*, 221–25; *Aeronautics* 6, no. 2 (February 1910): 62; 6, no. 3 (March 1910): 81; Jerome S. Fanciulli Collection, box 3, folder 9: 1910 contract of sale; *Los Angeles Herald*, 1/10/1910, 1.
27. RoA, 6009, ex. 389; 7003, ex. 1132; *Morning Oregonian* (Portland), 1/22/1910, 18; 1/25/1910, 1, 14; 2/14/1910, 16; *Oregon Daily Journal* (Portland), 1/16/1910, sec. 6, 6; 1/30/1910, sec. 2, 7.
28. *Morning Oregonian* (Portland), 1/30/1910, sec. 4, 4; 1/31/1910, 14; 2/1/1910, 20; 3/4/1910, 13; *Oregon Daily Journal* (Portland), *1/16/1910, sec. 6, 6;* 1/30/1910, sec. 2, 7.
29. Roseberry, *Glenn Curtiss*, 234; Jerome S. Fanciulli Collection, box 3, folder 1: 1912 Fanciulli anticipated testimony; *Buffalo (N.Y.) Commercial*, 1/21/1910, 2.
30. Trimble, *Hero of the Air*, 79; *Independent* (Santa Barbara, Calif.), 1/22/1910, 4; *Los Angeles Herald*, 1/25/1910, 1; RoA, 6021, ex. 397; *Evening Tribune* (San Diego), 1/25/1910, 8; *San Francisco Call*, 12/14/05, 6; 1/17/1909, 47; *San Diego Union*, 1/26/1910, 8.
31. *Bakersfield Californian*, 1/29/1910, 1; *Fresno (Calif.) Morning Republican*, 1/22/1910, 12; 2/1/1910, 12; 2/2/1910, 12; 2/4/1910, 16; 2/12/1910, 9; *Arizona Republican* (Phoenix), 2/11/1910, 1; 2/14/1910, 1; 2/16/1910, 6; 2/18/1910, sec. 2, 1; *Tombstone (Ariz.) Weekly Epitaph*, 2/20/1910, 2; *Arizona Daily Star* (Tucson), 2/18/1910, 6; 2/20/1910, 8; *El Paso (Texas) Herald*, 2/24/1910, 10; *San Francisco Call*, 2/28/1910, 10; Jerome S. Fanciulli Collection, box 3, folder

1: 1912 Fanciulli anticipated testimony; RoA, 6025, ex. 401; *Independent-Journal* (San Rafael, Calif.), 9/6/1958, M3; *Oakland (Calif.) Tribune*, 1/22/1910, 3; *Morning Oregonian* (Portland), 2/13/1910, sec. 1, 12; 2/20/1910, sec. 1, 12; sec. 4, 4; 2/23/1910, 14; 3/2/1910, 20.

32. *Tacoma (Wash.) Daily News*, 1/20/1910, 6.
33. RoA, 5998-99, ex. 381; *Morning Oregonian* (Portland), 1/19/1910, 18; 1/29/1910, 13; 2/22/1910, 13; 2/23/1910, 14; 2/25/1910, 13; *Independent* (Santa Barbara, Calif.), 1/22/1910, 4; *Los Angeles Herald*, 1/25/1910, 1; Jerome S. Fanciulli Collection, box 3, folder 3: 1912 copy of accounts.
34. *Vancouver (Wash.) Columbian*, 3/1/1910, 1; *Morning Oregonian* (Portland), 2/23/1910, 14; 2/26/1910, 8; 2/28/1910, 10; 3/1/1910, 7; 3/3/1910, 7.
35. *Morning Oregonian* (Portland), 3/3/1910, 7.
36. *Morning Oregonian* (Portland), 3/2/1910, 20; 3/5/1910, 12.
37. *San Francisco Call*, 2/28/1910, 10; *Morning Oregonian* (Portland), 3/6/1910, 8; RoA, 6026, ex. 402.
38. *Morning Oregonian* (Portland), 3/6/1910, 1, 8.
39. *Morning Oregonian* (Portland), 3/6/1910, 1.
40. *Morning Oregonian* (Portland), 3/8/1910, 12; 3/13/1910, sec. 3, 11.
41. RoA, 6025, ex. 401; *Tacoma (Wash.) Times*, 3/17/1910, 1.
42. *Seattle Daily Times*, 3/13/1910, 1; 3/14/1910, 2; *Centralia (Wash.) Daily Chronicle*, 3/21/1910, 1.
43. RoA, 5800, ex. 179; *Seattle Daily Times*, 3/21/1910, 3; Casey, *Curtiss*, 224.
44. *Morning Oregonian* (Portland), 3/29/1910, 12; 4/2/1910, 11.

CHAPTER 6. FLYING LESSONS

1. Curtiss and Post, *Curtiss Aviation Book*, 87; Roseberry, *Glenn Curtiss*, 321–22; *Nashville American*, 4/6/1910, 5; *Jackson (Miss.) Daily News*, 4/1/1910, 6.
2. *Jackson (Miss.) Daily News*, 4/1/1910, 6; Roseberry, *Glenn Curtiss*, 263–64; Trimble, *Hero of the Air*, 83.
3. In 2010, Cdr. Robert Coolbaugh, USN (Ret.), a naval aviator and commercial pilot, built a replica of a 1911 Curtiss pusher airplane and taught himself to fly it; see http://YouTu.be/PnmGZwl5wkU. Commander Coolbaugh generously shared details of his experiences with it in an email exchange with the author in March 2015.
4. *Post-Standard* (Syracuse, N.Y.), 4/2/1910, 1; *New York Times*, 4/8/1910, 3; *Aeronautics* 7, no. 3 (September 1910): 92–95; Trimble, *Hero of the Air*, 81.
5. *Indianapolis Star*, 3/5/1910, 8; Crouch, *Bishop's Boys*, 426–27.
6. *Morning Oregonian* (Portland), 4/13/1910, 1.
7. Coolbaugh, email correspondence with the author, March 2015.
8. *Morning Oregonian* (Portland), 4/14/1910, 15.
9. RoA, 7003–5, ex. 1132.
10. *Morning Oregonian* (Portland), 4/14/1910, 15; Curtiss and Post, *Curtiss Aviation Book*, 246.

11. *Morning Oregonian* (Portland), 4/14/1910, 15.
12. Coolbaugh, email correspondence with the author, March 2015; Curtiss and Post, *Curtiss Aviation Book*, 238–39, 290.
13. *Morning Oregonian* (Portland), 4/18/1910, 5.
14. *Morning Oregonian* (Portland), 4/28/1910, 13.
15. *Morning Oregonian* (Portland), 4/28/1910, 13; Portland Aeroplane Company, Records of the Secretary of State, Index to Incorporations, no. 14753, Oregon Historical Society, Portland, Ore.; U.S. Census, 1910, Portland, Ore.
16. *Morning Oregonian* (Portland), 5/10/1910, 6; *Medford (Ore.) Mail Tribune*, 5/15/1910, 14.
17. *Medford (Ore.) Mail Tribune*, 5/20/1910, 3. For more than a week, the *Mail Tribune* consistently reported Ely's first name as "Paul."
18. Eugene B. Ely Scrapbooks, NHHC, S–005, folder C (Ely's postcard to Mabel, postmarked May 19, 1910, Sutherlin, Oregon).
19. *Morning Oregonian* (Portland), 5/20/1910, 1.
20. *Daily Capital Journal* (Salem, Ore.), 5/26/1910, 5; *Portland Aeroplane Company v. C. T. Colt, M. Valerius and Charles E. Hatfield*, Circuit Court, Douglas County, Oregon (complaint filed May 24, 1910, dismissed without prejudice June 13, 1911), Box 193, No. 538, Oregon State Archives, Salem, Ore.
21. *Medford (Ore.) Mail Tribune*, 5/22/1910, 13; 5/27/1910, 3.
22. *Medford (Ore.) Mail Tribune*, 5/25/1910, 1, 5; 10/11/1910, 1.
23. *Medford (Ore.) Mail Tribune*, 5/27/1910, 1.
24. Casey, *Curtiss*, 61, 64–66; Roseberry, *Glenn Curtiss*, 262–64; Trimble, *Hero of the Air*, 82–83.
25. Curtiss and Post, *Curtiss Aviation Book*, 104; Casey, *Curtiss*, 67; Roseberry, *Glenn Curtiss*, 273–78, 280; Trimble, *Hero of the Air*, 84–86.
26. *Morning Oregonian* (Portland), 6/2/1910, 4.
27. *Galveston Daily News*, 6/1/1910, 3.
28. *Medford (Ore.) Mail Tribune*, 5/30/1910, 1.
29. *San Francisco Call*, 4/21/1910, 4; 4/24/1910, 52; 5/2/1910, 4; *Santa Cruz (Calif.) Evening Sentinel*, 4/23/1910, 1; *Fresno (Calif.) Morning Republican*, 5/1/1910, 9; *Evening Tribune* (San Diego), 5/2/1910, 3; *Seattle Daily Times*, 5/2/1910, 2; *Aeronautics* 6, no. 6 (June 1910): 197; 7, no. 2 (August 1910): 53.
30. *San Francisco Call*, 5/14/1910, 5; *San Diego Union*, 5/14/1910, 2.
31. Coolbaugh, email correspondence with the author, March 2015; *Medford (Ore.) Mail Tribune*, 6/5/1910, 1, 5, 8; 6/6/1910, 1.
32. *Medford (Ore.) Mail Tribune*, 7/17/1910, 1.
33. *Arkansas Democrat* (Little Rock), 5/22/1910, 8; *Post-Standard* (Syracuse, N.Y.), 6/1/1910, 8; *Wayne (Kans.) Journal*, 5/20/1910, 3; *Springfield (Mo.) Republican*, 6/14/1910, 1; *New York Times*, 6/14/1910, 1–10; *Philadelphia (Pa.) Inquirer*, 6/14/1910, 1; *St. Louis (Mo.) Globe-Democrat*, 6/19/1910, 7; Jerome S. Fanciulli Collection, box 2, folder 14: affidavit, ex. C, 3.

34. *New York Times*, 6/15/1910, 2.
35. *Eugene (Ore.) Guard*, 6/7/1910, 1; 6/10/1910, 1; 6/11/1910, 1; 6/18/1910, 7; 6/20/1910, 1; *Medford (Ore.) Mail Tribune*, 6/10/1910, 7; *Morning Oregonian* (Portland), 6/20/1910, 5.
36. *La Grande (Ore.) Evening Observer*, 6/14/1910, 6.

CHAPTER 7. OUTLAW

1. Crouch, *Bishop's Boys*, 426, 428; *Galveston Daily News*, 3/4/1910, 4; *Montpelier (Ind.) Evening Herald*, 3/8/1910, 1.
2. *Los Angeles Herald*, 4/30/1910, 14; *Indianapolis News*, 5/26/1910, 12.
3. *Kansas City (Mo.) Star*, 9/6/1896, 4; 6/30/1910, 7; *Garnett (Kans.) Journal*, 12/24/1897, 4; *Daily Times* (New Brunswick, N.J.), 7/24/1899, 7; *Philadelphia Times*, 12/4/1900, 8; 4/21/1901, 20; 4/26/1901, 8; 4/28/1901, 20; *New York Times*, 12/23/1900, 21; 1/13/1901, 18; 1/15/1901, 8; *Boston Post*, 5/19/1901, 20.
4. *Washington (D.C.) Post*, 8/5/1906, Mag., 3; *Indianapolis News*, 1/11/1910, 5.
5. *Mathews (Va.) Journal*, 10/6/1910, 3; *Oregon Daily Journal* (Portland), 11/18/1910, 5.
6. Crouch, *Bishop's Boys*, 428–29; *Aeronautics* 7, no. 2 (August 1910): 42.
7. Jerome S. Fanciulli Collection, box 3, folder 6: J. L. Gribble contract; *New York Times*, 6/19/1910, 6.
8. *Minneapolis Journal*, 6/20/1910, 9; *Billings (Mont.) Times*, 6/16/1910, 2; *Billings (Mont.) Daily Gazette*, 6/16/1910, 3; 6/20/1910, 1; *Billings (Mont.) Evening Journal*, 6/20/1910, 1.
9. *Billings (Mont.) Daily Gazette*, 6/16/1910, 3; 6/17/1910, 1; *Anaconda (Mont.) Standard*, 6/16/1910, 1; *Billings (Mont.) Evening Journal*, 6/17/1910, 1.
10. *Billings (Mont.) Daily Gazette*, 6/17/1910, 1; 6/18/1910, 1; 6/19/1910, 1.
11. *Billings (Mont.) Evening Journal*, 6/20/1910, 1; *Billings (Mont.) Daily Gazette*, 6/19/1910, 1; 6/21/1910, 4.
12. *Minneapolis Journal*, 6/20/1910, 9; 6/21/1910, 8; *Bismarck (N.D.) Daily Tribune*, 6/23/1910, 8 (Ely's first name given as "Ray").
13. *Aeronautics* 7, no. 2 (August 1910): 46.
14. RoA, 7003–5, ex. 1132; *Independent-Journal* (San Rafael, Calif.), 9/6/1958, M3.
15. *Minneapolis Journal*, 6/23/1910, 2; *Minneapolis Tribune*, 6/23/1910, 1.
16. *Minneapolis Journal*, 6/23/1910, 1; *Minneapolis Tribune*, 6/21/1910, 1; 6/22/1910, 1.
17. *Minneapolis Journal*, 6/23/1910, 2.
18. *Minneapolis Tribune*, 6/23/1910, 1, 2; *Minneapolis Journal*, 6/23/1910, 1, 2.
19. *Minneapolis Tribune*, 6/24/1910, 1–2; *Minneapolis Journal*, 6/24/1910, 1, 7.
20. *Minneapolis Tribune*, 6/25/1910, 1–2.
21. *Minneapolis Tribune*, 6/25/1910, 3; 6/26/1910, 1–2; *Minneapolis Journal*, 6/26/1910, 9.
22. Roseberry, *Glenn Curtiss*, 285–86.
23. *Rochester (N.Y.) Democrat and Chronicle*, 8/4/1910, 1.

24. Jerome S. Fanciulli Collection, box 2, folder 16: Fanciulli, letter to Curtiss, April 4, 1910; RoA, 1775–76.
25. *Williamsburg (Iowa) Journal-Tribune*, 6/30/1910, 2.

CHAPTER 8. ON THE TEAM

1. *International Gazette* (Buffalo, N.Y.), 7/8/1922, 1; *Duluth News Tribune*, 6/28/1910, 5; 6/29/1910.
2. *Duluth News Tribune*, 6/28/1910, 1; *Springfield (Mo.) Republican*, 6/14/1910, 1; *Waterloo (Iowa) Times-Tribune*, 6/29/1910, 10; Minneapolis Journal, 6/30/1910, 8; Sioux County Herald (Orange City, Iowa), 7/6/1910, 1.
3. *New York Times*, 6/28/1910, 5; Roseberry, *Glenn Curtiss*, 283–84; Trimble, *Hero of the Air*, 87–88.
4. *Minneapolis Journal*, 6/30/1910, 10.
5. *Duluth News Tribune*, 6/30/1910, 5; 7/1/1910, 5.
6. *Minneapolis Journal*, 6/30/1910, 8; *Waterloo (Iowa) Times-Tribune*, 7/2/1910, 11.
7. *Eau Claire (Wis.) Leader*, 7/1/1910, 4; *Aeronautics* 7, no. 2 (August 1910): 48.
8. *Lincoln (Neb.) Daily News*, 5/12/1910, 7.
9. *Daily Telegraph* (Atlantic, Iowa), 7/2/1910, 6; *Sioux County Herald* (Orange City, Iowa), 7/6/1910, 1; Jerome S. Fanciulli Collection, box 2, folder 14: Draft affidavit, ex. C.
10. *Aeronautics* 7, no. 2 (August 1910): 48; *Waterloo (Iowa) Times-Tribune*, 6/29/1910, 10.
11. *Sioux County Herald* (Orange City, Iowa), 7/6/1910, 1; *Lowell (Mass.) Sun*, 7/1/1910, 14.
12. *Inter Ocean* (Chicago, Ill.), 6/29/1910, 3; 7/4/1910, 10; 7/6/1910, 3; *Indianapolis News*, 6/29/1910, 10; *Chicago Tribune*, 7/3/1910, sec. 2, 3; 7/5/1910, 3; 7/6/1910, 3.
13. *Omaha (Neb.) Daily Bee*, 5/25/1910, 7; *Omaha (Neb.) Daily News*, 6/24/1910, 1; 7/4/1910, 3; *Winnipeg (Manitoba) Tribune*, 6/23/1910, 7; *Manitoba Free Press* (Winnipeg), 7/13/1910, 7.
14. *Williamsburg (Iowa) Journal-Tribune*, 7/28/1910, 5; 7/14/1910, 2; 10/27/1910, 1.
15. *Manitoba Free Press* (Winnipeg), 7/13/1910, 7; 7/15/1910, 8.
16. *Manitoba Free Press* (Winnipeg), 7/15/1910, 1, 20; 7/22/1910, 1; Kipling, "With the Night Mail."
17. *Manitoba Free Press* (Winnipeg), 7/16/1910, 1; *Vancouver (B.C.) World*, 3/26/1910, 1, 20; *Winnipeg (Manitoba) Tribune*, 7/16/1910, 7; *Iowa City Citizen*, 7/22/1910, 1.
18. *Manitoba Free Press* (Winnipeg), 7/18/1910, 1; *Des Moines (Iowa) News*, 7/16/1910, 3; *North Adams (Mass.) Transcript*, 7/16/1910, 1; *Colorado Springs Gazette*, 7/16/1910, 2; *Berkeley Daily Gazette*, 7/16/1910, 1; *New York Times*, 7/17/1910, 2; *San Antonio Light and Gazette*, 7/17/1910, 6.
19. *Iowa City Citizen*, 7/19/1910, 1; 7/22/1910, 1; *Winnipeg (Manitoba) Tribune*, 7/18/1910, 2; *Cedar Rapids (Iowa) Evening Gazette*, 7/20/1910, 1.

20. *Manitoba Free Press* (Winnipeg), 7/18/1910, 1; *Winnipeg (Manitoba) Tribune*, 7/18/1910, 2; 7/20/1910, 1.
21. *Manitoba Free Press* (Winnipeg), 7/21/1910, 1; 7/22/1910, 1; 7/23/1910, 21; 7/26/1910, 11; *Winnipeg (Manitoba) Tribune*, 7/21/1910, 5.
22. *Aeronautics* 7, no. 2 (August 1910): 45; *New York Times*, 7/13/1910, 1.
23. *New York Times*, 7/9/1910, 1; RoA, 6041, ex. 421; Roseberry, *Glenn Curtiss*, 284–85; Trimble, *Hero of the Air*, 92.
24. Eugene B. Ely Scrapbooks, NHHC, S–005, folder A, 6.
25. *Omaha (Neb.) Daily Bee*, 7/21/1910, 7; 7/24/1910, 1; 7/28/1910, 1; 7/23/1910, 1; *Lincoln (Neb.) Evening News*, 7/22/1910, 4; 7/28/1910, 3; *New York Times*, 7/23/1910, 5; *Galveston Daily News*, 7/25/1910, 3; *Omaha (Neb.) Daily News*, 7/21/1910, 1; 7/22/1910, 1.
26. *Rochester (N.Y.) Democrat and Chronicle*, 7/27/1910, 11, 15; 7/26/1910, 16; *Omaha (Neb.) Daily Bee*, 7/28/1910, 1.
27. *Rochester (N.Y.) Democrat and Chronicle*, 8/4/1910, 14; Jerome S. Fanciulli Collection, box 3, folder 10: August 1910 lease.
28. Jerome S. Fanciulli Collection, box 3, folder 5: Agreement between Fanciulli and Charles Bryce, August 3, 1910; *Rochester (N.Y.) Democrat and Chronicle*, 7/30/1910, 14; 7/31/1910, 21; 8/4/1910, 14; 8/5/1910, 18; 8/7/1910, 22; 8/9/1910, 15; *Brooklyn (N.Y.) Daily Eagle*, 8/7/1910, sporting, 4.
29. *Rochester (N.Y.) Democrat and Chronicle*, 8/9/1910, 15.
30. *Rochester (N.Y.) Democrat and Chronicle*, 8/5/1910, 18; 8/8/1910, 14; 8/9/1910, 15.
31. Eugene B. Ely Scrapbooks, NHHC, S–005, folder B, 20 (photograph of Ely standing by an automobile with Glenn and Lena Curtiss, with Mabel's caption: "Gene & Mr. & Mrs. Curtiss. Trip from N.Y. to Buffalo"); *New York Times*, 8/12/1910, 3; *Amsterdam (N.Y.) Evening Recorder and Daily Democrat*, 8/13/1910, 3.

CHAPTER 9. LOFTIER GOALS

1. *Philadelphia Inquirer*, 8/14/1910, 6; *Aeronautics* 7, no. 3 (September 1910): 91.
2. *New York Times*, 8/19/1910, 2.
3. *New York Times*, 8/11/1910, 1; 8/12/1910, 3; 8/16/1910, 4; Crouch, *Bishop's Boys*, 430.
4. *New York Times*, 8/12/1910, 5; 8/16/1910, 4; Crouch, *Bishop's Boys*, 430; Corn, *Winged Gospel*, 9.
5. *New York Times*, 8/19/1910, 2; *Aeronautics* 8, no. 1 (January 1911): 2.
6. RoA, 6041, ex. 421; *New York Times*, 8/12/1910, 3.
7. *New Castle (Pa.) News*, 8/12/1910, 15; *Brooklyn (N.Y.) Daily Eagle*, 8/18/1910, 3.
8. *Brooklyn (N.Y.) Daily Eagle*, 8/18/1910; 3 8/19/1910, 1; 8/20/1910, 16.
9. *New York Times*, 8/19/1910, 2.
10. *New York Times*, 8/16/1910, 4; 8/19/1910, 2.
11. *New York Times*, 8/20/1910, 16; *Sun* (New York, N.Y.), 8/20/1910, 2; Eugene B. Ely Scrapbooks, NHHC, S–005, folder B, 31 (only known

photograph of Mabel in flight, with her caption: "Mabel Ely in air with Bud Mars").

12. *Cincinnati Enquirer*, 8/20/1910, 3; *Brooklyn (N.Y.) Daily Eagle*, 8/20/1910, 16.
13. *Independent-Journal* (San Rafael, Calif.), 9/6/1958, M3; *Davenport (Iowa) Democrat and Leader*, 8/13/1911, 15; *Sun* (Medford, Ore.), 6/3/1911, 1.
14. *Independent-Journal* (San Rafael, Calif.), 9/6/1958, M3; *Davenport (Iowa) Democrat and Leader*, 8/13/1911, 15.
15. *Brooklyn (N.Y.) Daily Eagle*, 8/20/1910, 16; *Cincinnati Enquirer*, 8/20/1910, 3; *Sun* (New York, N.Y.), 8/20/1910, 2; *New York Times*, 8/20/1910, 16.
16. *Charlotte (N.C.) News*, 8/21/1910, 1; Casey, *Glenn Curtiss*, 70; Trimble, *Hero of the Air*, 90.
17. *Oakland (Calif.) Tribune*, 8/21/1910, 18; *New York Times*, 8/20/1910, 16.
18. *Brooklyn (N.Y.) Daily Eagle*, 8/23/1910, 16.
19. *Brooklyn (N.Y.) Daily Eagle*, 8/24/1910, sport, 3; *New York Times*, 8/24/1910, 6; 8/25/1910, sporting, 2; 8/26/1910, 3.
20. *New York Times*, 8/28/1910, 28; *Brooklyn (N.Y.) Daily Eagle*, 8/28/1910, local, 1, 6.
21. Eugene B. Ely Scrapbooks, NHHC, S–005, folder B, 24 (photograph of Ely at the wheel of his airplane, with Mabel's caption: "Gene starting on trip from Sheapshead to hotel Man"); *Aeronautics* 7, no. 4 (October 1910): 129. Augustus Post, who was at Sheepshead, repeated the story in Curtiss and Post, *Curtiss Aviation Book*, 113.
22. *Galveston Daily News*, 8/29/1910, 2; *Brooklyn (N.Y.) Daily Eagle*, 8/29/1910, 16; *Washington (D.C.) Post*, 8/29/1910, 3; *Los Angeles Herald*, 8/30/1910, 3.
23. *New York Times*, 8/28/1910, 28.
24. Roseberry, *Glenn Curtiss*, 288; Trimble, *Hero of the Air*, 90.
25. *Iowa City Citizen*, 9/14/1910, 1; *Naugatuck (Conn.) Daily News*, 9/24/1910, 1.
26. *Rock Island (Ill.) Argus*, 9/8/1910, 8; 9/9/1910, 6; *Williamsburg (Iowa) Journal-Tribune*, 9/15/1910, 1; Eugene B. Ely Scrapbooks, NHHC, S–005, folder B, 61, 67 (photographs show Ely at Rock Island, accompanied by his stepmother Mabel, wife Mabel, stepbrother Paul, sister Maidie, and father Nathan).
27. *Rock Island (Ill.) Argus*, 9/9/1910, 6.
28. *Rock Island (Ill.) Argus*, 9/15/1910, 5; *Quad-City Times* (Davenport, Iowa), 6/19/2001, B1–2.
29. *Rock Island (Ill.) Argus*, 9/15/1910, 5.
30. *Rock Island (Ill.) Argus*, 9/16/1910, 8; 9/17/1910, 5; 9/19/1910, 5.
31. Eugene B. Ely Scrapbooks, NHHC, S–005, folder B, 2 (photograph of Petersen at the wheel of Ely's airplane, Rock Island); 12 (photograph of Mabel at the wheel of Ely's airplane, Maidie beside her, with Mabel's caption: "Mrs. Ely & Miss Ely, Rock Island"); *Fort Wayne (Ind.) Journal-Gazette*, 9/25/1910, supp., 7; *Independent-Journal* (San Rafael, Calif.), 9/6/1958, M3.

32. *Roanoke (Va.) Times*, 9/23/1910, 1; *Times Dispatch* (Richmond, Va.), 9/23/1910, 6; Eugene B. Ely Scrapbooks, NHHC, S–005, folder B, 34 (photograph of Ely's machine loaded on a flatcar, with Mabel's caption: "Hauling machine up the mountain to jump off at Roanoke, Va."; contradicting sources reporting that the machine was hauled up the Mill Mountain Incline railway).
33. *Belvidere (Ill.) Daily Republican*, 9/30/1910, 1; *Poughkeepsie (N.Y.) Daily Eagle*, 9/29/1910, 5–6; 9/30/1910, 5; 10/1/1910, 5; Jerome S. Fanciulli Collection, box 3, folder 3: Undated summary of the Curtiss Exhibition Company's first year.

CHAPTER 10. ENDURANCE

1. *Fort Wayne (Ind.) Journal Gazette*, 4/25/1909, 20; J. A. Edgerton, editorial, published in, among other places, *Logansport (Ind.) Pharos Tribune*, 7/15/1910, 7.
2. Jerome S. Fanciulli Collection, box 3, folder 6: Air Race Contract.
3. *New York Times*, 7/8/1910, 1; 7/16/1910, 1; 9/27/1910, 1.
4. Roseberry, *Glenn Curtiss*, 289; *New York Times*, 7/26/1910, 5; 9/23/1910, 1; 10/5/1910, 6.
5. *Evening Record* (Greenville, Pa.), 9/30/1910, 1; *Rock Island (Ill.) Argus*, 9/15/1910, 5; Crouch, *Bishop's Boys*, 429.
6. *Monroe (La.) News-Star*, 10/4/1910, 8; *Post-Standard* (Syracuse, N.Y.), 10/8/1910, 4; *Bismarck (N.D.) Tribune*, 10/2/1910, 1, 6; *Lowell (Mass.) Sun*, 10/3/1910, 4.
7. *Oregon Daily Journal* (Portland), 9/11/1910, 12; *New York Times*, 7/16/1910, 1; 9/29/1910, 1; 10/2/1910, 1; *Inter Ocean* (Chicago, Ill.), 10/2/1910, 5; 10/3/1910, 2.
8. *Inter Ocean* (Chicago, Ill.), 10/9/1910, 9.
9. *New York Times*, 7/8/1910, 1; *Elyria (Ohio) Evening Telegram*, 10/8/1910, 1; *New York Times*, 10/4/1910, 1; 10/5/1910, 6; *Chicago Tribune*, 10/4/1910, 24.
10. *Chicago Tribune*, 10/4/1910, 24; 10/5/1910, 25.
11. *New York Times*, 10/6/1910, 1, 4; *New Castle (Pa.) News*, 10/7/1910, 1.
12. *New York Times*, 10/7/1910, 1, 5; *Chicago Tribune*, 10/7/1910, 21; *Inter Ocean* (Chicago, Ill.), 10/3/1910, 2; 10/7/1910, 10.
13. *Inter Ocean* (Chicago, Ill.), 10/7/1910, 10; Curtiss and Post, *Curtiss Aviation Book*, 113–14 n.1.
14. *Inter Ocean* (Chicago, Ill.), 10/7/1910, 10.
15. *New York Times*, 10/8/1910, 1.
16. *Chicago Tribune*, 10/8/1910, 3; *New York Times*, 10/9/1910, 1.
17. *Chicago Tribune*, 10/8/1910, 3; *New York Times*, 10/8/1910, 1.
18. *New Castle (Pa.) News*, 10/8/1910, 10; *Tacoma (Wash.) Times*, 10/8/1910, 1.
19. *Oakland (Calif.) Tribune*, 10/9/1910, 1; *San Francisco Examiner*, 10/9/1910, 1–2; *New York Times*, 10/9/1910, 2.
20. *Chicago Tribune*, 10/9/1910, 3.

21. *Chicago Tribune*, 10/9/1910, 3.
22. *New York Times*, 10/9/1910, 1–2; 10/10/1910, 2; *Washington (D.C.) Times*, 10/9/1910, 3; *Inter Ocean* (Chicago, Ill.), 10/9/1910, 9.
23. *New York Times*, 10/10/1910, 2; *Cincinnati Enquirer*, 10/10/1910, 2; Casey, *Curtiss*, 50, 70–71; Roseberry, *Glenn Curtiss*, 289–91; Trimble, *Hero of the Air*, 91, 94–95; Eugene B. Ely Scrapbooks, NHHC, S–005, folder A, 92, 94; folder B, 66 (photographs of the machine that Ely flew from Chicago, showing *Banshee*'s V-8 engine and its distinctive ailerons on the trailing edges of the wings).
24. *Times* (London), 10/10/1910, 9; *Inter Ocean* (Chicago, Ill.), 10/10/1910, 1–2; *Cincinnati Enquirer*, 10/10/1910, 2.
25. *New York Times*, 10/10/1910, 2; *Cincinnati Enquirer*, 10/10/1910, 2.
26. *Chicago Tribune*, 10/10/1910, 1; *Galveston Daily News*, 10/10/1910, 1; *New York Times*, 10/10/1910, 1; *Cincinnati Enquirer*, 10/10/1910, 2; *Chicago Evening Post*, 10/10/1910, 1.
27. *Washington (D.C.) Herald*, 10/10/1910, 1; *New York Times*, 10/10/1910, 1–2.
28. *New York Times*, 10/11/1910, 1; *Asheville (N.C.) Gazette News*, 10/10/1910, 1.
29. Curtiss, "Aeroplane for the Navy," 1816–17; Curtiss and Post, *Curtiss Aviation Book*, 197.
30. *Charlotte (N.C.) News*, 10/10/1910, 1; *New York Times*, 10/11/1910, 1; *Chicago Evening Post*, 10/10/1910, 1; *Chicago Tribune*, 10/11/1910, 22; *Iowa City Citizen*, 10/11/1910, 1.
31. *New York Times*, 10/11/1910, 1; *Washington (D.C.) Post*, 10/11/1910, 2; *Chicago Tribune*, 10/11/1910, 22.
32. *New York Times*, 10/12/1910, 2; *Chicago Evening Post*, 10/12/1910, 2.
33. *New York Times*, 10/12/1910, 2; *Inter Ocean* (Chicago, Ill.), 10/10/1910, 1.
34. Curtiss, "Aeroplane for the Navy," 1816; Curtiss and Post, *Curtiss Aviation Book*, 114.
35. *Chicago Tribune*, 10/12/1910, 22; *St. Joseph (Mo.) Gazette*, 10/12/1910, 7.
36. *New York Times*, 10/12/1910, 1–2; 10/13/1910, 1; *Chicago Evening Post*, 10/12/1910, 2.
37. *Washington (D.C.) Post*, 10/12/1910, 2; *Ligonier (Ind.) Leader*, 10/20/1910, 5; *Waterloo (Ind.) Press*, 10/13/1910, 1; *Fort Wayne (Ind.) Journal-Gazette*, 10/16/1910, part 1, 14.
38. *New Castle (Pa.) News*, 10/13/1910, 12; Jerome S. Fanciulli Collection, box 3, folder 6: Contract, September 14, 1910.
39. *New Castle (Pa.) News*, 10/13/1910, 12; 10/14/1910, 5.
40. *Waterloo (Ind.) Press*, 10/20/1910, 5; *Chicago Evening Post*, 10/12/1910, 2.

CHAPTER 11. THE WAR IN THE AIR

1. *Inter Ocean* (Chicago, Ill.), 10/2/1910, 5; *Daily Mail* (London), 7/11/1908, 5; 12/10/1908, 7; *Grandview (Manitoba) Exponent*, 8/27/1908, 6; *Buffalo (N.Y.) Sunday News*, 10/11/1908, 2.
2. Wells, *War in the Air*, 129, 149, 169.

3. Paine, *Sea and Civilization*, 563; *South Carolina* IV and *Michigan* II, in *DANFS*; Memorandum for the Secretary of the Navy, December 2, 1908, National Archives and Records Administration (NARA), RG 80, file 26983–20; Turnbull and Lord, *History of United States Naval Aviation*, 4–5.
4. Memorandum for the Secretary of the Navy, 1st Endorsement, August 16, 1909, NARA, RG 80, file 26983–20:1; Zimmerman, "Naval Aviation in the Tidewater," 38; van Deurs, *Wings for the Fleet*, 9.
5. *Spokane (Wash.) Press*, 9/9/1910, 6; Howe, *George von Lengerke Meyer*, 3, 392, 418, 446–47, 456, 468.
6. Stein, *From Torpedoes to Aviation*, 154–57, 159; *Louisiana* III, in *DANFS*; Library of Congress, Manuscript Division, Washington Irving Chambers, Papers, box 4: Chambers, letter to Admiral Dewey, September 24, 1913.
7. *Hearings before the Committee on Naval Affairs*, 2223; "The German Plan to Invade America," *American Heritage* 53, no. 6 (November/December, 2002): 18; Howe, *George von Lengerke Meyer*, 256.
8. Howe, *George von Lengerke Meyer*, 440; *Washington (D.C.) Herald*, 2/26/11, lit., 2; McCullough, *Wright Brothers*, 238–39.
9. *Corona (Calif.) Independent*, 10/19/1909, 7; Washington Irving Chambers Papers, box 11: Chambers, draft letter to George Platt, December 14, 1910.
10. Library of Congress, Manuscript Division, George van Deurs Papers, box 4: Unpublished biographical sketch; Washington Irving Chambers Papers, box 3: Orders, October 21, 1910; box 15: Chambers, letter to Ellyson, January 24, 1911.
11. *Washington (D.C.) Post*, 5/28/1910, 3.
12. Roseberry, *Glenn Curtiss*, 279; Curtiss and Post, *Curtiss Aviation Book*, 124.
13. *New York World*, 6/30/1910, 1–2; 7/1/1910, 1–2.
14. *New York World*, 7/1/1910, 2.
15. Casey, *Curtiss*, 61; *Aeronautics* 7, no. 2 (August 1910): 44–45; *Hamburg (Iowa) Reporter*, 7/22/1910, 7; Roseberry, *Glenn Curtiss*, 284; Trimble, *Hero of the Air*, 89; *Middlebury (Ind.) Independent*, 8/12/1910, 7.
16. *New York Times*, 7/31/1910, 3; 8/1/1910, 1.
17. *New York Times*, 8/3/1910, 7; *Air-Scout* 1, no. 1 (November 1910): 10; *Fort Wayne (Ind.) Sentinel*, 8/5/1910, 12; *Ogden (Utah) Standard*, 8/2/1910, 8; *Los Angeles Herald*, 8/3/1910, 2; *Portsmouth (N.H.) Herald*, 8/3/1910, 4.
18. *Portsmouth (N.H.) Herald*, 8/3/1910, 4; *Brooklyn (N.Y.) Daily Eagle*, 8/7/1910, 1.
19. *Portsmouth (N.H.) Herald*, 8/3/1910, 4; *Tribune* (Altoona, Pa.), 8/8/1910, 1; *New York Times*, 8/19/1910, 2.
20. Curtiss, "Aeroplane for the Navy," 1815–17.
21. Curtiss, "Aeroplane for the Navy," 1815–17.
22. *New York Times*, 8/21/1910, 2.
23. Lenger, "Conquest of the Air," 32–33.
24. Rotch, *Conquest of the Air*, 169–70.
25. Lenger, "Conquest of the Air," 35–37; *Boston Sunday Post*, 9/11/1910, 2; *Scientific American* 103, no. 12 (September 17, 1910): 216.

26. Lenger, "Conquest of the Air," 35–37; *Coffeyville (Kans.) Daily Journal*, 9/3/1910, 1; *Brooklyn (N.Y.) Daily Eagle*, 9/4/1910, 4; *New York Times*, 9/10/1910, 3.
27. *New York Times*, 9/6/1910, 5; *Chicago Tribune*, 9/13/1910, 7; *Boston Globe*, 9/14/1910, 1, 3, 6; *Wilmington (N.C.) Morning Star*, 9/16/1910, 1; Lenger, "Conquest of the Air," 38.
28. *New York Times*, 9/19/1910, 4.
29. *Washington (D.C.) Post*, 10/12/1910, 6; *New York Times*, 9/19/1910, 4.
30. *Air-Scout* 1, no. 1 (November 1910): 23; *Arms and the Man* 48, no. 26 (September 29, 1910): 556; 49, no. 3 (October 20, 1910): 44; *New York Times*, 1/22/1911, sport, 1.
31. *Washington (D.C.) Herald*, 9/23/1910, 2; *San Francisco Call*, 9/23/1910, 1; *Air-Scout* 1, no. 1 (November 1910): 23.
32. *Air-Scout* 1, no. 1 (November 1910): 23; Washington Irving Chambers Papers, box 9: Rudolf Geyer, letter to Navy Department, September 12, 1910; Chambers, letter to Rudolf Geyer, September 29, 1910; Chambers, letter to John Barry Ryan, September 29, 1910; John Barry Ryan, letter to Chambers, October 4, 1910.
33. *Raleigh (N.C.) Times*, 9/30/1910, 1; *Washington (D.C.) Post*, 9/30/1910, 7; Howe, *George von Lengerke Meyer*, 418–19; Stein, *From Torpedoes to Aviation*, 159–60.
34. Washington Irving Chambers Papers, box 3: Rear Adm. Richard M. Watt, memo to Secretary of the Navy, October 11, 1910.
35. Washington Irving Chambers Papers, box 11: Capt. Hutchinson I. Cone, memo to Secretary of the Navy, October 7, 1910; *Chester* I, in *DANFS*.
36. Washington Irving Chambers Papers, box 6: Chambers, memorandum, October 10, 1910.
37. *Chester* I, in *DANFS*; Washington Irving Chambers Papers, box 6: Endorsement referring matter to General Board, October 13, 1910; box 11: W. P. Potter, memorandum, October 11, 1910; R. Wainwright, memorandum, October 12, 1910; box 20: "Brief Summary of the First Steps in the Development of Naval Aeronautics" (1917), 3.
38. Washington Irving Chambers Papers, box 20: "Brief Summary of the First Steps in the Development of Naval Aeronautics" (1917), 3.
39. *Washington (D.C.) Post*, 10/13/1910, 3; *Washington (D.C.) Herald*, 10/16/1910, sec. 1, 6.
40. *Washington (D.C.) Herald*, 10/15/1910, 1; 10/16/1910, sec. 1, 6; *Washington (D.C.) Post*, 10/15/1910, 3.
41. Washington Irving Chambers Papers, box 6: Endorsement, October 14, 1910.

CHAPTER 12. **BELMONT STAKES**

1. *Ottawa (Ont.) Journal*, 9/16/1910, 16; *Daily Times* (New Philadelphia, Ohio), 9/20/1910, 5; *St. Louis (Mo.) Star*, 10/16/1910, 1–2; *Cleveland Plain Dealer*, 10/16/1910, part 2, 1; 10/17/1910, 1.

2. *Allentown (Pa.) Democrat*, 10/17/1910, 2; Curtiss and Post, *Curtiss Aviation Book*, 76; Roseberry, *Glenn Curtiss*, 293.
3. Washington Irving Chambers Papers, box 3: Rear Adm. Richard M. Watt, memo to Secretary of the Navy, October 11, 1910.
4. Washington Irving Chambers Papers, box 3: Beekman Winthrop, memo to Richard M. Watt and Capt. Hutchinson Cone, October 13, 1910; Capt. Hutchinson Cone, memo to Secretary of the Navy, October 17, 1910; Richard M. Watt, memo to Secretary of the Navy, October 21, 1910; box 6: Endorsement by General Board, October 14, 1910; Trimble, *Hero of the Air*, 97.
5. Casey, *Curtiss*, 72; *New York Times*, 10/23/1910, 2; 10/27/1910, 3; Chambers, "Aviation and Aeroplanes," 163, 167; Washington Irving Chambers Papers, box 3: Orders, October 21, 1910; Lord, "History of Naval Aviation," 14.
6. Casey, *Curtiss*, 72; Curtiss and Post, *Curtiss Aviation Book*, 115.
7. Casey, *Curtiss*, 72; Roseberry, *Glenn Curtiss*, 186; Trimble, *Hero of the Air*, 94, 98.
8. *New York Herald*, 10/23/1910, sec. 1, part 3, 1; Casey, *Curtiss*, 72.
9. Roseberry, *Glenn Curtiss*, 292–93; Trimble, *Hero of the Air*, 97; *New York Times*, 10/23/1910, sec. 1, part 3, 2; Chambers, "Aviation and Aeroplanes," 169.
10. *New York Times*, 10/4/1910, 2.
11. *New York Times*, 10/25/1910, 2; Roseberry, *Glenn Curtiss*, 293.
12. *Chicago Tribune*, 10/23/1910, 6; *Washington (D.C.) Post*, 10/23/1910, 1; *New York Times*, 10/23/1910, part 3, 1–2.
13. *New York Times*, 10/23/1910, 2; *Washington (D.C.) Post*, 10/23/1910, 1; Chambers, "Aviation and Aeroplanes," 168 (Chambers is mistaken in his report when he states that Moisant's flight was thirty miles; other sources report that it was ten miles each way to Hicksville and back).
14. Washington Irving Chambers Papers, box 3: 10/21/1910 orders; Chambers, "Aviation and Aeroplanes," 163.
15. *New York Times*, 10/25/1910, 1–2.
16. *Sun* (Baltimore, Md.), 10/25/1910, 2; *Salt Lake Tribune* (Salt Lake City, Utah), 10/25/1910, 11; *Lincoln (Neb.) Evening News*, 10/24/1910, 1; *New York Times*, 10/25/1910, 2; *Times* (London), 10/25/1910, 6.
17. *New York Times*, 10/26/1910, 1–2.
18. *Sun* (New York, N.Y.), 10/28/1910, 1; Eugene B. Ely Scrapbooks, NHHC, S-005, folder B, 4, 77 (photographs documenting the single-surface racer: alternate views).
19. *New York Times*, 10/26/1910, 1; 10/27/1910, 1; *Sun* (New York, N.Y.), 10/26/1910, 1; 10/27/1910, 1–2; 10/28/1910, 4; *New-York Tribune*, 10/27/1910, 1, 5; *Boston Globe*, 10/28/1910, 3; *Boston Evening Transcript*, 10/29/1910, 1; *World's Work* 21, no. 2 (December 1910): 13, 720–21.
20. Roseberry, *Glenn Curtiss*, 293.
21. *New York Times*, 10/25/1910, 1; 10/28/1910, 1.
22. Chambers, "Aviation and Aeroplanes," 165–66; *Washington (D.C.) Herald*, 10/30/1910, 5.

23. Eugene B. Ely Scrapbooks, NHHC, S–005, folder B, 22 (photographs documenting Moisant's collision with Harmon's Farman, with Mabel's caption: "Bleriot smashed into Farman. N.Y. Moissant in collision with Harman").
24. *World's Work* 21, no. 2 (December 1910): 13, 720–21; *New York Times*, 10/31/1910, 1, 2.
25. *News* (Frederick, Md.), 11/3/1910, 8.
26. *New York Times*, 11/1/1910, 1–2; *Washington (D.C.) Herald*, 11/1/1910, 1.
27. *World's Work* 21, no. 2 (December 1910): 13, 720–21.
28. *New York Times*, 11/1/1910, 1.
29. *Washington (D.C.) Herald*, 9/18/1910, 1; *Raleigh (N.C.) Times*, 11/1/1910, 2; Washington Irving Chambers Papers, box 3: Orders, November 1, 1910.
30. *New York Times*, 11/5/1910, 3; *Raleigh (N.C.) Times*, 11/1/1910, 2.
31. *Raleigh (N.C.) Times*, 11/2/1910, 6; *New York Times*, 11/3/1910, 2; *Fort Wayne (Ind.) Sentinel*, 11/2/1910, 1.
32. *New York World*, 11/2/1910, 4.
33. *New York Times*, 11/4/1910, 1; *Brooklyn (N.Y.) Daily Eagle*, 11/3/1910, 2.
34. *New York Times*, 11/3/1910, 1; *New York World*, 11/3/1910, 1; *Washington (D.C.) Post*, 11/3/1910, 1.

CHAPTER 13. THE RACE WITH THE FLOATING ZOO

1. *Washington (D.C.) Post*, 11/3/1910, 1.
2. *Washington (D.C.) Post*, 11/3/1910, 1; *Brooklyn (N.Y.) Daily Eagle*, 11/3/1910, 2; *New York World*, 11/3/1910, 1; *New York Times*, 11/3/1910, 1.
3. *New York World*, 11/7/1910, 6; *Washington (D.C.) Post*, 11/3/1910, 1; *Fort Wayne (Ind.) Journal Gazette*, 11/9/1910, 5.
4. Curtiss and Post, *Curtiss Aviation Book*, 116.
5. *Washington (D.C.) Herald*, 11/4/1910, 2; *Lowell (Mass.) Sun*, 11/3/1910, 9.
6. Washington Irving Chambers Papers, box 3: Orders, November 2, 1910; *New York World*, 11/3/1910, 1; *New York Times*, 11/4/1910, 2; *Washington (D.C.) Herald*, 11/4/1910, 2.
7. Hale, "Paper Relating to Auxiliary German Navy."; *Brooklyn (N.Y.) Daily Eagle*, 11/3/1910, 2.
8. *Indianapolis News*, 11/4/1910, 18.
9. Washington Irving Chambers Papers, box 3: Annulment, November 4, 1910.
10. *New York Times*, 11/4/1910, 1; *Washington (D.C.) Herald*, 11/4/1910, 2; *News* (Frederick, Md.), 11/4/1910, 2; *Tacoma (Wash.) Times*, 11/4/1910, 3; *Indianapolis News*, 11/4/1910, 18; *Washington (D.C.) Times*, 11/5/1910, 7; *Sun* (Baltimore, Md.), 11/5/1910, 10; *Aero* 1, no. 6 (November 12, 1910), 7; *Washington (D.C.) Post*, 11/5/1910, 4; *Virginian-Pilot* (Norfolk, Va.), 11/5/1910, 3; *Edgefield (S.C.) Advertiser*, 10/26/1910, 4; *Greenwood (S.C.) Journal*, 11/2/1910, 6.
11. *New York Times*, 11/4/1910, 2; 11/5/1910, 1; Washington (D.C.) Post, 11/5/1910, 1.
12. *New York World*, 11/5/1910, 16.

13. *New York World*, 11/7/1910, 6.
14. Washington Irving Chambers Papers, box 11: Undated draft of speech to Aeronautical Society, "The Development of Naval Aviation," delivered on April 27, 1911; box 20: "Brief Summary of the First Steps in the Development of Naval Aeronautics" (1917), 2.
15. Washington Irving Chambers Papers, box 20: "Brief Summary of the First Steps in the Development of Naval Aeronautics" (1917), 2; Lord, "History of Naval Aviation," 14–15; *Washington (D.C.) Herald*, 11/11/1910, 1.
16. *Charlotte (N.C.) News*, 11/13/1910, 1; *News and Observer* (Raleigh, N.C.), 11/15/1910, 1; *Birmingham* I, in *DANFS*; *Annual Reports of the Navy Department for the Fiscal Year 1911*, 76; *Charlotte (N.C.) Observer*, 11/7/1910, 1; *Washington (D.C.) Post*, 11/7/1910, 12; *Boston Post*, 11/7/1910, 1; *Washington (D.C.) Times*, 11/6/1910, 1.
17. van Deurs, *Wings for the Fleet*, 17–18.
18. National Archives and Records Administration, RG 24–118, USS Birmingham deck log, 87-88 (11/7/1910); *Annual Reports of the Navy Department for the Fiscal Year 1911*, 76.
19. *New York World*, 11/8/1910, 1; *Charlotte (N.C.) News*, 10/24/1910, 1; 11/10/1910, 1
20. *New York World*, 11/5/1910, 16; *Charlotte (N.C.) Daily Observer*, 11/25/1910, 2.
21. *New York World*, 11/11/1910, 4.
22. *Brooklyn (N.Y.) Daily Eagle*, 11/4/1910, 3; *New York World*, 11/8/1910, 1; 11/11/1910, 4.
23. Washington Irving Chambers Papers, box 3: Lt. Nathaniel H. Wright report, November 17, 1910, 1.
24. *New York World*, 11/8/1910, 1; 11/9/1910, 6; 11/11/1910, 4; 11/12/1910, 1; USS *Birmingham* deck log, 91–96 (11/9/1910–11/11/1910); Washington Irving Chambers Papers, box 16: Lt. William McEntee, undated memo to Chambers.
25. *Washington (D.C.) Post*, 11/6/1910, 6; *Philadelphia Inquirer*, 11/9/1910, 18; *Sun* (Baltimore, Md.), 11/10/1910, 11; 11/11/1910, 10; *Washington (D.C.) Herald*, 11/10/1910, 1; 11/11/1910, 1; 11/12/1910, 2; *Iowa City Citizen*, 12/21/1910, 1; *Davenport (Iowa) Democrat and Leader*, 11/14/1910, 2.
26. *Augusta (Ga.) Chronicle*, 11/23/1910, 5; *Winston-Salem (N.C.) Journal*, 11/9/1910, 6; *New York World*, 11/12/1910, 1; 11/13/1910, 2; *Charlotte (N.C.) News*, 11/12/1910, 1.
27. *New York World*, 11/12/1910, 1; *Asheville (N.C.) Citizen*, 11/12/1910, 1; *Brooklyn (N.Y.) Daily Eagle*, 11/12/1910, 1; *Boston Post*, 11/12/1910, 1; *Charlotte (N.C.) Observer*, 11/12/1910, 1.
28. *Brooklyn (N.Y.) Daily Eagle*, 11/12/1910, 2; *Sun* (Baltimore, Md.), 11/13/1910, 16.

CHAPTER 14. SHIP TO SHORE

1. *New York World*, 11/13/1910, 2.
2. *New York World*, 11/13/1910, 2; *Raleigh (N.C.) Times*, 11/12/1910, 1; *New York Times*, 11/13/1910, 8; Curtiss and Post, *Curtiss Aviation Book*, 116–17.
3. *New York World*, 11/13/1910, 2; *New York Times*, 11/13/1910, 8; 11/14/1910, 2; Washington Irving Chambers Papers, box 3: Orders, November 12, 1910; *Sun* (Baltimore, Md.), 11/13/1910, 16; Chambers, "Aviation and Aeroplanes," 174–75.
4. *Washington (D.C.) Post*, 11/15/1910, 1–2, 9; *Annual Reports of the Navy Department for the Fiscal Year 1911*, 76.
5. Chambers, "Aviation and Aeroplanes," 175; Washington Irving Chambers Papers, box 3: Lt. Nathaniel H. Wright, report, November 17, 1910, 1.
6. *Bailey* II, in *DANFS*; Washington Irving Chambers Papers, box 19: Chambers, letter to Ensign Archer Allen, February 10, 1911; Chambers, "Aviation and Aeroplanes," 176.
7. *New York Times*, 11/14/1910, 2; *Wichita Beacon*, 11/14/1910, 9; USS *Birmingham* deck log, 102 (11/14/1910); *Roe* I, *Stringham* I, and *Terry* I, in *DANFS*.
8. Chambers, "Aviation and Aeroplanes," 175.
9. Washington Irving Chambers Papers, box 3: Lt. Nathaniel H. Wright, report, November 17, 1910, 2.
10. Washington Irving Chambers Papers, box 3: Lt. Nathaniel H. Wright, report, November 17, 1910, 2.
11. Washington Irving Chambers Papers, box 3: Lt. Nathaniel H. Wright report, November 17, 1910, 2; Chambers, "Aviation and Aeroplanes," 176, 195; *Aeronautics* 7, no. 3 (September 1910): 92; *New York World*, 11/15/1910, 2.
12. *New York World*, 11/15/1910, 2.
13. USS *Birmingham* deck log, 102 (11/14/1910).
14. *Washington (D.C.) Post*, 11/15/1910, 1; *Washington (D.C.) Times*, 11/15/1910, 1–2; *York (Pa.) Daily*, 11/15/1910, 1; *Leavenworth (Kans.) Times*, 11/15/1910, 1; *Salt Lake Herald-Republican* (Salt Lake City, Utah), 11/15/1910, 1; *San Francisco Call*, 11/15/1910, 1; Washington Irving Chambers Papers, box 16: *New York World*, wireless telegram to Guy Mason c/o Chambers, November 14, 1910; *New York World*, 11/15/1910, 2.
15. *New York Times*, 11/15/1910, 1; Washington Irving Chambers Papers, box 3: Lt. Nathaniel H. Wright report, November 17, 1910, 3–4.
16. Washington Irving Chambers Papers, box 3: Chambers, report to Secretary of the Navy, November 23, 1910.
17. Roseberry, *Glenn Curtiss*, 337–38.
18. *Washington (D.C.) Times*, 11/15/1910, 1; *New York Times*, 11/24/1910, 1; *Charlotte (N.C.) Observer*, 11/24/1910, 1.
19. Washington Irving Chambers Papers, box 16: Secretary Meyer, letter to Ely, November 17, 1910.
20. Chambers, "Aviation and Aeroplanes," 177.

21. *Washington (D.C.) Times*, 11/15/1910, 1–2; Washington Irving Chambers Papers, box 3: Lt. Nathaniel H. Wright report, November 17, 1910, 2; box 19: Chambers, letter to Gen. James Allen, February 10, 1911.

CHAPTER 15. STAR-DUST FALLING

1. *Elyria (Ohio) Evening Telegram*, 8/17/1910, 6; *Santa Ana (Calif.) Register*, 8/12/1910, 3; *Oregon Daily Journal* (Portland), 11/18/1910, 5.
2. *New York Times*, 8/12/1910, 3; *Oakland (Calif.) Tribune*, 8/14/1910, 18; Buist, "Miracles of Flight," 411, 414.
3. *Gettysburg (Pa.) Times*, 9/9/1910, 2; *San Francisco Call*, 9/15/1910, 3.
4. Buist, "Miracles of Flight," 411; Library of Congress, Manuscript Division, Wilbur Wright and Orville Wright Papers, General Correspondence: Hoxsey, Arch, 1910, 1928, image 5 ([Wilbur Wright], letter to Hoxsey, September 19, 1910); *Nebraska State Journal* (Lincoln), 9/16/1910, 8; *San Francisco Call*, 11/18/1910, 3.
5. Mortimer, *Chasing Icarus*, 138, 184, 210; *Brooklyn (N.Y.) Daily Eagle*, 1/1/1911, local, 1.
6. *New York Times*, 11/17/1910, 6; *San Francisco Call*, 11/18/1910, 3; *Washington (D.C.) Herald*, 11/18/1910, 1; *Washington (D.C.) Post*, 11/17/1910, 3; 11/19/1910, 3; *News and Observer* (Raleigh, N.C.), 11/18/1910, 1.
7. *News and Observer* (Raleigh, N.C.), 11/17/1910, 1; 11/18/1910, 1; *Charlotte (N.C.) Daily Observer*, 11/24/1910, 1; Hoffbeck, "Shooting Star," 333; *Montgomery (Ala.) Advertiser*, 3/22/1910, 9.
8. Washington Irving Chambers Papers, box 14: Fanciulli, letter to Chambers, November 29, 1910; Curtiss and Post, *Curtiss Aviation Book*, 118–19; Lord, "History of Naval Aviation," 32; *Hawaiian Gazette* (Honolulu), 12/2/1910, 3; Trimble, *Hero of the Air*, 102.
9. *Annual Reports of the Navy Department for the Fiscal Year 1910*, 23; *Los Angeles Herald*, 12/25/1910, 4; Chambers, "Aviation and Aeroplanes," 182; Lord, "History of Naval Aviation," 14.
10. Washington Irving Chambers Papers, box 14: Chambers, letter to Curtiss, December 19, 1910; *San Francisco Call*, 12/21/1910, 3.
11. *San Francisco Call*, 12/17/1910, 3; 12/18/1910, 29–30; 12/19/1910, 2; *Los Angeles Herald*, 12/15/1910, 2.
12. *Hawaiian Gazette* (Honolulu), 12/2/1910, 1; 12/9/1910, 1; 12/16/1910, 1; *Hawaiian Star* (Honolulu), 12/13/1910, 6; 12/19/1910, 8; *Aircraft* 1, no. 12 (February 1911): 440–41; *San Francisco Call*, 12/21/1910, 12.
13. *Oakland (Calif.) Tribune*, 12/25/1910, 26; Jerome S. Fanciulli Collection, box 2, folder 17: Curtiss, letter to Fanciulli, February 17, 1911.
14. *Cincinnati Enquirer*, 12/3/1910, 1; *Aeronautics* 8, no. 2 (February 1911): 60; *Times-Democrat* (New Orleans, LA), 12/2/1910, 11; 12/3/1910, 7; 12/4/1910, part 2, 7; 12/5/1910, 3, 11; 12/7/1910, 7; *Daily Record (Columbia, S.C.)*, 12/8/1910, 3; *State* (Columbia, S.C.), 12/9/1910, 9; *Charlotte (N.C.) News*, 12/9/1910, 6.

15. *New Orleans Times-Democrat*, 12/12/1910, 11.
16. *Atlanta Constitution*, 12/16/1910, 10.
17. *Atlanta Constitution*, 12/13/1910, 3; 12/14/1910, 12; 12/18/1910, sports, 1.
18. Jerome S. Fanciulli Collection, box 2, folder 16: Fanciulli, letter to Curtiss, December 24, 1910.
19. Jerome S. Fanciulli Collection, box 2, folder 16: Fanciulli, letter to Curtiss, December 13, 1910; Fanciulli, night telegram to Curtiss, December 8, 1910.
20. *Aircraft* 1, no. 12 (February 1911): 441; *Los Angeles Herald*, 12/24/1910, 14; Jerome S. Fanciulli Collection, box 2, folder 17: Curtiss, letter to Fanciulli, March 8, 1911; Casey, *Curtiss*, 75–76.
21. Jerome S. Fanciulli Collection, box 2, folder 16: Fanciulli, letter to Curtiss, December 24, 1910.
22. *Washington (D.C.) Post*, 12/15/1910, 3; *Los Angeles Herald*, 12/15/1910, 1; *Morning Echo* (Bakersfield, Calif.), 12/16/1910, 3; Curtiss and Post, *Curtiss Aviation Book*, 119, 126; Lord, "History of Naval Aviation," 32; van Deurs, *Anchors in the Sky*, 55–56; Washington Irving Chambers Papers, box 15: Chambers, letter to Ellyson, January 11, 1911; Trimble, *Hero of the Air*, 97–118.
23. *Los Angeles Herald*, 12/25/1910, sec. 1, 1, 4.
24. *Los Angeles Herald*, 12/26/1910, 1.
25. *Los Angeles Herald*, 12/27/1910, 1, 7; *Ogden (Utah) Standard*, 12/27/1910, 5.
26. *Los Angeles Herald*, 12/28/1910, 1.
27. *Los Angeles Herald*, 12/29/1910, 1.
28. *Los Angeles Herald*, 12/30/1910, 1, 3; 12/31/1910, 7.
29. *Los Angeles Herald*, 12/30/1910, 3; 12/31/1910, 1, 7.
30. *Los Angeles Herald*, 12/30/1910, 3; 12/31/1910, 1, 7; *Hawaiian Gazette* (Honolulu), 1/3/1911, 3.
31. *Evening World* (New York, N.Y.), 12/30/1910, 1; *Washington (D.C.) Herald*, 12/31/1910, 1; *New York Times*, 1/1/1911, 1.
32. *El Paso Herald*, 12/31/1910, 1; *New York Times*, 1/1/1911, 1.
33. Wilbur Wright and Orville Wright Papers, General Correspondence: Knabenshue, Roy, 1908–1911, images 44–46 (undated letter from January 1911).
34. *Cincinnati Enquirer*, 1/1/1911, 1–2; *Washington (D.C.) Post*, 1/1/1911, 7.
35. *San Francisco Chronicle*, 1/5/1911, 1, 4; *Salt Lake Tribune* (Salt Lake City, Utah), 1/20/1911, 9; *San Francisco Call*, 1/5/1911, 16.
36. *Brooklyn (N.Y.) Daily Eagle*, 1/1/1911, local, 1.
37. Office of Information Services, *Chronology of American Aerospace Events*, 104; *Philadelphia Inquirer*, 11/20/1910, sec. 1, part 2, 8; 1/8/1911, sec. 2, 4.

CHAPTER 16. THE DOVE TO THE ARK

1. *Lowell (Mass.) Sun*, 11/3/1910, 9; Washington Irving Chambers Papers, box 14: Chambers, letter to Curtiss, December 19, 1910; *Washington (D.C.) Times*, 11/23/1910, 3; *Washington (D.C.) Post*, 11/24/1910, 9.
2. *San Francisco Call*, 1/2/1911, 11; 1/5/1911, 16; 1/6/1911, 5; *San Francisco Chronicle*, 1/5/1911, 3; 1/9/1911, 1.

3. *San Francisco Examiner*, 1/2/1911, 4; 1/7/1911, 3; *San Francisco Chronicle*, 12/30/1910, 4; *Tacoma (Wash.) Times*, 12/30/1910, 1; Cole and Schreiner, "Willard," 189; Charles Willard, letter to Capt. Dean Veremakis, September 15, 1972, collection of the author.
4. *San Francisco Chronicle*, 1/1/1911, 50; 1/2/1911, 11; *San Francisco Examiner*, 1/2/1911, 4.
5. *Pittsburgh* II (formerly *Pennsylvania*), in *DANFS*; Zogbaum, *From Sail to Saratoga*, 170; *Annual Reports of the Navy Department for the Fiscal Year 1912*, 111 (movements of vessels); *Oakland (Calif.) Tribune*, 1/5/1911, 6.
6. van Deurs, *Anchors in the Sky*, 56; *San Francisco Call*, 1/2/1911, 11; Washington Irving Chambers Papers, box 15: Ellyson, memorandum to Secretary of the Navy, January 4, 1911; *San Francisco Chronicle*, 1/5/1911, 1; 1/6/1911, 16.
7. *San Francisco Chronicle*, 1/1/1911, 27; 1/5/1911, 1; *San Francisco Call*, 1/5/1911, 16; 1/9/1911, 5.
8. *San Francisco Examiner*, 1/8/1911, 3; *San Francisco Call*, 1/5/1911, 16; *San Francisco Chronicle*, 1/5/1911, 1.
9. *Bismarck (N.D.) Daily Tribune*, 1/6/1911, 1; *Fort Wayne (Ind.) Journal Gazette*, 1/5/1911, 5.
10. Casey, *Curtiss*, 76–79; *San Francisco Call*, 1/6/1911, 5; 1/9/1911, 1.
11. *San Francisco Chronicle*, 1/5/1911, 3; 1/6/1911, 16; *Oakland (Calif.) Tribune*, 1/5/1911, 6; *San Francisco Call*, 1/9/1911, 1 (photo).
12. Zogbaum, *From Sail to Saratoga*, 172–74.
13. Chambers, "Aviation and Aeroplanes," 192; Keith-McHenry-Pond Family Papers, BANC MSS C-B 595, carton 11: book 15, 1269, Bancroft Library, University of California, Berkeley; Chesneau, Aircraft Carriers of the World, 22.
14. Chambers, "Aviation and Aeroplanes," 192.
15. Chambers, "Aviation and Aeroplanes," 192; Washington Irving Chambers Papers, box 15: Ellyson, letter to Chambers, February 1, 1911; *San Francisco Chronicle*, 1/2/1911, 11; *San Francisco Call*, 1/2/1911, 11; 1/6/1911, 5; *San Francisco Examiner*, 1/2/1911, 4.
16. Vergara, Hugh Robinson, 2, 26-27; *San Francisco Chronicle*, 1/1/1911, 50; Lord, "History of Naval Aviation," 17–18; Cole and Schreiner, "Willard," 189.
17. National Archives and Records Administration, RG 24–118, USS *Pennsylvania* deck log, 420 (1/9/1911); *Annual Reports of the Navy Department for the Fiscal Year 1912*, 111 (movements of vessels); Keith-McHenry-Pond Family Papers, BANC MSS C-B 595, carton 11: book 15, unnumbered page (photograph of Captain Pond, Curtiss, Ely, and others inspecting the platform on USS *Pennsylvania*, with a guard rail and a guide rail visible, January 9, 1911); Chambers, "Aviation and Aeroplanes," 192; *San Francisco Examiner*, 1/10/1911, 3; Cole and Schreiner, "Willard," 189–90.
18. Chambers, "Aviation and Aeroplanes," 192–93; Naval History and Heritage Command, NH #77588 (photograph showing that five metal hooks were fixed to the airplane's central skid, contradicting Captain Pond's report stating that there were three pairs); *Aeronautics* 8, no. 3 (March 1911): 96.

19. *San Francisco Chronicle*, 1/1/1911, 50; 1/5/1911, 1, 3; 1/6/1911, 16; *Oakland (Calif.) Tribune*, 1/1/1911, 18; 1/6/1911, 14.
20. *San Francisco Call*, 1/9/1911, 1–3; *San Francisco Examiner*, 1/9/1911, 1, 2, 4; *San Francisco Chronicle*, 1/8/1911, 81, 83; 1/9/1911, 1.
21. *San Francisco Call*, 1/12/1911, 3; *San Francisco Examiner*, 1/10/1911, 3.
22. *San Francisco Call*, 1/11/1911, 1, 3.
23. Curtiss and Post, *Curtiss Aviation Book*, 120–21.
24. Washington Irving Chambers Papers, box 15: Ellyson, memorandum to Secretary of the Navy, January 17, 1911; Ellyson, letter to Chambers, January 18, 1911; Ellyson, memorandum to Secretary of the Navy, January 31, 1911.
25. *San Francisco Call*, 1/17/1911, 2; San Francisco Chronicle, 1/16/1911, 2.
26. *San Francisco Call*, 1/17/1911, 1–2; *San Francisco Chronicle*, 1/17/1911, 1, 3.
27. *San Francisco Chronicle*, 1/17/1911, 3; *San Francisco Call*, 1/18/1911, 2.
28. Bonnalie, "Eugene B. Ely," 40; Zogbaum, *From Sail to Saratoga*, 179; Chambers, "Aviation and Aeroplanes," 195.
29. *San Francisco Call*, 1/19/1911, 2.
30. USS *Pennsylvania* deck log, 438 (1/18/1911); *San Francisco Call*, 1/19/1911, 2; *San Francisco Examiner*, 1/19/1911, 30; Chambers, "Aviation and Aeroplanes," 193.
31. *San Francisco Examiner*, 1/19/1911, 31–32; *San Francisco Call*, 1/19/1911, 3; Chambers, "Aviation and Aeroplanes," 193, 195.
32. Chambers, "Aviation and Aeroplanes," 193, 195; Vergara, *Hugh Robinson*, 27.
33. Naval History and Heritage Command, NH #82737 (photograph showing Ely's airplane on final approach, the right wing slightly higher as a result of the updraft).
34. USS *Pennsylvania* deck log, 438 (1/18/1911); *San Francisco Examiner*, 1/19/1911, 30–31; *San Francisco Call*, 1/19/1911, 3; Chambers, "Aviation and Aeroplanes," 193, 195.
35. Zogbaum, *From Sail to Saratoga*, 178–79; Chambers, "Aviation and Aeroplanes," 193–94.
36. *San Francisco Call*, 1/19/1911, 1–2; Vergara, *Hugh Robinson*, 28; *Independent-Journal* (San Rafael, Calif.), 9/6/1958, M4; Zogbaum, *From Sail to Saratoga*, 179; Chambers, "Aviation and Aeroplanes," 193.
37. *San Francisco Examiner*, 1/19/1911, 29–32; USS *Pennsylvania* deck log, 438 (1/18/1911); Chambers, "Aviation and Aeroplanes," 194; *Mountain Democrat* (Placerville, Calif.), 1/28/1911, 4.
38. *San Francisco Chronicle*, 1/19/1911, 4; *San Francisco Examiner*, 1/19/1911, 29.
39. *Seattle Daily Times*, 7/20/1911, 2; *Salt Lake Tribune* (Salt Lake City, Utah), 2/13/1911, 2; *San Francisco Examiner*, 1/19/1911, 29, 31; *San Francisco Call*, 1/20/1911, 6; *Independent-Journal* (San Rafael, Calif.), 9/6/1958, M4; Zogbaum, *From Sail to Saratoga*, 179; Chambers, "Aviation and Aeroplanes," 193, 195; *San Francisco Call*, 1/19/1911, 2; *Mountain Democrat* (Placerville, Calif.), 1/28/1911, 4.

40. *Washington (D.C.) Post*, 1/19/1911, 1; *New York World*, 1/19/1911, 3; *San Francisco Examiner*, 1/19/1911, 52; *Hawaiian Star* (Honolulu), 2/3/1911, 8; *Macon (Ga.) Daily Telegraph*, 10/3/1911, 16; Chambers, "Aviation and Aeroplanes," 194.
41. *San Francisco Call*, 1/27/1911, 6; *Greensboro (N.C.) Daily News*, 1/28/1911, 4; *New-York Tribune*, 2/26/1911, part 2, 2.
42. *Philadelphia Inquirer*, 1/22/1911, part 3, 4.
43. *Fort Wayne (Ind.) Journal Gazette*, 1/19/1911, 1; *San Francisco Chronicle*, 1/10/1911, 5; *Humboldt Times* (Eureka, Calif.), 5/27/1911, 1; *Post-Standard* (Syracuse, N.Y.), 1/19/1911, 1; *New York Times*, 1/19/1911, 1; *Washington (D.C.) Post*, 1/19/1911, 1; *Elyria (Ohio) Evening Telegram*, 1/19/1911, 1; Chambers, "Aviation and Aeroplanes," 194.
44. Curtiss and Post, *Curtiss Aviation Book*, 122.

CHAPTER 17. **WATER AND AIR**

1. *San Francisco Call*, 1/20/1911, 5, 6; 1/21/1911, junior, 5; 1/23/1911, 1, 2; *Oakland (Calif.) Tribune*, 1/22/1911, 23; *San Francisco Chronicle*, 1/23/1911, 2.
2. *San Francisco Chronicle*, 1/26/1911, 16.
3. *New York Times*, 1/31/1911, 1; *Paulding* [I], in *DANFS*; Washington Irving Chambers Papers, box 19: Fanciulli, letter to Chambers, January 6, 1911; Chambers, letter to Lt. Cdr. Yates Stirling Jr., January 14, 1911.
4. Washington Irving Chambers Papers, box 19: Hayden (commandant of the Key West naval station), undated note to Chambers; *New York Times*, 1/24/1911, 3; Chambers, "Aviation and Aeroplanes," 185.
5. *Salt Lake Tribune* (Salt Lake City, Utah), 1/20/1911, 9; *San Francisco Call*, 1/17/1911, 1; 1/22/1911, 31; 1/24/1911, 7; *San Francisco Chronicle*, 1/17/1911, 3; *Tacoma (Wash.) Times*, 1/31/1911, 1.
6. *Bulletins of the Aerial Experiment Association* 9 (September 7, 1908), 4; Curtiss and Post, *Curtiss Aviation Book*, 221; Roseberry, *Glenn Curtiss*, 143–47; Trimble, *Hero of the Air*, 43.
7. Washington Irving Chambers Papers, box 15: Ellyson, memorandum to Secretary of the Navy, January 28, 1911; Curtiss and Post, *Curtiss Aviation Book*, 130–32; *San Francisco Call*, 1/27/1911, 4; Roseberry, *Glenn Curtiss*, 313–14; Trimble, *Hero of the Air*, 112.
8. Keith-McHenry-Pond Family Papers, box 11, book 15: 1269; *Oakland (Calif.) Tribune*, 1/27/1911, 6; *Aeronautics* 8, no. 3 (March 1911): 86.
9. Washington Irving Chambers Papers, box 14: Chambers, letter to Curtiss, December 19, 1910; box 15: Chambers, letter to Ellyson, January 24, 1911.
10. Chambers, "Aviation and Aeroplanes," 177, 182; Lord, "History of Naval Aviation," 19.
11. *Arizona Republican* (Phoenix), 1/29/1911, 1.
12. Washington Irving Chambers Papers, box 15: Ellyson, letter to Chambers, February 1, 1911.
13. *San Francisco Chronicle*, 1/30/1911, 3.

14. *Humboldt Times* (Eureka, Calif.), 5/28/1911, 1
15. Coolbaugh, email correspondence with the author, March 2015.
16. *Humboldt Times* (Eureka, Calif.), 5/27/1911, 1.
17. *New York Times*, 1/26/1911, 1; 1/31/1911, 1; *Tacoma (Wash.) Times*, 1/26/1911, 1.
18. *Washington (D.C.) Post*, 1/31/1911, 3; *New York Times*, 1/31/1911, 1.
19. *New York Times*, 1/31/1911, 1; Chambers, "Aviation and Aeroplanes," 185–89; Washington Irving Chambers Papers, box 19: Chambers, letter to James Allen, February 10, 1911; Lord, "History of Naval Aviation," 19–20.

CHAPTER 18. TWISTS AND CORKSCREWS

1. *San Francisco Examiner*, 1/24/1911, 1.
2. Washington Irving Chambers Papers, box 16: Ely, letter to Chambers, January 30, 1911.
3. *Washington (D.C.) Herald*, 2/3/1911, 4; *Galveston Daily News*, 2/7/1911, 1; Washington Irving Chambers Papers, box 15: Ellyson, letter to Chambers, February 1, 1911; Chambers, letter to Ellyson, February 8, 1911.
4. Washington Irving Chambers Papers, box 20: Midn. Frank Loftin and Midn. Ralph F. Wood, letter to Chambers, February 9, 1911; Chambers, letter to Midn. Frank Loftin and Midn. Ralph F. Wood, February 14, 1911; Chambers, letter to E. W. Paynter, October 5, 1911.
5. RoA, 6097–99, ex. 444; 6101–2, ex. 445; 6103, ex. 447; Jerome S. Fanciulli Collection, box 2, folder 17: Curtiss, letter to Fanciulli, February 22, 1911; Crouch, *Bishop's Boys*, 435.
6. Chambers, "Aviation and Aeroplanes," 196; RoA, 6122, ex. 461.
7. *New York Herald*, 1/5/1911, part 3, 9; Jerome S. Fanciulli Collection, box 2, folder 17: Fanciulli, note to Curtiss, January 5, 1911; Curtiss, letter to Fanciulli, January 12, 1911.
8. Jerome S. Fanciulli Collection, box 2, folder 17: Fanciulli, letter to Curtiss, February 15, 1911; Curtiss, letter to Fanciulli, February 17, 1911; Curtiss, letter to Fanciulli, February 22, 1911.
9. Jerome S. Fanciulli Collection, box 2, folder 17: Curtiss, letter to Fanciulli, February 17, 1911; Curtiss, letter to Fanciulli, February 22, 1911.
10. Jerome S. Fanciulli Collection, box 2, folder 15: Curtiss, letter to Fanciulli, April 11, 1911.
11. *Oakland (Calif.) Tribune*, 1/27/1911, 12; 2/6/1911, 16; *Sacramento Star*, 2/2/1911, 3; 2/6/1911, 2, 7; *San Francisco Call*, 2/6/1911, 7; 2/7/1911, 7; *Ogden (Utah) Standard*, 2/6/1911, 5.
12. *Salt Lake Tribune* (Salt Lake City, Utah), 2/12/1911, 1–2; 2/13/1911, 1.
13. *Salt Lake Tribune* (Salt Lake City, Utah), 2/13/1911, 2.
14. *Tacoma (Wash.) Times*, 5/23/1911, 7; *San Francisco Chronicle*, 2/13/1911, 14; *Fort Wayne (Ind.) Sentinel*, 2/13/1911, 8; *Middletown (N.Y.) Daily Times-Press*, 2/13/1911, 5; *Washington (D.C.) Post*, 2/13/1911, 12; *San Francisco Examiner*, 2/14/1911, 1.

15. *Salt Lake Tribune* (Salt Lake City, Utah), 2/13/1911, 1; *San Francisco Chronicle*, 2/19/1911, 26; *Tacoma (Wash.) Times*, 5/23/1911, 7; *Aircraft* 2, no. 3 (May 1911): 84.
16. Washington Irving Chambers Papers, box 16: Chambers, letter to Ely, February 9, 1911.
17. *Goodwin's Weekly* (Salt Lake City, Utah), 2/18/1911, 8; Trimble, *Hero of the Air*, 118; Washington Irving Chambers Papers, box 15: Chambers, letter to Lieutenant Ellyson, January 11, 1911; box 16: Chambers, letter to Ely, February 9, 1911.
18. *Salt Lake Tribune* (Salt Lake City, Utah), 2/14/1911, 8; 2/15/1911, 9; 2/16/1911, 1; 2/17/1911, 1; *Salt Lake Telegram* (Salt Lake City, Utah), 2/17/1911, 12; 2/18/1911, 6.
19. *Salt Lake Tribune* (Salt Lake City, Utah), 2/18/1911, 1, 11; 2/19/1911, sport, 1; *Salt Lake Telegram*, 2/18/1911, 6.
20. Jerome S. Fanciulli Collection, box 2, folder 17: Fanciulli, letter to Curtiss, February 15, 1911; Washington Irving Chambers Papers, box 15: Chambers, letter to Lieutenant Ellyson, February 8, 1911.
21. Casey, *Curtiss*, 94–95; Curtiss and Post, *Curtiss Aviation Book*, 132–33; Washington Irving Chambers Papers, box 15: Lieutenant Ellyson, letter to Chambers, February 14, 1911; Jerome S. Fanciulli Collection, box 2, folder 17: Curtiss, letter to Fanciulli, February 17, 1911.
22. Washington Irving Chambers Papers, box 15: Lieutenant Ellyson, letter to Chambers, February 14, 1911; Curtiss and Post, *Curtiss Aviation Book*, 133.
23. Washington Irving Chambers Papers, box 15: Lieutenant Ellyson, memorandum to Secretary of the Navy, February 17, 1911; Curtiss and Post, *Curtiss Aviation Book*, 134.
24. Washington Irving Chambers Papers, box 16: Chambers, letter to Ely, February 9, 1911; box 15: Lieutenant Ellyson, telegram to Chambers, February 17, 1911; Jerome S. Fanciulli Collection, box 2, folder 17: Curtiss, letter to Fanciulli, February 17, 1911.
25. Oath and Enlistment Papers of Eugene Burton Ely, California National Guard, California State Archives, Sacramento; *Aero* 1, no. 22 (March 4, 1911): 164.
26. Washington Irving Chambers Papers, box 16: Nathan D. Ely, letter to Secretary of the Navy, February 24, 1911.
27. Washington Irving Chambers Papers, box 4: Chambers, memo, February 11, 1911; box 15: Chambers, letter to Lieutenant Ellyson, February 16, 1911.
28. Washington Irving Chambers Papers, box 16: Assistant Secretary Winthrop, letter to Nathan Ely, March 1, 1911.
29. Washington Irving Chambers Papers, box 4: Chambers, letter to Admiral Dewey, September 24, 1913; box 9: Chambers, letter to E. L. Jones, December 5, 1911.
30. Washington Irving Chambers Papers, box 15: Chambers, letter to Lieutenant Ellyson, March 11, 1911.
31. Washington Irving Chambers Papers, box 4: Orders, March 13, 1911.
32. *San Francisco Call*, 3/19/1911, 50, 72; 3/17/1911, 14; *San Francisco Examiner*, 3/20/1911, 1; *San Francisco Chronicle*, 3/20/1911, 3.

CHAPTER 19. **WAR MACHINE**

1. *Washington (D.C.) Herald*, 3/13/1911, 3; 3/15/1911, 4; Casey, *Curtiss*, 76; Jerome S. Fanciulli Collection, box 2, folder 15: Curtiss, letter to Fanciulli, April 11, 1911; folder 17: Fanciulli, telegram to Curtiss, March 17, 1911.
2. RoA, 6105-6, ex 449.
3. Washington Irving Chambers Papers, box 15: Ellyson, letter to Chambers, February 22, 1911; Ellyson, letter to Chambers, March 31, 1911; Jerome S. Fanciulli Collection, box 2, folder 15: Curtiss, letter to Fanciulli, April 11, 1911.
4. Washington Irving Chambers Papers, box 15: Ellyson, letter to Chambers, March 5, 1911; RoA, 6104-5, ex. 448; *Oakland (Calif.) Tribune*, 3/18/1911, 1.
5. Jerome S. Fanciulli Collection, box 2, folder 17: Curtiss, letter to Fanciulli, March 8, 1911; Fanciulli, telegram to Curtiss, March 17, 1911; Curtiss, letter to Fanciulli, March 29, 1911.
6. Oath and Enlistment Papers of Eugene Burton Ely, California National Guard, California State Archives, Sacramento; *Chronicle Telegram* (Elyria, Ohio), 4/13/1911, 7.
7. RoA, 6104, ex. 447; Jerome S. Fanciulli Collection, box 2, folder 17: Fanciulli, letter to Curtiss, March 27, 1911; Curtiss, letter to Fanciulli, March 29, 1911; folder 15: Curtiss, letter to Fanciulli, April 11, 1911.
8. Jerome S. Fanciulli Collection, box 2, folder 15: Curtiss, letter to Fanciulli, April 11, 1911; folder 17: Curtiss, letter to Fanciulli, April 17, 1911.
9. *Los Angeles Times*, 3/30/1911, 14.
10. *Ogden (Utah) Standard*, 4/7/1911, 2; *Salt Lake Tribune* (Salt Lake City, Utah), 4/8/1911, 1.
11. *San Francisco Call*, 4/9/1911, 17; *Oakland (Calif.) Tribune*, 4/9/1911, 35; *Salt Lake Tribune* (Salt Lake City, Utah), 4/11/1911, 1, 13; Trimble, *Hero of the Air*, 117–18; Roseberry, *Glenn Curtiss*, 315; Casey, *Curtiss*, 96–98.
12. *Salt Lake Tribune* (Salt Lake City, Utah), 4/11/1911, 1, 13; Roseberry, *Glenn Curtiss*, 317.
13. *Aeronautics* 8, no. 5 (May 1911): 182; Washington Irving Chambers Papers, box 15: Ellyson, letter to Chambers, March 5, 1911; Roseberry, Glenn Curtiss, 254-55, 258-59; Trimble, *Hero of the Air*, 81, 118; Jerome S. Fanciulli Collection, box 2, folder 17: Fanciulli, telegram to Curtiss, March 6, 1911; Curtiss, letter to Fanciulli, March 8, 1911.
14. Jerome S. Fanciulli Collection, box 2, folder 17: Curtiss, letter to Fanciulli, March 8, 1911; Fanciulli, letter to Curtiss, March 27, 1911.
15. *Salt Lake Tribune* (Salt Lake City, Utah), 4/13/1911, 6; *Bakersfield Californian*, 4/10/1911, 9; 4/17/1911, 1, 9.
16. *San Antonio Express*, 4/20/1911, 7; *Aeronautics* 8, no. 6 (June 1911): 213; *Manitoba Free Press* (Winnipeg), 7/16/1910, 1; Casey, *Curtiss*, 76.
17. *New York Times*, 4/21/1911, 2.
18. *Aeronautics* 8, no. 6 (June 1911): 213; Burge, "Diary of V. L. Burge," 30; *San Antonio Light*, 4/23/1911, 1; *Galveston Daily News*, 4/21/1911, 1; 4/23/1911, 4.

19. *San Antonio Light*, 4/30/1911, 4; *Galveston Daily News*, 4/21/1911, 1; 4/30/1911, 2; *Nevada State Journal* (Reno), 4/21/1911, 8; *New York Times*, 4/27/1911, 2; 4/30/1911, parts 3–4, 12; *Sun* (New York, N.Y.), 4/28/1911, 1; *Aeronautics* 8, no. 6 (June 1911): 202; Burge, "Diary of V. L. Burge," 30.
20. *Brooklyn (N.Y.) Daily Eagle*, 4/26/1911, 16; *Aeronautics* 8, no. 4 (April 1911), 129; no. 5 (May 1911): 158-59; no. 6 (June 1911), 210; *New York Times*, 4/9/1910, 9.
21. Washington Irving Chambers Papers, box 9: Hudson Maxim, invitation to Chambers, April 16, 1911; box 11: "The Development of Naval Aviation."
22. *Aeronautics* 8, no. 4 (April 1911): 129; *San Antonio Light*, 4/28/1911, 1.
23. Washington Irving Chambers Papers, box 15: Ellyson, report to Secretary of the Navy, March 31, 1911.
24. RoA, 6105–6, ex. 449; *Galveston Daily News*, 4/30/1911, 2; Washington Irving Chambers Papers, box 15: Ellyson, letter to Chambers, March 17, 1911; Ellyson, letter to Chambers, February 14, 1911; Ellyson, letter to Chambers, February 22, 1911; Ellyson, letter to Chambers, February 25, 1911; Curtiss and Post, *Curtiss Aviation Book*, 239.
25. Foulois, *Memoirs*, 86, 91; Curtiss and Post, *Curtiss Aviation Book*, 242; *San Francisco Call*, 5/11/1911, 18; Burge, "Diary of V. L. Burge," 30.
26. *New York Times*, 4/30/1911, parts 3–4, 12; *Wichita Daily Eagle*, 4/19/1911, 3; *Galveston Daily News*, 5/1/1911, 5; *Topeka (Kans.) Daily Capital*, 5/13/1911, 6; *Fort Worth Star-Telegram*, 5/15/1911, 2.
27. Burge, "Diary of V. L. Burge," 30; Foulois, *Memoirs*, 92; *Galveston Daily News*, 5/3/1911, 1; *New York Times*, 5/4/1911, 5.
28. Jerome S. Fanciulli Collection, box 2, folder 17: Curtiss, letter to Fanciulli, May 14, 1911.
29. Foulois, *Memoirs*, 92.
30. *Wichita Beacon*, 5/6/1911, 1; *Wichita Daily Eagle*, 5/5/1911, 1.
31. *Leavenworth (Kans.) Times*, 5/6/1911, 1; *San Antonio Light*, 5/6/1911, 3; 5/22/1911, 12; *Carnegie (Okla.) Herald*, 5/11/1911, 2; *Fort Leavenworth (Kans.) News*, 5/12/1911, 1; *Davenport (Iowa) Democrat and Leader*, 5/7/1911, 13; *Wichita Beacon*, 5/8/1911, 5; *Wichita Daily Eagle*, 5/7/1911, 1.
32. *Topeka (Kans.) Daily Capital*, 5/13/1911, 6; *Kansas City (Mo.) Times*, 5/12/1911, 16; *Williamsburg (Iowa) Journal-Tribune*, 5/11/1911, 7.
33. Trimble, *Hero of the Air*, 121; U.S. Congress, Joint Resolution to Designate May 8, 1986, as "Naval Aviation Day," Public Law 99–292, U.S. Statutes at Large 100 (198), 416.
34. *Aeronautics* 8, no. 6 (June 1911): 213; Burge, "Diary of V. L. Burge," 31; Foulois, *Memoirs*, 92–93; *San Antonio Light*, 5/11/1911, 1.
35. *Eureka (Calif.) Herald*, 5/15/1911, 8.
36. Foulois, *Memoirs*, 94; Manning, *History of Military Aviation in San Antonio*, 5, 9.

CHAPTER 20. FULL CIRCLE

1. *Washington (D.C.) Herald*, 5/12/1911, 3; Washington Irving Chambers Papers, box 15: Paul Beck, letter to Curtiss, May 12, 1911; Ellyson, letter to Chambers, May 15, 1911.
2. *Fort Worth Star-Telegram*, 5/15/1911, 2; Jerome S. Fanciulli Collection, box 2, folder 17: Curtiss, letter to Fanciulli, May 14, 1911.
3. *Des Moines (Iowa) News*, 5/21/1911, 12; Jerome S. Fanciulli Collection, box 2, folder 17: Fanciulli, letter to Curtiss, June 7, 1911; Curtiss, letter to Fanciulli, May 14, 1911.
4. Jerome S. Fanciulli Collection, box 2, folder 17: Fanciulli, letter to Curtiss, June 7, 1911.
5. Jerome S. Fanciulli Collection, box 2, folder 17: Fanciulli, letter to Curtiss, June 7, 1911.
6. Jerome S. Fanciulli Collection, box 2, folder 17: Fanciulli, letter to Curtiss, June 7, 1911; Foulois, *Memoirs*, 92.
7. Foulois, *Memoirs, 93*, contradicting the board of officers' report reprinted in *Aeronautics* 8, no. 6 (June 1911): 213.
8. *Greensboro (N.C.) Daily News*, 5/26/1911, 1; *New York Times*, 5/28/1911, parts 3–4, 12.
9. *Eureka (Calif.) Herald*, 5/18/1911, 5; 5/27/1911, 1, 4, 8.
10. *Humboldt Standard* (Eureka, Calif.), 5/27/1911, 8; 5/29/1911, 1.
11. *Eureka (Calif.) Herald*, 5/27/1911, 1; 5/28/1911, 3; *Humboldt Times* (Eureka, Calif.), 5/28/1911, 1; *San Francisco Examiner*, 5/28/1911, 1; *San Francisco Call*, 5/28/1911, 36; *Humboldt Standard* (Eureka, Calif.), 5/27/1911, 1.
12. *Eureka (Calif.) Herald*, 5/27/1911, 4; *Humboldt Times* (Eureka, Calif.), 5/27/1911, 1.
13. *Eureka (Calif.) Herald*, 5/29/1911, 1.
14. Jerome S. Fanciulli Collection, box 2, folder 17: Fanciulli, letter to Curtiss, May 19, 1911; Curtiss, telegram to Fanciulli, May 28, 1911.
15. Jerome S. Fanciulli Collection, box 2, folder 17: Fanciulli, letter to Curtiss, June 7, 1911; Curtiss, telegram to Fanciulli, May 28, 1911.
16. *San Francisco Examiner*, 4/18/1911, 12.
17. Jerome S. Fanciulli Collection, box 2, folder 17: Fanciulli, letter to Curtiss, June 7, 1911; *Eureka (Calif.) Herald*, 5/15/1911, 8; *Daily Capital Journal* (Salem, Ore.), 5/29/1911, 1.
18. Jerome S. Fanciulli Collection, box 2, folder 17: Fanciulli, letter to Curtiss, June 7, 1911.
19. Jerome S. Fanciulli Collection, box 2, folder 17: Fanciulli, letter to Curtiss, June 7, 1911.
20. *Medford (Ore.) Mail Tribune*, 6/5/1910, 1; 5/25/1911, 7; 5/28/1911, sec. 2, 3; 6/4/1911, 1.
21. Jerome S. Fanciulli Collection, box 2, folder 17: Curtiss, letter to Fanciulli, May 14, 1911; *Medford (Ore.) Mail Tribune*, 5/31/1911, 1; 6/1/1911, 1; 6/2/1911, 1; 6/4/1911, 1, 6.

22. *Medford (Ore.) Mail Tribune*, 6/4/1911, 1.
23. *Medford (Ore.) Mail Tribune*, 6/4/1911, 6; 6/5/1910, 1, 8; 6/6/1910, 1; 6/4/1911, 1, 6.
24. Jerome S. Fanciulli Collection, box 2, folder 17: Fanciulli, letter to Curtiss, June 7, 1911.
25. Jerome S. Fanciulli Collection, box 2, folder 17: Fanciulli, letter to Curtiss, June 7, 1911.
26. Roseberry, *Glenn Curtiss*, 435.
27. Jerome S. Fanciulli Collection, box 2, folder 17: Curtiss, letter to Fanciulli, June 12, 1911.
28. *Medford (Ore.) Mail Tribune*, 6/4/1911, 1; *Aero* 3, no. 2 (October 14, 1911): 41; no. 11 (December 16, 1911): 216.
29. Jerome S. Fanciulli Collection, box 2, folder 17: Fanciulli, letter to Curtiss, June 7, 1911; *Oregon Daily Journal* (Portland), 6/4/1911, 2; 6/5/1911, 18; *Eureka (Calif.) Herald*, 5/29/1911, 1; *Daily Capital Journal* (Salem, Ore.), 5/11/1910, 8; 6/5/1911, 1; *Morning Oregonian* (Portland), 6/5/1911, 5.
30. *Morning Oregonian* (Portland), 6/4/1911, sec. 3, 9; *Oregon Daily Journal* (Portland), 6/5/1911, 6; *Morning Oregonian* (Portland), 5/28/1911, sec. 4, 4.
31. Portland Aeroplane Company, Records of the Secretary of State, Index to Incorporations, no. 14753, Oregon Historical Society.
32. *Oregon Daily Journal* (Portland), 6/3/1911, 1; 6/7/1911, 6; *Morning Oregonian* (Portland), 6/7/1911, 17.
33. *Morning Oregonian* (Portland), 6/7/1911, 17.

CHAPTER 21. **SPIRAL GUIDE**

1. Trimble, *Hero of the Air*, 93; *Mount Airy (N.C.) News*, 4/13/1911, 1.
2. *Washington (D.C.) Post*, 5/6/1911, 3; *New York Times*, 5/6/1911, 14; *Washington (D.C.) Herald*, 5/6/1911, 1, 3.
3. *Aeronautics* 8, no. 6 (June 1911): 223; *Washington (D.C.) Post*, 5/8/1911, 2.
4. *Wilkes-Barre (Pa.) Record*, 6/3/1911, 14; 6/5/1911, 7; Chambers, "Aviation and Aeroplanes," 169; Washington Irving Chambers Papers, box 15: Ellyson, memorandum to Secretary of the Navy, January 31, 1911.
5. *Montreal (Quebec) Star*, 6/26/1961, 3; *New York Times*, 3/15/1915, 5; *San Francisco Examiner*, 3/15/1915, 4; "Lincoln Beachey," https://www.findagrave.com/memorial/7038456; *Fitchburg (Mass.) Sentinel*, 6/19/1911, 10; Jerome S. Fanciulli Collection, box 2, folder 17: Curtiss, letter to Fanciulli, June 12, 1911.
6. Trimble, *Hero of the Air*, 21; *Wilkes-Barre (Pa.) Record*, 6/2/1911, 5; *Wilkes-Barre (Pa.) Times-Leader*, 6/2/1911, 18; *Aeronautics* 9, no. 1 (July 1911): 23.
7. *Humboldt Times* (Eureka, Calif.), 5/27/1911, 3.
8. *Anaconda (Mont.) Standard*, 5/7/1911, 13; 6/15/1911, 13; *Salina (Kans.) Daily Union*, 6/10/1911, 4; 6/15/1911, 1; *Bismarck (N.D.) Daily Tribune*, 6/10/1911, 8; Jerome S. Fanciulli Collection, box 2, folder 17: Curtiss, letter to Fanciulli, June 12, 1911.

9. *Butte (Mont.) Inter Mountain*, 6/9/1911, 1; *Anaconda (Mont.) Standard*, 6/10/1911, 6–7.
10. *Anaconda (Mont.) Standard*, 6/10/1911, 7; *San Francisco Call*, 3/14/1909, 38; *Seattle Daily Times*, 5/5/1911, 16.
11. *Anaconda (Mont.) Standard*, 6/10/1911, 7; *Great Falls (Mont.) Daily Tribune*, 6/16/1911, 7.
12. *Butte (Mont.) Inter Mountain*, 6/12/1911, 5; *Anaconda (Mont.) Standard*, 6/13/1911, 2.
13. *Anaconda (Mont.) Standard*, 6/13/1911, 2; 6/14/1911, 7, 11; *Santa Cruz (Calif.) Evening Sentinel*, 11/8/1911, 4; *Butte (Mont.) Inter Mountain*, 6/14/1911, 5.
14. *Anaconda (Mont.) Standard*, 6/14/1911, 7; 6/15/1911, 6; *Great Falls (Mont.) Daily Tribune*, 6/15/1911, 6; *Butte (Mont.) Inter Mountain*, 6/15/1911, 5; 6/16/1911, 5; 6/17/1911, 1.
15. *Anaconda (Mont.) Standard*, 6/15/1911, 11.
16. *Great Falls (Mont.) Daily Tribune*, 6/16/1911, 7; 6/17/1911, 7; *Great Falls (Mont.) Leader*, 6/15/1911, 1; 6/17/1911, 1; 6/19/1911, 3.
17. *Kalispell (Mont.) Journal*, 6/22/1911, 1; *Daily Missoulian* (Missoula, Mont.), 6/22/1911, 6; 6/27/1911, 5; *Fergus County Argus* (Lewistown, Mont.), 6/30/1911, 1.
18. *Missoula (Mont.) Sentinel*, 6/29/1911, 8; *Daily Missoulian* (Missoula, Mont.), 6/27/1911, 5; 6/28/1911, 1; 6/29/1911, 7.
19. *Boston Post*, 6/18/1911, 6; *New York Times*, 6/23/1911, 14.
20. *New York Times*, 6/28/1911, 1; *Topeka (Kans.) Daily Capital*, 6/30/1911, 8.
21. *Sandusky (Ohio) Star-Journal*, 6/22/1911, 4.
22. *Washington (D.C.) Herald*, 7/1/1911, 6.

CHAPTER 22. OFF GUARD

1. *Reno (Nev.) Evening Gazette*, 7/4/1911, 1–2; 7/5/1911, 1, 8; *San Francisco Call*, 7/5/1911, 5; *Morning Oregonian* (Portland), 7/5/1911, 1.
2. *Nevada State Journal* (Reno), 5/24/1911, 1; 7/11/1911, 4; 7/12/1911, 5.
3. National Guard of California, 1912 Annual Muster Roll, March 18, 1912, Headquarters, Coast Artillery Corps; *San Bernardino County (Calif.) Sun*, 7/7/1911, 1; *San Francisco Chronicle*, 7/6/1911, 6; *San Francisco Call*, 7/7/1911, 2; *Reno (Nev.) Evening Gazette*, 7/7/1911, 10.
4. *San Francisco Chronicle*, 7/13/1911, 11.
5. *Morning Oregonian* (Portland), 7/10/1911, 14; *Sun* (New York, N.Y.), 6/18/1911, 2; *Oregon Daily Journal* (Portland), 7/11/1911, 3.
6. *Oakland (Calif.) Tribune*, 7/15/1911, 11; *Lethbridge (Alberta) Daily Herald*, 7/3/1911, 7; 7/13/1911, 7; 7/15/1911, 1, 8.
7. *Oakland (Calif.) Tribune*, 7/17/1911, 9; *San Francisco Examiner*, 7/19/1911, 2.
8. *Evening Kansas-Republican* (Newton, Kans.), 7/17/1911, 7; *Vancouver (B.C.) World*, 7/19/1911, 8; *Seattle Daily Times*, 7/20/1911, 1–2.
9. *Seattle Daily Times*, 7/17/1911, 2; 7/18/1911, 15; 7/19/1911, 1, 10; 7/20/1911, 1; *Seattle Star*, 7/21/1911, 1, 4; *Vancouver (B.C.) World*, 7/21/1911, 1; *Annual Reports of the Navy Department for the Fiscal Year 1911*, 22.

10. *Seattle Daily Times*, 7/19/1911, 10; 7/20/1911, 7; 7/23/1911, 16.
11. Jerome S. Fanciulli Collection, box 3, folder 3: Fanciulli, Statement, October 1, 1911, 4; *New York Times*, 7/22/1911, 2; *Seattle Daily Times*, 7/23/1911, 16; Morehouse, "Hamilton," 161.
12. *Washington (D.C.) Post*, 7/29/1911, 2; 7/30/1911, sec. 2, 2; Jerome S. Fanciulli Collection, box 2, folder 17: Fanciulli, letter to Curtiss, June 7, 1911; *Washington (D.C.) Herald*, 7/29/1911, 1.
13. *Washington (D.C.) Herald*, 7/30/1911, 1–2; *Washington (D.C.) Post*, 7/31/1911, 12; *New York Times*, 7/30/1911, C, 6.
14. *Washington (D.C.) Post*, 7/31/1911, 12; *Washington (D.C.) Herald*, 7/31/1911, 2.
15. *Washington (D.C.) Herald*, 7/30/1911, 2; 8/1/1911, 2; 8/2/1911, 2; *Washington (D.C.) Post*, 8/1/1911, 2.
16. *Brooklyn (N.Y.) Daily Eagle*, 8/3/1911, 11; 8/6/1911, sport, 12; *New York Times*, 8/6/1911, 1; *Washington (D.C.) Herald*, 8/6/1911, 3; *Aeronautics* 9, no. 3 (September 1911): 91.
17. *Chicago Tribune*, 8/8/1911, 7; *Dixon (Ill.) Evening Telegraph*, 8/9/1911, 4; *Evansville (Ind.) Press*, 8/9/1911, 1; *Inter Ocean* (Chicago, Ill.), 8/13/1911, 1, 2.
18. *New York Times*, 7/15/1911, 1; *Chicago Tribune*, 7/15/1911, 1; *Oakland (Calif.) Tribune*, 7/15/1911, 11.
19. *Inter Ocean* (Chicago, Ill.), 8/13/1911, 2.
20. *Chicago Tribune*, 8/16/1911, 3; 8/18/1911, 3.
21. *Inter Ocean* (Chicago, Ill.), 8/13/1911, 2; 8/14/1911, 3; *New York Times*, 8/13/1911, sec. C, 7.
22. *Inter Ocean* (Chicago, Ill.), 8/14/1911, 3; Washington Irving Chambers Papers, box 15: Ellyson, letter to Chambers, August 19, 1911.
23. *Inter Ocean* (Chicago, Ill.), 8/14/1911, 3; *New York Times*, 8/13/1911, C, 7; *Chicago Tribune*, 8/15/1911, 1; Washington Irving Chambers Papers, box 15: Ellyson, letter to Chambers, August 19, 1911.
24. *Inter Ocean* (Chicago, Ill.), 8/14/1911, 3.
25. *Chicago Tribune*, 8/16/1911, 1–3; *Aeronautics* 9, no. 3 (September 1911): 92; *Inter Ocean* (Chicago, Ill.), 8/16/1911, 1–2; Washington Irving Chambers Papers, box 15: Ellyson, letter to Chambers, August 19, 1911.
26. *Inter Ocean* (Chicago, Ill.), 8/17/1911, 1–2.
27. *Inter Ocean* (Chicago, Ill.), 8/16/1911, 1–2; *Chicago Tribune*, 8/16/1911, 1–2; *Aeronautics* 9, no. 3 (September 1911): 92; Washington Irving Chambers Papers, box 15: Ellyson, letter to Chambers, August 19, 1911.
28. *Chicago Tribune*, 8/16/1911, 1; *Inter Ocean* (Chicago, Ill.), 8/16/1911, 1; *Chicago Examiner*, 8/16/1911, 1.
29. *Inter Ocean* (Chicago, Ill.), 8/16/1911, 2; 8/17/1911, 3; *San Francisco Examiner*, 8/16/1911, 1; *Chicago Tribune*, 8/18/1911, 2.
30. *Inter Ocean* (Chicago, Ill.), 8/17/1911, 3; *Chicago Tribune*, 8/16/1911, 3.
31. *Inter Ocean* (Chicago, Ill.), 8/17/1911, 2.
32. *Chicago Tribune*, 8/17/1911, 3; *Inter Ocean* (Chicago, Ill.), 8/17/1911, 2.

33. *Chicago Tribune*, 8/18/1911, 2; *Inter Ocean* (Chicago, Ill.), 8/20/1911, 1; 8/21/1911, 1.
34. *Inter Ocean* (Chicago, Ill.), 8/17/1911, 2; 8/22/1911, 1; *Chicago Tribune*, 8/16/1911, 3; 8/19/1911, 2.
35. *Great Falls (Mont.) Daily Tribune*, 6/16/1911, 7.
36. Jerome S. Fanciulli Collection, box 2, folder 18: Curtiss, letter to James Plew, August 25, 1911; *Chicago Examiner*, 8/16/1911, 1; *Inter Ocean* (Chicago, Ill.), 8/16/1911, 1.

CHAPTER 23. **FULL MEASURE**

1. Lenger, "Conquest of the Air," 36; *Boston Globe*, 8/26/1911, 1–2.
2. *New York Times*, 8/27/1911, 4; *Brooklyn (N.Y.) Daily Eagle*, 8/27/1911, sporting, 4; *Indianapolis Star*, 8/27/1911, 5; *Boston Globe*, 8/27/1911, 1, 8.
3. *Boston Globe*, 8/27/1911, 1; *New-York Tribune*, 8/29/1911, 3.
4. *Boston Globe*, 9/2/1911, 1, 4; 9/4/1911, 4.
5. *Boston Globe*, 9/5/1911, 4; 9/7/1911, 4; *Fort Wayne (Ind.) Sentinel*, 9/4/1911, 1; *Indianapolis Star*, 9/5/1911, 3.
6. *New Castle (Pa.) News*, 9/1/1911, 12; *Fort Wayne (Ind.) Daily News*, 9/1/1911, 7; *Evening News* (San Jose, Calif.), 12/14/1911, 4; RoA, 6080, ex. 435; *Aero* 3, no. 11 (December 16, 1911): 216.
7. *Boston Journal*, 9/6/1911, 12; *Brooklyn (N.Y.) Daily Eagle*, 9/4/1911, 7; 9/9/1911, sporting, 2; *New York Herald*, 9/11/1911, sec. 1, part 3, 1; *Philadelphia Inquirer*, 9/11/1911, 1.
8. *Chicago Tribune*, 9/14/1911, 2; *St. Johnsbury (Vt.) Caledonian*, 9/13/1911, 1; 9/20/1911, 1, 6.
9. *New-York Tribune*, 9/17/1911, 12; *New York Herald*, 9/17/1911, sec. 2, 9; *Brooklyn (N.Y.) Daily Eagle*, 9/18/1911, sporting, 2; *New York Times*, 9/18/1911, 2; *Elmira (N.Y.) Star-Gazette*, 9/21/1911, 9; 9/23/1911, 5.
10. *Brooklyn (N.Y.) Daily Eagle*, 9/1/1911, 11; *New York Times*, 9/24/1911, sporting, 1–2.
11. *Indianapolis Star*, 9/25/1911, 2; *Sun* (New York, N.Y.), 9/25/1911, 2; *New York Times*, 9/25/1911, 11.
12. *Sun* (New York, N.Y.), 9/25/1911, 1; *Aero* 3, no. 2 (October 14, 1911): 38.
13. *Brooklyn (N.Y.) Daily Eagle*, 9/26/1911, 2; 10/1/1911, editorial, 2; *Repository* (Canton, Ohio), 9/17/1911, 19; *Salem (Ohio) News*, 9/21/1911, 8; 9/27/1911, 8; 9/28/1911, 1; *Sun* (New York, N.Y.), 9/28/1911, 1; *Wichita Beacon*, 10/24/1911, 4.
14. Casey, *Curtiss*, 79–81; Roseberry, *Glenn Curtiss*, 319; Trimble, *Hero of the Air*, 123.
15. *Salem (Ohio) News*, 9/29/1911, 8; 9/30/1911, 1, 8; *Sun* (New York, N.Y.), 10/1/1911, 3; 10/2/1911, 12; *Brooklyn (N.Y.) Daily Eagle*, 10/1/1911, sporting, 10; 10/2/1911, sporting, 2; *New York Herald*, 10/1/1911, sec. 1, part 3, 9; 10/2/1911, sec. 1, part 3, 14.
16. *Brooklyn (N.Y.) Daily Eagle*, 8/30/1911, 11; *Anaconda (Mont.) Standard*, 10/1/1911, 1; *Tacoma (Wash.) Times*, 10/3/1911, 7; *New York Times*, 10/3/1911, 1.

17. *Outing* 59, no. 1 (October 1911): 123; *Scientific American* 105, no. 16 (October 14, 1911): 337.
18. Jerome S. Fanciulli Collection, box 2, folder 14: affidavit of Jerome Fanciulli, 9; folder 18: Curtiss, letter to Fanciulli, October 17, 1911; box 2, Trimble, *Hero of the Air*, 119.
19. *Davenport (Iowa) Democrat and Leader*, 10/6/1911, 15.
20. *Davenport (Iowa) Democrat and Leader*, 10/8/1911, 28.
21. *Rock Island (Ill.) Argus*, 10/9/1911, 8; *Evening Times-Republican* (Marshalltown, Iowa), 10/11/1911, 4; *Muscatine (Iowa) Journal*, 10/19/1911, 2; *National Democrat* (Des Moines, Iowa), 10/12/1911, 2; *Davenport (Iowa) Democrat and Leader*, 10/10/1911, 11.
22. *Charlotte (N.C.) News*, 10/19/1911, 1.
23. *Atlanta Constitution*, 10/1/1911, C, 6; 10/8/1911, M, 20; *Macon (Ga.) Daily Telegraph*, 9/30/1911, 8; 10/13/1911, 1.
24. *Macon (Ga.) Daily Telegraph*, 10/12/1911, 1.
25. Telegram from Eugene Ely to Mabel Ely, October 14, 1911, reproduced in Miller, *Eugene Ely*, 281; *Macon (Ga.) Daily Telegraph*, 10/13/1911, 1; 10/14/1911, 1.
26. *New York Times*, 10/15/1911, 1, 8.
27. *Macon (Ga.) Daily Telegraph*, 10/15/1911, 1; 10/17/1911, 1, 9; 10/18/1911, 1.
28. *Macon (Ga.) Daily Telegraph*, 10/18/1911, 10; 10/19/1911, 1; *Atlanta Constitution*, 10/19/1911, 4.
29. *Williamsburg (Iowa) Journal-Tribune*, 10/26/1911, 1; *Macon (Ga.) Daily Telegraph*, 10/20/1911, 1, 2, 9; *Washington (D.C.) Post*, 10/20/1911, 1; *New York Times*, 10/20/1911, 1; *San Francisco Chronicle*, 10/20/1911, 1; *Indianapolis Star*, 10/20/1911, 1; *Muscatine (Iowa) Journal*, 10/20/1911, 1.
30. Jerome S. Fanciulli Collection, box 2, folder 18: Fanciulli, letter to Aviation Editor, October 19, 1911.
31. Jerome S. Fanciulli Collection, box 2, folder 18: Fanciulli, letter to Aviation Editor, October 19, 1911.
32. *New York Herald*, 10/20/1911, sec. 1, part 3, 1.
33. *Marion (Ohio) Daily Mirror*, 10/7/1911, 5; Putnam Museum, Davenport Iowa (photograph dated October 8, 1911, showing the front elevator); Eugene B. Ely Scrapbooks, NHHC, S–005, folder E, 100, 101 (photographs of the wreckage of Ely's machine, showing no evidence of a front elevator); *Daily Times* (Davenport, Iowa), 10/23/1911, 1; *Macon (Ga.) Daily Telegraph*, 11/8/1911, 6.
34. *Macon (Ga.) Daily Telegraph*, 10/20/1911, 2.
35. *New York Times*, 10/23/1910, sec. 1, part 3, 2; Casey, *Curtiss*, 82-83; *Macon (Ga.) Daily Telegraph*, 10/20/1911, 2.
36. *Inter Ocean* (Chicago, Ill.), 10/20/1911, 1, 3.
37. *Macon (Ga.) Daily Telegraph*, 9/30/1911, 8; 10/21/1911, 4.
38. Keith-McHenry-Pond Family Papers, BANC MSS C-B 595, carton 11: book 16, 1361.
39. *Aeronautics* 9, no. 5 (November 1911): 154; *Scientific American* 105, no. 20 (November 11, 1911): 427.

40. *Edgefield (S.C.) Advertiser*, 10/26/1910, 4; *Charlotte (N.C.) News*, 12/9/1910, 6; *Macon (Ga.) Daily Telegraph*, 10/8/1911, 7; 10/21/1911, 8; 7/27/1912, 10; *Muscatine (Iowa) Journal*, 10/20/1911, 1.
41. *Atlanta Georgian and News*, 10/20/1911, 6; *New Orleans Item*, 10/20/1911, 1; *Seattle Daily Times*, 10/23/1911, 6.
42. *Philadelphia Inquirer*, 10/22/1911, sec. 2, 8.
43. Washington Irving Chambers Papers, box 14: undated draft telegram.
44. Letter from Georgia State Fair Association to Mrs. Eugene Ely, October 20, 1911, reproduced in Miller, *Eugene Ely*, 289.
45. *Tacoma (Wash.) Times*, 5/25/1911, 7; *Elyria (Ohio) Evening Telegram*, 5/27/1911, 1; Roger-Bloche, *Monument aux aviateurs*, Salon des Artistes Français, 1911, http://salons.Musee-Orsay.fr/index/notice/462199.
46. Eugene B. Ely Scrapbooks, NHHC, S-005, folder E, 100–102 (photographs of Ely's wrecked airplane and of the sculpture of the fallen flier).

CHAPTER 24. THE WORLD BEFORE HIM

1. *New York Times*, 10/21/1911, 6; *Macon (Ga.) Daily Telegraph*, 10/20/1911, 1; *Williamsburg (Iowa) Journal-Tribune*, 10/26/1911, 1; *Daily Times* (Davenport, Iowa), 10/20/1911, 1; 10/21/1911, 6.
2. *Williamsburg (Iowa) Journal-Tribune*, 10/26/1911, 1; *Daily Times* (Davenport, Iowa), 10/23/1911, 4; *Muskegon (Mich.) Chronicle*, 10/25/1911, 2.
3. *Williamsburg (Iowa) Journal-Tribune*, 10/26/1911, 1.
4. *Register and Leader* (Des Moines, Iowa), 10/30/1911, 3; San Francisco Superior Court, Probate Case No. 18875; *San Francisco Call*, 1/14/1912, 19; *San Francisco Chronicle*, 2/24/1912, 3; *Oakland (Calif.) Tribune*, 2/25/1912, 17, 19; *New-York Tribune*, 1/25/1912, 1; *Aero* 3, no. 23 (March 9, 1912): 456; *Oakland (Calif.) Tribune*, 2/24/1912, 13–14.
5. *Oakland (Calif.) Tribune*, 8/28/1912, 10; 12/21/1918, 5; *Morning Oregonian* (Portland), 8/29/1912, 3; *Evening News* (San Jose, Calif.), 8/28/1912, 5; *Anaconda (Mont.) Standard*, 8/29/1912, 13; *Colorado Springs Gazette*, 8/29/1912, 5; *Mariposa (Calif.) Gazette*, 4/20/1918, 1; *San Francisco Examiner*, 12/21/1918, 10.
6. *Oakland (Calif.) Tribune*, 11/20/1920, 2; *San Francisco Examiner*, 11/20/1920, 4; *San Francisco Chronicle*, 3/30/1921, 11; 4/18/1921, 7.
7. *Independent-Journal* (San Rafael, Calif.), 9/6/1958, M4; U.S. Post Office Department, *Postage Stamps of the United States*, 185.
8. *Independent-Journal* (San Rafael, Calif.), 3/28/1960, 1; *Journal Herald* (Dayton, Ohio), 12/16/1965, sec. 1, 14; *South San Francisco Enterprise-Journal*, 6/23/1976.
9. Stein, *From Torpedoes to Aviation*, 186; Washington Irving Chambers Papers, box 22: Chambers, form letter, 1913.
10. *Oakland (Calif.) Tribune*, 3/8/1913, 4; *Boston Post*, 3/15/1915, 1, 7; *Bakersfield Californian*, 3/15/1915, 1–2; *Salt Lake Tribune* (Salt Lake City, Utah), 3/15/1915, 1; Roseberry, *Glenn Curtiss*, 307.

11. *New York Times*, 7/27/1944, 17.
12. von Schaezler/Ely Scrapbooks (photograph of President Herbert Hoover presenting Nathan with the Distinguished Flying Cross posthumously awarded to his son); U.S. War Department, *Army Retired List 1930*, 769; "Distinguished Flying Cross," Naval History and Heritage Command, http://history.navy.mil/browse-by-topic/heritage/awards/decorations/distinguished-flying-cross.html; Trimble, *Admiral William A. Moffett*, 39; *Waterloo (Iowa) Daily Courier*, 2/17/1933, 5; U.S. Congress, "An Act to authorize the posthumous award of a distinguished flying cross to Eugene B. Ely," S. 433, 72nd Congress, 2nd Session (1933), 1717.
13. Information regarding the disposition of Ely's Distinguished Flying Cross is from David D'Onofrio, email correspondence with the author, February 2014–May 2015.
14. Turnbull and Lord, *History of United States Naval Aviation*, 19; Chesneau, *Aircraft Carriers of the World*, 9, 11; Chambers, "Aviation and Aeroplanes," 175.
15. Chesneau, *Aircraft Carriers of the World*, 12–13, 85; Crouch, *Wings*, 359; Gilbert, *First World War*, 355.
16. Chesneau, *Aircraft Carriers of the World*, 2, 12, 14, 205; Crouch, *Wings*, 362; *Ranger* IX, in *DANFS*.
17. *Langley* I, *Wright* I, *Wright* II, and *Wright* III (T-AVB-3), in *DANFS*; Chesneau, *Aircraft Carriers of the World*, 198, 261.
18. Chesneau, *Aircraft Carriers of the World*, 22; *Pensacola News*, 10/5/1981, 1; *News and Observer* (Raleigh, N.C.), 12/19/1994, 2C; Zobel and Zobel, "Those Magnificent Men," 53; *Gazette* (Cedar Rapids, Iowa), 10/21/2011, 5A.
19. Washington Irving Chambers Papers, box 11: "The Development of Naval Aviation."
20. National Air and Space Museum, Washington, D.C., documentation of accession no. 115248, acquired July 14, 1931.
21. National Air and Space Museum, N. D. Ely, letter to museum, June 20, 1931; *San Francisco Examiner*, 1/19/1911, 30.

SELECTED BIBLIOGRAPHY

MANUSCRIPTS AND ARCHIVAL MATERIAL

Burge, V. L. "Diary of V. L. Burge, 1909–1912." Fort Wood, NY: n.d. http://media.defense.gov/2013/Nov/22/2001329857/-1/-1/0/burge%20diary.pdf

California State Archives, Sacramento, Calif.

National Guard of California, Coast Artillery Corps

Oath and Enlistment Papers of Eugene Burton Ely, March 22, 1911

1912 Annual Muster Roll, Headquarters, March 18, 1912

Glenn H. Curtiss Museum, Hammondsport, N.Y.

Lois G. Durr (Eugene Ely's niece), private collection

Iowa County, Certificate of Live Birth 1/166-11 (November 6, 1886) for "Eugene H. Eally".

Jerome S. Fanciulli Collection, McDermott Library, Special Collections, University of Texas at Dallas.

Keith-McHenry-Pond Family Papers, BANC MSS C-B 595, Bancroft Library, University of California, Berkeley.

Library of Congress, Manuscript Division, Washington, D.C.

Bulletins of the Aerial Experiment Association (AEA)

Chambers, Washington Irving, Papers

Minutes of the Meetings of the Aerial Experiment Association

van Deurs, George, Papers

Wright, Wilbur and Orville Wright, Papers

Lord, Clifford L. "The History of Naval Aviation, 1898–1939." Office of the Deputy Chief Naval Operations (Air), Washington, D.C., Naval Aviation History Unit, 1946.

National Archives and Records Administration (NARA), Washington, D.C.

RG 24–118: USS *Birmingham* deck log

RG 24–118: USS *Pennsylvania* deck log

RG 80, 26983–20: Memorandum for the Secretary of the Navy, December 2, 1908

RG 80, 26983–20:1: 1st Endorsement, August 16, 1909

Naval History and Heritage Command (NHHC), Washington, D.C.

Aviation Biography Collection

Eugene B. Ely Scrapbooks

Dictionary of American Naval Fighting Ships (*DANFS*), http://history.navy.mil/research/histories/ship-histories/danfs.html

Oregon Historical Society, Portland, Ore.
Records of the Secretary of State, Index to Incorporations, no. 14753, Portland Aeroplane Company, 1910.
Oregon State Archives, Salem, Ore.
Portland Aeroplane Company v. C. T. Colt, M. Valerius and Charles E. Hatfield, Circuit Court, Douglas County, Oregon (complaint filed May 24, 1910; dismissed without prejudice, June 13, 1911), box 193, no. 538.
Peter C. Petersen Sr. Collection, Putnam Museum, Davenport, Iowa
Smithsonian Institution, Washington, D.C.
National Air and Space Museum (NASM), Archives Division
Documentation of accession no. 115248, July 14, 1931 (propeller from USS *Birmingham* flight)
Biographical Technical Files, Eugene B. Ely
A. Roy Knabenshue Collection, biographical note
Morehouse Collection, Eugene B. Ely biography
von Schaezler/Ely Scrapbooks (Eugene Ely's stepmother, Mabel von Schaezler Ely, and stepbrother, Paul von Schaezler Ely), William and Paul Henderson and Ann Stamets, private collection.
Willard, Charles F. Letter to Capt. Dean Veremakis, September 15, 1972. Collection of the author.

PUBLIC DOCUMENTS

Annual Reports of the Navy Department for the Fiscal Year 1910. Washington, D.C.: U.S. Government Printing Office, 1910. http://catalog.HathiTrust.org/Record/012202882.
Annual Reports of the Navy Department for the Fiscal Year 1911. Washington, D.C.: U.S. Government Printing Office, 1912. http://catalog.HathiTrust.org/Record/012202882.
Annual Reports of the Navy Department for the Fiscal Year 1912. Washington, D.C.: U.S. Government Printing Office, 1913. http://catalog.HathiTrust.org/Record/012202882.
Herring-Curtiss Co. v. Curtiss
Plaintiff's Brief on Appeal from Judgment Entered in Steuben (New York) County Clerk's Office, May 21, 1923, decision on appeal reported at *Herring-Curtiss Co. v. Curtiss*, 223 App. Div. 101, 227 N.Y.S. 489 (N.Y. App. Div. 1928). http://books.Google.com?id=U8K5lqS6my8C.
Record on Appeal (RoA) from *Herring-Curtiss v. Curtiss*, judgment entered May 21, 1923, by the Steuben County (New York) Clerk's Office, decision on appeal reported at *Herring-Curtiss Co. v. Curtiss*, 223 App. Div. 101, 227 N.Y.S. 489 (N.Y. App. Div. 1928).
Vol. 1–2 (0001–1469). http://books.google.com?id=j-FpJlBtdiwC.
Vol. 3–4 (1469–2860). http://books.google.com?id=9SEyYvDA7HUC.
Vol. 5–6 (2861–4298). http://books.google.com?id=_61WjBKeps8C.

Vol. 7–8 (4299–5705). http://books.google.com?id=EwXe4XPwKA0C

Vol. 9–11 (5706–7026, supp.). http://books.google.com?id=e5LCTMl2wSUC

Iowa County Atlas: York Township, 1886. http://digital.lib.UIowa.edu/islandora/object/ui%3Aatlases_12416

Iowa State Census. 1895, Iowa City Township. http://FamilySearch.org/ark:/61903/1:1:VTSF-QPN.

Iowa State Senate. *Journal of the Senate.* 34 GA (1911), January 9–12, 1911. http://www.legis.iowa.gov/docs/publications/YSJL/855223.pdf.

National Oceanic and Atmospheric Administration (NOAA). *A Study of Earthquake Losses in the San Francisco Bay Area: Data and Analysis. A Report Prepared for the Office of Emergency Preparedness.* Washington, D.C.: U.S. Government Printing Office, 1972. http://books.Google.com?id=SjXrO4Uca6kC.

National Personnel Records Center (NPRC). National Archives and Records Administration, St. Louis, Mo. http://Archives.gov/personnel-records-center.

Office of Information Services. *A Chronology of American Aerospace Events* (Air Force Pamphlet 0000210-1-1). Washington, D.C.: Dept. of the Air Force, 1959. http://archive.org/details/chronologyofamer00wash.

San Francisco, California, Superior Court. *In the Matter of the Estate of Eugene B. Ely, Deceased*, Probate Case No. 18875, Decree Vesting Entire Estate in Widow, Oct. 19, 1915, Vol. 319, p. 65.

Supplemental List of Owners of Motor Vehicles and Names of Chauffeurs Registered in the Office of the Secretary of State. Sacramento, Calif.: W. W. Shannon, Superintendent State Printing, 1906. http://archive.org/details/registermotor00unse

Supplemental List of Owners of Motor Vehicles and Names of Chauffeurs Registered in the Office of the Secretary of State. Sacramento, Calif.: W. W. Shannon, Superintendent State Printing, 1907. http://archive.org/details/registermotor00unse

U.S. Census.

1900, San Francisco, Calif. http://FamilySearch.org/ark:/61903/1:1:M9GW-KH6.

1910, English Township, Iowa. http://FamilySearch.org/ark:/61903/1:1:MGMW-311.

1910, Portland, Ore. http://FamilySearch.org/ark:/61903/1:1:MLYB-MN4.

1910, San Antonio, Texas. http://FamilySearch.org/ark:/61903/1:1:M2QJ-YN9.

U.S. Congress.

An Act to authorize the posthumous award of a distinguished flying cross to Eugene B. Ely, S. 433, 72nd Congress, 2nd Session (1933), 1717.

Hale, Eugene. "Paper Relating to Auxiliary German Navy." S. 174, 60th Congress, 1st Session (1908), Document No. 174.

Hearings before the Committee on Naval Affairs of the House of Representatives on Sundry Legislation Affecting the Naval Establishment, 1929–1930. Washington, D.C.: U.S. Government Printing Office, 1930.

"A joint resolution to designate May 8, 1986, as 'Naval Aviation Day.'" Pub. L. No. 99-292, 100 Stat. 198. http://congress.gov/bill/99th-congress/house-joint-resolution/569.

U.S. Patent #821,393: "Flying Machine," O. & W. Wright, May 22, 1906. https://image-ppubs.USPTO.gov/dirsearch-public/print/downloadPdf/0821393.

U.S. Post Office Department. *Postage Stamps of the United States.* Washington, D.C.: U.S. Government Printing Office, 1962. http://archive.org/details/postagestampsofu00unit_0.

U.S. War Department. *Army Retired List, 1930.* Washington, D.C.: Government Printing Office, 1930.

BOOKS AND ARTICLES

Abbott, Edward. "Cambridge." In Samuel Adams Drake, *History of Middlesex County, Massachusetts,* vol. 1, 305–58. Boston: Estes and Lauriat, 1880. http://books.Google.com?id=QGolOAyd9RMC&pg=PA305.

Anderson, John D., Jr. *A History of Aerodynamics and Its Impact on Flying Machines.* New York: Cambridge University Press, 1997.

Bonnalie, A. F. "Eugene B. Ely, 34 Years Ago, First Proved Practicability of Aircraft Carrier." *U.S. Air Services* 30, no. 1 (January 1945): 12–40. http://books.Google.com/books?id=0FJVAAAAYAAJ&pg=PA13.

Bonney, Walter T. "Chiefs of the Army Air Force 1907–1957." *The Pegasus* 26, supp. (July 1957). Reprinted in *Airpower Historian* 7, no. 3 (July 1960): 129–42. http://JSTOR.org/stable/44513065.

Bradford, William. *[History] Of Plimoth Plantation.* Boston, Mass.: [State Library of Massachusetts], 1651. http://mass.gov/info-details/bradfords-manuscript-of-plimoth-plantation

Buist, H. Massac. "Miracles of Flight." *Electrician and Mechanic* 22, no. 6 (June 1911): 411–19. http://catalog.HathiTrust.org/Record/100560427.

Bulfinch, Thomas. *Bulfinch's Mythology.* New York: Grosset and Dunlap, 1913. http://books.Google.com?id=NKcwAQAAMAAJ.

Casey, Louis S. *Curtiss: The Hammondsport Era, 1907–1915.* New York: Crown, 1981.

Chambers, Washington Irving. "Aviation and Aeroplanes." U.S. Naval Institute *Proceedings* 37, no. 1 (March 1911): 163–207. http://books.Google.com?id=6xNLAAAAYAAJ&pg=PA163.

Chesneau, Roger. *Aircraft Carriers of the World, 1914 to the Present: An Illustrated Encyclopedia.* London: Arms and Armour Press, 1992.

Chevillot, Catherine. "Réalisme optique et progrès esthétique: La fin d'un rêve." *Revue de l'Art* 104 (1994): 22–29.

Cole, Martin, and H. L. Schreiner. "Charles Willard: The Exhibition Years." *Journal of the American Aviation Historical Society* 19, no. 3 (Fall 1974): 177–91.

Corn, Joseph. *The Winged Gospel: America's Romance with Aviation.* New York: Oxford University Press, 1983.

Crouch, Tom D. *The Bishop's Boys: A Life of Wilbur and Orville Wright.* New York: W. W. Norton, 1990.

———. *Wings: A History of Aviation from Kites to the Space Age.* New York: W. W. Norton, 2003.

Curtiss, Glenn H. "The Aeroplane for the Navy." *Columbian* 2, no. 6 (September 1910): 1815–18. http://catalog.HathiTrust.org/Record/000528676.

Curtiss, Glenn H., and Augustus Post. *The Curtiss Aviation Book*. New York: Frederick A. Stokes, 1912. http://books.Google.com?id=MDBMAAAAIAAJ.

"Distinguished Flying Cross." Naval History and Heritage Command. http://history.navy.mil/browse-by-topic/heritage/awards/decorations/distinguished-flying-cross.html

Downer, Harry E. *History of Davenport and Scott County, Iowa*. 2 vols. Chicago: S. J. Clarke, 1910. http://books.Google.com?id=kzREAQAAMAAJ.

Drake, Samuel Adams. *History of Middlesex County, Massachusetts*. 2 vols. Boston: Estes and Lauriat, 1880. http://books.Google.com?id=QGolOAyd9RMC.

Duncan, Robert Gordon. *Goths and Vandals of the Wemme Cases*. Portland, Ore.: August Wemme, 1932.

Ely, Heman. *Records of the Descendants of Nathaniel Ely*. Cleveland, Ohio: Short & Forman, 1885. http://books.Google.com?id=CbDhAAAAMAAJ.

"An Epitome of the Work of the Aeronautic Society of New York from July, 1908, to December, 1909." *Bulletin of the New York Aeronautic Society* 1 (1910). http://catalog.HathiTrust.org/Record/102671204.

Foulois, Benjamin D. *From the Wright Brothers to the Astronauts: The Memoirs of Benjamin D. Foulois*. New York: McGraw-Hill, 1968.

Gale Research Company. *Library of Congress and National Union Catalog Author Lists, 1942–1962: A Master Cumulation*. 152 vols. Detroit, Mich.: Gale Research, 1971. http://archive.org/details/libraryofcongres0000unse_x0g4.

"The German Plan to Invade America—Newly Revealed: How Kaiser Wilhelm Planned to Keep America from Becoming a Global Power." *American Heritage* 53, no. 6 (November/December 2002): 18.

Gilbert, Martin. *The First World War, A Complete History*. New York: Henry Holt, 1994.

Goddard, Stephen B. *Colonel Albert Pope and His American Dream Machines: The Life and Times of a Bicycle Tycoon Turned Automotive Pioneer*. Jefferson, N.C.: McFarland, 2000.

Goss, William Henry. *A Sketch of the Life and Death of Llewellynn Jewitt*. London: Bemrose and Sons, 1887. http://books.google.com?id=txoLAAAAYAAJ.

Hill, William E. *The Oregon Trail: Yesterday and Today*. Caldwell, Idaho: Caxton Press, 1987.

Hoffbeck, Steven R. "Shooting Star: Aviator Jimmie Ward of Crookston." *Minnesota History* 54, no. 8 (Winter 1995): 331–41.

Howe, M. A. DeWolfe. *George von Lengerke Meyer, His Life and Public Services*. New York: Dodd, Mead, 1919. http://books.Google.com?id=ypoejLPuylQC.

Jones, Keith R. "If Only in Another Time: The Story of the DeVaux-Hall Motors Corporation." Research paper, University of Michigan at Ann Arbor, December 16, 1999.

Kipling, Rudyard. "With the Night Mail." *McClure's Magazine* 26, no. 1 (November 1905): 23–35. http://catalog.HathiTrust.org/Record/000548741.

Lenger, John. "Conquest of the Air." *Harvard Magazine* (May–June 2003): 32–37.

Lockley, Fred. *History of the Columbia River Valley from the Dalles to the Sea*. 3 vols. Chicago: S. J. Clarke, 1928. http://catalog.HathiTrust.org/Record/001269171.

Mahan, Louis F. "Eugene B. Ely—His Racing Days." *Foundation* 6, no. 2 (Fall 1985): 73–76.

Manning, Thomas A., ed. *A History of Military Aviation in San Antonio*. San Antonio: N.p., 2000. http://books.Google.com?id=upffAAAAMAAJ.

McCullough, David. *The Wright Brothers*. New York: Simon & Schuster, 2015.

Miller, William M. *Eugene Ely, Daredevil Aviator: First Shipboard Landing and Takeoff*. New York: McFarland, 2014.

Mills, Herbert. "When Aviators Are Up in the Air, Figuratively." *San Francisco (Calif.) Call*, April 9, 1911, 8.

Morehouse, Harold E. "The Flying Pioneers: Charles K. Hamilton, Early Balloonist—Curtiss Exhibition Pilot." *Journal of the American Aviation Historical Society* 14, no. 3 (Fall 1969): 125–27.

Mortimer, Gavin. *Chasing Icarus: The Seventeen Days That Changed American Aviation*. New York: Walker Books, 2009.

Olcott, William Tyler. *Star Lore of All Ages*. New York: G. P. Putnam's Sons, 1911. http://books.Google.com?id=6_IRAAAAYAAJ.

Oldham, Chuck, ed. *Air Power at Sea: A Century of US Naval Aviation 1911–2011*. Norfolk, Va.: Navy League of the United States Hampton Roads Council, 2011.

Paine, Lincoln. *The Sea and Civilization: A Maritime History of the World*. New York: Alfred A. Knopf, 2013.

Roseberry, C. R. *Glenn Curtiss: Pioneer of Flight*. New York: Doubleday, 1972.

Rotch, A. Lawrence. *The Conquest of the Air*. New York: Moffat, Yard, 1909. http://books.Google.com?id=y6sJAAAAIAAJ.

Stein, Steven K. *From Torpedoes to Aviation: Washington Irving Chambers and Technological Innovation in the New Navy, 1876 to 1913*. Tuscaloosa: University of Alabama Press, 2007.

Stevens, Walter. *St. Louis, the Fourth City, 1764–1911*. 2 vols. St. Louis, Mo.: S. J. Clarke, 1911. http://catalog.HathiTrust.org/Record/008652674.

Thomas, John R. "The Question Concerning Patent Law and Pioneer Inventions." *Berkeley Technology Law Journal* 10, no. 1 (1995): 35–103.

Trimble, William F. *Admiral William A. Moffett: Architect of Naval Aviation*. Annapolis, Md.: U.S. Naval Institute Press, 2007.

———. *Hero of the Air: Glenn Curtiss and the Birth of Naval Aviation*. Annapolis, Md.: U.S. Naval Institute Press, 2010.

Turnbull, Archibald D., and Clifford L. Lord. *History of United States Naval Aviation*. New Haven, Conn.: Yale University Press, 1949. http://catalog.HathiTrust.org/Record/004413748.

Union Historical Company. *The History of Iowa County, Iowa*. Des Moines, Iowa: Birdsall, Williams, 1881. http://books.Google.com?id=G3wUAAAAYAAJ.

van Deurs, George. *Anchors in the Sky: Spuds Ellyson, the First Naval Aviator*. New York: Presidio Press, 1979.

———. *Wings for the Fleet: A Narrative of Naval Aviation's Early Development, 1910–1916*. Annapolis, Md.: U.S. Naval Institute Press, 1966.

Vergara, George L. *Hugh Robinson, Pioneer Aviator.* Gainesville: University Press of Florida, 1995.

Warner, Beers, and Co. *History of Portage County, Ohio.* Chicago, Ill., 1885. http://archive.org/details/bub_gb_RVDWAAAAMAAJ.

Weis, Frederick Lewis. *Early Generations of the Family of Robert Harrington.* Worcester, Mass.: privately printed, 1958. http://Archive.org/details/earlygenerations00weis.

Wells, H. G. *The War in the Air.* New York: Grosset & Dunlap, 1908.

Winchester, Jim. *A Chronology of Aviation: A Day-by-Day History of a Century of Powered Flight.* London: Amber Books, 2007.

Zimmerman, Dwight Jon. "Naval Aviation in the Tidewater." In *Air Power at Sea: A Century of US Naval Aviation 1911–2011*, edited by Chuck Oldham, 38–49. Norfolk, Va.: Navy League of the United States Hampton Roads Council, 2011.

Zobel, Hiller B., and John H. Zobel. "Those Magnificent Men: 100 Years of Naval Aviation." *American Heritage* 60, no. 4 (Winter 2011): 46–53.

Zogbaum, Rufus. *From Sail to Saratoga: A Naval Autobiography.* Rome, Italy: privately printed, 1950.

CORRESPONDENCE/INTERVIEWS

Coolbaugh, Cdr. Robert, USN (Ret.), email correspondence with the author, March 2015.

Daly, John, Studebaker E-M-F expert, email correspondence with the author, March 2014.

D'Onofrio, David, U.S. Naval Academy, Nimitz Library, Special Collections and Archives, email correspondence with the author, February 2014–May 2015.

Leisenring, Rick, Curator, Glenn H. Curtiss Museum, Hammondsport, N.Y., email correspondence with the author, May 2012–August 2016.

MISCELLANEOUS MATERIALS

San Francisco Blue Book, San Francisco: Hoag, Charles C., pub. 1906. http://archive.org/details/sanfranciscoblue06sanf.

"1911 Coolbaugh Curtiss Pusher in Flight." YouTube, http://YouTu.be/PnmGZwl5wkU.

"Lost Film from 1906" (San Francisco). YouTube, http://YouTu.be/ZdvRNdGlgzY.

Additional information and resources are at JohnZobel.com.

INDEX

ABOUT THE AUTHOR

JOHN HILLER ZOBEL was an author, recovering attorney, and accomplished athlete. He practiced law for twenty years in Seattle before becoming a full-time writer and parent in 2007. His first book, *A Slight Change of Plans*, published in 1998, was a P. G. Wodehouse–style romantic comedy. He earned a BA in English from Harvard College in 1981 and received his law degree from Stanford Law School in 1985. He died unexpectedly on the summit of Aconcagua in Argentina in January 2017.

THE NAVAL INSTITUTE PRESS is the book-publishing arm of the U.S. Naval Institute, a private, nonprofit, membership society for sea service professionals and others who share an interest in naval and maritime affairs. Established in 1873 at the U.S. Naval Academy in Annapolis, Maryland, where its offices remain today, the Naval Institute has members worldwide.

Members of the Naval Institute support the education programs of the society and receive the influential monthly magazine *Proceedings* or the colorful bimonthly magazine *Naval History* and discounts on fine nautical prints and on ship and aircraft photos. They also have access to the transcripts of the Institute's Oral History Program and get discounted admission to any of the Institute-sponsored seminars offered around the country.

The Naval Institute's book-publishing program, begun in 1898 with basic guides to naval practices, has broadened its scope to include books of more general interest. Now the Naval Institute Press publishes about seventy titles each year, ranging from how-to books on boating and navigation to battle histories, biographies, ship and aircraft guides, and novels. Institute members receive significant discounts on the Press' more than eight hundred books in print.

Full-time students are eligible for special half-price membership rates. Life memberships are also available.

For more information about Naval Institute Press books that are currently available, visit www.usni.org/press/books. To learn about joining the U.S. Naval Institute, please write to:

Member Services
U.S. NAVAL INSTITUTE
291 Wood Road
Annapolis, MD 21402-5034
Telephone: (800) 233-8764
Fax: (410) 571-1703
Web address: www.usni.org